About Island Press

Since 1984, the nonprofit organization Island Press has been stimulating, shaping, and communicating ideas that are essential for solving environmental problems worldwide. With more than 1,000 titles in print and some 30 new releases each year, we are the nation's leading publisher on environmental issues. We identify innovative thinkers and emerging trends in the environmental field. We work with world-renowned experts and authors to develop cross-disciplinary solutions to environmental challenges.

Island Press designs and executes educational campaigns, in conjunction with our authors, to communicate their critical messages in print, in person, and online using the latest technologies, innovative programs, and the media. Our goal is to reach targeted audiences—scientists, policy makers, environmental advocates, urban planners, the media, and concerned citizens—with information that can be used to create the framework for long-term ecological health and human well-being.

Island Press gratefully acknowledges major support from The Bobolink Foundation, Caldera Foundation, The Curtis and Edith Munson Foundation, The Forrest C. and Frances H. Lattner Foundation, The JPB Foundation, The Kresge Foundation, The Summit Charitable Foundation, Inc., and many other generous organizations and individuals.

The opinions expressed in this book are those of the author(s) and do not necessarily reflect the views of our supporters.

GASLIGHT

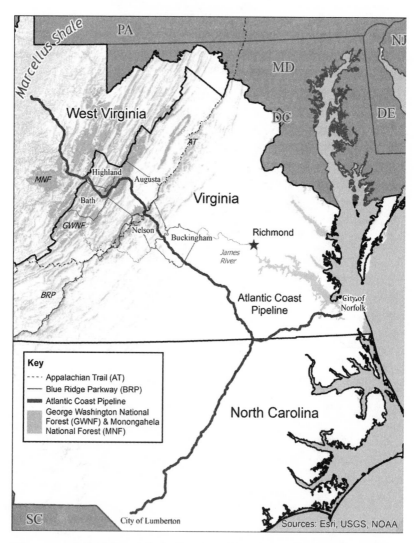

The route of the Atlantic Coast Pipeline. (Courtesy of Dan Shaffer, ABRA)

Gaslight

The Atlantic Coast Pipeline and
the Fight for America's Energy Future

Jonathan Mingle

ISLANDPRESS | Washington | Covelo

Library of Congress Control Number: 2023949502

All Island Press books are printed on environmentally responsible materials.

Manufactured in the United States of America
10 9 8 7 6 5 4 3 2 1

Keywords: Allegheny–Blue Ridge Alliance; Appalachian Mountains; climate
activism; climate change; Dominion Energy; Duke Energy; electrification;
Federal Energy Regulatory Commission (FERC); fossil fuels; fracking;
Hurricane Camille; Inflation Reduction Act (IRA); Joe Manchin; Marcellus
Shale; methane; Mountain Valley Pipeline; natural gas; renewable energy;
Southern Environmental Law Center

For Quinn, Vivien, and Liza

Power concedes nothing without a demand.
It never did and it never will.
  —Frederick Douglass

Contents

A Note to the Reader

"Whoever gave it the name 'natural gas'? Now there was a marketing coup!"

Cheryl LaFleur, former chair of the obscure but powerful Federal Energy Regulatory Commission, had a point. The world's fastest-growing fossil fuel has some built-in branding advantages.[1]

Consider a lump of coal. Chances are you picture a crumbly, carbonaceous rock that leaves everything it touches smudged, smoky, smeared. Now consider the words "natural gas." The first thing that comes to mind might be a neat blue flame dancing on your stovetop or in the pages of a kitchen design catalogue. In surveys, when Americans are asked what they associate with the words "natural gas," most mention words like "clean" and "energy."[2] It's worth taking a moment to ponder why that's the case.

"Natural gas just sounds so . . . natural," LaFleur noted. And who doesn't like natural?

But natural gas is the sibling of coal and oil, derived from the same raw materials: long-dead organisms trapped deep underground. Natural gas is a fossil fuel extracted with chemicals and heavy machinery, refined and compressed and pumped across thousands of miles to be burned in basement furnaces and kitchen stoves and power plants, producing an array of pollutants from nitrogen oxides to volatile organic compounds to carbon dioxide.[3] So it's fair to wonder, like Cheryl LaFleur, just how this other carbon-rich substance acquired its label.

It turns out that the term was coined in the early nineteenth century to differentiate gas that occurred "naturally"—that is, seeping out of the ground—from "town gas," which was manufactured from coal in a rather nasty process in urban factories.[4] This era also gave rise to the first generation of gas utilities. "Gas light companies" spread from Norfolk to Atlanta, New York to Baltimore, supplying manufactured gas and, later, "natural gas" to city streetlamps. Before long, they veined their way into America's businesses and homes—more than 75 million, at last count.

One consequence of this inherited terminology is that, today, relatively few people think about exactly what they are burning when they turn on their stove.

"Years ago, I had some people in my office talking about methane leaks," said LaFleur, whose former job involved weighing the merits of some of America's most consequential energy projects. "These were people from well-known, respected environmental groups." One of them asked if she knew that natural gas emits methane. "I said, 'I'm pretty sure natural gas *is* methane!'"

She was right on that score too. But when asked how they feel about "methane" or "methane gas," Americans of all political persuasions report much more negative feelings. Their strongest associations: "global warming," "greenhouse," and "climate change." Methane is emitted from a variety of human and natural sources, from fossil fuel production to agriculture to wetlands. In this book, "natural gas" and "methane" and "gas" and "fossil gas" will all be deployed to refer to the same substance: the colorless, odorless gas with the chemical formula CH_4 that is lighter than air, easy to ignite, and traded as one of the world's most prized commodities. These words are used interchangeably—partly for convenience and partly to illustrate how words can serve to clarify or cloud what we're really talking about when we talk about "natural gas."

Prologue

The People vs. the Pipeline

D. J. Gerken (center) and Greg Buppert (far right) on the steps of the US Supreme Court after oral arguments on February 24, 2020. (Nancy T. Sorrells)

1

Nancy Sorrells sat down in the gallery of the Supreme Court of the United States, looked around the storied chamber, and took a moment to marvel at just how far she and her neighbors had come.

It was February 24, 2020. Nearly six years had passed since Dominion Energy, one of the biggest power companies in the country, had unveiled its plans to build a natural gas pipeline from West Virginia's fracking fields across Virginia to eastern North Carolina.[1] At 42 inches in diameter, the pipeline would be the largest to ever cross Appalachia's rock-ribbed ridges. At close to 600 miles in length, it would be nearly as long as the Blue Ridge Mountains themselves. And with a price tag that had swelled to $8 billion, its owners would have a strong incentive to keep gas flowing through it for decades to come.

Sorrells, a publisher and historian who lived in a Shenandoah Valley hamlet a few miles from the project's path, helped lead one of the dozens of grassroots groups that had banded together to fight it since 2014. She and a small contingent had traveled to Washington, DC, the night before, with plans to rise at three in the morning and wait for tickets to hear oral arguments in their case, *Atlantic Coast Pipeline LLC and U.S. Forest Service v. Cowpasture River Preservation Association*. But they discovered a long line of people already winding around First Street and East Capitol, angling to be among the fifty members of the public admitted.[2]

Throughout the night, fellow pipeline fighters from Virginia and West Virginia clustered together in small groups, chatting, sharing thermoses of tea, stamping their feet in the darkness. When Dominion routed its pipeline through their communities, the company had roused—and unified—a diverse group of citizens from across the political spectrum in opposition: retirees, innkeepers, farmers, scientists, physical therapists, pastors, nurses, teachers, builders, former lobbyists, engineers, and entrepreneurs. With temperatures hovering just above freezing, some wrapped themselves in sleeping bags and reclined on folding chairs to grab brief snatches of sleep.[3] A member of Sorrells's group stayed in line, while the rest retired for the night. At 5:00 a.m., having secured just one ticket between them, the group decided that Sorrells should be the one to use it. After all, few had been more relentless in the struggle against Dominion's pipeline or more confident that they could defeat it.

For years, Sorrells had been telling everyone that the Atlantic Coast Pipeline was not inevitable—that, if they kept fighting, their band of Davids could overcome Dominion's Goliath. In every email she sent, every flyer she handed out, she included the sentence: "This pipeline is not a done deal."

And here, she thought, was the proof. Nearly everyone had expected Dominion—the most politically powerful company in Virginia—to steamroll them. "At the very beginning it was like we were just a little drop in the ocean," she said. But after years of contending in courtrooms, street protests, shareholders' meetings, newspaper opinion pages, and under the fluorescent lights at every conceivable kind of county or state or federal public hearing, they had stymied the largest fossil fuel pipeline project to come out of Appalachia.

And they had forced Dominion to appeal to the highest court in the land for permission to build its gas line through Virginia's mountains.

Once the justices had taken their seats, Sorrells's first thought was: *There's Ruth Bader Ginsburg, this is unreal.* But as she listened to the oral arguments unfold, her excitement was tempered by a dawning realization: they were going to lose this case.

Many of the grassroots groups opposing Dominion's pipeline were represented by the Southern Environmental Law Center, a nonprofit legal organization based in Charlottesville. As was common practice, SELC had hired a veteran counsel with experience before the Supreme Court to argue the case. As he jousted with the justices, Sorrells kept jotting down notes and thinking of points she wished he would make.

"It wasn't a bad argument," she said. "But he didn't make those points, because he hadn't lived it for six years."

☼

From her home at the western foot of the Blue Ridge, a few miles from where Dominion planned to drill a mile-long tunnel through the mountains, Sorrells had been living it since the day it was announced.

In the fall of 2014, Dominion had mailed a flyer to residents of communities along the project's proposed route through western Virginia. Like a coach collecting opponents' taunts on the locker room bulletin board to motivate her players, Sorrells had held on to it ever since.[4] Printed in large font, against a backdrop of forested mountains and lush valleys stretching west of the Blue Ridge, was a bold claim: "The Atlantic Coast Pipeline will change everything. And nothing."

This slogan encapsulated Dominion's sales pitch: its gas conduit would supercharge collective prosperity, at virtually no cost. The company sought to convince everyone—local landowners, lawmakers, investors, regulators—that the ACP was essential to meet growing demand for gas, lower energy bills for its customers, and cut its own carbon emissions as it replaced older coal-burning power plants. And, moreover, that it could safely bury its pipe across the region's steep, slide-prone slopes.[5]

But for many who lived in its path, that tagline offered an inverted reflection of their darkest fears. They feared that, in terms of concrete economic benefits, the pipeline would change nothing. Local businesses wouldn't be able to tap its gas even if they wanted to, unless they paid a $5.5 million connection fee.[6] Construction jobs would be temporary, largely filled by crews from Oklahoma and Texas. Many local residents got their power from local cooperatives, not Dominion.

And on the other side, they worried the project really would change everything. That it would threaten life and limb, water quality, property values, local businesses, ecosystems, the very stability of their beloved mountains themselves, and their children's ability to live safely among them. They worried about dwelling within the "blast radius" of a potential rupture and explosion. And many feared the climate consequences of a fossil fuel project with an eighty-year lifespan.

"The pipeline will be virtually invisible," Dominion's flyer promised. "There are 2.5 times more miles of underground natural gas pipelines than interstate highways in Virginia. Yet few people ever notice."

Yet few people ever notice. Those five words were, in retrospect, an inadvertent Rosetta stone for understanding the gambit of the Atlantic Coast Pipeline and the broader narrative driving the gas building boom that had engulfed America for more than a decade. Dominion was just one of many energy companies making big bets on gas. The success of those investments depended on convincing people that there were few, if any, costs or risks worth paying any mind.

That line was intended to soothe locals' anxieties—to suggest that, after construction crews packed up and left, all they would see was a grassy strip that resembled a golf course fairway. But it could also be read as as an admission that, if you looked closely enough, maybe there *was* something to see—cause for concern rather than comfort—going on down there. Nancy Sorrells, for instance, knew that beneath the flyer's verdant vista, where Dominion planned to string its pipe, was a vast network of limestone caves, sinkholes, and underground rivers connected to downstream drinking water supplies around the region, from Washington to Richmond.

And in fact, from Pennsylvania to Virginia, people already in the fracking-and-pipeline boom's crosshairs had been noticing for years. It was hard to ignore a massive trench being dug in your yard or farm or community, and giant pipes laid in it. And once you saw that messy process up close, it was hard not to wonder about some of the other, less obvious consequences—and about the strength of the industry's broader case for building more gas infrastructure.

According to Dominion and many other energy companies, the argument for natural gas was a slam dunk. As the flyer noted, burning gas to generate electricity produced half the carbon emissions of burning coal. This talking point undergirded the familiar claim that gas was a "bridge fuel" to a cleaner, climate-safe future—a metaphor repeated so often, in news stories and politicians' stump speeches and CEOs' conference keynotes, that it had hardened into orthodoxy.

It was indeed a fact that gas power plants produced less carbon dioxide than coal plants. But those selling the "bridge" needed people to *not* notice some other facts. For one, that the metaphor was floated by the gas industry itself way back in 1988, as climate change first burst into public consciousness, helpfully proffering their product as "the least harmful alternative while the world looks for other, longer-lasting solutions to the 'greenhouse' effect.'"[7] And secondly, that we all seemed to be stuck on their bridge, with no end in sight.

Bridges, of course, are meant to deliver you somewhere else. Three decades later, gas had dethroned coal as the leading source of power.

America had become the world's top producer and exporter of natural gas. Meanwhile, in the period between 1988 and 2020, humans had added more carbon dioxide to the atmosphere than in all of human history up to that point. Yet the industry continued to tout gas as the only sure route to a greener future. Exhibit A: the Atlantic Coast Pipeline, perhaps the most ambitious project yet.

By 2020, plenty of people had long since taken notice of some other salient facts too. Investing finite capital into gas meant fewer dollars available for renewables and a slower transition to clean energy. Building more gas infrastructure risked locking in decades of future carbon dioxide emissions.[8] Gas wasn't the only alternative to coal: wind, solar, batteries, and energy efficiency were readily available and getting cheaper by the month. The six years since Dominion had launched its pipeline had been the six hottest years since recordkeeping began. And more gas meant more emissions of a climate-warming super-pollutant.

Because natural gas, you see, is methane.[9] And methane is a greenhouse gas that packs eighty-six times the heat-trapping power as carbon dioxide over a twenty-year period. Some scientists have called it "carbon dioxide on steroids."[10]

Methane is responsible for a third of the global temperature rise since preindustrial times. Since 2007, methane levels in the atmosphere had surged at twice the rate of carbon dioxide concentrations.[11] Alarmed by this spike, climate scientists warned that unless methane emissions were wrestled downward, the world's efforts to keep global warming under 2 degrees would fail.[12] That would push us past tipping points from which there might be no returning, rendering unrecognizable the friendly climate that humans have evolved with—an outcome that really *would* change everything.

Dominion's project—if built—would play no small role in bringing about that reality. Because, like all gas pipelines, the Atlantic Coast Pipeline would be a very large and long-lived methane delivery device.

Picture an enormous, 42-inch-wide interstate-scale cigarette lighter that keeps working for a century. At one end: the fracking wells of the Marcellus Shale. At the other: dozens of gas power plants and hundreds of thousands of burner tips in furnaces, water heaters, and kitchen stoves. In between: a vast metallic spaghetti of gas field gathering lines and large-diameter pipelines and local distribution lines.

On its journey through all those pipes and valves and fittings—as any plumber could tell you—some methane would inevitably escape. If all the gas in the Marcellus Shale were to be exploited, methane leaks alone would likely equal three times the total annual carbon dioxide emissions of the United States—making the Marcellus the largest "methane bomb" in the world, according to researchers.[13] The methane that did make it to the end of the pipe would feed machines designed to convert that gas into carbon dioxide—the primary driver of climate change.

Simple facts, derived from the laws of physics. But physics has a hard time competing with public relations.[14]

☼

The word "methane" did not appear on Dominion's flyer. Nor was it uttered in the chambers of the Supreme Court. As Nancy Sorrells listened, the oral arguments were starting to sound like a sophomore philosophy class: the justices seemed more interested in the metaphysics of trails than the physics of gas pipes.

At issue was whether the law allowed Dominion to build its pipeline at Reeds Gap, its chosen spot for crossing the Blue Ridge, where the Appalachian Trail ran through national forest land. The government's lawyer, defending the Forest Service, repeated his core argument (which aligned with that of Dominion's lawyers) that the company could bore underneath the iconic footpath because the "trail is not land." This idea didn't sit well with Justice Elena Kagan. "Nobody makes this distinction in real life," she countered. A slightly surreal debate over the nature of a trail ensued, with musings from Justices Samuel Alito and Stephen Breyer. *Is a trail inseparable from the land that it traverses? Is it something that lies on top of the ground, but separate from it, like a ribbon? Does it go to the center of the earth?*

Then Chief Justice John Roberts chimed in and unintentionally cut to the heart of the matter. If the court ruled against Dominion, he worried aloud, would it "erect an impermeable barrier to any pipeline from the area where the natural gas, those resources are located and to the area east of it where there's more of a need for them?"[15] In other words, would the Appalachian Trail become a wall preventing energy companies from tapping the vast fossil fuel reserves lying underneath Appalachia?

As he listened, Greg Buppert's thoughts paralleled those of his client, Nancy Sorrells, sitting a few dozen feet away. The odds, he had to admit, were not looking good.[16] Roberts wasn't the only justice peppering his lead counsel with skeptical questions.

Buppert, a senior attorney for the Southern Environmental Law Center, had started scrutinizing Dominion's proposed pipeline—and its risks to the region's water, air, climate, citizens, and economy—in the summer of 2014. At the time, Dominion had confidently predicted that the pipeline would be finished, with 1.5 billion cubic feet of gas flowing through it each day, by the end of 2018. But here it was, the winter of 2020, and not a single piece of the Atlantic Coast Pipeline had been laid in Virginia's soil. The project was at least three years behind schedule. Construction had been mostly halted since late 2018, thanks to a series of successful legal challenges mounted by SELC, their grassroots clients, and partner organizations in the region. Buppert was a seasoned environmental attorney, but at the outset he knew little about the 1938 Natural Gas Act or interstate pipelines. Over the past six years, he liked to joke, he had acquired an inadvertent PhD in both subjects. And to his now expertly trained ear, most of the justices seemed inclined to side with Dominion.[17]

Buppert and his colleagues—led by D. J. Gerken, SELC's lead litigator on the case since 2018—had argued that, because the Appalachian Trail was administered as a unit of the National Park System, Dominion would need special authorization from Congress to cross it at Reeds Gap. A federal appellate court had agreed, citing a hundred-year-old federal law that prohibited drilling or pipelines on National Park lands. Dominion had appealed, and now the justices would determine whether it needed that act of Congress to greenlight its plan—a time-consuming and uncertain prospect.[18] The legal questions were narrow and technical, winding through a thicket of competing interpretations of obscure statutes. But for a moment, the chief justice had gestured toward the much wider stakes of the morning's debate.

The premise embedded in Roberts's question was that America would need more methane gas, and more pipelines to transport it, for many years to come. This conviction was widely shared beyond the conservative-leaning Supreme Court: support for the natural gas construction frenzy underway across the country had become a fixed feature of the landscape of bipartisan elite opinion.

But that very premise—that building the Atlantic Coast Pipeline was good for America, that there was a *need* for its gas that outweighed all the risks it posed to the region's people, forests, climate, and economy—was the delusion that Greg Buppert and his colleagues had spent years trying to dispel. With the patience of a master builder, he had painstakingly assembled a case—still waiting to be heard by another federal appeals court—that challenged Dominion's rationale for the project *and* the methodology the federal government used to determine whether a gas pipeline was, in its arcane phrasing, in "the public convenience and necessity."

In his view, *that* case was the main event. But no one was writing headlines about it. Instead, all eyes—Wall Street, the gas and utility industries, energy analysts, and environmental advocates—were trained on the Supreme Court.

As the oral arguments wrapped up, Buppert still had reason to be heartened.[19] Justice Ruth Bader Ginsburg had noted that the case before them addressed only one of *four* fatal flaws that the appeals court found in the Forest Service permit. Wouldn't this question about who could authorize crossing the Appalachian Trail be "moot," she wondered, if federal courts ruled the pipeline couldn't proceed due to those various other shortcomings? Until the Forest Service fixed them all, ACP LLC would still lack permission to cross the national forests.

And even if those problems were resolved, Dominion would still lack seven *other* critical permits—several of which the SELC and its allies had already successfully challenged.

If they lost this high-profile battle—if, as media outlets were already speculating, a Supreme Court win for Dominion breathed new life into their embattled pipeline—Nancy Sorrells and her fellow activists were determined to press on. The larger war was still up for grabs—and the stakes were high.

They were fighting for their homes, their neighbors, their children's futures. The six-year-long fight—longer than the Civil War—that had converged on this contested spot atop the Blue Ridge Mountains was also a struggle to shape the trajectory of the US energy system for decades to come. Dominion and other energy companies wanted Sorrells and, indeed, all Americans to see projects like the Atlantic Coast Pipeline as a "bridge" to a better world—to a clean energy future.

But when they looked closely, many saw something that looked more like a fuse. With a blast radius that enveloped, and extended far beyond, their beloved Virginia hills.

Part I

The Public Necessity

John Ed Purvis on the land in Shipman, Virginia, that has been in his family since 1768. (Marcie Gates-Goff/BlueRidgeLife.com)

Chapter One

The Burning Spring

On March 9, 1669, John Lederer walked west out of Jamestown in the company of three Native guides. The German physician and explorer had been tasked by Virginia's colonial governor with finding promising routes through the distant mountains to boost the fur trade and perhaps establish a "western passage" to California and its fabled Spanish mines of silver and copper, rumored to be just a few weeks' march away.

On the sixth day of their journey, Lederer's party crested a hill about a dozen miles northeast of what is now Charlottesville and glimpsed the mountains to the west. At this sight, Lederer's companions prostrated themselves and prayed, crying out in reverence for the mountains: "God is nigh!"

After four more days of walking—past "great herds of red and fallow deer" and "bears crashing mast like swine"—and a difficult climb, Lederer became the first European to set foot atop the Blue Ridge and see the Allegheny Highlands beyond. The view filled him with awe—and disappointment. Mountains stretched westward as far as he could see. Daunted by the thick tangle of trees and cliffs below, he returned to Jamestown.

The following year Lederer set out again with the same mission and a much larger contingent of twenty Englishmen and five Native guides. They traveled to where the Rockfish River flows into the James at the southeast corner of what is today Nelson County, Virginia. A community of Monacan Indians, who lived in a series of villages along the river, greeted them. Lederer asked the locals for directions, as one does. An old man grabbed a stick and traced in the dirt two well-trod routes they could take.[1]

Lederer's English companions rebuffed this advice and insisted on pressing ahead in a straight westward line dictated by their compass, heedless of obstacles in their way. (This didn't sit well with Lederer, but he was outvoted.) After a week of rough going over "steep and craggy cliffs," the party reached a place where the Mahock Indians purportedly lived, likely near present-day Lynchburg. But Lederer found no sign of the tribe. This journey, too, would end without discovery of an easy route through the mountains.

On returning east, Lederer briefed his sponsors, penned an account of his travels, and drew an annotated map. "They are certainly in a great errour," he wrote, "who imagine that the Continent of North America is but eight or ten days journey over from the Atlantick to the Indian Ocean." There were a lot more mountains in Virginia to cross, he reported, than people realized.[2]

Lederer hadn't been the first to try. From the day that European colonists first set foot in Virginia, they dreamt of western riches and saw the mountains as something to be overcome to tap them.

In 1607, soon after landing near what would become Jamestown, Captain Christopher Newport attempted to press inland along the James River. The Powhatan who lived there tried to talk him out of it. They warned that a day and a half above the falls (around present-day Richmond) the Englishmen would encounter the Monacans, their enemies, and that they would find nothing to eat and hard going in *Quiranck*, their name for the Blue Ridge. Newport made later forays into Monacan territory in search of gold and silver and a passage to the South China Sea, to no avail.[3]

As for the Mahock, they vanished from the historical record after 1728. In their only previously recorded encounter by Europeans, in

1608, Captain John Smith and his men stumbled into a group of them near the Rappahannock River. The Mahock attacked with a volley of arrows. After a skirmish and a chase, Smith found a wounded warrior left behind named Amoroleck. While his men treated the man's wounds, Smith asked what he knew of the land west of the mountains. Nothing, he replied, just that the sun lives there. Smith asked him why the Mahock had attacked. "We heard that you had come from the underworld to take our world from us," Amoroleck answered.[4]

It would be several decades before the settlers found something they prized in the mountains themselves. In 1742 another adventurer found a coal seam on a tributary of the Kanawha River, near present-day Charleston, West Virginia. And then, in 1773, George Washington caught wind of a peculiar spot several miles upstream.

He had a keen interest in the Allegheny Highlands, after exploring them on foot as a young surveyor and an officer during the French and Indian War. While commanding the Continental Army in 1780, after years of maneuvering and petitions, Washington finally secured ownership of 250 acres along the Little Kanawha River. (Back then it was all part of Virginia, so Thomas Jefferson, the colony's governor, ceded the lands jointly to Washington and another former army officer.)[5]

Washington had coveted the tract, he explained years later in his will, "on account of a bituminous Spring which it contains, of so inflammable a nature as to burn as freely as spirits, and is as nearly difficult to extinguish."

The "Spring" was basically a hole in the ground that exhaled a steady stream of natural gas; when filled with rainwater, it seemed to boil, and the surface of the water could be set aflame.[6]

The source of the "Burning Spring," as it came to be known, was not fully understood at the time. Washington didn't know exactly how, but he intuited that these vapors would one day make the land more valuable—that booms would come.[7]

Designed in a Week

In the winter of 2014, Brittany Moody was taking a break during a company training workshop in Richmond when Leslie Hartz, a senior vice president at Dominion Energy, approached her with a request.

"Hey, I'm gonna need you to route a pipeline. How long do you think it'll take you to complete it?"

"I'll have it done in a week," Moody replied.

As a manager of engineering projects with Dominion Transmission, the company's gas transportation subsidiary, Moody knew pipelines. She had mapped several before. She had even grown up with one running through her family's backyard in West Virginia. Moody assumed this project would be like others she had worked on. But when she found out it would be at least 550 miles long and 42 inches in diameter—far bigger than any she had designed—she began to worry that she had overpromised.

Moody set to tracing digital lines across the pixelated contours of the Allegheny and Blue Ridge Mountains on her computer screen. Eventually she settled on what seemed the most efficient path: a line connecting the spider's web of gas-gathering lines in the fracking fields of northern West Virginia with the coastal city of Norfolk and the towns along the Interstate 95 corridor of eastern North Carolina, ending near the town of Lumberton, just shy of the South Carolina border.

When it was done, she had nearly delivered on her pledge. It took just over a week to design the initial route of what would become the Atlantic Coast Pipeline.[8]

To the uninitiated, that might not seem like adequate time to lay out the optimal route for the largest-ever gas pipeline to cross Appalachia's steep terrain, two national forests, the karst-riddled Shenandoah Valley, the world's second-oldest mountain range, the Blue Ridge Parkway, the Appalachian Trail, and the James River, all while cutting through thousands of private parcels—each representing an easement to be secured through negotiation or the use of eminent domain.

But Leslie Hartz and her boss, Dominion CEO and chairman Thomas F. Farrell II, had their reasons for moving quickly. A twenty-first-century gold rush was underway, and Dominion was determined to become one of its key players.[9] If it moved quickly, it could own and operate its very own lucrative modern-day Western Passage. Because, while the mountains that John Lederer had spied were still an imposing obstacle, they concealed a prize that fired the imaginations of Virginia's contemporary elites: vast quantities of methane.

The Allegheny Mountains were formed around 300 million years ago, thrust to Earth's surface as Africa collided with North America to form the supercontinent Pangaea. Prior to that slow-motion crash, countless organisms had lived and died and sunk to the bottom of a shallow inland sea that covered Appalachia for millions of years. As sediment piled above, heat and pressure transformed that carbon-rich stuff into methane and other gases, trapped in tiny crevices in the rock. That layer-cake matrix—known to today's geologists as the Marcellus Shale—contains more than 200 trillion cubic feet of gas.[10] A thousand feet thick, extending roughly 600 miles from West Virginia to New York, it is one of the world's largest gas fields. And a few thousand feet beneath it lies another immense gas-rich formation: the Utica Shale.

That methane had remained mostly bottled up snugly in its subterranean crevices, sandwiched between impervious veins of limestone, until a Texan named George Mitchell came along. With the support of the US Department of Energy—which placed a long-running, taxpayer-financed bet on his idea—Mitchell spent years developing a technique called hydraulic fracturing.[11] To "frack" a shale, crews drill down and then horizontally, then inject a huge amount of sand and water laced with proprietary chemical lubricants at high pressure to shatter the rock. As gas flows out of the resulting fissures, they pump it to the surface. Fracking enabled drillers to reach a mile deep and thousands of feet sideways into oil and gas deposits long thought inaccessible or too costly to tap. It proved to be the key that would unlock the ancient methane entombed in the Appalachian underworld.

Throughout the 1980s and 1990s, while his fellow oil barons scoffed, Mitchell refined his new technique in Texas. But once fracking's effectiveness became obvious, its use accelerated in the early 2000s, as a bevy of wildcatters made their way into the hollows and hilltop farms of Pennsylvania, Ohio, and West Virginia.

The turning point came with the 2008 financial crash. In its wake, with record-low interest rates and corporate wreckage all around them, shell-shocked investors hunting for bigger returns to rebuild their portfolios set their sights on shale formations like the Marcellus, North

Dakota's Bakken, and the Eagle Ford and Permian Basin in Texas. Banks funneled cash to brash new companies like Chesapeake Energy, which hungrily bought up leases from local landowners. On the strength of its Marcellus holdings, Chesapeake—founded by a risk-loving Oklahoman named Aubrey McClendon—quickly became the second-biggest gas producer in the US (after ExxonMobil), and Pennsylvania became the second-biggest gas-producing state (after Texas).[12]

By 2010, the frackers were producing too much gas. They needed to expand their markets—to gin up demand for their hydrocarbons among consumers and companies. But to reach those customers, they would need to move methane out of the mountains to population centers near the coast. The gas producers needed a conduit that would trace Lederer's journeys in reverse. In fact, they needed several.

Pipeline companies answered the call with zeal. As in any commodity boom, fortunes were being made. Firms raced to capitalize, and new interstate pipelines popped up like mushrooms after a spring rain. There was the Rover Pipeline (Pennsylvania to Ohio to Michigan), the PennEast Pipeline (Pennsylvania to New Jersey), the Atlantic Sunrise Pipeline (Pennsylvania), the Constitution Pipeline (Pennsylvania to New York), and the Mountaineer Xpress Pipeline (West Virginia). And there was the Mountain Valley Pipeline, proposed by a consortium led by one of the biggest fracking companies in Appalachia, slated to start near the same point of origin as Dominion's project and cross the Blue Ridge farther south. The CEO of the company behind the Rover Pipeline, a Texas billionaire named Kelcy Warren, summed up the situation when he told investment analysts in a moment of candor that "the pipeline business will overbuild until the end of time."[13]

Amid this frenzy of activity, in the winter of 2014, Duke Energy—a utility giant based in North Carolina—had floated its own request for proposals to build a new pipeline to supply Marcellus gas to new power plants it was planning to build. That spring, Dominion and Duke decided to join forces. Dominion, as the majority owner, would lead the construction and operation of the project.

Under Tom Farrell's leadership, Dominion had become a poster child for the nation's ongoing "dash for gas." He moved aggressively to expand the company's gas portfolio, gobbling up storage facilities and distribution utilities from Ohio to Utah and seeking federal approval to build a facility in Maryland to export supercooled liquefied gas around the world.[14] But its new pipeline would be an even bigger undertaking.

As a piece of physical infrastructure, Dominion's was perhaps the most ambitious gas pipeline project in US history. The company would need to secure at least a dozen state and federal permits, billions in financing, and thousands of easements all along the route.

To the casual observer these might seem like daunting obstacles. But Dominion's leaders had cause for their confidence. Getting the newly fabled Marcellus riches to market had taken on the cast of a national mission. The story of "cheap, abundant, clean natural gas" had acquired seemingly unstoppable momentum. To many who lived in the project's corridor, it seemed that the force of this narrative—combined with Dominion's unparalleled clout—would be irresistible. More than enough to bulldoze a path straight across the mountains to the sea.

A Fragile Domain

Imagine one day you receive a letter in the mail. It informs you that a large energy company is planning to build a pipeline through your property. That surveyors will be coming out soon. That they'd like you to sign and return the enclosed permission form for them to do so. But that whether you do or not, the surveyors will be coming onto your land anyway. Because a state law gives them the power to do so without your permission.

Your likely response might be, *Well, damn.* Whatever your feelings about natural gas, if you have any, like most people, you are none too excited at the prospect of having your yard dug up and giant pipes full of pressurized, highly flammable gas buried in it.

Your next thought might be, *Well, there's nothing I can do about it.* Because you know that said energy company is the most powerful and politically connected company in your state.

This was the scenario that played out for John Ed Purvis—and hundreds of other landowners in Nelson County, Virginia—as he checked his mailbox one day in May 2014.

The letter he found there explained that his property was among those in a "potential route corridor" for Dominion's new pipeline, that the company planned to begin surveying on July 1, and that "we are notifying you so that we can begin keeping you informed throughout this process and because surveys will be conducted on your property."

Purvis assumed—not unreasonably—there wasn't much he or anyone else could do about it. Enclosed with the letter was a copy of Virginia Code 56-49.01, the "Right-to-Trespass" statute passed in 2004, allowing pipeline companies to survey private property, whether the owners want them to or not.[15]

The Purvis land lay just east of the county seat of Lovingston, not far from where John Lederer passed through on his first journey. Locals knew it as "Purvis Hollow." Purvis lived in the house his grandfather built in 1904, the same house where he was born in 1932. Around the county, Purvis was a familiar sight in his customary ball cap and bib overalls, whether stopping to chat at the local store or attending meetings of Nelson's school board, on which he sat for seventeen years, gaining a reputation as a civic-minded fiscal conservative and a man of deep integrity. He tended a herd of beef cattle and farmed the same hilly acres as seven generations of Purvises before him, ever since an Englishman named George Purvis built a homestead there in 1768.

His family's tenure on the land preceded George Washington's acquisition of the Burning Spring by 12 years, the signing of the United States Constitution by two decades, and Congress's passage of the Natural Gas Act by 170 years. That law empowered the Federal Energy Regulatory Commission (FERC) to authorize projects it deemed to be "required by the present or future public convenience and necessity"— an archaic way of saying that a pipeline was in the public interest. With that approval came the awesome power of eminent domain.

A permit from FERC gave Dominion the authority to seize land so it could clear a 125-foot-wide construction right-of-way—roughly the width of a four-lane highway—from Harrison County, West Virginia, all the way to Robeson County, North Carolina.

For about 30 miles, it would cut right through the heart of Nelson County. Dominion's crews would excavate a 12-foot-deep trench, lay the pipe in it, and bulldoze fill on top of it. Once in place, the permanent right-of-way would be 50 feet wide. No trees could grow within it. Nothing larger than a garden shed could be built atop it.

The forever-ness of this arrangement rankled Purvis: a future foreclosed on. Half of the acreage he would lose was in timber. "Once that timber is cut down for the pipeline it can never grow back," he told a neighbor. Dominion would either mow or spray herbicides to make sure of it, as tree roots would threaten the integrity of its pipe. To add insult to injury, Dominion would take permanent ownership of an easement across his land, even as he and his descendants had to keep paying taxes on it.

John Ed Purvis had experienced eminent domain before—from both sides of the equation. As a member of the school board, he had been involved in building new elementary and middle schools, which required claiming land to expand roads and parking and for the buildings themselves. The Purvises had themselves lost pasture and hayfields years back when the state needed to widen a road. They gave it up willingly, as long as they were fairly compensated, because it served the public. To John Ed Purvis, it just seemed like common sense that eminent domain should be reserved for projects that everyone could benefit from. Roads and highways, schools and parks, water facilities and power lines. When it came to the pipeline, there was no public good in it that he could see.[16]

But he also saw this invasion as an affront to his heirs and ancestors alike. "It just tears me all to pieces to see this land, they're going to desecrate so much of our property," he told one neighbor. "We've got it running fairly close to the graveyard down here, best we can tell."

Purvis and his wife Ruth had four children, all of whom had stayed in Virginia. His daughter Elizabeth lived a mile away and taught at the elementary school. Purvis's overriding concern, she said, was "to be a good steward of the land." He knew the contours of that land, how water flowed through it, where cattle liked to bed down, what species of timber grew in its folds, like few others.

She watched with concern as spring turned to summer and her father became more distraught. He began losing sleep. The pipeline was all he could think about. "He worried constantly."[17]

He fretted about contamination of the family's water—they drank from a well, like just about everybody in Nelson. How would they irrigate fields and care for their cattle? "I'm concerned for my family," he told a local reporter. Elizabeth and her family had built a home nearby on the family's land; he feared for their water too. "I may kick the bucket anytime and be planted in that graveyard down there, and my concern is for the children and grandchildren."[18]

Watching her 82-year-old father agonize was painful enough for Elizabeth.[19] Their interactions with Dominion's land agents hadn't been all that friendly or helpful either. But what really steamed her was the response he got from some county officials, who appeared all too ready to give up. After one public meeting, she recalled, two of the five elected supervisors approached Purvis and told him, "We're so sorry this is gonna happen to you. But you can't stop it. Get the best price for your timber that you can."

She knew they meant well, that they cared about her father—but she was incredulous that they didn't plan to fight. "They were just rolling over."[20]

Rick Webb Goes Fishing

On a May morning in 2014, Rick Webb decided to go fishing. He had the time, after all.

After a career spent monitoring the recovery of brook trout in Appalachian streams, Webb was three months into retirement. He decided to try catching some brookies on Benson's Run, one of his favorite streams in the George Washington National Forest.

He climbed into his Toyota pickup and drove down the long gravel driveway of the home that he shared with his wife Susan, the one he had built himself over many years, near the West Virginia border. Webb headed east through the heart of Highland County, along the distinctive folds of what geologists called the Valley and Ridge complex. In cross-section, that stretch of Virginia looks like a rough green sea, with parallel waves of long, heavily forested, north–south ridges cresting above troughs of lush valleys.[21]

Webb knew that folded terrain as intimately as just about anyone alive. Except for a stint in college at William and Mary, not far from

Jamestown, he had lived his entire life within the view that once lay at John Lederer's feet. He had grown up in Waynesboro, exploring and fishing the small, cold creeks that tumbled down the western slope of the Blue Ridge.

That passion had eventually led him to his life's work: leading two concurrent, long-term monitoring studies of Virginia's mountain streams. For twenty-five years, the shaggy-bearded, soft-spoken scientist had collected samples from remote headwaters all over the state. This work entailed hiking to a set of 65 streams every three months since 1987; once a decade, he and his colleagues fanned out to survey all 450 streams tracked in their larger study. Some required 20-mile round-trip hikes. Many had only been touched by human activity in the form of acid rain.[22]

The data that Webb and his colleagues painstakingly gathered and analyzed told a clear story: in most streams, hard-hit brook trout populations were slowly recovering from decades of acid rain caused by air pollution from midwestern power plants. The 1990 amendments to the Clean Air Act had imposed limits on sulfur dioxide and other pollutants from power plants. Webb's work helped show that the law was, albeit gradually, working.[23]

Now that he had finally handed the reins over to colleagues, he could focus on catching a few trout himself. After a few hours chasing the brookies of Benson's Run, he packed his rod and headed home. On the way, he stopped at the post office in Monterey, the tiny town— population 139, elevation 2,894 feet—that served as Highland's economic hub and county seat.

An acquaintance hailed him in the lobby with a question: "Hey, have you heard about the pipeline?"

Word was going around that Dominion Energy was planning to build a large gas pipeline through Highland County and central Virginia, all the way to the coast. Locals had been getting letters requesting permission for surveyors to come on their land. Not much other information had been made public. Confusion and apprehension reigned.

This was all news to Webb. Before he drove home, he asked around and managed to track down a hard copy of the map that Dominion had sent to the county's board of supervisors. It was low resolution, depicting the entire route from West Virginia down through eastern North Carolina on one page. But Webb could see clearly enough that it crossed some of Highland's steepest ridges and remote watersheds, untrammeled areas in the Monongahela and George Washington National Forests, the Shenandoah Valley, and the Blue Ridge—the wild places he had dedicated his career to protecting.

Then he peered closer at the map in his hand. Sure enough, the route went right through the headwaters of the stream he had just spent the day fishing. *Well, I know what I'm going to be doing for the next year or two,* he said to himself.[24]

Long-delayed carpentry projects would have to wait a while longer. Beekeeping, another passion, would have to take a back seat too. As it turned out, he was off by several years. It wouldn't be until the next decade that Rick Webb could focus on making honey or catching brook trout again.

Webb v. Fury

Webb devoted that first summer of his retirement to doing what he did best: research.

He pored over maps of the likely route. He read up on environmental regulations governing pipeline construction. He called experts and asked about industry techniques for controlling erosion and runoff on steep slopes. He even went up in a two-seater airplane with a pilot friend to peer down at other pipelines being built in similar terrain in West Virginia.

And he got up to speed on the nitty-gritty elements of the pipeline construction process. It sounded like a kind of large-scale open-heart surgery. First, crews would stake out the right-of-way. Then they would remove all trees, rocks, and debris within its boundaries. Operators of large backhoes or huge machines called "wheel trenchers" would scour out soil, rock, and gravel to a depth of 10 to 12 feet. If they hit shallow bedrock, they would hammer or blast deep enough that the pipe could be buried at least 3 feet beneath the finished surface. Truckers would haul in 40-foot lengths of pipe and set them next to the trench. Welders would join them together. Each joint would be visibly inspected and x-rayed before being coated with anti-corrosion epoxy. Each "string" of pipe would then be lowered into the ground on a bed of sand or some other padding material. Then workers would backfill the trench, finishing with topsoil on top, roughly graded to the contour of the land. The pipe would be filled with locally sourced water at very high pressures and tested for leaks.[25] After that, the right-of-way would be seeded with grass and pollinator-friendly plants.

As a beekeeper, Webb could appreciate that last gesture. But everything else he was learning flashed warning signs. That standard process had been developed in relatively flat places like Oklahoma or Texas. Dominion's pipeline would cross some wickedly steep terrain. Crews would need to blast and flatten narrow ridgelines to accommodate both the pipe trench and a workspace for their machines. *Where would they put all the material they removed?* To trench across streams, they would either build temporary dams or divert water through a hose while they dug. *How would they keep sediment-choked runoff from moving downstream?*

The more he studied the route, the more Webb feared for the region's drinking water too. The whole area was underlaid by karst—a subterranean network of porous limestone riddled with hidden rivers, fissures, sinkholes, and caverns. Groundwater flowed throughout it all. Any contamination would move through it as through a sponge, spreading to private wells and municipal water supplies.

He realized that the pipeline could also spell disaster for the brook trout. The fish was finally bouncing back in remote streams around the region. But it was, he said, as if "the pipeline was routed to maximize the harm to the best of what remains" of remaining native trout habitat in Virginia.

All in all, it struck him as a terrible place to bury a large pipe full of methane—and a cockamamie way to spend several billion dollars. The terrain was just too tough, too erosion-prone, too laced with fragile streams in a region with weather that was too wet, to boot.

He was skeptical that anyone could lay a pipe through that landscape in a way that complied with both existing laws and regulations *and* the laws of physics. It was as though Dominion were promising to build a road to the moon.

Webb couldn't help wondering if the map he had gotten hold of wasn't the result of some miscommunication: maybe the engineers simply hadn't informed Dominion's leadership about the challenges they would encounter. Once they studied those obstacles, like John Lederer turning back atop the Blue Ridge, they would surely abandon this risky venture.

His wife Susan wasn't surprised to see him working around the clock just a few months into retirement. "Rick's been like that since we married," she told me. "'The world's going to hell, got to do something about it.'"

She didn't seem surprised by his conviction that the pipeline could be stopped either. Webb had gone toe to toe with a giant energy company before—and won. In the late 1970s the couple lived near Elkins, West Virginia, and ran a small nonprofit that sampled streams for pollution from nearby coal mining operations. Webb filed complaints with state and federal regulators claiming that 7 miles of native brook trout streams had been destroyed due to mining practices in the area. The coal company operating in that area sued him for defamation—a so-called SLAPP suit (for Strategic Lawsuit Against Public Participation), a popular corporate strategy to silence critics by weighing them down with crushing legal costs. The 31-year-old Webb fought it all the way to West Virginia's Supreme Court, which ruled in his favor.

The resulting decision, *Webb v. Fury*, sounds like a professional wrestling grudge match, but it would become a widely cited precedent, protecting the public's right to report potential violations of the law by coal companies, or any other companies. He hadn't set out to become a standard-bearer for the free speech rights of everyday citizens. He simply wanted to protect West Virginia's brook trout streams from becoming collateral damage of the fossil fuel industry.

Forty years later, the same principle applied when Webb studied Dominion's plans. "This is some of the best remaining wild landscape in the East," Webb would tell anyone who would listen. "And they are planning to cut right through the heart of it."

But when he said as much to friends and neighbors he ran into, almost all of them offered the same two responses. The first was agreement: it seemed that no one in Highland—where most people's livelihoods depended on farming or tourism—wanted a gas pipeline coming through their county.

The other sentiment Webb encountered over and over was resignation. "There's no stopping it," people would tell Webb ruefully, "because it's being pushed by Dominion."[26]

This attitude reached to the top of the county government. When asked for comment by the *Recorder*—the plucky local newspaper that broke the news in May 2014 about the project before any other media outlet—one Highland County board of supervisors member responded: "Holy cow, what else can you say?"[27]

"There might be nothing we can do," he added. "It's going to sock us."

The Lords of Virginia

Dominion. In Virginia, the name was synonymous with power, in both senses of the word.

Dominion Energy was a Fortune 500 corporation, one of the biggest energy companies in the country, the second-largest utility holding company in the US by market valuation, and the second-most profitable.

Most knew Dominion as their only available source of electricity: it owned the monopoly power utility that served two-thirds of all Virginians. Fewer were aware that Dominion was a natural gas giant too. Under the leadership of Tom Farrell—its disciplined and demanding CEO and chairman—the company had grown rapidly, acquiring gas pipelines, storage facilities, and distribution utilities around the country. Dominion made its money from stringing both pipes *and* wires, from moving molecules *and* electrons.[28]

Dominion claims a pedigree longer than any other energy company in America. Its corporate roots stretch back to 1787, when the Upper

Appomattox Company was granted a charter—with trustees that included George Washington and James Madison—by the Virginia General Assembly to build canals for hauling goods to the Tidewater region. Two centuries and many corporate transformations later, Dominion had accumulated enormous sway over the lawmakers who met blocks away from its own high-rise headquarters in Richmond.[29]

Over the decades, the company had developed a playbook for getting its way—whether it was higher electricity rates or approval for large, lucrative power plants.[30] With a market capital valuation of nearly $70 billion in mid-2014, it had massive resources to spend on media campaigns, attorneys at white-shoe law firms, and hiring former senior staffers from the federal agencies or governors' offices that they now lobbied. Dominion had long been the state's biggest corporate donor to political candidates and leaders on both sides of the aisle.[31] The company took advantage of Virginia's unusually lax campaign finance laws to shower Democratic and Republican legislators alike with contributions and perks like all-expenses-paid golf and hunting trips.

In 2014, Dominion seemed at the peak of its powers within its home state. The company's logo was ubiquitous: it loomed over Richmond from the top of its twenty-story office tower, graced the promotional materials for the annual Charity Classic golf tournament and the annual Riverrock Music Festival on the James River (both of which Dominion sponsored), and greeted theatergoers in the lobby of Richmond's largest performance venue—which would soon be renamed the Dominion Energy Center for the Performing Arts.

Its CEO, meanwhile, was widely viewed as the most influential man in Virginia. Tom Farrell was at the center of Virginia's political and cultural power centers. He served on the boards of Virginia's most prestigious philanthropic and education institutions—including the University of Virginia, which had employed Rick Webb for most of his career.[32] He sat on the board of the state's other iconic corporate behemoth, also based in Richmond: the tobacco company Altria (formerly known as Philip Morris, before it rebranded after a legal settlement for its decades of denial that its products caused cancer). Farrell was childhood friends with former governor Bob McDonnell; Farrell's brother-in-law was chairman of McGuireWoods, Virginia's leading corporate law firm, and a former state attorney general; Farrell's own son was a Republican state legislator.[33]

But beyond the personal reach of its CEO, Dominion's longstanding grip on Richmond was so firm, so obvious, that there was no sense in pretending otherwise. In 2015, a Dominion spokesman couldn't name for a reporter a single piece of legislation in the preceding five years in which the company didn't get what it wanted from the Virginia General Assembly.[34] During the same 2015 session in which Virginia legislators approved a bill freezing in place a large rate hike on Dominion's customers, they also passed and presented a resolution to Farrell expressing their gratitude "for the company's commitment to service."[35] (It would later come to light that the new law let Dominion overcharge its customers by as much as $426 million in 2016.)

For all these reasons, a Dominion representative wasn't being hyperbolic when he reportedly told landowners along the path of its new pipeline in Augusta County that they should quickly sign easement agreements because "we're a billion-dollar company, and we're going to put the pipeline wherever we want to put it."[36]

Everyone's Favorite Fossil Fuel

There was another reason why people thought tending bees might be a more productive use of Rick Webb's time than poring over pipeline regulations.

He was swimming against the ineluctable current of mainstream— and elite—opinion.

"Natural gas is, in many ways, the ideal fossil fuel," read the first line of a 2014 study guide for high school students produced by the US Department of Energy.[37] Natural gas, in the wake of the financial crisis, had become the great American comeback story—the fossil fuel almost everyone could love, used in everything from fertilizer to plastic to power plants. It was suddenly cheap and abundant, thanks to the ingenuity, pluck, and persistence of fracking pioneers like George Mitchell. The post-recession frenzy of drilling and pipeline-building had created jobs in economically depressed swaths of Pennsylvania, Ohio, and West Virginia. And it burned cleaner than coal, producing fewer health-damaging air pollutants and less climate-warming carbon dioxide.

Gas—or, rather, the brand of "natural gas" that had been carefully constructed like a shiny, impenetrable shell encasing the actual molecule composed of one carbon and four hydrogen atoms—seemed to offer something for everyone. It was every politician's fantasy: *Abundant! Cheap! Job-generating! Environmentally friendly! Made in America!*

This consensus had crystallized into its purest form by late January 2014—not long before Brittany Moody sat down to devise the initial route of the Atlantic Coast Pipeline—when President Barack Obama visited Congress to deliver his sixth State of the Union address.[38] He devoted substantial time to singing the praises of natural gas: "The all-of-the-above energy strategy I announced a few years ago is working, and today, America is closer to energy independence than we've been in decades. One of the reasons why is natural gas—if extracted safely, it's the bridge fuel that can power our economy with less of the carbon pollution that causes climate change."

Obama didn't use the word "fracking"—it had already become too controversial to say out loud. But he and other politicians enthusiastically embraced the "all of the above" slogan that oil and gas giant BP had rolled out in 2006 to convince customers that fossil fuels could work hand-in-hand with renewable energy. (The campaign's ads featured an image of several answers listed on a multiple-choice test: oil, natural gas, wind, solar, biofuels, and energy efficiency, with "all of the above" checked at the bottom.)

In 2007 and 2008, Obama had campaigned on his pledges to tackle climate change. Pursuing a clean energy agenda was, he said time and again, one of his top priorities.[39] Once in office, he presided over a head-spinning surge in the production and export of fossil fuels. And he didn't shy away from taking credit for it. A decade later, he would say during a speech in Texas, "That whole, suddenly America's like the biggest oil producer and the biggest gas—that was me, people . . . just say thank you, please."[40]

In the intervening years, to square that circle, Obama used his presidential bully pulpit time and again to portray the natural gas boom as a win for the climate.

"The natural gas boom has led to cleaner power, and greater energy independence," Obama said in his 2012 State of the Union address. He pledged to "take every possible action to safely develop this energy."

In March of that year, Obama gave another speech in the Oklahoma oil town of Cushing to prove his fossil fuel bona fides. "We've added enough new oil and gas pipeline to encircle the Earth and then some," he boasted, before warning that even more would be needed. "In fact, the problem in a place like Cushing is that we're actually producing so much oil and gas in places like North Dakota and Colorado that we don't have enough pipeline capacity to transport all of it to where it needs to go—both to refineries, and then, eventually, all across the country and around the world."[41]

Obama was trying to thread a delicate political needle. The fight over the Keystone XL oil pipeline was intensifying. A committed coalition of Native Americans, Nebraska ranchers, and other residents along its route had emerged to fight the project, which would ferry crude from Canada's tar sands straight through their irrigation and drinking water sources on its way to refineries on the Gulf Coast for export. The White House was drawing fire from these grassroots groups and climate activists on one side and Republicans on the other (who decried his "anti-energy agenda" for not rubber-stamping Keystone without delay).[42]

All the same, on his party's "all of the above" energy menu, the main entrees remained oil and gas. During his 2012 reelection campaign, Obama studiously avoided discussing climate change, for fear of alienating moderate voters. In a presidential debate with his opponent Mitt Romney in October 2012, he responded to attacks on his support for the fossil fuel industry by touting the record levels of oil and gas produced on federal lands on his watch. "We continue to make it a priority for us to go after natural gas," the president said. "We've got potentially 600,000 jobs and a hundred years' worth of energy right beneath our feet with natural gas. And we can do it in an environmentally sound way . . . natural gas isn't just appearing magically; we're encouraging it and working with the industry."[43]

As a shot of economic adrenaline coming on the heels of the financial crisis, the timing of the fracked gas gusher was impeccable. The sugar high of jobs—most temporary, but still, they were jobs—was something Obama could brag about to an increasingly polarized electorate in key swing states like Pennsylvania and Ohio, as he faced an intractable Republican opposition after the 2010 midterms. Gas was crowding out coal in the power sector, but the coal industry's clout and workforce had been shrinking for years anyway.

What's more, unfettered access to cheap energy had long been viewed by many Americans as a birthright of sorts—as revealed every time gasoline prices rose and politicians' poll numbers tanked in response. The siren song of gas was irresistible. It let Obama and other leaders claim to have reconciled the false choice that had long been another enduring trope in American political discourse: the economy versus the environment.

Most people don't spend their evenings reading policy papers about lifecycle carbon emissions. Instead, they take their cues from voices they trust. This rhetoric—coming from the first US president to, avowedly, take the problem of climate change seriously—helped cement the idea of natural gas as a form of "clean energy" in the minds of many Americans.

Years later, Cheryl LaFleur, Obama's nominee to lead the Federal Energy Regulatory Commission—perhaps the most influential but overlooked climate actor within the federal government—would summarize the thinking that prevailed in Washington, DC, this way to me: "At that time, gas was seen as the environmental savior."[44]

With natural gas, they could have it both ways.

A Bridge Made of Methane

But the soaring rhetoric cloaked an awkward fact: natural gas is a fossil fuel.

And leaders were offering it up as a solution to an accelerating crisis—the warming of the planet—*primarily caused by fossil fuels.*

Even as Obama touted his oil and gas record, scientists were pointing out that natural gas might actually prove to be an "all of the above" approach to making climate change worse: via the carbon dioxide produced when it was burned, via the methane that leaked during its production and transport, via the renewable energy investments it crowded out, and via the fossil energy production it locked in for decades to come.[45]

"We really have to be quite careful about the language we use to frame things," climate scientist Kevin Anderson told the *New York Times* in 2011. Natural gas, he said, "is not a positive thing, it's just less negative." In fact, he added, it was "a very bad fuel" with "very high emissions indeed . . . not as high as some other fossil fuels, but given where we need to be, to compare it with the worst that's out there is very dangerous."[46]

Anderson wasn't the only one ringing alarm bells.[47] In 2011, Robert Howarth and Anthony Ingraffea, scientists at Cornell University, published an analysis suggesting that gas produced by fracking might be, in fact, *dirtier* than coal once you tallied up all the methane that likely leaked into the atmosphere.[48]

The entire premise of the "bridge fuel" idea, they implied, rested on sleight of hand: gas only appeared cleaner than coal if one ignored all the methane quietly streaming out of wells, pipelines, compressor stations, distribution lines, and even appliances like furnaces and stoves. And if enough methane leaked to nearly cancel out any benefits from the massive coal-to-gas switch underway, then natural gas was, in Howarth's words, a "bridge to nowhere."[49]

The data painted a troubling picture. In February 2014, a peer-reviewed study in *Science*, drawing on twenty years of methane measurements, concluded that the Environmental Protection Agency's leak estimates were too low by 25 to 75 percent.[50] Another key *Science* paper followed, revealing that, in 2015, the amount of methane leaking across the US oil and gas supply chain was 60 percent greater than the EPA's estimates.[51] In October 2014 an international team of researchers published a study in *Nature*, the world's other leading academic journal, warning that building out a gas-heavy global energy system would likely not reduce greenhouse gas emissions in the coming decades; most of their models projected an *increase* in total climate-warming pollution in a scenario of "abundant gas."[52]

Those concerns struggled to get a hearing, though. There were louder voices in the room.

In 2013, Obama tapped Ernest Moniz, a physicist at MIT, to be his new secretary of energy. One of Moniz's claims to fame was leading a yearlong project that produced a report titled *The Future of Natural Gas*. It recommended channeling more private investment and government R & D dollars into natural gas. Moniz and his coauthors confidently asserted that extracting and burning more shale gas would be, on balance, *good* for the climate because it would reduce the use of more carbon-intensive coal. They shrugged at the environmental consequences as "challenging but manageable."[53]

"Much has been said about natural gas as a bridge to a low-carbon future, with little underlying analysis to back up this contention," Moniz said at a 2011 press conference to launch the report. "The analysis in this study provides the confirmation—natural gas truly *is* a bridge to a low-carbon future."

It was little noticed at the time, or in the ensuing years, but the MIT report's primary funder was the American Clean Skies Foundation, a nonprofit that functioned as a pro–natural gas front group, founded by Aubrey McClendon, the CEO of Chesapeake Energy.[54]

The revelation that the MIT analysis was largely financed by the nation's most aggressive fracking firm—and the second-biggest gas producer—did nothing to blunt its impact. Instead, the heavily footnoted document was widely cited by its intended audience of policymakers, politicians, energy analysts, and investors as ironclad evidence—from one of the world's most prestigious research institutions—of the wisdom of expanding the country's gas infrastructure. Moniz testified to the Senate Committee on Energy and Natural Resources that summer, at a hearing convened expressly to air the report's findings, soon after its release.[55]

Moniz went on to serve as energy secretary for the remainder of Obama's time in office. He was proud enough of the *Future of Natural Gas* report that he would later have it painted into the background of his official Department of Energy portrait.[56] (Years later, he would remain one of the highest-profile proponents of Obama's "all of the above" energy strategy; in 2018, he would go on to join the board of Southern Company, after it became a partner in the Atlantic Coast Pipeline.)

But the Obama administration's eager embrace of the "bridge fuel" trope still wasn't enough for some fossil fuel boosters.

Soon after his 2014 speech, the Brookings Institution—the most august and influential of DC think tanks—published a letter by one of its fellows addressed directly to the president. It exhorted Obama to go even further, to capitalize on "your energy moment" by making it easier to extract, pipe, and export methane to secure and spread American influence abroad: "While I welcome your prescience, I would argue that rather than being a bridge, gas *is* the future."[57]

Chapter Two

An Energy Superhighway

"It's what you'd call the Saudi America of natural gas."

Chet Wade opened his presentation by thus singing the praises of the Marcellus Shale—after first noting that his employer, Dominion Energy, was "the second most admired company in the industry."

Several dozen residents of Highland County stared back at him from their seats in the gallery of the Monterey courthouse. They had turned out to hear Wade, Dominion's vice president for corporate communications, and his colleagues explain why the company wanted to route its pipeline through their county, which billed itself as "Virginia's Switzerland."

Demand for cheap Marcellus gas was insatiable, Wade claimed. Homeowners, manufacturers, and power producers in densely populated eastern Virginia and North Carolina desperately needed it to heat their homes, fire industrial furnaces, and push coal out of the grid, he said. That's why the pipeline would be a good thing for everyone: "It helps the economy."[1]

"Gas offers opportunities to counties that don't have it," his colleague Emmett Toms chimed in, adding that Highland stood to gain much-needed tax revenues. Toms pointed out, for good measure, that Dominion had donated $13,000 to a local high school scholarship fund. Before taking questions, he walked folks through what they could expect to see after construction was done. He cued up a slide with a photo of grassy meadows striping through dense forest, with elk peaceably grazing atop a pipeline right-of-way. His final slide: a close-up photo of steak and potatoes heaped on a plate.

For a moment, the Highlanders silently absorbed these visuals, suggestive of . . . hunting opportunities? Jobs? Theirs being a rural, largely conservative county with not a whole lot of new economic activity on its horizon—people mostly depended on farming, timber harvests, and vista-seeking tourists for their livelihoods—an outsider could be forgiven for assuming this kind of broad-brush sales pitch might find a receptive audience.

But at least one longtime resident sitting in the front row just rested his head on his hand in amazement. Rick Webb marveled at the implication that Highland should be *grateful* to be in the path of Dominion's proposed megaproject. His astonishment quickly curdled into indignation.

"It was just so insulting," he would say later, referring to the images of food and elk—a species that hadn't been found in the region since John Lederer's time. "In my view they showed profound disrespect for the people they were talking to. You think we don't care about anything other than bare survival around here?"[2]

But Webb was even more disturbed by the absence of technical detail in the presentation. He sat next to Brittany Moody, the lead designer—"She seemed like a very nice person"—but no one on Dominion's team had mentioned how they planned to deal with the steep terrain for which Highland was named. Nor had they explained how they would avoid puncturing the karst formations—the Swiss cheese under Virginia's Switzerland—through which much of western Virginia's water supply percolated. When those issues were raised by his elected supervisors, Webb only heard vague answers that sounded to him like "trust us."

The back-and-forth confirmed his suspicion that Dominion didn't really grasp the terrain—either physical *or* human—that it was dealing with.[3]

A few rows behind Webb—sitting next to Nancy Sorrells and Greg Buppert, both busy jotting down notes—Lew Freeman had listened closely to the sales pitch too. As a local resident who prized the wild spaces of Highland County, he was concerned. As someone who had helped craft his fair share of public relations campaigns, he was un-impressed. Though he was now happily retired and living on several leafy acres near the West Virginia border, Freeman had spent much of his career as a lobbyist, representing the plastics industry—and before that, the oil and gas industry—on Capitol Hill in Washington.

Freeman listened as local officials peppered Dominion's team with anxious queries about emergency response in the event of a rupture, about protecting water supplies, about road traffic and property values and how often they would use eminent domain. He noticed that the company's emissaries had a quick response for each question but never really answered it.

"It reminded me of a guy on a street corner with a monkey on a leash and a folding table and three cups," Freeman said. "And it was Tom Farrell who was moving the cups around. That was an early impression I had of their style: the guy who's selling snake oil at the fair."[4]

"All Revved Up, Unlikely to Win"

The following week, Dominion's team continued its barnstorming tour of western Virginia, with information meetings in two other rural counties that the pipeline would traverse before tunneling under the James River and onward to North Carolina.

Highland, Augusta, and Nelson Counties had their demographic, economic, and topographic differences, but they had plenty in common too: each was dense with steep mountains, wooded hollows, Baptist churches, family-run farms, and—on balance—a conservative-leaning electorate. (Each county would go on to vote for Donald Trump in 2016, by comfortable margins.)

In Nelson, Wade, Toms, and their colleagues ran through the same sales pitch—and a nearly identical slideshow presentation (including the slide with the meat and potatoes) to a standing-room-only crowd in the middle school auditorium. On their way in, Dominion's team had walked past dozens of locals in NO PIPELINE t-shirts, several of whom held signs that read "NO EMINENT DOMAIN FOR CORPORATE GAIN" (and one with a sketch of Gandalf from *Lord of the Rings* with the caption: "You shall not pass"). Only 25 percent of Nelson's 225 landowners on the route had granted access to surveyors to set foot on their property. Perhaps cognizant of that fact, Toms downplayed the role of eminent domain in the process.[5]

"It's a last resort and we are able to negotiate successfully with 95 percent of property owners," he said. Toms reminded everyone that the company hadn't yet decided whether to pursue the project. But then he sketched out Dominion's expected timetable: approval by federal regulators in 2016, construction in 2017 and 2018, a pipe full of gas by the end of 2018.

After the presentation, dozens of Nelsonians voiced their frustration that Dominion's gas train seemed to be leaving the station before they had even been told where it was heading. They raised concerns about the project's purpose, safety, and impacts on water quality and property values. One resident who lived on the proposed route wondered if the gas would ultimately be exported overseas. "I see no benefit in this for Nelson County," she said. Another described how he had once witnessed a 24-inch gas line explode in California and the "incredible inferno" that resulted. What would an explosion on a 42-inch pipeline look like, he asked, and how would *that* be put out? Another Nelsonian who had worked in construction for forty years took issue with Dominion's entire approach:

> "It seems like what these people did is they took a giant magic marker and said, 'All right let's start in West Virginia and we'll come down here in Virginia, this looks nice and we'll end up here in North Carolina.' Then they decided to survey where they put the mark. They are doing it ass-backwards. First you go out and survey and find out if it's even feasible where you want to put the pipeline before you draw the line. And I highly recommend these people take a hike"—the crowd laughed—"but also take a hike over the Blue Ridge Parkway and see the kind of terrain they have to deal with. It's nothing but rock with two inches of dirt on it. They will be blasting for months and months."[6]

The following night, Dominion's team presented on the other side of the Blue Ridge, to another large, restive crowd in neighboring Augusta County. The reception was even frostier.

A conservative member of the board of supervisors named Tracy Pyles gave a fifteen-minute stem-winder of a monologue, chiding Dominion for colluding with lawmakers in Richmond to foist the unwanted pipeline on Augusta residents. Alluding to the 2004 state law that gave gas companies the authority to send surveyors onto private property without permission, Pyles challenged Wade and Toms to reveal "the contributions that Dominion and all your subsidiaries and all the gas lobbies that are out there, spent on our legislature, our executive officeholder and on elections for the period of July 1st 2003 through December 31st 2004."

"Let's see how much money went to these guys," he said to loud applause.[7]

Nancy Sorrells marveled at Pyles's performance. He had been her "nemesis" during her own tenure on the board of supervisors: they had, she said, disagreed on just about everything. But on the question of Dominion's pipeline, they seemed in perfect alignment.

Sorrells was also struck by her neighbors' collective fury and skepticism. Some wondered aloud why Dominion was investing in a huge gas project instead of spending on more solar projects. Many emphasized their concerns about the county's water supply. "People wanted to know 'How many jobs, really? How much taxes, really? Is this thing going to explode?'"

From where she was sitting, Dominion's late summer western Virginia charm offensive had floated like a lead balloon. "Dominion just got booed out of those places," Sorrells said. "You could tell they were just unnerved by it."[8]

But would it matter? That's where most of her neighbors parted ways with her. They could—and should—rage against it, many agreed, but in the end, Dominion would prove too powerful.[9] The local *Staunton News Leader* ran an editorial after the raucous meeting. Its headline reflected the prevailing mood, with its mix of outrage and resignation: "Residents All Revved Up, but Unlikely to Win."

"It's disconcerting to watch and those who oppose the pipeline probably have a few more plays to make," the editorial board wrote. "They'll be loud, public and probably futile. It's tough to see how they'll trump a major utility which holds governmental power and has its sights on building this pipeline, regardless of who does or doesn't want it in their backyard. Even David had a rock to throw at Goliath."[10]

Seeds of a Strategy

On a steamy August afternoon, Greg Buppert left his office on Charlottesville's downtown mall, got into his 2007 Honda Accord, and headed west out of town.

His route paralleled the old Three Notch'd Road cut by colonial settlers in the 1730s from Richmond all the way through the Blue Ridge and took him onward through the Shenandoah Valley, over the twisting two-lane roads that crossed the Valley and Ridge complex, past the roadside monuments on the heights of Shenandoah Mountain where the Union and Confederate armies once jockeyed for position, and then down onto the sleepy main street of Monterey. It was a drive he would come to know well.

Two weeks earlier, Buppert had made it for the first time, to hear Dominion's public relations team make their pipeline pitch to the people of Highland County.

He had gone to size up his likely opponent. After that meeting had ended, Lew Freeman walked with Buppert to their cars and made a prediction: "This is going to end up in court."

If so, that would be Buppert's department. Dominion was, at least publicly, still weighing whether to pursue the project, but his employer, the Southern Environmental Law Center, was already gearing up for a fight.

Fights needed soldiers. This time Buppert would be the one making the pitch to the citizens of Highland County. He would try to sell them on their own agency—to persuade them that they had both the means and opportunity to oppose this project if they wanted to. Rick Webb would take the stage after him, to describe the physical and regulatory hurdles in the project's path.

Lew Freeman introduced them to an audience of nearly one

hundred. A tenth of Highland's adult population had gathered in a former elementary school to hear what the two men had learned from their respective summer crash courses of study: Buppert's on the eye-glazing subjects of regional gas markets, pipeline permitting, and the 1938 Natural Gas Act; Webb's on the more pulse-quickening topic of pipe-laying through steep, sensitive, unstable Appalachian terrain. Buppert could sense their anxiety. Like doctors laying out treatment options after an unwelcome diagnosis, he and Webb planned to offer them a path forward.[11]

The clean-cut 41-year-old lawyer and the shaggily bearded 65-year-old scientist cut different figures, but they shared a few qualities. Each had a soft-spoken, low-key bearing that masked a steely resolve and an eye for details that others tended to overlook. And neither was easily intimidated.

The lawyer went first. Buppert demystified the thicket of acronyms that loomed before them: NEPA (National Environmental Policy Act), USFS (United States Forest Service), FWS (Fish and Wildlife Service), EIS (environmental impact statement), DEQ (Virginia's Department of Environmental Quality), ESA (Endangered Species Act). He explained the various ways that ordinary citizens could navigate this bureaucratic obstacle course of state and federal agencies—to make their concerns known, to protect their property, to assert their rights under the law. He explained the intricacies of NEPA and how it required agencies like the Forest Service to review the environmental impacts of major infrastructure projects.

And then he gave a quick tutorial on the most important letter combination of all: FERC. A harsh-sounding syllable that would soon become a familiar sound in that part of Virginia, muttered with the tone one uses when stubbing a toe.

The Federal Energy Regulatory Commission, Buppert explained, would weigh the possible benefits of the project—say, purported lower costs for consumers—against the downsides—say, reduced property values and damage to local agriculture. "It's like a trial," he told the Highlanders, but in practice, FERC focused much more on the economic benefits of a project than environmental impacts. He described how the Natural Gas Act authorized FERC to, in turn, authorize companies like Dominion to invoke the power of eminent domain—a subject on everyone's mind.

Buppert hammered home one key point: they had to get in the arena if they wanted to fight.

"You have to participate as an intervenor if you might file legal action later," he said. By registering as "intervenors" with FERC, they could get their concerns formally placed on the record. This would give them legal standing should they later decide to pursue lawsuits on the environmental, safety, health, or other issues they raised. (Those comments would also be some of the bricks with which Buppert and his team at SELC would assemble their legal arguments down the road.)

Then Rick Webb took over the mic. "There are serious problems with this project," he began. He cued up on a screen Dominion's pictures of elk grazing on a pipeline corridor. "This is what they showed at meetings," Webb said. "Sort of a nicely mowed city park." Then he showed them some photos of what actual pipeline construction looked like: a huge, muddy, open wound. Football field–wide trenches, heavy machinery, brown pools of water everywhere.

And those were images of smaller lines out west. Webb explained that Dominion had never built a 42-inch-pipeline. In fact, no one had ever built a pipeline of that size across Appalachia's mountains before—for good reason. Trenching through Oklahoma prairie was one thing. West Virginia's vertiginous ravines were entirely another. Even the best available construction techniques couldn't prevent erosion and runoff in this kind of landscape. Peeling open so many miles of earth, on 60-degree slopes frequently hammered by torrential rains, would threaten streams, ecosystems, and people's water supplies, Webb said, no matter how careful the construction crews were. There would be serious damage, he concluded. The only question was how much damage people—and regulators—were willing to accept.

Greg Buppert shared the scientist's skepticism that the project, as currently laid out, could comply with state and federal environmental regulations. He was also skeptical that there was any economic need at all for this pipeline. Its capacity was greater than the demand for gas in all of Virginia that year. He speculated that the larger economic rationale for the pipeline was vulnerable to legal attack. Buppert wanted to make that case before a panel of judges—before the pipe was laid in the ground and the question became moot.

SELC was smaller and more regionally focused than well-known groups like the Natural Resources Defense Council or the Sierra Club, but it had more legal muscle and resources than the local conservation and grassroots groups they often worked with. Still, its annual budget—fueled by individual donations and foundation grants—was just $30 million, a rounding error for a company like Dominion or Duke.

The lawyers of SELC were quite familiar with those two firms. In 2007, the organization had won a case before the Supreme Court, successfully arguing that the Clean Air Act required Duke Energy to install new pollution control technology on coal power plants. And SELC attorneys were also going toe to toe with Dominion, pressing lawmakers and regulators to require the utility to clean up toxic coal ash ponds at its largest coal power plants.[12]

Buppert and his colleagues had already identified a few reasons to wade into this new fight. "The immediate hook for us was the fact that it was going through the National Forest," he said. Protecting public lands was their bread and butter, but the group had also begun pushing for policies to encourage utilities to adopt more renewable energy. In their view, the pipeline represented a giant leap in the wrong direction.

That evening, the seeds of a strategy for fighting the pipeline were being planted in western Virginia. While Rick Webb would spend the years ahead making the case that the Atlantic Coast Pipeline *could not* be built and still comply with existing laws, Buppert would pursue a parallel tack, arguing that the project *should not* be built—because there was no economic need for it and because it would lock Virginians into eighty years or more of fossil fuel dependence.

This strategy would further take shape in the months and years to come, with the input of dozens of organizations, and it wouldn't lack in ambition. But if they succeeded, there was a chance it would strike at the foundation of the "bridge" fuel building spree unfolding not just in Appalachia but across the US.

After the meeting, Buppert drove back home to Charlottesville on

a series of twisting two-lane roads, plunging up and over mountain after mountain. The drive roughly paralleled the route that the pipeline
would take.

"I felt like I always had to be in the driver's seat on a trip out to
Highland County," he told me. "If I wasn't driving, I would get nau-
seous." You didn't have to be an expert to see how hard it would be to
lay a pipeline safely across that terrain. "You only have to do this drive
a couple times to realize that Rick was really on to something."[13]

Buppert had no doubt that Webb was right when he said that
Dominion's pipeline would be an unprecedented undertaking.

But Buppert hadn't told the audience that he and a colleague had
been reading up on other pipelines for the past two months and had
come to a dispiriting conclusion. "We couldn't find a single example of
a situation where citizens were able to mount an effective opposition
to a gas pipeline," he told me.

If the Virginians in its path came together to stop it—well, that
would be unprecedented too. They would be pioneers.

"A Game-Changer for the Commonwealth"

"What we are going to announce today is a game-changer for the commonwealth of Virginia."

Governor Terry McAuliffe beamed out at the cameras and phones
held aloft by reporters to record the moment. It was the morning of
September 2, 2014. Outside it was a sweltering 101 degrees—the warmest September reading in Richmond since 1954—but inside the briefing room, the men in dark suits at the podium looked at ease. They
were there to make it official: Dominion was indeed going to build a
new interstate gas pipeline.[14]

And, McAuliffe promised, it would be an "an energy super-highway
to fuel our new economy."

The room—packed with Virginia's power brokers, state agency
heads, legislators, and corporate elites—erupted in applause. Standing
next to him, Dominion CEO Tom Farrell smiled beneficently.

"We will now have direct access to the most affordable and abundant supplies of natural gas anywhere in the United States of America,"

the governor said. "This project will mean lower energy costs for all Virginia customers, both electricity and natural gas costs." Virginia was finally going to become a major player in the nation's gas boom. "Up until this announcement, Virginia was not able to play in that game," McAuliffe said, "because we didn't have the pipeline to make us competitive."

And this new pipe would be *big*, he crowed, "one of the largest that has ever been built in decades."

Then the governor ad-libbed a line in Farrell's direction: "As long as we've got this trench dug in parts of the Commonwealth, maybe—I hate to surprise you—but maybe we could throw a little fiber-optic cable in that as well . . . what do you think about that?"[15]

Tom Farrell smiled again indulgently. The garrulous McAuliffe, a native of New York, was relatively new to Richmond's self-consciously genteel ways. But he was a veteran Democratic Party operative and a legendary fundraiser, close to some of the most powerful politicians in the country—he once told a reporter he had 18,632 names in his Rolodex.[16] In other words, he was someone Farrell could work with. Dominion had been the leading corporate contributor to McAuliffe's campaign, and to his inaugural celebration.

McAuliffe's riffing also offered him a chance to savor the moment. For Farrell this day represented the culmination of years of strategic bets on gas, going all the way back to Dominion's 2000 acquisition of the Pittsburgh-based pipeline giant Consolidated Natural Gas—a deal he spearheaded during his tenure as the firm's general counsel. Farrell was having a big year. In June 2014, Dominion had finished converting one of its oldest coal-fired power plants, Bremo Bluff, to run on natural gas. Dominion was on the cusp of getting federal approval to build a facility in Maryland to export gas to energy-hungry countries like India and Japan. And that winter, Farrell had seen a long-held personal goal come to fruition, when the film he had cowritten, produced, and financed—a Civil War drama that offered a sympathetic portrayal of young Confederate soldiers—debuted in Richmond. (It garnered mixed reviews.)

And now he was launching his biggest, boldest venture of all.

The Atlantic Coast Pipeline, the governor continued, would support manufacturing, recruit new industries to the state, and generate over a billion dollars in economic activity. As McAuliffe unspooled his superlatives, the press conference took on the air of a ribbon-cutting, as though the men were unveiling something that had already been built.

"I look forward to working with Tom and Hank and the other players and other stakeholders to make sure we complete the safest, most environmentally responsible and locally cooperative pipeline ever built in the history of the United States of America," McAuliffe concluded. He reached out and shook Tom Farrell's hand, then yielded the microphone.

"In each century of America's history we have seen a handful of key infrastructure developments leading to new opportunities and prosperity," the CEO observed. "In the nineteenth century we have railroads, the steam engine, and the beginning of steel manufacturing. In the twentieth century we have the automobile assembly line, the Internet, and, from my perspective the most important of all, the electric grid. In the twenty-first century the expansion of our natural gas pipeline network looks to be one of those key infrastructure developments."

The ACP would now take its rightful place among this civic pantheon of great progress-enabling infrastructure leaps in American history. Tom Farrell then made an explicit promise, one that communities along the path of the pipeline would later recall with some bitterness: "We will work closely with landowners and other stakeholders to find the best possible route, one that minimizes the impact on natural, cultural, and historic resources but still meets our operational needs."[17]

On the same day, a newly formed citizens' group in Nelson County sent out press releases to 123 news outlets declining that offer. "This pipeline is not in the public interest," said Ernie Reed of Friends of Nelson. "We, along with our partners in the counties along the route, intend to fight the pipeline until the project is dead."[18]

That same month, the Allegheny–Blue Ridge Alliance (ABRA) was formally launched. The alliance had started coalescing in July, with the meeting of a dozen or so concerned citizens around a table in the Staunton public library. By October, it encompassed twenty-five grassroots and conservation groups spanning the westernmost

Virginia counties on the route, all dedicated to working together to oppose the ACP. Before long, the alliance also counted among its members well-established organizations like the Chesapeake Climate Action Network, which advocated for a just transition away from fossil fuels in the Virginia, Maryland, and Washington, DC region, and Appalachian Mountain Advocates, a nonprofit public interest law outfit with long experience fighting mountaintop coal removal and the fracking industry in West Virginia. Lew Freeman, with his expertise in running complex organizations, had been tapped to lead the nascent alliance; Nancy Sorrells, Ernie Reed, and Greg Buppert were all founding members of its steering committee.

The Southern Environmental Law Center had formally entered the arena too. The organization assigned a team of lawyers and paralegals to work on challenging the Atlantic Coast Pipeline. And Buppert would lead them.

Meanwhile, Dominion reached out to Bob Burnley, a former head of Virginia's Department of Environmental Quality (the state's version of the federal Environmental Protection Agency), about consulting on the project.

"My reaction was," Burnley told me, "'Well, okay, if this is going to be done, I wouldn't normally bet against Dominion when they set their mind to doing something. . . . I can be a part of this and have some input in how it's done so it can be done in the most environmentally responsible way possible.'" So, he signed on as an environmental consultant.

Before long, Burnley invited Lew Freeman out to lunch in Staunton. The former oil and plastics lobbyist was on one side fighting the fossil gas project, while the former environmental regulator was on the other side, working to help get it built. Burnley wanted to allay the pipeline resisters' fears—"My objective is to see that it's the most environmentally responsible pipeline ever built," he said—and find ways to work together to minimize the project's impact. But he also wanted to disabuse them of any notions that they could stop it. "It's going to be built," Burnley said, according to Freeman—and he didn't think it would be the last one either.

Tom Farrell Goes to Wall Street

The day after the press conference, Tom Farrell traveled north to unveil the new project to perhaps his most essential audience: Wall Street.[19]

Each September, energy executives descended on Midtown Manhattan for an energy industry conclave hosted by Barclays, the international bank, where they presented to analysts, asset managers, and other financial gurus. These were the people who could make or break a company's plans for growth. They shaped wider perceptions of the prudence of a firm's investments in ways that would, in turn, influence everything from its credit rating to its ability to access debt financing to its stock price. They needed careful tending.

As Farrell launched into his prepared remarks, a slide appeared on the screen behind him, showing a stylized map of the Atlantic Coast Pipeline. John Lederer's hand-drawn map from 1670 had far more detail. This one had no towns or cities, no mountains, no Benson's Run or Appalachian Trail or James River—just a thick red line angling arrow-straight across Virginia and doglegging down into North Carolina. The only other features were shaded areas indicating the Utica and Marcellus Shales, arcing northward from West Virginia.[20]

The pipeline, Farrell noted, would give Dominion "access to the most prolific and cost-competitive natural gas supply in the US." What's more, it was "along an independent new route."[21] Every easement Dominion purchased and held in perpetuity would become part of its new asset. This kind of "greenfield" pipeline was far more valuable than one that used existing rights-of-way or co-located with, for example, the utility's electric transmission corridors.

The previous day's news had already been well received on Wall Street. The new project seemed like another smart gas bet by Dominion. Its combination of low risks with a generous 14 percent guaranteed rate of return could scarcely be found in any other class of investment. One prominent financial analysis website praised the move, noting that Marcellus and Utica gas "creates a need for massive, multi-year new investment in transportation infrastructure and natural gas downstream solutions (LNG export terminals, gas-fired power generation, petrochemical facilities, etc.)."[22]

Investors and financial analysts can be guilty of groupthink, but they can also size up an opportunity with ruthless clarity. The bankers in the audience knew quite well that two striking trends had defined the US energy sector since 2007. One, average US electricity demand had remained flat, as businesses and consumers were becoming more efficient.[23] Two, a dizzying surge of fracked shale gas had flooded the market. It wasn't so much that end users needed more gas; all that supply needed more demand. As the author of that analysis observed, the gas boom itself *"creates the need"* for more customers. The tail was wagging the dog.

The Atlantic Coast Pipeline would be a piece of long-lived infrastructure that itself would create a rationale for new, long-lived gas power plants. Once in place, the pipeline would help justify even more gas power plants, much in the way suburban owners of new pickup trucks look for excuses to go to Home Depot to buy stuff in need of hauling.

Wall Street's analysts also knew that, as proof of broader economic need, federal regulators would be satisfied by "precedent agreements"—private contracts with companies that committed to receive a certain share of a pipeline's capacity. Farrell told his audience that such twenty-year deals had already been inked with "multiple end-use customers."

Dominion had spent much of 2014 claiming that customers in Virginia and North Carolina were desperate for more Marcellus gas. Those customers, it would turn out, were themselves: Dominion's and Duke's own subsidiary power companies would receive most of the gas coming through the new pipe. They would be both seller *and* buyer (or "shipper" in the industry lingo). Financially, at least, there would be few leaks. It was a neatly closed loop.

Farrell also walked the analysts through an update of Dominion's Cove Point LNG project in Maryland. Once it received approval from FERC, construction would begin on a facility that would ship molecules of methane to other nations interested in cheap American energy. And then Farrell hinted at an even richer future that awaited.

He cued up a slide that showed "future pipeline takeaway opportunities" from Appalachia's shale formations. They added up to more than 10 billion cubic feet per day—more than five times the capacity of the Atlantic Coast Pipeline—and equaling nearly 15 percent of the country's total natural gas consumption.

His takeaway message: the gas-fueled growth opportunities would keep on expanding. His company intended to do its part to bring that methane to market. It would be a service to the nation, and more to the point, a rewarding undertaking for anyone who owned shares of Dominion Energy.

Tom Farrell already seemed to be looking ahead, as though the mountains of Virginia were a mere speed bump, to the Atlantic Coast and perhaps even beyond. First, they just had to build the pipeline.

Chapter Three

America's Homeplace

"Haven't you guys ever heard of Camille?"

Vicki Wheaton's question drew a blank stare from the chipper Dominion staffer. She had driven over the mountain from her home in Nelson County to attend the company's "open house" meeting about the new pipeline project in Augusta County, a week after Farrell and McAuliffe's grand unveiling in Richmond.

Other locals wandered around her, drifting from table to table, seeking more information about what the pipeline would mean for their lives and livelihoods and land. Dominion staffers in polo shirts smiled out at them from behind tables strewn with fact sheets meant to preempt their concerns—about economic impacts, safety measures, how the survey process works.

Dominion had finally released a more detailed map of its intended route, now displayed on poster boards around the room. Wheaton, a retired nurse, lived in a home near the route but not on it. Like many other Nelsonians, she was dismayed to discover that it cut up and over Roberts Mountain, which she could see from her front yard, and then straight down through Davis Creek—a quiet hollow that happened to be the place hardest hit by one of the most intense rainfall events in American history.

When she repeated the question—"Haven't you heard of Camille?" —to a few other smiling Dominion representatives, she received the same quizzical looks. Another staffer offered something about their "world-class" engineering and how most folks never even noticed after the pipe was in the ground.

And it suddenly dawned on Vicki Wheaton: this company was planning to excavate a 12-foot-deep trench through the ground zero of Nelson County's unthinkable loss, near the homes of people still racked with the trauma nearly half a century later. And its planners didn't seem to realize it. Her incredulity soon gave way to outrage. Did they not know that they would be disturbing hallowed ground— ground that had proven, time and again, to be prone to catastrophic flooding?[1]

A Promise to Tinker Bryant

On the evening of August 19, 1969, the remnants of Hurricane Camille, the second most powerful hurricane to ever make landfall in the United States, arrived unannounced in central Virginia.

After battering Mississippi and Louisiana, the storm had weakened as it moved inland, until the jet stream grabbed and carried it east across Appalachia. It started raining around dinnertime. For the next eight hours, Camille emptied its contents on the eastern slopes of the Blue Ridge.

In Nelson County, the epicenter of the deluge, 28 inches of rain were officially recorded; some folks later reported finding 55-gallon barrels, which hold 31 inches of water, filled to the brim. So much rain sheeted down that people had to cover their faces with their shirts just to breathe. Birds drowned in flight and dropped at their feet. Entire mountainsides turned to liquid. On dozens of slopes, avalanches of soil—a cement-like slurry that contained car-sized boulders and entire trees, roots and all—rocketed toward homesteads full of sleeping families below.

The residents of Nelson County woke on August 20 to an unrecognizable, apocalyptic landscape. The storm had done things no one had thought possible: relocated entire barns, parked cars in treetops, swept houses clear from their foundations and 20 miles downstream. Many ravines and river bottoms became death traps. Nelson had lost nearly 1 percent of its population—128 people—in the space of eight hours. Thirty-three were never found. They still lay entombed by Camille's debris somewhere in the surrounding hills.[2]

Those who lived in the hollows along Davis Creek had suffered the most. The US Weather Bureau estimated that the creek—normally a few inches deep and narrow enough to jump across—had reached, in some places, 75 feet deep and 500 feet wide. When rescuers made their way into the valley over the next few days, they found just three of the hollow's thirty-five homes still standing.

Nelsonians would come to refer to the event simply as "the Flood." It became a terrible hinge in their lives: there was before Camille and after Camille. Some were so traumatized they never spoke about it again.

Vicki Wheaton had not experienced Camille herself. When the storm hit, she was a 14-year-old kid in Florida. In the mid-1980s, when she first decided to move to Nelson County, she wasn't even sure where she was—the place just called to her.

She was in her early thirties, living with her husband and young daughter in Atlantic City, New Jersey, when she went to visit her parents in Petersburg, Virginia. She was trying to wean her daughter at the time, so her parents told her to leave the child and get out of the house for the day. Wheaton took an aimless drive along the Blue Ridge Parkway and then down Route 56 into an impossibly scenic valley below. As she pulled out onto the flats of the Tye River Valley, the iconic Blue Ridge peaks of the Priest and Three Ridges loomed on either side, cradling apple orchards and hayfields, giving the impression of one huge, lush embrace.

Suddenly, her fancy new car ("I was married to lots of money!") started making a "crazy ass noise." She stopped on the side of the two-lane road, right in the center of the valley, and got out, thinking it was about to explode.

"I'm standing outside the car," she recalled, "and I'm looking around. And I just heard, you know, 'This is it.'"[3]

She got back in the car. The noise stopped. She pulled into the next gas station, at Mac's store, and asked the guys there to check it out. They told her everything looked fine.

Vicki Wheaton believes in the universe sending signals. She and her then-husband, eager to escape the congestion of New Jersey, had been scouting for places to move. She called him and said: "Look, I don't know, but this is where we're moving." He came down with her to Nelson some weeks later to check it out and agreed. They made the move and, soon after, Vicki met Tinker Bryant, the cousin of the man who had sold them their land.

Vicki and Tinker, then in his mid-sixties and retired, became fast friends. They drank coffee on his front porch and Wheaton listened to his stories. Frank Bryant Jr., known to all as Tinker, had been a radio operator for the US Navy in the Pacific during World War II. After the war he returned home to the family farm and took over his father's mail route—which happened to be the same route his grandfather had worked—making a 70-mile daily round trip through southwest Nelson in his two-door Chevrolet.[4] Many folks who had lived through the Flood didn't much like to talk about it. Tinker seemed to make an exception for the high-spirited Wheaton, who had the friendly but forthright manner you find in the most capable nurses. He entrusted her with his story of unimaginable loss.

In August 1969, Bryant was living in a modest home with his wife Sarah Grace Marshall and their daughters on the banks of Hat Creek, not far from where he had grown up. He told Vicki how, on the night Camille struck, a wall of water and debris engulfed his house and he had somehow grabbed a tree and clung to it for hours. How, when morning came, there was no sign of Sarah or three of their children. How he had frantically tracked down his neighbor, who happened to be the county sheriff, to help. How they assembled a small search party and made their way to the river's junction with Hat Creek, where they found pieces of Tinker's house and possessions—mattresses, pillows, a child-sized suitcase—scattered about, but no trace of his family. How Sarah and three of their five daughters were among the 128 Nelson residents who lost their lives that night.[5]

Tinker went on to remarry. His two surviving daughters, who had been away at summer jobs, had children—his eight grandchildren—and lived nearby. He lived out the rest of his life not far from the home Camille had destroyed. One day, Tinker turned serious mid-conversation and asked Wheaton to make him a promise. He was getting old, he said, but she had most of her life ahead of her. He wanted her to do whatever she could to help others avoid the kind of loss and pain that he had experienced. The rawness of his emotion, decades later, left a profound impression on her.[6]

"I agreed to his terms," Wheaton said.

"It Will Never Happen"

After Tinker Bryant died in 2009 at the age of 84, Wheaton's promise took on the form of a fixation on the floodplains of Nelson County. She decided to push for tougher restrictions on what could be built in those areas, so that when extreme rains struck again—as they surely would—people wouldn't be caught in the path of deadly deluges.

Wheaton soon became a self-educated expert on zoning regulations and flood risk maps issued by the Federal Emergency Management Agency. (As it happens, FEMA was created partly in response to lessons learned from the response to Camille; so were Nelson County's first zoning laws). She hectored county and state officials, waging a lonely campaign for stricter floodplain protections.

Once she heard about the Atlantic Coast Pipeline, her quest took on heightened urgency. She kept thinking about what might happen if a storm with even a fraction of Camille's strength hit Nelson with the pipeline buried under dozens of its streams and rivers. *How could emergency personnel reach people who needed help? In the event of a rupture, would fires and explosions impede rescue efforts? Would the resulting pollution be dangerous to breathe, or infiltrate water supplies and communities downstream?* She talked to experts at Virginia Tech and other universities, who told her that such a scenario could lead to serious loss of life.[7]

County officials were resistant. Her friends and fellow organizers were skeptical that anything would come of her efforts. But she pressed ahead anyway, with the singular focus of someone trying to defuse a bomb as a timer ticks down.[8]

She had left Dominion's pipeline information meeting in Augusta County with a newfound resolution. The following night, she attended another "open house" at the Nelson high school. The company's friendly, polo shirt–clad representatives were there again, assuring worried landowners that the route would be wiggled as needed—"like a piece of spaghetti"—to accommodate any discoveries of archaeological sites or family cemeteries.

Wheaton quizzed a few more staffers with the same question—"Have you ever heard of Camille?"—and got the same blank look. Nearby, a Dominion employee was explaining to another Nelson resident, after being informed about the horrors that had visited Davis Creek in 1969, "Well, we have a procedure to follow should we find human remains."[9]

Wheaton had heard enough.

"You will never come through my county," she said to one of them, with a firmness and confidence that would later, on reflection, surprise her. "It will never happen."

And then she walked out and headed home.

Chosen Ground

Many neighbors shared her defiance, if not her certainty about the outcome. By September's end, Nelson County had emerged as the epicenter of resistance to the Atlantic Coast Pipeline.

Drivers on Nelson's winding roads were used to seeing the familiar signs for breweries and vineyards and even more numerous Baptist churches, along with hand-lettered yard signs that read "Thank you Jesus" and "Cast thy burden upon the Lord." But that fall no one could miss a new species of sign proliferating like kudzu on the roadsides. They were bright blue, and in big white block letters they read: "NO PIPELINE." The slogan was even painted on the sides of a few barns.[10] Here and there were also a few placards that read: "REMEMBER CAMILLE—NO PIPELINE."

For the denizens of Richmond or Washington who glimpsed those signs on their way to Wintergreen, the local ski resort, or to drink in mountain views along with their hard ciders and IPAs at one of

Nelson's fast-proliferating craft beverage establishments, the area might seem like a quiet backwater. The governor of Virginia seemed to share that impression.

"Nelson County—I think it's our smallest population county in Virginia," Terry McAuliffe replied to a caller on a radio show that winter, who had asked him to weigh in on the proposed route of the Atlantic Coast Pipeline, which, for thirty-some of its 600 miles, would wend through the heart of Nelson.[11]

McAuliffe was way off: Nelson's 474 square miles of narrow hollows, sweeping valleys, and steep wooded slopes were home to nearly fifteen thousand souls, making it more populous than thirty-three other Virginia counties. Among his other responsibilities, the governor was the booster-in-chief of the commonwealth, whose longstanding slogan (coined in the summer of 1969) for luring outside visitors was "Virginia Is for Lovers." McAuliffe probably didn't realize it, but the state's most famous cultural export had once been Nelson County—America's favorite "homeplace."

Between 1972 and 1981, tens of millions of Americans had a concentrated dose of Nelson beamed into their living rooms each week in the form of *The Waltons*. The beloved television show chronicled the lives of a tight-knit, mountain-dwelling family in rural Virginia during the Great Depression. Through hard times, the Walton family ekes out a materially modest but happy life on their homestead—the "homeplace"—at the foot of the Blue Ridge. The narrator is John-Boy, the earnest eldest son who serves as an alter ego for Earl Hamner Jr., the novelist and screenwriter who created the show from his own memories of growing up in Nelson. In a speech called "Nelson County in Hollywood," Hamner once quoted an episode where John-Boy calls home "an island, a refuge, a haven . . . of love."

"That's Nelson County to me," Hamner concluded.[12]

As sentiments go, it's a bluntly nostalgic instrument, one that could live comfortably on a Hallmark card. But if you polled Nelson residents today, you wouldn't find much disagreement. That feeling prevails across its varied demographics, spanning all of America's familiar and confounding political, cultural, and economic divides.

Ron Enders and Ellen Bouton moved to Nelson County in 1974,

soon after they married, for precisely that reason: to fall in love with the land. They settled in an old farmhouse in Afton on 50 rolling acres near a tributary of the Rockfish River. They were members of a group that founded a nearby intentional community called Shannon Farm, part of a larger wave of folks who had alighted in the area: back-to-the-landers in search of cheap acreage, open space, the chance to live closer to nature.[13] They planted a large vegetable garden and tended the land while Ron led a nonprofit that helped people with intellectual, developmental, and other disabilities find jobs, and Ellen worked as a professional archivist for the National Radio Astronomy Observatory. They raised their children and became part of the civic fabric of the area.[14]

Although they had lived in Nelson for forty years, they were still "come-heres."

In Nelson, as in many parts of Virginia's hill country, there were "from-heres" (also known as "been-heres") and "come-heres." Even if you'd lived in Nelson for half a century, you were still a come-here and always would be.

The from-heres, meanwhile, had roots sunk many generations deep. They had family legends accumulating in thick layers tied to every knob and knoll on their land. They could trace their tenure back to the Civil War, to the Revolution, or even, like John Ed Purvis, to the original English land grants in the mid-1700s. (Members of the Monacan Indian Nation, the federally recognized tribe whose ancestors have lived in these hills for thousands of years, might raise their eyebrows at the distinction.[15])

These labels weren't a source of overt tension—more of a winking reference to the pride-in-place you find in country dwellers all over. When it came to the big questions, the come-here/from-here line largely dissolved. Both demographics shared a fierce attachment to their chosen ground, whether by birth or by choice, however deep in time their roots went. As Elizabeth Purvis Shepard noted of their come-here neighbors in Nelson County: "Maybe they didn't have all the generations of family on a piece of property, but their property meant just as much to them too."[16]

Back in May 2014, Ron Enders, recently retired, had finally gotten around to tackling a long-planned project: digging an irrigation pond. One day he checked his mail to find the same letter that had greeted John Ed Purvis, advising him that he could expect surveyors on his land by July 1. Instead of firing up the tractor, he sat down to write a few emails; the pond would have to wait.

Over the next few days, he called up neighbors he knew and searched the county's records to find contact information for those he didn't. He drove up quiet back roads and knocked on doors. If someone answered, he asked: "Did you get a letter about this pipeline?"

Some had and didn't know what to make of it. Some hadn't and were surprised to hear about it. A handful told him they wouldn't mind taking the money for an easement. But most expressed vehement opposition to the idea of Dominion's land agents or surveyors coming onto their land.

Slowly, Enders pieced together a rough sense of the route. He came to call it his "Dragon Map."[17] Highlighted in red, the parcels took the shape of a curling form with a large head hugging the Blue Ridge Parkway, a thin body crossing Route 151, and a tail snaking south through the Rockfish River Valley. He came to suspect that Dominion did not want landowners to talk to each other or know who else was on the route. Some told him they were shown partial maps by surveyors but weren't permitted to take a photo or make a copy; others had asked about neighbors on the route, only to be told that information was "privileged and private."

But he persisted, and the dragon kept growing in size: when he confirmed from another landowner that they had been contacted, he colored in their parcel on the map in red. And he began hearing their stories too.

Kathy and Martin Versluys had received the same letter. Since the mid-1980s they had owned and run a bed-and-breakfast on a scenic road that twisted its way through the center of the county, roughly following the clear-running Rockfish River. The initial pipeline route slashed diagonally across their property.

One afternoon in early June, Kathy answered the door to find a representative from a land agency contracted by Dominion. As they stood on her front porch, he made his pitch and tried to assuage her fears. He explained what it would look like during construction and afterward. How the pipe would be buried 3 feet deep (except where they had to bore through the mountain). How she could mow her grass over it but wouldn't be able to build anything bigger than a shed within the permanent right-of-way. How the crews would spray herbicides to keep trees from growing atop it. How the company would pay a one-time fee for the easement, and for any incidental damages done to their property. How that fee would be negotiated directly with Dominion.[18]

Versluys wanted to know about the chances of a leak or a rupture, and whether her inn was inside the 1,100-foot "blast radius" she had read about—the area within which everything would be incinerated in the event of a severe explosion. How, she asked, would Dominion access the pipe for regular maintenance or checking leaks?

"They don't worry about that," the man replied dismissively. The pipes were stainless steel, treated with a special coating so they don't corrode, he said. "They'll last for twenty, thirty, forty years."

"What about after that?" Versluys asked.

"Well, are you gonna be around after that?" he shot back.

The Friends of Nelson

On June 8, 2014, more than 120 people crowded into the Memorial Library (named in remembrance of those who died during Camille) in the county seat of Lovingston. They filled every available seat and stood three deep along the walls. The agenda was Dominion's pipeline—what it meant for Nelson County, and what they could do about it.

Ernie Reed stood before them. The 55-year-old had a veteran educator's alert and easy manner at the head of a classroom. In addition to being the founder of an alternative school in Charlottesville, Reed was the president of Wild Virginia, a nonprofit conservation group. Thanks to his connections with groups in Pennsylvania that had been resisting fracking and pipeline development for years, Reed knew more than most of his neighbors about FERC and the other distant bureaucracies they would be dealing with. For decades, Reed had owned a piece of land in central Nelson, where he had built a small house. It, too, was on the route.

As he spoke, the crowd hung on his every word. The room was charged with bottled-up anxiety: people were desperate for information. As they passed around a clipboard to share their names, phone numbers, email addresses, they fired questions at Reed: *How many days did people have left to reply to Dominion's letter? Where could people find a digital version of Dominion's route map? Who should they call to learn about legal options for fighting eminent domain? Was Dominion building this pipeline just so it could export gas to Asia? Who had a fast enough internet connection to compile all the names on the clipboard into one master email list?*

Everybody's first step, Reed advised, should be writing back to deny permission for surveyors to come on their land. And the second step: connect with each other. There were already small groups forming— they all needed to get on the same page and reach out to neighbors who might not be online.

"There's really no better way of organizing than by talking to your neighbors," Reed said.

He noted that the Forest Service—another "landowner" on Dominion's chosen route—had learned about it the same way everyone else did: a letter in the mail. And then he made two prescient predictions.

"We are more of an obstacle than they see the federal agencies being," Reed said, referring to Dominion. "We all have more power, I think, than (the agencies) do."[19]

Things snowballed from there. A week later, at the board of supervisors monthly meeting, 13 citizens rose to speak out against it. At the next meeting, 23 people offered public comments against it. At the end of June, 150 people assembled at the Rockfish Valley Community Center to start planning their own campaign of resistance. Out of those meetings, Friends of Nelson was officially born.[20]

The founding members didn't have time to overthink things—they simply started *doing*. They intuited that they were in a race, of sorts, to reach landowners before Dominion did. The core group, including Ron Enders and Ernie Reed, formed subcommittees for monitoring the route and environmental impacts, for communications and media, for legal issues. Volunteer teams took on a range of tasks: handing out flyers in stores, staffing an information table at the farmers' market, writing press releases, planning music festivals to draw more people in and raise money, printing stickers and T-shirts and yard signs. Throughout the summer, interest in the pipeline fight surged. Donations flowed in, along with offers to host fundraising events from local breweries and vineyards. Friends of Nelson's Facebook group had gained 806 members in its first thirty days.

The specter of the dragon had mobilized the Nelson countryside: come-heres, from-heres, liberals, conservatives, innkeepers, entrepreneurs, nurses, therapists, brewers, farmers, loggers, teachers, retirees. They had been randomly thrown together by the digital line that Brittany Moody and her colleagues had snapped across their mountains. They had different backgrounds, income levels, political viewpoints, long-term goals, and immediate concerns. But the Friends of Nelson wanted to create a big tent that welcomed anyone and everyone opposed to the ACP, whatever their motivation—property rights, safety, concerns about local or global pollution—partly because they knew the fight could take years. "What we had in common was that our homes and properties were threatened, and we wanted to stop the pipeline," said Enders.

In their anxious late-night web scrolling, the Purvis family caught wind of all this hubbub. John Ed and his daughter Elizabeth went to some Friends of Nelson meetings. They talked with Ron Enders. He gave them his growing list of folks who had gotten Dominion's letter and provided templates of a certified letter that they could use to deny survey requests. (Saying no to surveyors, he explained, could buy time to negotiate restrictions on the use of heavy equipment, or document special features on one's property, like old family gravesites, that deserved consideration.)

The Friends of Nelson reminded John Ed Purvis there was another avenue available to him: to fight. "And we started feeling like maybe there was some kind of hope, if we collectively put all our heads together, and had the right legal expertise, maybe something could happen," Elizabeth said.

The group's overarching priority was convincing everyone that, despite the power and influence of Dominion, the Atlantic Coast

Pipeline was not inevitable. The most important prerequisite for action was a belief that you could change the outcome. To that end, Friends of Nelson made a key choice early on. Every time they issued a press release, or Ellen Bouton—who became the group's tireless webmaster and archivist—published a post on their website, they would refer to it as the "proposed pipeline."[21] That language would help remind everyone that it wasn't in the ground yet. Until it was, the Atlantic Coast Pipeline would exist only in the imaginations of Tom Farrell and Terry McAuliffe and Wall Street financiers—and in the speculative scenarios of the prefiling application documents that Dominion submitted to FERC in September 2014.

And as long as there was no methane flowing through a pipe in the ground, the future was still up for grabs.

"They are counting on you to just feel defeated and just rolling over to let them do what they plan to do," said Elizabeth Purvis Shepard. The more isolated you felt, the more likely you were to throw up your hands in resignation. But the reverse was true too: she noticed that all the meetings and conversations with folks from Friends of Nelson were improving her dad's spirits. "It helped him to be with other people that were fighting, that had concerns like he did," she said.[22]

The profound thing they gave him: "It was making him feel less alone."

Chapter Four

All the Hornets' Nests

On a late January afternoon in 2015 in the heart of Washington, DC, Cheryl LaFleur looked out at her audience, massed between the mahogany bars and floor-to-ceiling windows of the Holeman Lounge of the National Press Club's headquarters on Fourteenth Street.

The club was a venerable platform for big-name politicians and cultural figures—in the coming weeks it would host a keynote talk by the United Nations Secretary-General Ban Ki-moon and another by Senator Bernie Sanders, right before the launch of the latter's presidential campaign. But on that day the capacity crowd of Capitol Hill staffers, think tank fellows, reporters, and lobbyists had gathered to hear LaFleur, the chair of the Federal Energy Regulatory Commission and former utility executive.

"Now, I'm not a Washington lifer," she began somewhat apologetically. "But I am more or less an energy lifer, because I've been in the energy world for more than 30 years." And she had a warning for them from the energy world's turbulent front lines.

"We have a situation here," she said.

As LaFleur herself conceded, a tiny number of Americans could describe what FERC stood for, let alone what it does. That included the DC insiders in the room, so she took a moment to explain that FERC's five Senate-confirmed commissioners oversee the nation's two vast energy vascular systems: gas pipelines and the power grid. On the electricity side, they regulate hydropower facilities, wholesale power markets, and transmission across state lines; on the gas side, they permit interstate gas pipelines and coastal facilities for exporting liquefied gas. Critical stuff, but—let's face it—not the most riveting programming on C-SPAN.

But suddenly FERC was no longer boring. As the Bloomberg News editor who introduced her had observed, the packed room spoke volumes about how LaFleur's agency "has emerged from the bureaucratic shadows." Its decisions were now the stuff of headlines and high-profile Congressional hearings—and protests. There was mounting grassroots fury out there in the countryside. *That* was the situation. And it was being fueled by the proliferation of gas pipelines, which, LaFleur announced, were "facing unprecedented opposition from local and national groups including environmental activists."[1]

Just a few weeks earlier, a group of citizens from Nelson County had come knocking on the door of her DC office. A few weeks before that, *another* Nelson contingent had met with her fellow commissioner Norman Bay. And a few weeks before *that*, in November, yet another party led by Nancy Sorrells from Augusta County had come to meet LaFleur too. All three groups had tried to persuade the commissioners that their counties were a terrible place to put a 42-inch pipe full of methane.[2]

But the groundswell went beyond such polite, scheduled meetings. LaFleur painted an unnerving scene of citizens rattling both the digital and physical gates of her agency.

"These groups are active in every FERC docket," she said, "as they should be, as well as in my e-mail in-box seven days a week, in my Twitter feed, at our open meetings demanding to be heard, and literally at our door closing down First Street so FERC won't be able to work."[3]

That protesters could even locate their front door was, in and of itself, a surprising development. But the commissioners were now caught between two interconnected trends: methane's expanding footprint in the country's energy supply, thanks to the shale boom, and growing public concern about fossil fuel infrastructure, thanks to climate change.

This clash, LaFleur said, was the biggest issue confronting her agency. More and more Americans were expressing their own views on whether more methane was a good thing—and whether FERC was acting in their interest or merely providing a rubber stamp for the gas industry.

There was some striking data to support this latter charge. Since 1999, FERC had approved more than four hundred new pipeline projects. It had rejected only two.[4]

The commission would sometimes make a company tweak its route in deference to this wetland or that historical site, but it almost never said no outright. When it comes to the question of whether a natural gas pipeline is in the public interest, FERC's default answer—99.5 percent of the time—is yes.

One might expect a room full of journalists to ask about that lopsided track record. But it didn't come up during the Q and A session. LaFleur had been invited, rather, to address some big news: the Obama administration had recently proposed a new rule to regulate greenhouse gas emissions from power plants under the Clean Air Act. Conservative politicians were already saying the proposed Clean Power Plan would lead to rolling blackouts and higher bills. Climate activists were calling it a necessary step, but one that didn't go far enough. Washington's elite wanted to know: What did the head of FERC think about it?

LaFleur predicted that Obama's new rule would likely spur even *more* gas infrastructure, because new gas power plants were likely to be the easiest way for utilities to comply with it. "I think that our nation is going to have to grapple with our acceptance of gas generation and gas pipelines if we expect to achieve our climate and environmental goals," she said, voicing the consensus among DC decision-makers and, likely, a significant share of those listening.

In this analysis, the new rule—framed as the federal government's most significant step yet to fight climate change—would, paradoxically, serve to boost the flow of fossil fuels through the network of pipes that FERC oversaw. Whether the public wanted it or not, more gas was what they were going to get.

Which meant the Situation was only likely to intensify.

Joyce Burton Has an Epiphany

When Joyce Burton decided to leave New York for good, she knew where she wanted to wind up: in the mountains.

"I made a promise that every move I made would take me more rural." New York City to Long Island, then a little farther out on Long Island, then a suburb of Richmond, Virginia, for three years of training to be a physical therapist. "Then I ended up on a hippie commune!"

That's how she eventually found her way to Nelson County and Shannon Farm, the intentional community that Ron Enders and Ellen Bouton had helped start in the 1970s. There she found the more balanced approach to life she had been missing in the city—and some surprises too. "I would have laughed in your face if you had said I'd wind up building my own house on a commune, cutting firewood with a two-man saw, and splitting it myself," she said.

An avid hiker, Burton had been backpacking out west in the summer of 2014, when Friends of Nelson and other local resistance groups were forming. Before long, though, she would become one of the Situation's most determined actors.

When she returned home that fall, she was incensed to learn that Dominion was planning to plow right through Shannon Farm's communal land, including wetlands and mature beech forests they were trying to protect through a conservation easement. She worried, too, about their well water and safety risks. "I also thought it was insane that 'the system' would incentivize for-profit corporations to further invest in fossil fuels when there were other alternatives, but that ugly truth didn't particularly surprise me," she said.

Ron Enders shared his Dragon Map with her; then Dominion released its own more detailed digital map of the route. As Enders became involved in other aspects of FON's work, Burton threw herself into the volunteer role of reaching out to landowners. She proved a natural fit for the job; her work as an in-home physical therapist put her into contact with all kinds of people living among Nelson's hollows. In her late forties, diminutive and bespectacled with straight dark hair that she wore with a long braid and bangs that fell over her forehead, Burton radiated a kind of savvy sincerity. She was that rare person capable of both talking *and* listening intently, in quick succession.

And since she had learned about the pipeline, Burton had been in contact with all the local grassroots groups but hadn't formally aligned with any of them. Her philosophy was that whoever was interested in fighting Dominion's pipeline was a potential ally and therefore worth listening to.[5]

That's why, on a Sunday afternoon in late January 2015, she drove through a gate and up a long, winding road she'd never been on, just a couple miles from her home. She parked in the driveway of a mountaintop lodge that belonged to one of the prime movers behind yet another new Nelson-based organization. This one, called All Pain No Gain, had what its leaders described as a "very narrow" focus: "We want to convince Dominion to move to an alternate, responsible route. Period."

All Pain No Gain was the brainchild of Tom Harvey, a veteran national security official who had served in the first Bush administration before going on to a successful private sector career. Harvey was hosting a reception to present the new group's plan at his home, which had a jaw-dropping view of the Blue Ridge. (The ACP would stripe its way right through the middle of it.)

Burton walked into the grand home and was greeted by some familiar faces. Connie Brennan, one of Nelson's five elected supervisors, was there. So was Charlotte Rea, a retired US Air Force officer who lived nearby and had briefly served as the first president of Friends of Nelson; her property was on the pipeline's route. Nancy Sorrells, a former county supervisor herself, had come over the mountain, along with Travis Geary, a Tea Party stalwart and member of a large landowning family in neighboring Augusta County.

There were others there, too, whom Burton didn't know, presumably invited in the hopes they could write some large checks. Burton didn't have much money to give. She wasn't politically connected. But she was already a key figure in the nascent pipeline resistance, having swiftly become a kind of human switchboard for Nelson landowners—the person in touch with almost everyone else.

After a welcome from Tom Harvey, Brennan and Rea and then Sorrells and Geary shared the presentations they had given to FERC's commissioners a few weeks earlier. Then Harvey walked the group through the plan: raise a lot of money, secure meetings with elected officials, buy TV and digital and print advertisements in a massive media blitz, and lobby to shove the ACP onto a less objectionable route.[6] They had formed a 501(c)(3) and hired Navigators Global, a public relations firm with deep ties to decision-makers in DC, led by a powerful Republican lobbyist named Phil Anderson who had family land in the Afton area. The goal, according to Anderson, was to grab politicians "by the shoulders and say, 'Let's have a conversation about how this thing should go.'"[7]

Burton had reservations about this plan, but she figured that All Pain No Gain's influence campaign seemed as worthy an experiment as all the others. Then Harvey introduced Rick Webb, who was there to discuss his research into "responsible, alternative routes."

Other Friends of Nelson members had spent months researching options for co-locating the pipeline with existing electric transmission corridors or interstate highways, hoping to show FERC how Dominion could avoid plowing up virgin terrain. Burton had driven around, too, photographing various power line rights-of-way that already ran striping over the Blue Ridge as possible alternatives. So, she listened carefully as Rick Webb, in his methodical way, dismantled the entire premise of APNG's strategy.

Even if segments were moved onto existing rights-of-way, he explained, the project would face many of the same problems. No matter how much it was wiggled, the steel spaghetti would still traverse the karst-riddled Shenandoah Valley and the forested flanks of the Allegheny and Blue Ridge Mountains. And no matter how careful Dominion's crews were, he emphasized, there was no way to cross that terrain without flattening mountaintops, cutting through national forests, and threatening water supplies and critical habitat. "There are no good options for crossing the multiple steep ridges and karst valleys of the central Appalachians," he said.[8] In other words, there was no such thing as a "responsible" other route. They should focus on stopping the project altogether.

For all those reasons, as they walked out to their cars after the meeting, Webb told Joyce Burton that he couldn't get on board with the APNG campaign. (By that point he had already launched a four-letter acronym of his own: DPMC, the Dominion Pipeline Monitoring Coalition, a citizen-led effort to raise the alarm about all those issues he had raised.)

His analysis set up a clash of realisms. Webb was focused on the physical reality of the terrain, while Harvey's strategy was based on acceptance of the political landscape—of the imperative of swaying the few decision-makers who really mattered.

Which could be overcome more easily? Burton admired Webb's confidence and moral clarity but thought he was naïve. "I didn't think we could hope to do what he was talking about," she told me. Getting Dominion to move it onto existing rights-of-way seemed much more plausible.

A couple weeks later, though, Burton had an epiphany. She and a few others had driven to Harrisonburg to hear oral arguments in a case brought by five Nelson landowners against Dominion, challenging its authority to survey their property without their permission. After the hearing, Burton carpooled with two women spearheading other organizations, Marion Kanour of Free Nelson and Eleanor Amidon of the Pipeline Education Group. On the hour-long drive back home, they began discussing how to channel the grassroots energy in Nelson that Dominion had unleashed. Kanour asked Burton why she was involved with All Pain No Gain, a group that sought to merely shift the pipeline somewhere else—to make it someone else's problem.

"We just have to do what we can," Burton replied. "We're not going to be able to stop this. If we can get it co-located onto highways or existing corridors, I'm okay with that."

Kanour insisted their aim should be stopping the entire pipeline. A native of Norfolk, a former Marine and an ordained Episcopal priest, she was a recent "come-here" too. She had moved to a 15-acre Nelson farm in 2002 and become the pastor at a local church and an active community leader. As they talked, Burton's thinking shifted. Burton—who had studied for a time at the Jewish Theological Seminary in New York—found herself swayed by Kanour's moral argument.

"That conversation was a pivotal moment for me," she recalled. "We couldn't do this as a zero-sum game—it couldn't be something where I win, you lose. This needed to be something where we all win, or we all lose."

A Bittersweet Reprieve

Over the Christmas holidays of 2014, many Nelsonians had received, mixed in with their holiday cards, some less cheery mail: notifications that they were being sued by ACP LLC for refusing to allow its surveyors onto their land. All told, of the nearly 250 landowners Dominion was preparing to sue up and down the entire pipeline route, about half were in Nelson—because nearly 80 percent of Nelson residents still refused access.

Dominion hadn't won any more friends in the county when it mistakenly sued fourteen property owners who were *not* on its route, including the county's sheriff. "If they can't get the paperwork right, who's to say they can get [the pipeline] right," the sheriff, who remained opposed to the project, wondered.[9]

Plenty of their neighbors went on with their lives, dimly aware of all this fracas. But those in the pipeline corridor were digging in for a fight.

From its inception, Friends of Nelson had advised landowners to deny access to surveyors. They figured those individual legal challenges might slow the whole juggernaut down—and demonstrate to the fence-sitters that there were some Nelsonians, at least, who didn't see the pipeline as an inevitability.[10] Then, in February, Dominion surprised everyone when it announced that it was exploring new alternate routes—including one that would cross the Blue Ridge at Reeds Gap, right near the Wintergreen ski resort, which was the county's biggest employer and economic engine.[11] In one stroke, Dominion had roughly doubled the number of parcels in its sights—and with it, the number of Nelsonians taking notice.

The news came a day after John Ed and Ruth Purvis celebrated their sixty-first wedding anniversary. When the family found out, there was relief—maybe their land would be spared, after all—laced with sadness for neighbors who were now getting their own letters from Dominion. "I was so torn," said Elizabeth Purvis Shepard, "because I could see where they were moving it, and I knew who that would affect."[12]

John Ed Purvis still planned to say his piece, regardless, at a public meeting to be held a few weeks later by the Federal Energy Regulatory Commission. As the date approached, he sat down at his desk, took out a sheet of looseleaf paper and began writing:

NAME John E. Purvis
    DOB 1932
Opposed to pipeline because:
    1. Safety
    2. Contaminated water

He scratched a line through it and started again.

Born and raised in Nelson County . . . in home that grandfather built in 1904
    Except for four years in the air force
    My ancestor came to Fredericts [sic] from England arriving in 1739. He came to Nelson County in 1768. Purchased land, farmed his land and died in 1789
    I am the 7th generation to own this land

Unsatisfied, Purvis took another sheet of paper and began again.

I am opposed [sic] to pipeline for the following reasons:
    1. Fear of explosions
    2. Contaminated water
    3. Desication [sic] of landscape
    4. Lower property values
    5. Shipment of gas to foreign countries

6. Dis-regard of eminate [*sic*] domain
I love my land in the county of Nelson—I hate to see the beauty destroyed.

The Cove in the Corridor

"Our fathers and forefathers have worked, sometimes died, on this land to keep it," said Wisteria Johnson. "We don't want anybody to be able to come in and say, 'part of this belongs to me.'"[13]

Wisteria Johnson's ancestral land was not on Dominion's original pipeline route. But after sitting through the company's sales pitch at the board of supervisors meeting in August 2014, she had stood up to call on her elected officials to oppose the project anyway. She heard nothing good in it for Nelson County.

Johnson could trace her family's tenure in Harris Cove, a lush valley encircled by mountains, back to the 1880s—family stories suggested they were there long before that, but that's as far back as the written records go. Her father told her that, along with their Black and Irish forebears, some of their ancestors were Blackfoot, others Cherokee. "This was called Indian Cove," she said.

The family compiled a genealogy that stretched back beyond her Native American great-great-grandmother, and another great-great-grandmother who was an enslaved Black immigrant from Jamaica, to include an enslaved great-great-great-great-grandfather born in 1783. Their lives were hard in ways that are difficult to imagine—or document. But especially in the women's gazes, preserved in faded photographs and strands of stories passed down, one could make out their determination to stake out a home, author their own lives, make a refuge for their children in the Cove.

Over six feet tall, with her long gray hair in braids, Johnson's manner is both warm and wary, maternal and magisterial, all at the same time. "Now 'cove' is just a sophisticated word for 'holler,'" she said with a twinkle before turning serious. "There is a lot of peace up here."[14]

All through the fall and winter of 2015, after learning about the Atlantic Coast Pipeline, Johnson had a sense of foreboding. She kept telling herself, *We're going to get it, we're going to get it*.[15] So when

Dominion announced its new routes in February and she saw that one cut straight through the Cove, Johnson wasn't exactly surprised. But she was "stunned" all the same, she said, "like in any trauma." Next came anger, with the thought of how she would tell her children, and their children.

Her evenings were suddenly taken up with phone calls and texting neighbors, some of whom had been organizing for months to help people find lawyers, understand their rights when it came to refusing surveyors or negotiating easements, and ferret out more information from Dominion.

In those weeks, Johnson would walk the hills above her home, up the sloping pastures where the family's few dozen cattle grazed, until she reached the large, oblong boulder that sat atop a hill at the center of the Cove. The rock seemed to grow right out of the ground. She would run her hands over the circular depression and neat grooves—weathered but still distinct—where her great-great-grandmother once ground corn into meal.

That spot by the boulder afforded a sweeping view of the land and its features in all directions. The family cemetery just a stone's throw away. The rusting old press, where her great-grandfather had hitched his mule to grind sugarcane for making rum. Near it, the sloping rock formation where the clan would gather for reunions, summer barbecues, and fall bonfires, the children frolicking after dark. The graceful lines of Sugarloaf, Bailey, and Willoughby Mountains and the dark green folds in the forest canopy where four cold trout streams ran down from their forested ridges, past the house where she and her sister Liz had been raised—the house where she now watched her grandchildren play after school.

From that spot, the stories of Nelson County's two most profound transformations were also plainly legible. Off to the northeast, one could still see—when the chestnut oaks and hickories and tulip poplars were bare in winter—the scars where Camille had raked the upper flanks of Willoughby Mountain. Down below, running along the road, were the power lines installed by the local electric cooperative when Johnson was a child.

Her daughter Deanna Mitchelson had recently moved back home

from California with her husband and two young children. Deanna was planning to build a house at the foot of Willoughby—small and simple with a big porch wrapping around, a way to be inside and outside at the same time. After Dominion's announcement, Deanna shelved those plans.[16]

It was as though that future had been suddenly swapped out for another. Instead of hiring surveyors to mark out the dimensions of Deanna's foundation, the family was now debating how to respond when the pipeline surveyors showed up.

Both Liz's and Wisteria's houses would lay outside of the 1,100-foot "blast zone radius" within which everything would be vaporized in the event of an explosion. But they were within the 3,630-foot "blast evacuation radius"—meaning they would have to leave in the event of any leak or rupture. They worried, too, about water—that a spill of fuel or other contaminants during construction would leach into their well water, and that erosion triggered by the excavation would cloud the pristine streams that flowed down from the ridgetops. The top of Bailey would be bulldozed or blasted and widened to accommodate the required right-of-way. There would be access roads for all the heavy equipment. One would angle above Wisteria's house to reach the ridge, and another one would snake a half mile north of Liz's house to the top of Willoughby. There would be a steady parade of trucks going up, then hauling pieces of the mountain itself back down, down past her home, down past the grove where the old farmhouse— their original homeplace, the house where her great-grandmother had lived—now sat empty.

Johnson had moved back home to Nelson in 1977, after living in New York City for several years. Her first husband died soon after, at the age of 27, while she was pregnant with their third child, Deanna. She stayed for thirteen years, working as a social worker. In 1990, she left the Cove again to follow her second husband Brad Johnson, whose work for an insurance company took them to Illinois and California. In 2003, she moved back to the Cove for good.

Brad, who grew up in suburban New Jersey, took to the place readily but marvels at the depth of his wife's connection to the Cove. "I can understand it, but I can't *feel* it," he said. "I love the land, but I never thought I'd live in such a place." When friends from back home in New Jersey ask him what it's like living in the Cove, he asks if they've seen *The Waltons*. "That's what it's like," he tells them.[17]

It's an apt comparison, if *The Waltons* had actually looked like America: barefoot kids of Black, Native American, and Irish extraction working, playing, growing, and roaming the woods and fields. For Wisteria and her sister and their seven children and their grandkids, the Cove was the haven that Walton Mountain was for Earl Hamner's fictional clan—but in a world with plenty of extra obstacles.

Hamner's childhood home of Schuyler was just a few miles north. A few miles to the southwest was the childhood home of Edward Pollard, the white supremacist and originator of the Lost Cause narrative of the Confederacy, which glorified the secession of Southern states and denied that the Civil War was fought over slavery.[18] For each wholesome, uplifting tale found in a *Waltons* episode, there were plenty of stories of exploitation and discrimination to be unearthed in that part of Virginia.

"We're collectivists as a family," said C'ta DeLaurier, Wisteria's eldest daughter. "We recognize that we are here because of them [ancestors]. As an African American family, we have intentionally worked really, really hard to preserve that space. The people before us worked really, really, really hard to preserve that space."[19] A veteran educator and elementary school principal, she had been adamantly opposed to Dominion's overtures from day one.

"Change is inevitable, I get it," she continued. "In my mother's lifetime, they've not always had electricity. In my grandmother's lifetime, I'm not sure they had a functioning public road."

DeLaurier and her siblings grew up in the Cove, with the benefits of those large-scale civic and corporate investments. The project of bringing electricity to every part of Nelson—and most of rural America—had begun in the 1930s, catalyzed by the New Deal. Her mother Wisteria had memories of playing dominoes by the light of a kerosene lantern with her own grandfather before the power lines came. The family knew better than most how transformative certain infrastructure can be—and how it can be worth some sacrifice if its benefits are broadly shared.

"We now have running water, we have electricity, we have the phone," DeLaurier said. "Sometimes companies provide a service—I get that. But if you looked at the path of the pipeline, it didn't seem like it was providing anything for anyone along its path. It just seemed like a monster that was consuming ancient and sacred stuff."

On a mid-March afternoon in 2015, Wisteria Johnson guided a reporter from Richmond up to the boulder in the center of the Cove. She and her sister had been reluctant to invite the glare of the media into their world—they fiercely guarded their privacy. But they had decided that the situation demanded it. If the choice, at this stage, was letting a Dominion surveyor or a newspaperman on her land, Johnson would choose the latter. She pointed out where Deanna had planned to build her home, and traced the access roads Dominion would clear across the streams and springs hidden on the mountains' flanks.

"We had to fight to get the good stuff up here," Johnson told him. "The bad stuff is coming in without any invitation. It doesn't give anything to the people it's going through. The electricity gave us light. The phone gave us communication. The pipeline doesn't give us anything except heartbreak."[20]

FERC Comes to Nelson

Three days later, on March 18, 2015, nearly three hundred people filled the seats and crowded the aisles of the Nelson County middle school auditorium. They had come after work on a wintry evening to tell FERC where they stood on the matter of the Atlantic Coast Pipeline and to hear their neighbors do the same.

The mood was charged even before the meeting began. As people arrived, they discovered that Dominion had frontloaded the evening's lineup with its supporters. At least fifteen people had already signed up before 6:00 p.m., though public notices hadn't indicated that anyone should come earlier than 7:00 p.m. When the meeting began, the first nineteen out of twenty speakers—several from outside the county—rose to praise natural gas, Dominion, energy independence, and pipelines in general.

The crowd grew restive as it became clear that the TV crews putting together the evening news report would have a distorted picture of local support for the pipeline. A Dominion spokesman would later admit that company interns had stood in line to sign up pro-pipeline speakers. "It should surprise no one that we decided we could not let one side dominate the debate," he told the *Washington Post*.[21] "This is the county where the opposition has been the strongest," he explained to a local ABC News reporter.[22]

Will Fenton had only recently joined that resistance. He and his wife Lilia had learned in late February that Dominion's pipeline might now be coming into their lives. The couple had planned to open the brand-new Fenton Inn, just below Reeds Gap atop the Blue Ridge, that year. They had plowed all of their time and energy and much of their savings into the project. Will, a master carpenter, had spent the past three years felling, stripping, milling, and hand-carving trees from his land to craft the intricate building of his own design—a lifelong dream.

But the past year had brought a series of stressful developments. Russia had invaded and then annexed Crimea in Ukraine, where Lilia had grown up and still had family, in February 2014. And February 2015 had brought the news that Dominion planned to set up a yearlong, round-the-clock operation to drill a mile-long hole through the Blue Ridge, within a stone's throw of the inn they planned to advertise as a "peaceful refuge amidst stunning nature."[23]

The drilling would take place on land owned by the Wintergreen Resort right next door, though Dominion would also need a small corner of the Fentons' property. Crews would clear a large area for trucks and machines, parking, porta-potties, fuel tanks—all the stuff normally found on a large construction site, but not normally encountered next to a rustic mountain getaway.[24] Each foot drilled would produce 1.5 tons of rock debris (considered contaminated due to the lubricants used) to be hauled on the narrow road down to the Rockfish Valley. And for good measure, just across the road, crews would also blast the top of the mountain that sat squarely in the middle of their inn's sweeping view.[25]

The Fentons wondered if their business was doomed before it even got going.

In his youth Will Fenton had been a competitive powerlifter. Shy by nature, with a quiet intensity to his demeanor, he had relished the sport's psychological dimension, watching others underestimate him right up until the point he crushed them in competition. As he stood against the wall and listened to the proceedings unfold, he could feel that old warrior's mindset rising again.

Kevin Bowman, the 27-year-old "cumulative impact assessment coordinator and environmental protection specialist" sent by FERC to absorb Nelson County's mounting fury, had explained at the outset that his role was to moderate the meeting. He was not there to answer any questions. FERC was holding a series of ten scoping meetings, as required by law, to listen to the concerns of people in communities along the proposed route. "For us it's a learning process, it's where we educate ourselves about the project, potential issues and the environmental impacts," he said.

Bowman gestured toward a laptop displaying a timer and a digital recording device that would record their comments for the official record in the matter of Atlantic Coast Pipeline, Docket #PF15-6. Each speaker would have three minutes to say their piece before he cut them off.[26]

In those three-minute bites, Nelsonians gave him an earful. After the first twenty, the rest of the seventy-seven speakers voiced passionate opposition to the pipeline. One after another rose to share their fears at the prospect of a pipeline running just a few dozen feet from their front porches and water wells and family cemeteries or bisecting their farmlands and fruit orchards. Some worried about the economic fallout to the breweries, bed-and-breakfasts, and other businesses that anchored the county's thriving tourist industry. Others worried future storms might dislodge the steel pipe and its highly pressurized, highly flammable contents near their homes.

About halfway through the meeting, 82-year-old John Ed Purvis made his way to the microphone. He got straight to the point. He explained that he still lived in the house his grandfather built in 1904—the house where he was born. "I am opposed to the proposition that Dominion has made to us and Nelson County," Purvis said simply. "Thank you."[27]

Deanna Mitchelson rose to speak to a very specific fear: the destabilization of steep slopes ringing the Cove by blasting and construction. "These landslides can adversely affect the homes and lives of many families including my own," she said.

Her family knew from experience about that risk. Wisteria Johnson had been an 18-year-old about to leave for college on the day that Camille struck. She walked through the floodwaters with her mother to check on an elderly neighbor, only to find the woman crushed to death because her home had been pushed off its foundation and into a ravine.[28]

"My point is that they are life and death scenarios that, in my world, do not require the completion of a study," Deanna said. "It only requires common sense and a sincerity to do the right thing. It also requires some federal safety commissions to be strong enough to protect the people."

When it was her mother's turn to speak, Wisteria Johnson took a moment to compose herself. "I am afraid to start talking about our seventh-generation farms because I become very emotional, and so what I am going to try to do tonight is just stay general," she began. Then she turned her ire on FERC, directing her frustration at Bowman and his device. "What I wanted to get to, is that I am really disappointed. I had a vision of how commissioners—you know, *people*—would come and face the people tonight. Instead, we get a tape recorder and one or two people."[29]

Will Fenton stood in the back of the room, waiting for his turn to speak. Like Johnson, he had become fixated on that inert voice recorder—and what it said about the one-way relationship between the people and the government agency that was supposed to look out for their "convenience and necessity." People were pouring their deepest fears into it, but he was beginning to doubt much would come back out. In time he would come to regard all the hundreds of pages of written comments he and Lilia would submit to FERC, all the phone calls and pleas and letters, as so much "shouting in the wind."

After four hours, Bowman ended the meeting before Will Fenton and 124 others who had signed up had a chance to say their piece. Later, Fenton would sum up the evening thus: "That was the first time I've ever been bullied in a high school."

A Bright Gas-Fired Future

In 1978, Congress ordered FERC to set up an Office of Public Participation to help citizens get information about projects and give them more input into the permitting process. By 2015, FERC still hadn't created the office.

Congress had also directed the agency to create a landowner compensation program to help those of lesser means cover legal costs incurred in disputes with pipeline companies. That order had been ignored too.[30]

But FERC was keenly sensitive to the concerns and financial imperatives of the gas pipeline industry.

A few weeks after the Nelson scoping meeting, the lead story in the April 2015 issue of *American Gas Magazine*—published by the American Gas Association, the industry's biggest trade group—was an interview with Norman Bay, a veteran energy lawyer who had just replaced Cheryl LaFleur as FERC's chair.

Bay emphasized the importance of recognizing pipeline companies' needs, one of which was speed. "Timeliness is important because projects are capital intensive and the developer needs to know whether or not a project will be approved," he said. "We should always look for ways to streamline our own processes and do our work more efficiently."[31]

He was asked how he proposed to deal with upset citizens and frustrated landowners—that is, the Situation. Protesters should use the normal venues like formal comment periods and scoping meetings, he said, to share their views.

"FERC serves the public, and so, in a very real sense, everyone is a stakeholder in what we do," Bay elaborated. "We welcome all views, including the views of protesters, and I respect their First Amendment rights. That being said, there are permissible and impermissible ways to exercise those rights."

Then he gushed about the gas-driven prospects for the US energy industry. "This is such an exciting time to do energy work," Bay said. "The shale revolution has resulted in an abundant and low-priced natural gas supply to the point where LNG [liquefied natural gas] import facilities are being converted into LNG export facilities."

"The optimist in me believes that the energy future of the United States is very bright indeed," Bay concluded, "perhaps the brightest it has been in decades."

That year was on the way to becoming the hottest year ever recorded (up to that point). Given its authority over permitting very large, long-lived fossil fuel infrastructure projects—gas pipelines and LNG terminals—FERC's decisions were among the most consequential of any federal agency when it came to climate change. Yet—remarkably—FERC did not evaluate projects' total greenhouse gas emissions when it ruled on whether they were in the "public necessity."

Toward the end of the March FERC meeting, a Nelson resident named Michael Tabony had risen to speak. The pipeline wasn't going through his land, but he feared it would put his family at risk nevertheless—and he worried that FERC was ignoring this particular risk entirely. Tabony demanded that FERC study the emissions created from burning the ACP's methane, which "might be left in the ground if the ACP was not built."

"How much fossilized CO_2 will this amount of gas add to the atmosphere and how much additional warming with the addition of this gas falls to the earth of our grandchildren and their grandchildren?" he asked. "Before FERC can approve this project it is only sensible to know these things."[32]

But FERC had long waved off such concerns. When Romany Webb, a researcher at Columbia Law School, analyzed 125 pipeline approvals by FERC and their environmental impact assessments, she was surprised by how "cursory" the agency's analysis of climate impacts was.

For years, the commission had claimed that it didn't have a sound method for tallying up a pipeline's potential greenhouse gas emissions.

"They are often not considering upstream and downstream emissions, and certainly not quantifying those emissions," she told me, referring to pollution at each end of the pipe, from both gas production and end use. "FERC says, 'We don't know where the gas is going, so we can't calculate downstream emissions. That's such a cop-out to say that. It's well within their ability. They just choose not to do it."[33]

Nelson Goes to FERC

On May 21, the Federal Energy Regulatory Commission released its transcript of the March meeting at the high school. By that point Joyce Burton was becoming a FERC black belt, practiced at navigating the agency's labyrinthine, glitchy website. She had tracked almost every Nelson comment that went into FERC's digital maw, and now she saw what came out in the other direction: the transcript was riddled with errors. Some comments were unintelligible. Names were wrong, entire statements made no grammatical sense. The transcription had substituted "Formula Leo" for "El Niño" in Michael Tabony's comments.

Many Nelson residents were already furious that they hadn't gotten a chance to speak. Now, some of those who *had* were furious too.[34]

"Boy, were people pissed," Burton said. To many of them, the error-filled transcript made a mockery of FERC's purported commitment to public participation. How could they believe that FERC took their concerns seriously if it couldn't even write them down?

Some decided to travel to Washington to ensure that the commission could hear them more clearly. "FERC DOES NOT WORK" proclaimed a May 22, 2015 post on the Friends of Nelson website, calling for volunteers to join a week of protests outside of the commission's headquarters, organized by a coalition of anti–fossil fuel groups called Beyond Extreme Energy.[35]

Burton was among a dozen or so Nelson residents who carpooled to the capital. Throughout that week, they met people from all over the country who had *noticed* the gas pipelines being laid down and liquefied natural gas terminals sprouting up amid their communities. The Situation was getting louder.

Burton had never been part of this kind of protest before. She had attended two days of nonviolent direct action training, covering what to do if you got detained and how protests are staged so that some participants could choose ahead of time to be arrested. Burton was moved by some of the large murals and other artistic forms of protest that sprung up on the street. Other elements of the spectacle made her roll her eyes, such as the faux carousel with life-size photos of FERC commissioners riding on it, as part of one day's "FERCus" theme.

Whatever their methods, she sympathized with her fellow activists' goal of reframing the narrative around new fossil fuel projects, and with their larger argument that the true radicals weren't people taking time off work to wave silly signs in front of FERC but fracking outfits like Chesapeake and pipeline builders like Dominion, whose projects threatened to throw more fuel on the fires disrupting the friendly climate that humans had enjoyed for millennia.

On May 26, the protestors formed a blockade in front of FERC's office on First Street. FERC staffers walked past each day, avoiding eye contact. Burton and her companions had stopped at a Target earlier in the week to buy a large white sheet and a bunch of Sharpies. That night Burton and her friend Helen Kimble sent an email to everyone in Nelson she could think of, asking who wanted their names written down on a banner, stating their opposition to the construction of the Atlantic Coast Pipeline. She was deluged with replies.[36]

On the twenty-seventh, they joined a sit-in vigil in front of the commission's office. A contingent of Nelsonians drove up for the day. Vicki Wheaton and Kathy Versluys were there. Burton and Kimble held up the banner reading UNITED AGAINST THE PIPELINE, with two hundred names beneath it, and sat for hours in silence.

FERC's transcript was garbled, but the message sent back from Nelson County was clear enough.

Route Shifts and Regrets

In May, Dominion announced that its preferred route went straight through the Cove, angling up the ridge above Liz Miles's and Wisteria Johnson's homes. On July 15, the company made it official: that would be the route it submitted for approval to FERC. Two days later, the two women drove north to Charlottesville and walked into Dominion's local office.

For weeks, their neighbor Janice Jackson and Connie Brennan—the county supervisor most vocally opposed to the ACP—had been trying to arrange this meeting for them and other neighboring landowners. They sat through a lunch presentation by Dominion's engineers, who were cheerful as always. (To each friendly engineer she met, Brennan made a point of saying: "You should work on solar instead!") And then the landowners talked about what kept them up at night. Johnson went first, speaking frankly of her "distrust" since Dominion hadn't responded to earlier requests for a meeting—and since the route went straight through a predominantly Black community in the nearby hamlet of Wingina. The other landowners voiced their concerns about historic Native and African American sites, about safety and water quality. Why, they asked again, couldn't Dominion put its pipe in existing rights-of-way? Everyone exchanged contact information and promises to be in touch soon.[37]

For Johnson, it seemed like a small victory: they had met some of the individuals behind this invasion she dreaded—"put a face to the dragon"—and talked with them, honestly, as human beings. Those human beings had listened patiently and pledged to do what they could. Maybe, she thought, they would help.

The meeting soon yielded at least one concrete outcome: Dominion agreed to wiggle the route so it climbed up the ridge to Bailey sooner, a bit farther away from their homes and pastures. At first, she felt a bit of relief.

"We got the pipeline on the mountain instead of straight down through [the middle] of our property," she said. But when Johnson looked at the map, she was flooded with regret. "Once we got it on the mountain we realized, it's even worse up there."[38] Because it meant that even longer sections of ridgeline would be torn up, blasted, flattened, widened—and exposed to future Camilles.

Meanwhile, a dozen miles to the south, Andrew Gantt was celebrating. A former economist for the International Monetary Fund with a PhD from Harvard, Gantt owned 800 acres and a historic home in Wingina, just above the James River.

Gantt was a descendant of Joseph Cabell, one of the earliest colonial settlers of Nelson County. Cabell built a large plantation, and his sons were instrumental in setting up the James River and Kanawha Canal system, which was dug by enslaved people, to carry boats mostly piloted by other enslaved people.

"Virginia's government and Dominion doesn't seem to understand, *this is my land*," Gantt had said at the March FERC meeting. "My family has owned this land continuously since 1738—two generations before the establishment of the United States."[39] The history on Gantt's land goes much deeper than that. Archaeologists believe it is the site of Monahassanough, the westernmost of the five village settlements of the Monacan Indians, as described by Captain John Smith in a famed 1624 map. There is evidence that the site was inhabited as much as five thousand years ago but abandoned by the early seventeenth century. In his comments to FERC, Gantt had noted the extensive Monacan sites and artifacts on his and neighboring properties that were once part of Cabell's land grant. Gantt's property had hosted archaeological digs and was under consideration as a National Historic District.[40]

He initially thought the weight of all that history would be enough to push Dominion away from his property. "I told ACP that there was NO price which would make me wish to have the pipeline on my farm," Gantt told me via email. He had no particular objection to pipelines or to increasing the use of fossil fuels. He was incensed by the trammeling of property rights—especially when it came to a property that his family had held on to for centuries, even as Union Army soldiers occupied it during the Civil War.

Gantt bought Dominion stock so he could speak his mind at annual shareholders' meetings. But his real source of leverage was the land he held. Noting that Dominion had earlier pledged to respect conservation easements in their routing decisions, he set up a 330-acre easement of his own. Dominion, he said, objected: they couldn't work around every single landowner who placed an easement just to block the pipeline from coming through.

"The easement was a battle in itself: in my draft I included a provision prohibiting pipelines, powerlines, etc., and the AG [attorney general] of Virginia wrote me saying that that was illegal, but I negotiated my way out of that and it became part of my easement language," Gantt told me. When the route shifted away from his land, he was satisfied. "I got the route blocked through my own farm by 'going to the mat' in my opposition. It was the biggest 'battle' I've been in but I won."[41]

But his victory meant heartache for some of his neighbors. The route jogged east, through parcels belonging to landowners descended from people who were once enslaved on the plantation owned by Gantt's ancestors.

And it went right by the St. Hebron Baptist Church, founded in 1848, the oldest African American church in the county. The white clapboard-sided building sat atop a scenic ridge, surrounded on two sides by cemeteries and on another by two immense, stately chestnut oaks. St. Hebron, locals said, was a stop on the Underground Railroad, and under it lay buried some who had escaped from slavery but died of exhaustion before they could reach freedom.[42] Now it and its graves, marked and otherwise, lay in the pipeline's incineration zone.

Not in Anyone's Backyard

Dominion's new route had also shifted south of Afton, away from Tom Harvey's viewshed.

As it did, All Pain No Gain itself faded from view. The splashy media campaign ended. By August 2015, the group's Facebook page went quiet.

"It became obvious that it was not going to work," said Connie Brennan of the group's elite-focused strategy. Whatever APNG's founders thought about the extent of their influence, it quickly became apparent that Dominion had a lot more.[43]

Still, while Dominion had shed some opponents, it acquired new ones. The route would now emerge from the belly of the Blue Ridge right between the Fenton Inn and the Wintergreen Resort—which had officially announced its opposition. Jill and Richard Averitt owned a property in the valley below, where they planned to develop an eco-resort to accommodate the increasing numbers of visitors flocking to Nelson's popular breweries and cideries. Now they too were in the corridor; like the Fentons, they found their long-held plans in limbo. The Averitts would prove to be formidable adversaries for Dominion Energy.

Meanwhile, many of those who were no longer at risk stayed in the fight too. Dominion had managed to alienate both camps. Helen Kimble, one of Joyce Burton's neighbors at Shannon Farm, was also an early member (and, at one point, president) of Friends of Nelson. When Shannon Farm's lawyers called to congratulate them on no longer being in Dominion's sights, Kimble replied that she didn't feel like the fight was over.

"We had spent so much time looking into the impacts of this on the county in general, and the broader fossil fuel issues," said Kimble. "We were super charged up and motivated to do what we had to do." If anything, with the cloud removed from their own land, they had energy freed up to fight on. "We all knew what it was like to be told it was a fait accompli, just suck it up and try to get the best deal," she said. "We knew what that felt like, but we were no longer under the gun."[44]

The group's members had long shrugged off accusations that they were NIMBYs: "not in my backyard" types who opposed *any* kind of development, whether it was housing or industrial or commercial projects.[45] When it came to fossil gas pipelines, they were, if anything, NIABYs: they didn't think the pipe belonged in *anyone's* backyard.

In retrospect, Kimble would see the route shift as a tactical error on Dominion's part. She and Burton and Ron Enders and Ellen Bouton and Ernie Reed and many other founding members of Friends of Nelson—who lived along the now-abandoned original route—redoubled their efforts.

"They were stirring up a hornets' nest, and then turning to *another* hornets' nest," Kimble said. "But that first one is still mad!"

"The Greatest Effort in the Fight"

"What are you guys doing?"

Will Fenton looked up from his wrinkled map to find a middle-aged man sitting astride a road bike, taking a break from a late summer ride along the Blue Ridge Parkway. The man nodded quizzically at Fenton and his companion and their surveying equipment. Fenton explained that they were trying to figure out who owned the land under their feet, where the Appalachian Trail and parkway crossed the mountain.

"Why?" the man asked.

"Because Dominion wants to build a gas pipeline across them here. They say it's privately owned land. And they can't do it if it's National Park Service land."

The man shook his head. "Don't bother," he said. "You're wasting your time. You'll never beat them." Then he rode off.

Fenton watched him pedal away and turned back to studying his map. In June, Dominion had submitted a map to federal agencies claiming that the section of the Appalachian Trail that was in the pipeline corridor was on privately owned land. From everything he had seen, this could not be true. It had to cross on federal land. Now, armed with faded Park Service maps from the 1940s and permission to survey from the federal government, he was trying to prove this.[46]

He hadn't planned to become an amateur surveyor. It now came with the territory. For the past six months, the Fentons had logged many late nights getting up to speed on pipeline construction methods, researching the eminent domain process, learning how to become an "intervenor" with FERC—trying to push on every door they could think of. It was already becoming another full-time job on top of their existing full-time jobs: managing subcontractors, designing interiors, setting up billing systems, picking a menu, hiring staff, planning marketing, carving oak door panels. All while raising two kids.

Not long after his surveying expedition, Fenton met with Kevin Bowman, the FERC employee who had presided over the now-infamous March meeting. The two men sat at one of the hand-hewn tables he had built. The conversation was cordial. Bowman listened carefully as Fenton explained how his business would be affected and why he thought Dominion's route across the Appalachian Trail was legally suspect. After Bowman thanked him and left, Fenton felt momentarily satisfied: he had finally gotten to say his piece to FERC. But he had the distinct impression that his concerns would go nowhere—that Bowman was another polite government functionary checking boxes.

Not long after, Fenton sat down at the same table to talk with Greg Buppert, the senior attorney from the Southern Environmental Law Center. That conversation would prove more fruitful.

Back in May, Buppert had mentioned the Fentons' predicament in testimony he gave to Congress, when he told Republican lawmakers seeking to speed up permitting for gas pipelines that the public should have some say in the matter, some input on the question of what lies in the public interest. "For the public, there is little belief that these (pipeline) companies have anything other than their own self-interest at heart," Buppert had said.[47]

But the two men hadn't met until that September day. They sat and talked for hours about what Fenton had learned about the parkway and the trail crossing, poring over the old maps that Fenton had wrangled from officials.

"We may have something here," Buppert said in his careful, understated way. He wasn't sure if it would prove useful and didn't want to make any promises. But he had learned to be open to ideas from all quarters, and some of the best had come from his clients in Buckingham, Highland, Augusta, and Nelson. Nobody knew the ground—and what made it worth fighting for—better than they did.

Fenton, in turn, knew a bit about Buppert's organization: he had once helped build a house for the founder of SELC. But sitting there across from Buppert, he wasn't sure this mild-mannered lawyer could help him. Will Fenton's initial impression: Greg Buppert was very smart but maybe, like him, a little shy. Not necessarily the type to lead an army into battle. "When he came out here, I thought he looked more like a page turner," he'd say years later.

But he also knew from his powerlifting days not to draw too many conclusions from outward demeanor. He had competed against ex–football players, guys with swagger. "You don't always pick the guy that's going to win when you look at all these people," he said. "It's usually guys like myself, quiet and unassuming."[48]

The previous fall, in October 2014, when Buppert had his first and only face-to-face meeting with Dominion's team, he had received a clear message: the ACP was inevitable, and the company was not interested in discussing any alternatives to their chosen "greenfield" route. On September 18, 2015, Atlantic Coast Pipeline LLC officially submitted its application to the Federal Energy Regulatory Commission, with a route through Virginia that would eventually lead them all from Reeds Gap to the Supreme Court.

"That meeting was really important," Buppert told me years later of his afternoon at the Fenton Inn. "Will put the trail crossing issue on my radar screen."[49]

Media coverage had framed the brewing battle over the Atlantic Coast Pipeline as a "David versus Goliath story." But it would be more precise to say it was becoming a story of thousands of Davids versus Virginia's corporate Goliath. There was no protagonist—no single charismatic public face of the burgeoning resistance. There was, instead, a hive of hornets. Many hives, in fact, responding to their sense that their homes and futures and everything they valued were threatened. And, as hornets are wont to do, they were coordinating their efforts.

By late 2015, Will Fenton was coming to share the view expressed by another local a year earlier, in a letter to the Staunton newspaper.

"The argument that the pipeline matter will be decided by the FERC (i.e., the Federal government) is completely wrong," predicted the Augusta County resident. "It will be decided by the interest—Dominion or the citizens of Virginia—which puts the greatest effort into the fight."[50]

Part II

Ground Game

Trees felled by ACP crews near Wintergreen and the Fenton Inn in Nelson
County, Virginia. (Jonathan Mingle)

Chapter Five

Steep Slopes

" Anything I need to be aware of?"

Clyde Thompson considered the question and tapped out a reply.

"Probably," he began.

It was December 20, 2016, six weeks since Donald Trump had been elected president.

The political winds that had shifted so unexpectedly on Election Day were starting to blow through the headquarters of federal agencies throughout Washington, DC, including the stately Beaux-Arts structure jutting out onto the National Mall that housed the US Department of Agriculture. News reports suggested the new administration was preparing to populate some of those offices, from Interior to Energy, with fossil fuel industry boosters.[1] Trump's transition teams were already asking for lists of agency employees who worked on climate change.[2] Career staffers were left guessing what new directives might be coming their way.

Those winds had reached Thompson in Elkins, West Virginia, where he was completing his fifteenth year as supervisor of the Monongahela National Forest—and contemplating the time-sensitive email from his boss's boss, Glenn Casamassa, associate deputy chief of the US Forest Service.

Casamassa had a call scheduled that afternoon with his own superior at the Department of Agriculture. On the agenda: the Atlantic Coast Pipeline.

The pipeline was slated to cut a 21-mile swath through the Monongahela and George Washington National Forests in West Virginia and Virginia. A few days earlier, Casamassa had been visited by Dominion executives who wanted the Forest Service to "sync up" its permitting timetable with those of other federal agencies. Their concern: Clyde Thompson and his staff were holding things up.

Now Casamassa wanted Thompson, the Forest Service's lead contact for the ACP on behalf of both forests, to bring him up to speed.

Thompson and his team had spent nearly two years studying Dominion's construction plans for laying its 42-inch-wide conduit through some of the most flood- and erosion-prone topography in the US. After all that scrutiny, he explained, they were still worried that the risks of burying the pipeline in that terrain were far greater than the company's executives and engineers seemed to appreciate.

When Kent Karriker, an ecosystems specialist who worked under Thompson, first saw a map of Dominion's proposed route, his jaw had dropped in disbelief. Many had grades well over 40 percent—so steep you needed to grab hold of a tree to haul yourself up them. Some were more like cliffs than slopes: construction crews would have to secure their excavators to trees or bedrock with 200-foot-long cables and then lower them on winches. In some spots, workers would have to daisy-chain those winches together, one machine to the next, in a kind of excavator garland draping the mountainside.

Thompson, Karriker, and their colleagues had pressed Dominion for months to provide detailed designs for those stomach-churning inclines, laying out precisely how it would stabilize the soil both during and after digging.[3]

Because they were still waiting for that information, Thompson explained to Casamassa, the Forest Service had filed a letter in the official record stating that its final decision date on issuing a special use permit to ACP LLC was "To Be Determined."

That did not sit well with Dominion vice president Leslie Hartz. She seemed to think, Thompson wrote, that she could go up the hierarchy and negotiate a faster timetable directly with Casamassa or his superiors. But Thompson had told her that the rules were not "discretionary"—they couldn't just be waved away. There was a process they were legally required to go through. That, he explained, was why Hartz was "upset."[4]

No one had ever built a pipeline this big across that kind of terrain before. The stakes of getting this right were high.

Thompson reminded Casamassa that the goal of all their efforts was to demonstrate that they "have a reasonable chance of keeping the pipeline on the mountain and keep the mountain on the mountain."

Based on the expert analyses he had seen so far, he concluded: "I'm not optimistic."

The Obi-Wan Approach

Back in the spring of 2014, Clyde Thompson had learned about the Atlantic Coast Pipeline the same way most people had: he read about it in the newspaper. Unlike most people, however, Thompson oversaw the management of a million acres of public land.[5]

Tall and lean, with gray hair and a deeply lined face, Clyde Thompson had the affable, unflappable, wearily competent demeanor of a veteran administrator. He had been supervisor of the Monongahela since 2002, a length of tenure in one forest that was rare for an agency where administrators tended to be bounced around the country as they climbed the bureaucracy's ladder and pay scales.

Over the years, Thompson had dealt with all kinds of projects and fielded demands from plenty of "stakeholders" with strong opinions on how the "Land of Many Uses"—as the national forest tagline goes—should be used, from logging interests to hikers, hunters to conservation groups. And energy companies. His team had recently had a "positive" experience dealing with another company that wanted to upgrade an existing gas pipeline through the Monongahela.

Thompson was surprised Dominion hadn't reached out sooner. He would have liked a heads-up—a letter, a call, an email. Something.

When Dominion finally did contact his office and he saw a map of its proposed route, he immediately saw problems.

"They couldn't have picked a worse place than that first route," Thompson said.

Karriker, who had spent more than a decade at the Monongahela, had the same reaction. "They came to us with essentially a straight line drawn across the national forest," he said, "like they laid a ruler on the map."

Things went downhill from there. Because of the concern about erosion and landslides, Dominion was required to analyze soils at representative sites along the route. Thompson's staff repeatedly asked to see the qualifications of the subcontractors performing those surveys. A West Virginia–based Dominion lobbyist named Bob Orndorff pledged that they would provide a list of resumes before selecting them. When Dominion finally submitted that list—*after* the contractors had already gone out and dug pits in the forest—only one person named on it turned out to be a licensed soil scientist. But she told the Forest Service she had never been hired by Dominion. The people Dominion *did* hire had little expertise in soil analyses—rendering the surveys largely useless.[6]

For Thompson and his team, this strange bit of deception signaled a troubling willingness to cut corners. Dominion had submitted its route without carefully studying the soil and rock it would be disturbing along the way. This struck them as completely backward: they thought that what they learned from soil surveys should inform the development of the safest route for the pipeline.[7] "We were on edge because of that," said Karriker.

Meanwhile, Karriker tried to communicate another concern: the pipeline route would likely pose unacceptable (i.e., illegal) risks to the habitat of threatened and endangered species. He and his colleagues made it clear that Dominion would have to avoid both Cheat Mountain—the only known home to the eponymous Cheat Mountain salamander—and Shenandoah Mountain in the George Washington National Forest, home to the Cow Knob salamander, which likewise was found nowhere else in the world outside of its narrow ridgetop.[8]

Karriker was bemused by the way that Dominion's representatives never really addressed the points he raised but simply waved them away. "It was like that scene in Star Wars, with Obi-Wan saying, 'These aren't the drones you're looking for,'" he said. "That continued for a year and a half."

They finally got Dominion's attention with a letter on January 19, 2016, in which the Forest Service formally rejected the proposed route because it "did not meet minimum requirements" of laws protecting endangered species and mitigating environmental damage.[9]

The letter brought things to a screeching halt. Without a permit to cross the forests, Dominion had a major problem on its hands. The company scrambled to submit a new route. That one jogged about 15 miles farther south, but the Forest Service noted that it "only partially addressed the problems while creating new ones."[10] When Dominion filed yet another, longer alternative route the next month, it went through areas that the company had previously rejected as too steep and hazardous.[11]

"The elephant in the room throughout all of this is that you're going to do this really serious earth-disturbing construction going straight up the side of the mountain," Karriker said. "Gravity and water are uncompromising forces. There's just not much way to get across the central Appalachians west to east without encountering those kinds of problems."

And Dominion wanted to traverse some literally dizzying terrain. At one spot on Cloverlick Mountain in Pocahontas County, the grade exceeded 100 percent—so steep that Karriker was sick for two days after the exertion of hiking up it to inspect its soils and survey pits dug by Dominion's contractors.

"Some of these are so steep they are hard to stand on," Thompson told me. "You start digging in them and you hit a seep of water that works like lubricant on soil. You start thinking, 'How do you hold it? How do you keep it on the ground?'"

Veterans of West Virginia's highlands, Thompson and Karriker worried most about the confluence of steep grades and heavy rains. Monsoonal torrents regularly visited the Allegheny Mountains. As runoff percolated into the disturbed soil around the pipe, where would it go?

"Some of those places—I just don't see how you do it," Thompson said. "I wouldn't want to build my house there. I'd be worried every time it rained."

A History and Future of Atmospheric Violence

On June 23, 2016, rain started falling early in the morning across the mountains of central West Virginia and didn't stop for eighteen hours.

A series of powerful thunderstorms moving east from the Ohio Valley, brimming with moisture from the Great Lakes, had parked themselves over the basins of the Elk, Gauley, and Greenbrier Rivers—not far from the ACP's route. Some towns received 10 inches of rain and were partly submerged. Rivers surged to record-high levels. When the waters receded, hundreds of homes had been wrecked or washed away. The damage from one summer day's thunderstorms totaled more than a billion dollars. Twenty-three people died in the floods.[12]

It was the third-deadliest flood in the state's history and, according to the National Oceanic and Atmospheric Administration and the National Weather Service, a "thousand-year event."[13] While the volume of rain was unusual, the flooding was not. Heavy rains are the deadliest natural hazard that West Virginians face. Each of West Virginia's fifty-five counties reported at least fourteen floods in the quarter century preceding the 2016 floods. Since 1967, every county in the state has been declared a federal flood disaster area at least once, several as many as ten times.[14]

Torrential downpours have increased in intensity nationwide over the past several decades. Climate scientists are confident they will only become more severe as our world warms. For each degree (Celsius) of warming, the atmosphere holds 7 percent more water vapor—providing fuel for more powerful storms. In a 2017 report, the Army Corps of Engineers forecast that the largest increases in rainfall and stream flows would happen in West Virginia—specifically, in those areas that the ACP would traverse.[15] In fact, the region is already experiencing this shift: according to NOAA, extreme precipitation events have increased 55 percent since 1960.[16]

The June storms triggered hundreds of landslides throughout West Virginia. Clyde Thompson sent out teams to inspect damage in the

Monongahela. They found roads buried by slides or with gaping holes in them, exposing metal culverts and drainage pipes. Entire hillsides had given way, leaving scars hundreds of feet long and exposing bedrock. Staffers came across forty-eight landslides just while conducting random post-flood checks, without even looking for them.[17]

Engineers like to design for maximum stress, balancing cost with the need to withstand unlikely but extreme impacts. "From my perspective, it's like designing a campground for a Fourth of July crowd," said Thompson. But he thought Dominion wasn't even designing for the normal range of possible rainfall events that Central Appalachia saw in a typical year, let alone the supercharged storms of the future. "I never felt like we got to the point where they were designing it for *today's* weather, for normal fluctuations," said Thompson.[18]

Climate change hadn't even entered the analysis.[19] Left unsaid in all these discussions was yet another question: Would the pipeline's own methane and carbon dioxide emissions over time make the pipeline *itself* more vulnerable to extreme weather, like a snake eating its own tail?

"Best in Class"

In its filings to FERC, Dominion pledged that its construction crews and engineers would implement what it called "Best in Class" practices—a menu of engineering techniques to control erosion and stabilize slopes that promised to go above and beyond what regulations required.

Some were more specific than others, such as "slope breakers with diversion channels" and "targeted deep drains." Some were bold but rather crude: a measure to be deployed on the most precipitous slopes involved hammering in giant "soil nails"—steel spikes from 8 to 15 feet in length—to hold in place enormous sheets of heavy wire mesh. One option was simply called "Advanced Engineering," without further explanation.

"We told them many times, 'Show us how this is going to work and how you're going to prevent these problems,'" Karriker said. "All they would come back to us with was these so-called Best in Class measures."

The ACP planners used this phrase so often that years later Karriker would give a weary chuckle at its mere mention. It was invoked like some magic talisman. The pipe would stay on the mountain. The mountain would stay on the mountain. Why? Best in Class.

Thompson and Karriker were unsettled by Dominion's apparent disinterest in even knowing what the problems might be. What the pipeline engineers sent back to them—mostly basic profile drawings—didn't quiet their concerns. "It was not the kind of stuff we were used to, not detailed enough for these areas," Thompson said.

"There was just so much resistance to putting anything at all on paper and committing to it," Karriker said. Dominion's people seemed fixated on keeping the process moving along, rather than responding to the substance of their requests. These interactions left the Forest Service team wondering if Dominion saw steep slopes less as a problem of physics and engineering than one of public relations and persuasion.

In one meeting, Thompson said, he had to cut off a Dominion public relations official who was touting, yet again, their "Best in Class" program with an interjection: "It would make me feel better to hear you say you know how big a problem this could be."

"He didn't get it, he just kept on going," Thompson told me. "I would rather hear, 'We know this is a difficult route. We have some real challenges. Here's what we're doing to fix them and here's what we're doing to back this up.'" But the technical details were never forthcoming. "We just heard 'We've got the Best in Class.'"

The Forest Service's specialists weren't the only ones worried. Friends of Nelson had commissioned independent consultants—experts in soil science and geohazards—to analyze soil makeup and study some steep slopes on privately owned parcels in Nelson County along the ACP's route. In their final report, these consultants concluded that Dominion hadn't really studied the ground it was proposing to dig up. In its submissions to FERC, they wrote, Dominion had underestimated "the potential for debris flows in the very steep mountainous portions of Nelson County."[20] The Wintergreen Resort had asked yet another expert—an earth scientist who had been analyzing the geology of that part of the Blue Ridge since the 1970s—to review Dominion's plans. In his own report to FERC, he described Dominion's plan to drill near the Fenton Inn and Wintergreen as "inadvisable."

"The risk of failure is high," he warned.[21]

Later that fall, when FERC issued its draft environmental impact statement on the Atlantic Coast Pipeline—as required under the National Environmental Policy Act—the agency struck a curiously disinterested stance on all these questions. Across the entirety of the three-volume, 2,375-page document, the commission evinced little concern either about the risks that the pipeline would lock in decades of fossil fuel emissions or the risks of traversing slide-prone terrain in a fast-warming world. Its authors noted that pipelines are buried at least 3 feet deep, routinely inspected, and treated with special anti-corrosion external coatings and, therefore, the ACP "would not likely be significantly impacted by climate change."

All in all, the Atlantic Coast Pipeline would result in "some adverse effects" on the environment, the commission conceded, but these would be reduced to "less-than-significant levels" if Dominion took the steps it had proposed to mitigate risks.[22] (FERC took a similarly blasé approach to analyzing the ground that pipelines would cross. When a group of scholars analyzed several dozen FERC environmental reviews, they found that the agency recycled its own text with striking frequency. For pipelines sited in dramatically different landscapes, from Pennsylvania to Alabama, Texas to West Virginia, long sections read almost verbatim.[23])

That year, 2016, would set an all-time record high for global average temperature. But the primary federal regulator of interstate natural gas pipelines did not appear concerned with planning ahead for the warmer, wetter, wilder weather that was all but certain to test the integrity of those pipes. Invoking "Best in Class" seemed good enough for FERC, if not the US Forest Service.

"Give Them What They Want"

By the fall of 2016, Clyde Thompson was still holding his ground.

On October 24, he sent a thirty-page letter to ACP LLC and FERC outlining the Forest Service's request for site-specific designs for ten slopes—six in the George Washington and four in the Monongahela. These were spots so steep and potentially dangerous that citing generic best practices just wouldn't cut it—sites that the agency's experts flagged as potential "worst-case scenarios." What they needed, Thompson emphasized, were designs "tailored to the conditions of each site."[24]

Over the next few months, their request went unanswered. But their superiors heard plenty from Dominion.

"Once the presidential administration changed—even right after the election—there was an immediate shift of tone in the Washington office of the Forest Service," said Karriker.

On November 9, a day after Trump's shocking victory, Leslie Hartz met with Robert Bonnie—the man at the Department of Agriculture to whom the chief of the Forest Service reported—and pushed for the Forest Service to speed up its review process, to line up with FERC's timetable. Hartz met with Bonnie again in mid-December to make the same request. Then, on December 27, Hartz wrote to Clyde Thompson to lay out Dominion's preferred schedule.

That same day—a week after Thompson had warned Glen Casamassa that he was "not optimistic" that the pipe would stay on the mountain—his immediate supervisor made it clear that she shared Thompson's concerns. Dominion's timeline "is unrealistic and we have been trying to set that expectation," wrote Kathleen Atkinson, the regional forester for the Eastern Region, who oversaw seventeen national forests, including the Monongahela. She asked what Dominion's executives had discussed with Bonnie the previous week. Casamassa replied within the hour, explaining that the chief of the Forest Service and Bonnie had told him that Dominion wanted the agency to get a move on and issue its draft decision when FERC published its final environmental impact statement.

"Draft decision would be based on the present pipeline alignment," Casamassa wrote. That meant no more route changes. "I would anticipate that direction to be coming our way in as early as end of January," he added.[25] That meant that the Forest Service's longstanding concerns about steep slopes, landslides, and sediment in streams were about to disappear.

"It doesn't take a genius to figure out what he's saying," said Karriker, referring to the line in Casamassa's reply about "direction." "Once Trump gets inaugurated, he's gonna say, 'Give them what they want.'"[26]

The Era of "Alternative Facts"

On Friday, January 20, 2017, Donald J. Trump was sworn in as the forty-fifth president of the United States.

The crowds assembled on the National Mall for the occasion were thin, which apparently enraged the new president. The next day, his press secretary's first official statement was a series of brazen falsehoods about crowd size and accusations that the media had sought to understate it. On Sunday, Trump advisor Kellyanne Conway went on *Meet the Press* to spin her boss's newly declared war on reality as merely putting forth "alternative facts."[27]

This phrase quickly became infamous; it would be deployed frequently—and mockingly—as a label for the latest dubious claims from the new occupants of the White House. But inside federal bureaucracies, the crowd size episode triggered dread. The National Mall is overseen by the National Park Service, whose Twitter account was briefly shut down after it had retweeted a post comparing Obama's and Trump's crowd sizes. Trump himself called the acting director of the National Park Service to upbraid him and urge him to produce more flattering photographs.[28]

Those first days of the Trump era augured more serious gaslighting to come. Employees in federal agencies who worked on climate change began voicing fears that they would be punished for doing their jobs. By mid-February staffers at the Department of Agriculture were getting emails from superiors instructing them to avoid using the words "climate change" or "reduce greenhouse gases" in their work and communications altogether.[29]

After the inauguration fracas, "all the Interior folks were kind of nervous," Clyde Thompson told me. He didn't think the new atmosphere was conducive to rational decision-making about consequential projects, such as the Atlantic Coast Pipeline. "Everybody was kind of on edge. That doesn't help a process that should be calm and thoughtful."

A few weeks later, the Trump administration released a list of its top twenty infrastructure priorities. The Atlantic Coast Pipeline was on it.[30]

Trump had come under heavy criticism for a botched transition:

many key positions would remain unfilled for months across the federal bureaucracy. But soon after being installed at USDA, Trump appointees were already working overtime on behalf of energy companies.

In the weeks after the inauguration, Dominion executives and lobbyists met with newly installed senior advisors at the Departments of Agriculture and Interior. One ACP lobbyist emailed a political appointee at USDA to report on a "very productive meeting" with deputies to the new secretary of the interior "to sort through some regulatory issues at Interior that are slowing the permitting of the Atlantic Coast Pipeline Project."

"We've got some headaches at USDA as well," the lobbyist told the new staffer. "Is there a chance you might be available for a meeting next week to talk through some of the challenges we're facing?"[31]

The "headaches" likely referred to Clyde Thompson's persistent requests for more information. His demands threatened to delay Dominion's timetable, and delays were expensive. With every day that pipes sat in storage yards and subcontractors' crews were on standby, costs mounted and investors got more anxious.

In March, the company's frustrations spilled out into the open in the chambers of the US Senate. At a hearing on "Opportunities to Improve American Energy Infrastructure," Diane Leopold—a senior Dominion executive and longtime head of the company's natural gas business—lamented the fact that her company needed no fewer than eighteen different permits from federal agencies and that the National Park Service took fourteen months to review its twenty-two-page application to survey the area it wanted to drill under the Blue Ridge Parkway and Appalachian Trail. (Once permission was finally secured, she added, Dominion's team took only an afternoon to conduct its survey.)

"Though we rerouted 95 miles to meet its concerns, the Forest Service continues to move the goalposts with changing requirements and standards," Leopold griped.[32]

This "I'm going to talk to your manager" approach—not just venting to sympathetic senators but engaging the real decision-makers at Interior and Agriculture—would ultimately win the day. Dominion's pressure campaign culminated in what Karriker would later jokingly refer to as the "Mother's Day Massacre."

On a Friday in mid-May 2017, Karriker worked late into the day putting together a letter restating all the Forest Service's concerns about steep slopes and landslide risks. Instead of the ten site-specific designs they needed, Dominion had supplied them with two partial ones—quickly deemed inadequate by Thompson's in-house experts. This would be a last-ditch effort to get the information they had been seeking for years. Clyde Thompson reviewed and signed off on it, and it was filed as part of FERC's official docket, on Sunday morning, Mother's Day.[33]

Dominion responded with alacrity this time—though not with the long-requested information. That same afternoon, Hartz fired off a sharply worded email to Clyde Thompson. She was "surprised" to learn that the Forest Service was waiting for more information on steep slopes.

"I was under the clear impression that we were going to receive a letter saying that we had demonstrated our ability to construct on steep slopes" and that specific construction measures would be hashed out later in the process, Hartz wrote. "I don't understand this change in direction."[34]

This slightly peeved, panicky tone—*I thought this was taken care of*—was understandable, given that just three weeks earlier Leslie Hartz had stood and listened as her own boss, Diane Leopold, asserted during a press briefing that federal regulators' review of the Atlantic Coast Pipeline had "left no stone unturned, and it has addressed all of the important environmental and safety issues that have been raised. Rarely—if ever—has a project in our region received such intense scrutiny."

"This is a project where you can't cut corners," Leopold had pledged, "and we won't."[35]

Hartz's letter triggered reprimands from Thompson's superiors. "I got chewed out over that one," Thompson said. "Kent was right on. He put it out there. And folks didn't like the answer."

He was summoned to a meeting with the peeved regional forester in Milwaukee, who asked him why he signed off on the letter and didn't filter the information in it. Thompson, undeterred, calmly replied, "Because the information was correct."[36]

Karriker said he was expressly forbidden from communicating

on his own initiative with ACP's representatives. "We continued to have conference calls and meetings with Dominion," he told me. "We weren't allowed to press for anything."

Thompson had stood his ground but ultimately lost his purchase on the project's review process. His team had lost any meaningful influence over the planning of the Atlantic Coast Pipeline through public lands they managed. The steep slope designs would never become part of FERC's analysis of the project's risks because Dominion would never submit them—and the Forest Service stopped asking for them.

After that point, no federal agency would ask what "Best in Class" looked like in practice. The slogan itself would suffice for now. But Karriker and Thompson knew that terrain. They had stewarded it for decades. And they worried that, eventually, reality would catch up with the Atlantic Coast Pipeline.

The sudden, post-election about-face from the Forest Service had removed the last real obstacle for ACP's planners to move through the national forests. It would come back to haunt Dominion all the same.

Chapter Six

The Campaign to Elect a Pipeline

O utside the Hilton Scottsdale Resort and Villas, the Arizona sun was shining brightly. But inside, as an annual conference hosted by the American Gas Association kicked off, Bruce McKay pointed to dark clouds on the horizon for his industry.

"The problem is more serious than anyone in this room realizes," he warned.

It was October 9, 2017, and the temperature was already in the mid-80s by 9:00 a.m., as members of the nation's largest trade group for gas utilities settled in for the first of three days of "strategizing on key issues." McKay, a senior Dominion Energy lobbyist, was speaking on the day's first panel, billed as "tips on siting infrastructure in the age of 'keep it in the ground.'"[1]

If you had wandered in off the street, grabbed some lukewarm coffee, and sat down to listen to McKay, you'd be forgiven for concluding that the natural gas industry was in serious trouble. Yet his dire prognosis seemed out of step with the data. Less than a year into the Trump era, business was booming.

Gas had just eclipsed coal in 2016 as the country's primary fuel for making electricity.[2] The US was about to become a net exporter of methane. That year, 2017, would set a record for new interstate pipeline capacity added to the nation's gas delivery system. And federal regulators were being flooded with permit applications for even *more* new gas pipelines and LNG terminals.[3] In public comments and earnings calls, McKay's bosses, Tom Farrell and Diane Leopold, radiated confidence. They, along with just about everyone else, expected FERC to approve the Atlantic Coast Pipeline any day now.[4]

Among his peers, though, McKay could be candid. He was at pains to remind them that they faced a groundswell of opposition, and it wasn't just going to fade away on its own. The threat they all faced, he explained, was that "historically non-political processes (are) now political."[5] The groups pushing back against projects like his own employer's Atlantic Coast Pipeline were sophisticated, coordinated, determined—and their message was gaining wider traction. These activists were slowly making inroads in the halls of power.

Since 2012, a diverse coalition of citizens' groups had fought the Keystone XL oil pipeline. In 2015, nearing the end of his second term, President Obama finally rejected it for good. And now there was a growing movement afoot to "keep it in the ground," pushing for climate action by restricting the supply of fossil fuels and targeting major oil and gas producers like ExxonMobil, Shell, and BP.[6] The movement's leaders realized that one of the best ways to "keep it in the ground" was to keep new pipelines *out* of the ground. That meant calling out lesser-known but powerful firms like Enbridge, Williams, Duke, and Dominion that were building pipelines to ferry more hydrocarbons to more customers for many more decades to come.

McKay walked his audience through a scouting report on these agitators and how they were storming the halls of innocent regulators and pillorying firms like his, which were simply trying to keep the lights on. They were, he noted, adept at social media and planning events "staged for media consumption"; prone to using "outrage and intimidation"; and trying to "delegitimize the process" by claiming that companies like Dominion were "immoral, regulators corrupt, processes rigged."

Those might sound like pretty standard tactics deployed by protestors since the dawn of history. But this was a new and epic battle, McKay warned, for the "hearts and minds" of the American people. What was ultimately at stake was their industry's social license to operate. Renewables were getting inexorably cheaper. Citizens' concerns about pollution and climate impacts were mounting. Over the long run, the court of public opinion was where the real contest would play out. If the gas industry did not act to shore up that social license, it was at risk of fatally eroding—and perhaps one day collapsing altogether under this storm surge of resistance.

Still, in the spirit of lighting the candle rather than cursing the darkness, McKay noted, "We're all in this together." He then revealed some highlights from what he described as Dominion's "campaign to elect a pipeline."

He did not mention a letter sent by CEO Tom Farrell to Dominion's 76,000 employees, retirees, and shareholders earlier that year, urging them to consider candidates' stance on the pipeline when they voted in the Democratic primary.[7] But McKay did tick off some other key milestones in this "campaign": 150 letters to the editor, over 9,000 letters and cards mailed to FERC and elected officials, 11,000 phone calls to Governor McAuliffe and Virginia's two Democratic senators, and 250,000 pieces of direct mail taking Dominion's sales pitch of lower energy prices and more jobs directly to Virginians. His takeaway: "If you want fair media coverage you need to pay for it."[8]

Elite decision-makers had long ago embraced methane as a climate solution. But that didn't mean that the AGA's members should get complacent. People were paying more attention to the proliferation of gas infrastructure and applying coordinated pressure on government officials at every level. Scientists were shouting about methane leakage and other widening cracks in the carefully constructed narrative of natural gas as a Clean, Reliable, Abundant, Affordable Bridge Fuel—first proffered by the American Gas Association's leaders way back in 1988.[9]

Dominion seemed likely to win its own pipeline battle, but the assembled industry executives and lobbyists all risked losing the larger war for control of the Story. They had an insurgency on their hands. They had to respond accordingly.

Knitting Nannas and Other Radicals

Since 2015, on every other Wednesday, shoppers heading to the Whole Foods on Hydraulic Road in Charlottesville were greeted by a familiar sight: a cluster of people waving hand-lettered signs that read NO PIPELINE and HONK FOR CLEAN ENERGY NOW on the sidewalk in front of Dominion's local office across the street. Often there would be several grandmotherly looking women among them, settled into folding camp chairs, who would look up periodically from their knitting to smile and wave their own anti-ACP placards at the drivers.

Judy Matthews would sometimes glimpse these women—the Knitting Nannas, as they called themselves—through the window of her office. She had been working there, for Dominion's electric utility subsidiary, for over thirty years. Matthews liked her colleagues and took pride in her work: after all, Virginians really did need Dominion to keep their lights on. But ever since her own employer had sent agents to negotiate with her and her husband David about an easement for the pipeline, she had come to view those decades of work through a somewhat tinted lens. "Dominion's been good to me," she said. "But it put a bitter taste in my mouth."

In 2015, Judy and David had learned that the route was slated to come through their property just above Davis Creek. David had grown up just a few hundred yards downhill, in a house that was swept away in Camille's floodwaters. They felt insulted by the company's initial offers—it seemed like a pittance for what Dominion wanted to take, and for all the restrictions and risks they would have to live with. But as much as they wanted to speak their minds about what they saw as strong-arm negotiating tactics and scant benefits for Nelson County, they worried about repercussions for her job. So, when she saw the Knitting Nannas out there, she secretly wished she could join them.[10]

With their shawls and wool caps in their laps, they looked less like the dangerous radicals Bruce McKay had warned about and more like the gardening country-dwelling grandmas that many of them were. Their "knit-ins" were just one front of the multipronged effort by grass-roots groups across the region to put a dent in Dominion's prevailing narrative around the pipeline: that it was safe, that it would transport "clean" energy, that it was essential to fuel the region's prosperity, and that most people welcomed the project.[11]

But before they could change people's perceptions of either Dominion or its pipeline, these citizens' groups needed to get people's attention—no small task in the age of twenty-four-hour Netflix streaming, Twitter, and smartphones. That meant breaking through the noise and putting on events that reporters would write about.

They contested the narrative from every angle: in letters to the editor, in supervisors' meetings, on social media platforms. Occasionally they'd organize a larger rally and get on the evening news. On a sweltering July day in 2016, over sixty organizations had mustered more than six hundred people to march on the governor's mansion in Richmond to call on Terry McAuliffe to commit to clean energy and move Virginia away from fossil fuels.[12] A pilot from the Pipeline Air Force even flew over Dominion's annual Riverrock music festival in Richmond towing a NO PIPELINE banner for thousands of concertgoers to see. Friends of Nelson held a "music for the mountains" benefit concert and a "property rights revival" in a big tent with fire-and-brimstone-style preaching about eminent domain and the Constitution. In 2016, Allegheny–Blue Ridge Alliance member groups welcomed Indigenous activist leaders from Nebraska who had fought Keystone XL, who led them in planting traditional corn seeds held sacred by the Ponca Tribe—"seeds of resistance"—in the path of the ACP.

In a rural county, where you could go weeks without any spontaneous interactions with your neighbors, these gatherings had an added appeal: they offered a chance to come together.

Despite all these and many other efforts, they were losing. The ACP was behind schedule but mostly on track. The project's planners expected to soon have all the permits they needed. The Knitting Nannas and their allies were up against powerful forces: not just corporate inertia but a concerted effort to cement the fossil-fueled status quo in place.

In June 2014—several years into the nation's gas boom, but just as word was first spreading through Virginia's mountains about Dominion's pipeline—a controversial political communications consultant named Richard Berman had given a speech to a group of oil and gas executives in Colorado Springs. He outlined the toolbox he used to shape public perceptions of fossil fuels and other burning social and political issues, as part of his pitch to the assembled executives to bankroll a public relations campaign he called "Big Green Radicals," aimed at pushing back against groups protesting fracking in Pennsylvania and Colorado.[13]

Berman seemed to delight in revealing some of his dark arts to once and future clients. One of his objectives in his past work as a hired gun to crush labor unions and demonize environmental activists, he explained, was "taking away people's moral authority" through mockery or accusations of hypocrisy (e.g., pointing out that climate activists fly on planes and drive cars). His larger aim, he said, was to sow doubt and paralyze ordinary people's thinking on an issue like fracking—to move beyond the "factual debate" and get people "overwhelmed by the science and 'I don't know who to believe.'"[14]

"Think of this as an endless war," Berman exhorted the corporate leaders in the room. And if they won that war, if they succeeded in delegitimizing their opponents, he explained, "You get in people's mind a tie. They don't know who is right."

And a tie, he said, "basically ensures the status quo."

Ordinary people could, of course, look up the reports and learn from the legions of climate scientists and energy experts warning that, one way or another, some kind of radical change was inevitable. One or the other status quo had to give way: either a livable climate, or an economy designed around burning fossil fuels.

"I'll take a tie any day if I'm trying to preserve the status quo," Berman added for emphasis.

"Defeating Pipeline Insurgencies"

Efforts to preserve the status quo sometimes took on a more menacing cast.

In June 2016, Energy Transfer—the Dallas-based firm led by Kelcy Warren of "pipeline companies will overbuild until the end of time" fame—had begun construction on a 1,172-mile-long oil pipeline from

North Dakota to southern Illinois. The Dakota Access Pipeline would cut through lands sacred to the Lakota Sioux of the Standing Rock Reservation in South Dakota and under a lake they relied on for drink- ing water.

Under the leadership of Lakota and other Native groups who called themselves "water protectors," citizens assembled a camp at Standing Rock that soon swelled with Indigenous and environmental activists. They were met by a small army of riot gear–clad security forces, who sprayed the protestors with firehoses in freezing weather and used at- tack dogs to intimidate them. The brutal clampdown produced shock- ing images in national media and galvanized activists from around the country.[15]

For tactical lessons—and inspiration—Friends of Nelson and other Allegheny–Blue Ridge Alliance members kept close tabs on the events unfolding at Standing Rock. In September 2016, Nelson activists had hosted a "day of solidarity" with those fighting Dakota Access, aligned with the Standing Rock Sioux Tribe's National Day of Action. The following month police moved in and cleared the camp. The Trump administration fast-tracked permits, and in April 2017—the same month that 200,000 people marched from the Capitol to the White House calling for climate action—Dakota Access was completed.

It was soon revealed that a secretive international security firm called TigerSwan—formerly employed by the US military as a con- tractor in the global war on terror—had been hired by Energy Transfer to target protestors with surveillance techniques, working with police along the project's route. In internal reports, TigerSwan compared the water protectors to a "jihadist insurgency." Their solution: "aggressive intelligence preparation of the battlefield and active coordination be- tween intelligence and security elements are now a proven method of defeating pipeline insurgencies."[16]

The industry's "under siege" mentality long predated Standing Rock. In 2011, at a Houston-area energy industry conference, Matthew Pitzarella, an executive from Range Resources, one of the biggest gas drillers in the Marcellus, likened locals who opposed fracking and gas infrastructure to insurgents in war zones. Pitzarella noted that his com- pany had hired army combat veterans skilled in psychological warfare to deal with ornery landowners and recommended other companies do the same.[17]

At the same event, Michael Kehs, a vice president from Chesapeake Energy, used similar language: he described local citizens speaking out against the shale gas industry as a "strong activist insurgency."[18] While Range and Chesapeake were competitors, these men were fellow members of a larger public relations fraternity. Pitzarella was subchairman of America's Natural Gas Alliance, an industry-funded group that sought to boost public support for fracking.[19] The alliance had, in 2009, hired Hill and Knowlton, a public relations firm where Kehs used to work. Hill and Knowlton was notorious for its past work helping the tobacco industry sow doubt about the health risks of smoking. Less well known: the same firm advised the gas industry on how to contest the science showing that gas stoves emitted substantial amounts of nitrogen dioxide, a respiratory irritant known to exacerbate asthma. In a 1972 presentation to an AGA conference at Disney World in Florida, the Hill and Knowlton executive who led the firm's tobacco work gave gas executives tips on crafting the "massive, consistent, long-range public relations programs necessary" to dispel consumers' fears about the safety of their gas appliances.[20] (Hill and Knowlton would also go on to run campaigns for oil and gas majors like Shell, ExxonMobil, and Saudi Aramco and face heavy criticism for peddling climate misinformation.[21])

Sitting next to Kehs was an executive at Anadarko, another big fracking outfit, who took the belligerent rhetoric a step further.

"Download the U.S. Army-slash-Marine Corps Counterinsurgency Manual, because we are dealing with an insurgency," he said, as some in the audience gasped. "There are a lot of good lessons in there."[22]

He also recommended that audience members take an online course for public affairs professionals offered by Harvard and MIT called "Dealing with an Angry Public." It's not clear if he had read the book on which the course was based, the first paragraph of which reads:

There are many reasons for the public to be angry. Business and governmental leaders have consistently covered up mistakes, concealed evidence of potential risks, made misleading statements, and often lied. . . . But beneath these wrong-headed actions is bad advice. Whether by public relations experts or attorneys, decision-makers are often told to commit to nothing and admit nothing, to obscure and conceal rather than to clarify and reveal. The public is treated like an angry mob. Their concerns are brushed aside in order to maintain a good organizational image, regardless of the substance beneath the veneer.[23]

Marcellus vs. Maples

On the morning of March 1, 2016, Megan Holleran and her family watched quietly as a group of US marshals, clad in tactical vests and clutching semiautomatic weapons, escorted a crew of chainsaw-toting contractors onto their property in New Milford, Pennsylvania.

Flanked by a couple dozen protestors who had come to offer support, the Hollerans stood at a remove from the men as they fired up their saws. A federal judge had ordered them to keep at least 150 feet away—at penalty of fines and criminal charges—from the swath of their own property that he had awarded to the Constitution Pipeline, a planned 124-mile-long project to transport gas to Albany.

The Hollerans were placed in this peculiar bind—effectively prohibited from trespassing on their own land—when the Federal Energy Regulatory Commission approved the project in December 2014.

Normally, in early March the Hollerans would begin tapping their trees and boiling sap into syrup sold by their family business, North Harford Maple. Instead, they watched the men in hard hats cut down 90 percent of those sugar maples. After four days of felling, more than five hundred mature trees—some more than two hundred years old—lay in a tangle on the ground.

At the time, it wasn't clear that the Constitution Pipeline would ever get built: New York state regulators had denied it a key water quality certificate. Without it, construction couldn't move forward. But the judge had decided that delaying tree-felling would unfairly harm the energy companies behind the project (which included Duke Energy).

Holleran wasn't staunchly opposed to fracking. "I'm familiar with that whole industry," she told me. As a trained archaeologist, she herself had worked for consulting firms that contracted with pipeline companies on excavations. Like most people in that part of northern Pennsylvania, she had friends and neighbors who made their living in the industry. But like most Americans, Megan Holleran had never heard of FERC. When she and her family learned that the route came through their sugarbush, they were comforted by their assumption, she said, that "they can't use [eminent domain] unless the pipeline is for the public interest."[24]

"I thought that if we followed the rules, we were right, so we would win," she said. "Then you find out that's not really how it works." She was stunned to learn how cursory FERC's process for determining need for pipelines was, and how hard it was for landowners to communicate with the commission. "In the case of gas and oil infrastructure, they don't really need to prove it's in the public interest."

She was even more shocked that Constitution could be allowed to start clearing its right-of-way without the necessary permits in hand. The cruel irony of the pipeline's name wasn't lost on anyone. "When the trees came down, that was the ultimate feeling of being powerless," Holleran told me.

A few weeks after the maples were cut, Megan Holleran decided to go knock on FERC's door. As the pipeline's proponents might have it, their family business had been the unfortunate eggs broken to make an "affordable" energy omelet—but Holleran had a different breakfast food in mind to share with the federal energy regulators. She explained her strategy with a chuckle: "Everybody loves syrup."

On March 24, 2016, she and fellow protestors set up a pancake-cooking station on the sidewalk in front of the commission's office on First Street in Washington. She served up the last of her family's maple syrup to passersby—a symbolic invitation to talk about pipelines' impact on landowners like her, and on the climate.

"We followed all the rules," she said. "This could happen to anyone. FERC, come on down and chat with me. FERC has a chance to be accountable now."[25]

No one came down to chat—or eat pancakes. So Holleran and her companions sat in front of the entrance and refused to leave until they were arrested by Homeland Security agents.

Six weeks later, the entire Constitution Pipeline project was put on hold when New York state regulators denied it a key water quality certificate.[26] This had been widely expected; the Hollerans had pleaded with Constitution to wait until that decision was made. But at that point, of course, they couldn't put their two-hundred-year-old maples back in the ground.

The Legacy of "Mr. Gas"

Just after nine o'clock on the morning of March 2, 2016, Aubrey McClendon's Chevy Tahoe veered across the median of a busy road in Oklahoma City and crashed into a concrete bridge abutment. The car exploded into a ball of flame. He died instantly. Police would later learn he had been driving more than 40 miles per hour above the speed limit.[27]

The day before, as the Hollerans' maples fell, McClendon had been indicted on federal charges of price-fixing and violating antitrust laws.

The two events took place one day and 1,500 miles apart. But to understand why the Hollerans lost their business, one has to travel back to 1989, when McClendon and a friend founded Chesapeake Energy in Oklahoma with a $50,000 investment. There would likely be no PennEast, no Constitution, no Mountain Valley, no Atlantic Coast Pipeline without Chesapeake. Without the wells fracked by Aubrey McClendon—and the competitors he inspired—there would be no need for any of those steel arteries to ferry Marcellus methane out of Appalachia.

Everyone agreed that McClendon was a gifted salesman. He had gotten his start as a land man—the guy sent out to fast-talk landowners into signing leases for drilling.[28]

Two decades later, he became the country's highest paid Fortune 500 CEO. After a career of relentless risk-taking and reinventions, his mysterious death only added to his legend.[29] And his legacy was visible everywhere: from the enormous gas liquefaction facilities sprouting across the Gulf Coast to the well pads that dotted Appalachia's hilltops.

By the time of his death, he was the controversial face of the fracking industry—and self-appointed spokesman for natural gas. "I am not ashamed whatsoever to be the No. 1 pitchman for my product," he said in 2008, the year that Chesapeake became the second-biggest gas producer in the US—the same year that *Fortune Magazine* dubbed him "Mr. Gas."[30] "I believe in it with my heart and soul."

But over time, McClendon would become a victim of his own prowess. Investors flooded the shale patches with cash, leading to a profusion of drillers. As they produced more gas, prices dropped—and stayed there. Companies responded by borrowing more money and drilling for even more gas. The ensuing glut dropped prices even lower, crushing the balance sheets of many producers. Before long, Chesapeake was making more money from flipping leases—selling them to smaller operators at a profit—than from producing gas.[31]

The debt-fueled business model of Chesapeake and its ilk had been likened by some analysts to a Ponzi scheme.[32] Others called it "lighting money on fire." All the same, in the physical world, it pulled enormous quantities of methane out of the ground to be lit on fire.

But never quite enough for Aubrey McClendon. Throughout it all, he played the role of the high-living Pied Piper of American gas.[33] To keep the party going (Sotheby's auctioned off $55 million worth of bottles from his wine cellar[34]) McClendon needed gas demand to keep growing. But consumption in homes and businesses hadn't increased much since the 1990s. The only real growth was in the power sector—but utilities hadn't started their "dash for gas" in earnest yet.

So, in 2008, at the height of his power, McClendon worked every angle to promote the fuel. He launched his own pro-gas TV channel called Clean Skies TV. He lobbied relentlessly for policies to turn gas into a widely used transportation fuel and for cities to buy fleets that ran on compressed natural gas. Those efforts didn't pan out. So, while he preferred that his methane was burned closer to home, he tried another tack.

"If for some reason this country refuses to use this wonderful fuel . . . I have to put my gas up for sale to somebody," he said in 2009.[35]

That year, McClendon called Charif Souki, a former restaurateur turned energy entrepreneur. His company, Cheniere Energy, was on the verge of bankruptcy. Souki's very expensive bet on building a facility in

Louisiana to import gas from abroad had been ruined by the domestic glut produced by Chesapeake and its peers. McClendon invited Souki to a meeting at his lavish headquarters in Oklahoma City, where he offered a solution: "Why don't you build me an export terminal?"[36]

He suggested that Souki retool his facility to send gas in the *other* direction. By building liquefaction "trains" to supercool natural gas to negative 260 degrees Fahrenheit, Cheniere could then load Chesapeake's gas onto tanker ships that would carry it to Japan or India or wherever foreign industries might be hungry for American methane.

Souki went home, thought it over for a while, ran the numbers, and eventually rounded up investors. In April 2012, FERC approved Cheniere's application to build an export terminal on the Louisiana coast—the first to be constructed in the US in over fifty years. Souki's gamble paid off. Cheniere became both the dominant gas exporter and the single biggest buyer—the Walmart, if you will—of domestic gas.

It may have been a mere plan B for McClendon, but it birthed a new era for the industry—and upended global energy markets. By July 2014, over forty new proposals had been submitted by companies to the Department of Energy to export liquefied natural gas—including one from Dominion.

The second LNG export facility to be built in the US would be Cove Point in Maryland, another big gas bet placed by Tom Farrell.

The Greatest Trick

But Aubrey McClendon's most enduring legacy might be the widespread misconception that natural gas is an environmentally benign fuel. And his greatest coup—even bigger than his funding, via his American Clean Skies Foundation, of Ernest Moniz's influential *Future of Natural Gas* report—was his co-opting of key actors in the environmental movement.

By 2009, the big three green groups—the Sierra Club, the Natural Resources Defense Council, and the Environmental Defense Fund—had all come out in support of boosting gas use to wean America's power plants off coal.

In a 2008 interview, Carl Pope, head of the Sierra Club, laid out their thinking for the industry publication *Oil and Gas Investor*. "Use renewables as much as we can," he said. "Natural gas is the next-cleanest fuel, then we have oil and then we have coal . . . among the fossil fuels, natural gas is at the top."

McClendon not only welcomed this green embrace but helped engineer it. In 2012, *Time Magazine* revealed that the Sierra Club secretly took $26 million from Chesapeake Energy between 2007 and 2010.[37] For the fracking firm, this was peanuts. It scored a huge reputational return on a very small investment.

When the Sierra Club's national leadership celebrated fossil gas as a "bridge fuel" in 2009, some of its local volunteers in Appalachia were incensed. They lived near the frontlines of the gas boom, raising the alarm about contaminated water and polluted air and being able to light what came out of their faucets on fire.[38] The club's stance now made it easier for industry to marginalize their concerns. "It makes us look like the extremists that the industry wants to call us anyway," said a board member of the club's West Virginia chapter.[39]

When a new Sierra Club executive director took over in 2010, he turned down Chesapeake's offer of another $30 million. By 2012, with the story about to break, he apologized to the club's membership and pledged to never take gas industry money again.

But the damage had been done. The "clean" label that had been affixed to natural gas would prove difficult to unglue in many Americans' minds. Academics used it. Politicians waved it around every chance they got. Utilities printed it on their glossy annual reports. To anyone criticizing the "dash for gas" on climate grounds, companies like Dominion could simply point to endorsements from the Sierra Club and its ilk: *Look, even the environmentalists approve.*

As an analyst at Energy Innovation, a policy think tank that tracks the utility sector closely, told me: "The greatest trick the natural gas industry ever pulled was convincing everyone that it's 'clean.'"

Gastroturfing

The loss of public support from big green groups during Barack Obama's second term wasn't a fatal blow. The gas industry could always, as Richard Berman had advised, pivot to calling them "Big Green Radicals." Besides, it had plenty of other ways to get its message out.

In 2017, the American Gas Association launched a new media campaign called "Your Energy America." One of Your Energy America's priority projects was promoting the Atlantic Coast Pipeline, whose backers had close ties to the American Gas Association; Diane Leopold of Dominion sat on AGA's board, as did her counterparts at Duke and Southern.[40] Guided by a DC-based public relations firm, the new initiative ran digital advertisements and uploaded videos to YouTube, including one called "Meet Natural Gas" that described the fuel as "the friend that's always been there."[41]

Like other utility companies, Dominion had dipped its toes in these waters before. In 2015, it hired the Consumer Energy Alliance—another front group run by a public relations firm in Houston—to conduct pro-ACP polling that would suggest there was deep public support for the project.[42]

There was a certain pathos to these branding efforts. The taglines and names themselves—Consumer Energy *Alliance*, *Your* Energy America—struck a plaintive note. They sought to conjure up an invisible army of ordinary Americans—teachers, firefighters, nurses, innkeepers—who were simply *passionate* about methane, sitting at the kitchen table after the kids were in bed pondering ways to help the Chesapeakes and Dominions pump and burn more gas to improve everyone's lives. Imaginary counterparts to actual human beings like Joyce Burton, who had left her job to shepherd landowners through the regulatory and eminent domain wilderness, or Rick Webb, who was spending his retirement years designing citizen-led pipeline monitoring programs, or Will and Lilia Fenton, who were spending large sums and sleepless nights to protect their business. If the industry couldn't inspire their own grassroots movement, they could at least create the impression there might be one out there, somewhere.[43] These front groups were examples of "astroturfing"—campaigns concocted by consultants to create the appearance of citizens acting on their own initiative. The other evergreen strategy—honed during Big Tobacco's wars on the rock-solid science showing that smoking causes cancer—was to attack the credibility of their opponents.

Bruce McKay's "campaign to elect a pipeline" was aptly named: it had elements of a military campaign, influence campaign, and advertising campaign all rolled together. After word of his conference presentation in Arizona leaked, McKay was unapologetic when quizzed by a reporter about Dominion's efforts to engineer public perceptions of the Atlantic Coast Pipeline.

"We cannot just sit back and hope for the best and hope that the merit of our project will sell itself," McKay said. "Nowadays [regulators] are being bombarded by general citizenry, by elected officials who have asked to insert themselves into the process, and this debate swirls around."[44]

Tom Hadwin's Counter-Campaign

In 2015, a few of Tom Hadwin's neighbors called him up and asked if he would check out this whole pipeline deal. Did it make any sense to him? Did it all add up?

He told them he'd look into it and get back to them. By that point, Hadwin was a fellow member of the "general citizenry," enjoying semi-retirement and running a small consulting business, albeit an unusually well-informed one: he was a former energy utility executive.

Hadwin had worked for large utilities in Michigan and New York, leading teams permitting large-scale, billion-dollar energy projects. And when he studied the economic case for the Atlantic Coast Pipeline, it seemed like a project in search of a rationale. He just couldn't see any need for it.

"I think this is a really bad idea, for the customers and ultimately for the energy company itself," he reported back to his neighbors.[45]

Hadwin wrote a few op-eds and letters to the editor in which he said as much. "I thought I would work on this for a couple of months, write a few things and be on to something else," he recalled with a rueful smile. He could go back to focusing on his volunteer work mentoring local high school students and to thinking about the energy startup company he wanted to launch.

But he couldn't let go of it. The more he learned about the Atlantic Coast Pipeline—slated to come a few miles from his home in Augusta County—and about the way Dominion held sway in the Old

Dominion, the more incredulous he became. Dominion's pipeline, he thought, was so flagrantly unnecessary and profiteering that he couldn't rest until more people could see what he saw.

While other pipeline fighters would focus on environmental, health, and property risks, he would focus on the money. "When I was permitting these multibillion-dollar projects on the utility side, I saw time and attention given to the environmental impacts, but they didn't bear on the final decision made by the regulators," he told me. "It came down to need and economics. That influenced my approach from the beginning."[46]

The key decisions to greenlight, finance, and build the pipeline would be made by regulators, shareholders, and Wall Street investors. So those were the people he focused on reaching.

Hadwin knew quite well that FERC's commissioners nearly always sided with the energy industry because they interpreted their mandate as overseeing the orderly development of gas infrastructure. He also knew that all they required as proof of market demand for ACP's gas were "precedent agreements"—contracts with firms that committed to pay for a certain amount of the pipeline's capacity.

Hadwin traveled around the state, telling everyone he could that there was no demonstrated need for the Atlantic Coast Pipeline— and that customers would be paying for it for decades. The "energy superhighway," he contended, was a mere shell game. Lost in much of the media coverage about the project was a rather striking fact: almost 80 percent of that gas would go to power plants that were owned by Dominion's and Duke's own subsidiaries. It was a case, Hadwin thought, of naked self-dealing. And the risks of that investment would be borne almost entirely by Dominion's captive ratepayers.

Suddenly, as a volunteer, he found himself working six- or seven-day weeks. Hadwin submitted reams of detailed comments to Virginia's State Corporation Commission and heavily footnoted comments to FERC. He prepared dense analyses to share with financial analysts, whose calls he was always quick to return. He spoke at local chamber of commerce meetings and economic development conferences from Roanoke to Lynchburg to Hampton Roads. He lectured to local groups like Friends of Nelson. He went on radio shows. He wrote blog posts and letters to the editor.[47] He joined Greg Buppert and Nancy Sorrells on the steering committee of the Allegheny–Blue Ridge Alliance. The mileage on his hybrid Honda Accord began to rival the miles that Buppert was racking up on *his* Accord as he crisscrossed Virginia.

Why go to such lengths?

"I'm a utility guy," he'd tell his audiences. And he thought the ACP reflected poorly on the entire sector: "I'm embarrassed for the energy industry, the way it's been handled." Hadwin would insist that he had the best long-term interests of Dominion and Duke at heart too. "I want to look out for utilities. We need them to succeed."[48]

Tall and broad-shouldered with a crown of white hair and a courtly manner, Hadwin certainly looked the part of the retired utility executive. He was easy to spot among T-shirt-clad activists in his blue oxford shirt and loafers. He spoke with precision as he broke down the arcana of utility financial engineering for his lay audiences, holding up a rhetorical X-ray of the hidden incentive structures that had brought the pipeline into their lives.

"The Atlantic Coast Pipeline is just an ATM for Dominion," he would tell them. With energy sales flat over the previous decade, Dominion was looking to boost its profits, he explained. The pipeline would be a lucrative asset: FERC guaranteed its builders a 15 percent rate of return on their investment.

"That's what's driving this," he said. "Until we give our energy companies another way to make money besides just building, building, building things that we really don't need, they will continue to do so. Because the executives get paid by the shareholders. And the more they return to the shareholders the more they get paid."[49]

For each audience, Hadwin would hammer a few key points. One, demand for gas wasn't increasing, and existing demand could be met with existing infrastructure via existing rights-of way, such as the Columbia Gas line coming from West Virginia. The Transco pipeline, built decades earlier to bring gas from the Gulf Coast, ran right through the middle of Virginia and had excess available capacity. These projects were already built and paid for, so the gas they delivered would be much cheaper than gas from a new pipeline.

Two, Dominion's pledge that the ACP would provide cheaper gas could not be trusted because the company's estimates didn't include the cost of building the pipeline. In February 2015, Dominion had put out a study claiming the ACP would save the region's consumers $377 million per year, mostly from lower fuel costs for generating electricity. The only problem was this study did not incorporate the actual cost of transporting gas on the pipeline. (At one point, Hadwin said, he pointed this out during a conversation with Aaron Ruby, Dominion's public relations lead for the ACP. "His eyes got wide," Hadwin recalled, "and he said, 'What?' I said, 'Yeah, go back and look at it.' There were moments where a little doubt crept in.")

And three, even if the pipeline were *never actually used to deliver gas*, Dominion would get to charge its customers for the expense of building it anyway.

All of which helped explain why investors were so bullish: there was very little risk borne by Dominion Energy itself. "If Wall Street didn't support this project, Dominion wasn't going to build it," Hadwin said. "But they were wholehearted supporters because the revenue stream was so attractive. What this pipeline did for Dominion's ability to throw off dividends was dramatic. That's why they were doing it. They didn't need it. It was just a money machine for them."

Tom Farrell's Arithmetic

At Dominion's annual shareholders meeting in May 2016, a shareholder asked CEO Tom Farrell for his views on climate change—what with all the recent record-breaking heat and flooding—and on the newly inked Paris climate agreement. Just weeks earlier, 170 nations had signed the compact, agreeing to keep warming "well below" 2 degrees Celsius and "pursu[e] efforts to limit the temperature increase to 1.5° C above preindustrial levels." After years of fruitless negotiations, the nonbinding deal was hailed as a historic breakthrough. Now came the heavy lifting: governments and businesses needed to figure out how to deliver on the pledges. None had more work cut out for it than the energy sector, as the biggest source of climate-warming pollution.

But Farrell waved off the question. "I'll leave that to President Obama and Secretary Kerry," he said. "That's above my pay grade."[50]

Over the previous decade, Farrell had been paid at least $133 million.

According to SEC filings, his compensation was a combined $43,559,228 from 2014 to 2016 alone—making him one of the highest-paid CEOs in the world.[51] He also owned a million shares of Dominion stock.

During his presentation to fellow shareholders, Farrell hadn't said a word about emissions reductions targets. He did enthuse at length, however, about the Marcellus shale, which, he noted, "will provide gas for the balance of this century at least." (He briefly touted Dominion's environmental record, in the form of a complaint: "We're a leader, but people don't recognize it.")

In 2015, Dominion ranked dead last among US investor-owned utilities for renewable energy sales and energy efficiency savings.[52] In 2016, Dominion and Duke both generated less than 3 percent of their electricity from renewables, which put them near the very bottom of all regulated utilities. In 2017, Dominion ranked fiftieth out of the nation's largest fifty-one utilities in energy efficiency in an authoritative report by the American Council for an Energy-Efficient Economy.[53]

What was well within Farrell's pay grade was generating handsome returns for shareholders. And in those terms, Dominion *was* a leader, consistently scoring near the top of its class: in 2017, Dominion posted $9.6 billion in gross profits and nearly $3 billion in net profits.[54] Farrell's gas-focused strategy had so far paid off nicely. The company had recently placed another big bet, purchasing a gas distribution utility in Utah for $4.4 billion.

Whenever Farrell spoke about all the money his firm had sunk into fossil gas, he made it sound as logical as 2 + 2 = 4. A no-brainer. "It's just arithmetic," Farrell said in a July 2017 interview. "Gas is cheaper, it's more reliable, it's easier to move, and it's more environmentally friendly. Why wouldn't you do that?"[55]

As for wind, solar, and batteries—these technologies just weren't ready for prime time, in Farrell's view. He would return to this theme time and again: renewables had important roles as bit players in utilities' dance of keeping the lights on, but natural gas would be the star for a long time to come.

It was a tune that he had been singing ever since he first took the top job at Dominion. The pattern was set in 2008, when he told a meeting of the Republican Governors Association: "Wind and other alternative energy sources . . . are not ready to replace coal, natural gas and nuclear power as the work horses of our power fleet. As promising as renewable sources may be, they are not a panacea."[56]

As the years went by, renewables kept getting better, cheaper, more widely deployed. The cost of utility-scale wind power dipped below that of gas-fired power in much of the country back in 2011; large-scale solar became cheaper than gas in most areas in 2015. Energy experts expected these trends to continue.[57] Utilities in other parts of the country had already integrated much higher shares of renewable energy into their portfolios than Dominion. But you would not know that these changes were taking place if you listened to Tom Farrell.

In 2013: "America's newly abundant natural gas supplies offer the opportunity to address two goals at once—increasing the amount of affordable, reliable energy powering the world economy, and making progress on reducing greenhouse gas emissions."[58]

In 2015: "We've come a long way in a relatively short time with renewable energy, but we're still in the age of fossil fuels, whether we like it or not. . . . Seventy-five to eighty percent of it is going to come from fossil fuels, as I said, for many decades to come."[59]

In 2017: "Until somebody licks [electricity] storage on a very large scale, despite what a segment of our population wants to hear, you're going to have natural gas–fired power plants in play for decades to come."[60]

Tom Farrell was not blind to his customers' preferences. "All customers want us to go all in on renewable. Any poll data that we have, that comes up for top of the heap by far," he said in that 2017 interview—before predicting it would take yet *another* decade before large-scale solar power could be integrated in a way that ensured "reliability."[61]

Such statements called to mind the old joke about Brazil: it's the country of the future, and always will be. The renewably powered future was, to hear Dominion's leaders tell it, an ever-receding horizon.

Denial, Delay, Dominance

On June 1, 2017, President Donald Trump had announced that the US would become the only nation in the world to withdraw from the Paris agreement.[62] "We are a top producer of petroleum and the number-one producer of natural gas," he crowed later that month at an event. "With these incredible resources, my administration will seek not only American energy independence that we've been looking for so long, but American energy dominance."[63]

A month later, in an appearance at the US Chamber of Commerce's Global Energy Institute, Tom Farrell proclaimed: "We need to acknowledge we are an energy superpower and start acting like it, instead of trying to keep it all in the ground."[64]

In this more muscular rhetoric, it was hard not to hear an executive adapting to the changing songbook in DC. Energy independence was now "energy dominance." Climate was no longer a priority, not even a thing to be mentioned aloud.

And if it was, well, it was merely to point out that energy companies were not to blame. In March 2017, Tom Fanning—the CEO and chairman of utility giant Southern Company, the third corporate partner in the ACP venture—gave a televised interview in which he asserted that carbon dioxide was not the primary driver of climate change. "Is climate change happening? Certainly, it's been happening for millennia, that's not the issue, okay."[65]

Fanning's climate obfuscation was, in a sense, a company tradition.[66] In 1989, Southern became a founding member and leader of the Global Climate Coalition—an initiative created and funded by oil and gas, electric, automotive, chemical, and manufacturing companies with the goal of preventing legislative action to reduce greenhouse gases. The GCC—which also counted Dominion and Duke as members—quickly became a leading disseminator of climate disinformation.[67]

But nearly three decades later, Fanning's outspoken climate denial was out of step with the times; rejecting the science outright had become an outlier position. With total damages of well over $300 billion, 2017 would prove to be the costliest year of natural disasters in US history. For the first time, three Category 4 or higher hurricanes struck the US in one season, as Hurricanes Harvey, Irma, and Maria pounded Americans with rain and floods from Houston to South Carolina to Puerto Rico. Scientists pointed to the year's destruction as evidence of climate impacts arriving sooner, and with more force, than anticipated.[68]

It was getting harder and harder to wave away the evidence in front of everyone's eyes. Instead of insisting that climate change was nothing to be worried about, most utility leaders had accordingly adjusted their rhetoric. They advocated a cautious, plodding approach to the clean energy transition, rather than the all-out sprint scientists and experts were urging. Denial had largely given way to delay.

"Utilities Are Different"

"My philosophy is to make money. If I can drill and make money, then that's what I want to do."

To their detractors, Dominion and Duke and Southern were perhaps no different from any other corporation traded on Wall Street, with a core philosophy basically the same as the one articulated above by former ExxonMobil CEO and Trump cabinet member Rex Tillerson.[69] But as Tom Hadwin saw it, utilities were a distinct species from other such large corporations—or at least they *should* be.

"Utilities are different," he said. "They are given a monopoly to do something in the public interest."[70]

Monopoly utilities are indeed special creatures in the taxonomy of American capitalism. Where they operate, state laws grant them exclusive control over the provision of water or electricity or phone lines, recognizing the steep upfront cost of building all those pipes or wires, and the inefficiencies that would result if multiple firms jostled to provide those services.

The customers in their service areas, meanwhile, are "captive" ratepayers. Two-thirds of Virginia residents have no alternative: if they want to turn on their lights, they *have* to buy electricity from Dominion.

Energy utilities are guaranteed returns of 10 percent or more by state regulators on their capital investments. The more expensive the assets that they build and own, the more money they make. (Pro tip: a gas power plant costs much more than a solar array.) Being a regulated utility is, in other words, a sweet deal, with rates of return that are hard to find on Wall Street. But it is a *deal*: to earn those high returns, the utility is expected to provide an essential public service. Accordingly, in advertisements and speeches, utility leaders frequently invoke their sacred trust to supply customers with "reliable, affordable energy." Dominion Energy, Duke Energy, and Southern Company make most of their revenue from their regulated subsidiaries—monopoly power and gas providers—but, as holding companies, are themselves unregulated. Because they are shielded from competition, Tom Hadwin thought their leaders shouldn't pursue the same maximize-profit-at-all-costs approach that steers most of the publicly traded firms of the Fortune 500.

But that is the logic he had seen prevail in his industry ever since the 1980s, when the era of utility holding companies began. They behave, Hadwin said, as though they are answerable only to their shareholders, not their captive customers. He saw a flawed system, set up to reward Dominion's leaders for building more gas power plants and more pipelines to serve them, regardless of the need.

"Those executives are in the business to make the most" of those profit opportunities, Hadwin said. "I can't fault them for that. That's why we need to change the rules. I *can* fault them for telling us all sorts of stories that aren't true. But for them to try and pursue an economic avenue for their shareholders—that's what companies do."[71]

"What's happened here is the people that are supposed to make them do that responsibly—the regulators—have been asleep at the switch," he said.

One fall day in 2016, Hadwin drove to Richmond to try to jolt them awake. He sat in front of the three members of the State Corporation Commission—which must approve Dominion's requests for rate hikes and plans for new projects—and testified that the cost of building the Atlantic Coast Pipeline would ultimately be borne by Dominion's customers.

"It will be automatically passed through in utility bills," Hadwin said. Those customers would be on the hook to the tune of $2 billion or more while getting little to no benefit in return. Once FERC approved the company's pipeline, he said, the SCC would be the last line of defense to protect Virginia's captive citizen-ratepayers.[72]

He then got into an extended exchange with one commissioner, which concluded with him basically telling the regulators to do their job: "No one is speaking on behalf of the Virginia ratepayers and that, as I understand it, is the role of the State Corporation Commission."[73] (After this mic drop, attorneys who frequented these hearings told him it was the first time they had ever heard a commissioner question a public witness.)

As he drove over the Blue Ridge on his way back home, Hadwin passed near the entrance of an old railroad tunnel, designed nearly two centuries earlier by a French engineer named Claudius Crozet. Beginning in the early 1830s, Crozet advised his employers at Virginia's Board of Public Works to stop investing precious capital in canals and build railroads instead, as they would soon be a much cheaper way to move goods.[74] Virginia's elites ignored him; soon he was fired. But Crozet proved prophetic: investing in canals when the age of railroads had already arrived wrecked Virginia's finances and haunted its politics well into the twentieth century.[75]

Nearly two centuries later, Tom Hadwin was trying to warn Virginia's elites that they were making the same mistake, pouring finite resources into infrastructure that would soon be rendered obsolete by technological change—the rise of cheap renewables and storage—and by the inescapable policy imperative to cut emissions of climate-warming pollution. And he worried the public would wind up paying the price.

"The Project's Entire Purpose"

In February 2017, researchers at Oil Change International had estimated that the ACP would emit 67.5 million metric tons of greenhouse gases each year—equivalent to twenty coal power plants or 14 million passenger vehicles.

"Our analysis shows that both the Atlantic Coast Pipeline and the Mountain Valley Pipeline are climate disasters," said the lead author, Lorne Stockman, who also happened to live in Augusta County, Virginia. "They threaten communities along the route and they would cause massive increases in climate pollution."[76]

But when it looked at these projects, the federal government's regulators saw no climate risks at all. When the Federal Energy Regulatory

Commission released its final environmental impact statement for ACP during the summer of 2017, the agency claimed that the pipeline "will not contribute to [greenhouse gas] cumulative impacts or to climate change."

The commission denied that the pipeline would lead to more production of gas "upstream" by drillers like Chesapeake, and more consumption of it "downstream" by customers like Dominion Power—and therefore more carbon emissions compared to a universe in which there was no ACP. "If the proposed projects were not constructed, it is reasonable to assume that any new production spurred by such factors would reach intended markets through alternate pipelines or other modes of transportation."[77]

In other words, the pipeline couldn't exacerbate climate change because the methane that would leak out or get burned upon delivery was going to leak or get burned anyway. This reasoning led into a logical quagmire: if that gas was going to find a way to market anyway, then what was the need for the ACP?

FERC was essentially saying two contradictory things: that the Atlantic Coast Pipeline was needed to meet demand for gas (implying that if it weren't built, that demand couldn't be efficiently met) and that it would have no measurable effect on emissions. But even weirder was FERC's contention that it didn't know *how* to calculate the climate-warming pollution caused by the pipeline and therefore couldn't include emissions in its cost-benefit analysis—even though other federal agencies routinely used "social cost of carbon" calculations to do precisely that.[78]

The federal government was saying that the idea that Dominion's pipeline would add more greenhouse gases to the atmosphere was mere speculation—something as fundamentally unknowable as whether free will can exist in a world governed by cause and effect.

The very next month, a panel of federal judges swatted away this Alice-in-Wonderland reasoning. In a surprising decision related to a gas pipeline in Florida called Sabal Trail (co-owned by Duke Energy), the DC Circuit Court ruled that FERC must, under existing law, consider downstream greenhouse gas emissions as indirect impacts of the projects it reviewed.

The ruling read like a professor's unsparing comments on an essay by an undergraduate who hadn't done the assigned reading:

> What are the "reasonably foreseeable" effects of authorizing a pipeline that will transport natural gas to Florida power plants? First, that gas will be burned in those power plants. This is not just "reasonably foreseeable," it is the project's entire purpose, as the pipeline developers themselves explain. . . . It is just as foreseeable, and FERC does not dispute, that burning natural gas will release into the atmosphere the sorts of carbon compounds that contribute to climate change.[79]

Greg Buppert saw the ruling as a promising development for future pipeline reviews—and as a cautionary tale. Sabal Trail was already mostly in the ground, with methane already flowing through it. This was the outcome Buppert was keen to avoid: a favorable court decision after the fait accompli, a Pyrrhic victory with the pipe in Virginia's soil.

Just weeks earlier, Buppert and his colleagues had made their first formal move in the legal chess game they had been preparing for three years. They filed a motion with FERC, requesting a hearing on the entire premise underpinning the ACP, arguing that there was no new demand for gas to justify the project. And they had some new ammunition. In another State Corporation Commission hearing that summer, Buppert had gotten an expert witness for Dominion to effectively concede some of Tom Hadwin's most devastating points. The company's own director of strategic planning acknowledged that Dominion would pass pipeline costs through to its ratepayers—in the form of the "fuel cost adjustment" on their monthly electricity bills—regardless of whether the ACP's gas would ever be used to generate power.[80]

Dominion's own planning documents estimated the Atlantic Coast Pipeline would cost its customers $1.6 to 2.3 billion. Dominion also admitted that two new gas plants it was building in southern Virginia could be served by existing pipelines. And yet another bombshell dropped when Dominion revealed to the SCC that it had never actually studied whether it needed the pipeline at all to operate any of its gas power plants.[81]

Chet Wade had told Virginians from Highland County to Norfolk that better access to low-cost gas from the "Saudi America" of the Marcellus Shale would save its customers money. But by the time all costs were factored in, the price of that gas would likely be exorbitant. "One thing was apparent from the beginning: the ACP is the most expensive way to move gas somewhere," Buppert said.

Dominion, meanwhile, seemed to have plans to pump that methane even farther downstream than people realized. While speaking at a conference in South Carolina in September 2017, Dan Weekley, vice president of Dominion's southern pipeline operations, said that the Atlantic Coast Pipeline was not going to stop in North Carolina.

"Even though it dead-ends at Lumberton (North Carolina)—of course, 12 miles to the border—everybody knows it's not going to end in Lumberton," he said. It could head toward South Carolina's coast or farther inland, he said, depending on electricity generators' interest. "We could bring in almost a billion cubic feet a day into South Carolina. You tell me, we'll turn one way or the other."[82]

It was a moment of candor his bosses might have regretted. From the very beginning, Dominion and Duke had told FERC that most of the ACP's gas would fuel their own power plants in Virginia and North Carolina. But in filings submitted to their own state regulators, they had revised downward their own projections for new gas-fired power plants by about 400 million cubic feet per day—nearly a third of the total capacity of the ACP. Who would step in to make up the difference?

After Weekley's admission, Buppert wondered aloud to reporters, "Is the real intent to move most of the gas into South Carolina?"

Since 2014, residents along the route had voiced their suspicions that Dominion's long-term aim was perhaps to ultimately extend the pipeline to Georgia, where gas could be exported from an LNG facility on the coast. These concerns were always met with categorical denials from Dominion.

Its media relations team hurried to deny that the company was planning a southward expansion. Weekley, they said, wasn't available for interviews.

"Something Is Unraveling Here"

On October 13, FERC granted the Atlantic Coast Pipeline a certificate of public convenience and necessity. The approval surprised just about no one, and no one less than Greg Buppert.

What *was* surprising to Buppert and many other observers was the 2–1 vote. In the same ruling, FERC had approved the ACP's equally controversial Marcellus-birthed twin, the 300-mile-long Mountain Valley Pipeline. In a rare and stinging dissent, commissioner Cheryl LaFleur had voted against approving the two pipelines.

For one, she argued, they were redundant: both pipelines were meant to transport gas from the same region to "common destination markets." LaFleur criticized FERC's failure to consider the region as a whole and its overly narrow focus on "each project's specific stated goals." She worried that this approach increased the risk of overbuilding—of greenlighting projects that didn't really serve the public interest.[83]

"I believed FERC should take a fresh look at how it assessed need for pipelines," LaFleur told me. She thought the agency should zoom out to assess demand at the regional scale.

Her reasoning echoed arguments that Buppert himself had made in testimony he gave to Congress two years earlier, when he called for a region-wide analysis to determine whether these large gas pipelines were needed at all. "With FERC in particular, you can have the sense you're throwing paper into the wind," he told me. "When we saw the dissent, we said, 'We had an impact. The message is getting through.'"[84]

The other reason for her dissent, LaFleur said, was "the environmental impact, including the downstream climate impacts."

In late 2014, when activists pressed LaFleur and her fellow commissioners to weigh pipelines' total contributions to climate change, she had rejected their charge. It wasn't FERC's responsibility to tally up the emissions from burning or venting the methane that pipelines delivered, she said at the time.[85]

Like Tom Farrell, LaFleur was an attorney who had become CEO of a large gas and electric utility. And like him, she had once been a vocal proponent of the need for more gas. But by October 2017, her thinking had "evolved." She had begun to question her agency's failure to scrutinize pipelines' climate-warming emissions. FERC was comfortable speculating in fine-grained detail about how gas would be used downstream, as a demonstration of economic need, so why couldn't it tally up the climate-warming emissions from the *burning* of that gas downstream? (Let alone the methane that would likely leak from the pipe.)

"I thought: 'Something is unraveling here,'" she told me.

Since 2010, LaFleur had enjoyed a front-row view of America's gas building spree. The "situation" she had warned about nearly three years earlier at the Press Club had opened her eyes. When she took a close look at the Atlantic Coast Pipeline and the Mountain Valley Pipeline, she did not see projects in the "public necessity."

"She's not out there with an ideological agenda," said Gillian Giannetti, an attorney with the Natural Resources Defense Council who specializes in energy regulatory issues, referring to LaFleur's decision. "She could see the data simply didn't support that the project was needed.[86]

"There were tremendous environmental consequences, in terms of the sensitive terrain they were going through," LaFleur explained to me. "I couldn't go on record as supporting those pipelines. I said, 'Okay I'm going to take a stand, and start pushing back by saying no.'"[87]

A Winning Campaign

At the beginning of that week in October, Dominion lobbyist Bruce McKay had delivered his warning to gas industry colleagues in Arizona about the grassroots army they faced. By its end, his company had secured clearance from the federal government to build its long-planned pipeline, over the loud objections of the "general citizenry."

That same month ACP LLC secured $3.25 billion—roughly half the total cost of the project—in financing set up by Bank of America, with seventeen other banks participating.[88]

When Tom Hadwin and other pipeline opponents had met with a team from Bank of America earlier that year to make their case against the ACP, the bankers had pointed, in its defense, to Dominion's environmental initiatives.

"Well, that's what they're telling you in their reports, but what they're actually doing is ripping up unique habitat, overcharging their customers, and using your money to do it," Hadwin replied. He then squeezed all his various arguments for why the Atlantic Coast Pipeline was a poor investment into a ten-minute overview.[89]

"You've given us an awful lot to think about," the lead banker replied.

But Hadwin never heard back from them. ACP's backers had won a kind of shadow election with the financial sector. The country's biggest banks would not have lent billions if they didn't think Dominion's pipeline was a smart investment (made in what they might call a "favorable regulatory environment").

Like its next-door neighbor Dominion, Duke Energy had also been on a gas spending spree. In a November 3 earnings call, two weeks after the FERC approval, Duke CEO Lynn Good gave an update on her company's not one but *three* big gas pipeline projects: Constitution, Sabal Trail, and ACP. She was sanguine about their prospects, forecasting that both Atlantic Coast and Constitution would be up and running in 2019. Good predicted that the August ruling against Sabal Trail would be the gentlest of speed bumps. (She would be proved right: Sabal Trail never ceased operating.) She was similarly upbeat about resolving the legal tangle around the Constitution Pipeline, which had mowed down the Hollerans' maples. (She'd be wrong: Constitution would never be built.)

"We look forward to investing in this business and expanding our natural gas infrastructure for years to come," Good said.

"I think at times you've kind of characterized the company as keen or more keen to look towards gas into the future than perhaps electric," observed a Bank of America analyst on the call. "How are you thinking about that today in terms of your future in gas?"

"With the position that Duke holds as a company, the second largest consumer of natural gas, we see that as a growing opportunity for us," Good replied.

In other words, Duke was more bullish than ever on pipes, more than wires. "We're also pleased with the progress on Atlantic Coast Pipeline. I mean, that's a $2 billion investment for us, and we're anxious to get construction under way later this year."[90]

The project was behind schedule, but all the lights were finally turning green. Dominion and Duke had their permit from FERC and plenty of cash to spend. The Forest Service signaled it would issue its permit soon. And there was more good news from Virginia's off-year elections, which were often treated as a bellwether for the nation.

Democrat Ralph Northam had defeated his primary opponent (a vocal critic of both ACP and MVP) in June. Despite intense pressure from citizens and environmental groups, Northam had pledged his support for both pipelines, if regulators found they met environmental and safety standards. A month after Northam was elected governor by a comfortable margin, Dominion donated $50,000 to Northam's inaugural committee.[91]

So far, the arithmetic kept penciling out for Dominion Energy. The campaign to elect the pipeline seemed on the cusp of winning the day.

Chapter Seven

Full Nelson

"We are making excellent progress, particularly in the mountain areas."

It was January 29, 2018, and Tom Farrell had an upbeat status report on the Atlantic Coast Pipeline for the financial analysts on Dominion's quarterly earnings call.

Farrell ran through the milestones. By the end of 2017, Dominion had most of the permits it needed. Tree felling was already underway in parts of West Virginia and Virginia. That same week, the project had received two key permits from state regulators in West Virginia and North Carolina. Farrell expected that they would soon have two other critical approvals: one from the Army Corps of Engineers, and an erosion and sedimentation permit from Virginia regulators. With those in hand, Dominion could ask FERC for clearance to start construction on the full length of the pipeline.[1]

The good news extended beyond the recent pipeline approvals. Dominion's new $1.3 billion gas power plant in Greensville, Virginia—which would be the largest of its kind in the US—would be running by the end of the year.[2] The Cove Point LNG facility was fully built and undergoing testing; it would be ready to start shipping gas overseas

by March. Earnings growth was looking strong well into the next decade. Cash flow was robust. The bottom line: Dominion was moving
from strength to strength, and its gas-focused strategy was key to that
success.

The CEO opened the call up to questions. The tone was chummy.
"Congratulations on a good year," said Greg the bank analyst. "Thank
you, Greg," said Farrell. He predicted that gas would be flowing through
his company's pipeline by the second half of 2019. The dominoes were
all lining up and beginning to fall.

Don't Tap Out

There were, however, a few recalcitrant landowners left in Virginia's
mountains holding things up. But Dominion was taking steps to deal
with those obstacles too.

Two days later, on January 31, ACP LLC sued Fenton Family
Holdings LLC.

In its first eminent domain suit in Nelson County, Dominion
sought to condemn the northeast corner of the Fentons' property that
lay within the ACP's permanent right-of-way. The pipe would run
under that sliver of land before emerging from the mountain on a
parcel next door, owned collectively by Wintergreen Resort's property
owners. Thirty-one other landowners in Nelson County would soon
be served with similar lawsuits.[3] But the Fentons were a priority.

Of all 600 miles of the Atlantic Coast Pipeline, this one under
Reeds Gap was the crux move—both technically and legally. Boring
through the billion-year-old rock would take a year or more, depending
on whatever geological curveballs the mountain threw at the drilling
crews. Dominion needed to get going. The company wanted immediate access so it could begin tree felling next door, where it would prepare a workspace for equipment, workers, trucks, and soil and debris
storage.

The couple had refused all of Dominion's offers, ever since the first
one of $1,200. They had already gone to court to keep surveyors off
their land.[4] But now they were up against the wall.

Will and Lilia had opened the Fenton Inn several months later than they had planned. Since July 2016, business had been good. People came to celebrate wedding anniversaries and birthdays, to hike the nearby Appalachian Trail, bike the parkway, or ski at nearby Wintergreen. They had already witnessed a few surprise proposals and engagements by couples on weekend getaways. It was all lining up with the vision they had when they broke ground in 2012.

For someone who described himself as "shy and reserved," innkeeping might seem like an odd choice of profession. But the steady stream of guests fed Will Fenton's bottomless curiosity. He loved hearing about their lives and enthusiasms and tales from their careers as cancer researchers or FBI agents or entrepreneurs. The guests, in turn, would wander around in amazement at the miniature Bavarian village that he had created atop the Blue Ridge, replete with a store, a clock tower, a drawbridge, a theater, a "town square," a main street through it all, with rooms cantilevered over the alleys. He had purposely set everything at angles to open sightlines and give it the feel of a real village—a trick he learned on movie sets he had worked on. Around every turn lay intricately carved door panels, depicting scenes like a woodcutter returning from the forest. Wooden owls peeked out from various crannies in an homage to the day, almost fifteen years earlier, that he came across a wounded owl while bicycling on the parkway and brought it to a rehab center—a detour that had led him right past the "For Sale" sign on the property they now owned.

The inn itself was testament to the power of happenstance. Long before the owl led him to his dream building site, Fenton was working in historic restoration in New York in the mid-1990s. A gig working on the house of movie producer Ismail Merchant, who was filming *Jefferson in Paris* at the time, led him to a job as a carpenter at Monticello. Before long he was helping restore Thomas Jefferson's retreat at Poplar Forest and studying Jefferson's letters to puzzle out how to rebuild the house's complex octagonal roof structure—which would inspire his design of the Fenton Inn's lobby.

Despite all the bookings and the compliments, the innkeepers were distracted. On top of the angst caused by Russia's 2014 invasion of Ukraine's Crimea—where Lilia grew up—they had lost hundreds of hours to the pipeline fight: learning about the pipeline's potential impact on their business, researching alternative routes, writing letters to federal agency administrators, going to local activists' meetings. Once the inn was up and running, they kept grasping at new ways to fend off Dominion.[5]

After their guests were checked in and settled into their rooms, Will and Lilia would sit down at their computers and write emails to fellow Nelsonians on strategy, or reply to queries from their lawyers, or draft one of their many letters to FERC, like the ten-pager that Will filed in March 2017: "This is just the beginning of our ACP struggles. . . . We have only the rights we are willing to fight for in this world and not one bit more. The last two years plus have merely prepared us for the long battles ahead. Dear Dominion expect to be sued, repeatedly, expect to be shut down, sound checked, filmed, studied, sampled and tested. In the meantime I will [be] putting up solar panels."[6]

One of his many interests, along with Jefferson's writings and wood-carving techniques, was mixed martial arts. As his confrontation with Dominion intensified, there was one infamous match that Fenton kept thinking about. In 2011, two top Ultimate Fighting Championship fighters, Antônio Rodrigo Nogueira and Frank Mir, were locked in a brutal match. Late in the match, Nogueira moved to force a submission on Mir, who turned the tables quickly and put Nogueira in an inescapable arm-lock hold known as the *kimura*, which allows the attacker to isolate and apply escalating pressure to the shoulder and elbow joints.

Mir kept him locked. Nogueira refused to tap out. Mir broke his arm and won the match.

When asked later why he didn't surrender, Nogueira said, "I felt like I would get out of the submission and I knew I would keep trying my best to get out of it."

He thought he was still going to win.[7]

That fight left a strong impression on Fenton. Nogueira had let his opponent break his arm but didn't tap out. His spirit didn't break. (Nogueira had surgery and fought again ten months later, winning his next match.) The couple were of the same mind on this question—though at times Lilia was the one reminding Will of the need to dig in. At one early meeting about the pipeline at Wintergreen, she spied a television reporter. Lilia prodded Will to go tell her about their predicament. It was the last thing he wanted to do at that particular moment. "I'm tired and I have a headache," he told her.

"She looked at me and said, 'Grow some balls,'" Fenton recalled. He went and talked to the reporter, who would later bring her crew to the inn to tape a segment for the local evening news. "Quitting was not something that we could have dealt with well," Fenton observed. "I was told these stresses can break a marriage, and I would guess it could—or you fight harder together."[8]

Reeds Gap or Bust

There's a move in wrestling known as the full nelson.

It's a hold in which you use both arms to grip the back of your opponent's neck and immobilize their arms. The move is typically used to control an opponent so they can be flipped over, pinned, and defeated. Because of the danger it poses to the neck and spine, it's now banned in amateur and college wrestling.

Some say the name originates with a now-forgotten wrestler named Bobby Nelson; others claim it's a reference to a deft maneuver by the British admiral Horatio Nelson, who won the Battle of Trafalgar in 1805 by dividing his fleet and surrounding the enemy navies of the Spanish and French. Whatever the origin, it's a hold that envelops— and leaves the opponent with very few options for escape.

With its lawsuit against the Fentons and Wintergreen, Dominion was nearly complete in its encirclement of Reeds Gap—the spot it had settled on years earlier as the optimal place to cross the Blue Ridge. In the summer of 2017, Dominion had prevailed in a lawsuit that the landowner on the *other* side of the mountain—a dauntless octogenarian widow named Hazel Palmer—had pursued all the way to the Virginia Supreme Court.[9] On Palmer's land, the company would set up the cranes and other heavy equipment needed to string together, lift, bend, and install huge sections of pipe into the tunnel drilled from the Fentons' side.[10]

Will Fenton would periodically wonder how much Dominion was spending in billable hours to white-shoe law firms to fight for his small slice of mountainside. Whatever that bill amounted to, he reckoned it could have paid for a solar farm somewhere or smart grid technology or whatever else utilities were supposed to be doing. For the pipeline's planners, though, there was a logic to their fixation on Reeds Gap. In January 2016, the Forest Service had insisted that the ACP avoid the endangered creatures of Shenandoah Mountain. Dominion had come back with a new route that, if you zoomed out, didn't make a whole lot of sense. It doglegged and wiggled in inefficient-looking ways. It was longer and brought more landowners into the corridor. Those contortions ensured that its detours always brought it back to Reeds Gap. A shorter path would have continued farther south, east of Lexington. Why not just cross the Blue Ridge there?

Because Reeds Gap was the "optimum point for crossing the Appalachian National Scenic Trail," as Dominion executive Leslie Hartz had explained in an email to Clyde Thompson.[11] Because at Reeds Gap, the Appalachian Trail briefly traverses US Forest Service land, which meant Dominion's multibillion-dollar bet wouldn't hinge on a special act from Congress. (This theory would be challenged by Greg Buppert and his colleagues all the way to the Supreme Court, arguing that the Forest Service lacked that authority because the trail itself is administered by the National Park Service.)

According to Fenton, Dominion's engineers had told him that if the drilling failed for some technical reason, they would go for plan B: a "conventional trench" opencut crossing up and over the top. For Dominion, the strategy seemed to be Reeds Gap or bust.

The Low Points of Augusta County

Nancy Sorrells had a flat tire. But that wasn't what soured her mood. It was what she saw rolling by on Interstate 81 while she waited for AAA to come: truck after truck hauling huge sections of green 42-inch-diameter pipe.

It was an afternoon in late January 2018, and she had pulled over to a rest stop near Weyers Cave in northern Augusta County. She had been fighting the proposed pipeline for more than three years. But for the first time since she had started raising the alarm in 2014, she felt utterly dejected.

After all the late nights, miles logged, and comments submitted, seeing actual pipes streaming down the interstate hit Sorrells harder than she had expected. FERC had authorized Dominion's crews to start cutting trees along the western section of the route. She knew those trucks were heading to storage yards in West Virginia.

"It was probably the most depressing day I've had just sitting there watching that pipe," she said. "At that point we had done so much, but we hadn't won anything."[12]

Organizing against the pipeline had become a nearly full-time job on top of her full-time job as a publisher of a small press and historian. In that self-appointed role, she had attended to both the big picture and the smallest details. She sat on the steering committee of the Allegheny–Blue Ridge Alliance and designed flyers and posters. She had briefed FERC commissioners in person and lobbied elected officials and also served as Augusta's counterpart to Nelson's Joyce Burton, helping local landowners negotiate the moving of an access road a few dozen feet farther away from their front porch.

Sorrells let herself feel glum for a moment. Then she went back to making calls and writing emails about other pipeline-fighting irons in the fire, like securing protections for historic preservation in certain parts of Augusta and documenting various underground caves near the ACP route.

In Augusta County, she knew, one could always drop lower—literally. Her county had the most active sinkhole geology in Virginia. Sorrells's colleagues had worked with local officials and experts to map and list every known karst formation and sinkhole on the ACP's route; so far it was up to thirty.

Sinkholes formed wherever softer limestone dissolved under flowing water. They swallowed roads, cows, fences—even an entire section of a major street in the city of Staunton had collapsed one October 2001 day into a 45-foot-deep chasm. A 30-foot-wide sinkhole in 2015 not far from Sorrells's home had even exposed one of Dominion's buried transmission lines. In 2016 and 2017, nearby sections of Interstate 81 were shut down to fix sinkholes that had suddenly opened underneath the highway.

While she waited for help with her flat tire, she was heartened by one thought in particular: wherever those pipes were heading, it was not a pipe yard in her county.

A month earlier, as her husband drove them back from visiting family in Maryland over the holidays, she had been texting and emailing furiously to turn people out to perhaps the least appealing holiday gathering of all: a board of zoning appeals meeting. When that local body met each first Thursday of the month, attendance was understandably pretty sparse. But thanks to Sorrells and her colleagues, over 250 people turned out for the one in early January about Dominion's proposal to build a pipe storage and staging yard on a road named Scenic Highway on the west side of the Shenandoah Valley.

Of the forty-five citizens who spoke, forty opposed the pipe yard. Augusta County being farming country, many voiced fears about heavy traffic, noise, and pollution in an area that had long been set aside for agricultural use. "It's named Scenic Highway for a reason," said one local. "You going to rename the road? Because this is not going to be scenic after that."

But one young couple who rose to speak had more immediate concerns. They had just learned that their small organic farm, where they lived with their two children, would be surrounded on three sides by the pipe yard. They hadn't received any notice, they said, from Dominion about its plans to turn those fields into a 34-acre storage lot engulfing their farm with twenty-four-hour security and lighting, barbed-wire fencing, and four hundred employees coming and going every day— along with at least five hundred truckloads of pipe.

Sorrells had spoken after the young farmers. All her pent-up frustration seemed to pour out. "I feel like we have been bullied for about three and a half years," she said. "They talk about core values and high standards but they violate property rights, collapse bridges, tear up roads, kill livestock, pollute streams, and blame it all on the citizens."

The land was in an area zoned for agriculture, she said, but it could likely never be returned to farmland after use by Dominion, due to fuel dripping from vehicles, toxic runoff, and soil compaction. "Dominion has put people on the menu and not on the table at other hearings. Today, the citizens have a seat at the table. Dominion wants to break the rules, endanger our citizens and the economy, and change our landscape."[13] She asked the five members of the zoning appeals board to tell Dominion Energy that "they are not welcome at the table" by denying their permit.

To her surprise, the board voted to delay a decision until their next meeting.[14] The thought that the vote had taken the company by surprise, too, gave Nancy Sorrells some comfort.

Vicki Wheaton Finally Wins

Over on the other side of the Blue Ridge, in Nelson County, Ernie Reed was feeling upbeat.

Like Nancy Sorrells, Reed was a founding member of the ABRA steering committee. Since the alliance was launched in 2014, he too had sat in on the weekly conference calls in which the dozens of organizations that made up the alliance shared their news, lessons, and plans. He knew as well as she did that things weren't exactly going their way.

But he also knew that Greg Buppert and staff at SELC, in concert with Appalachian Mountain Advocates, a public interest legal group based in West Virginia, had filed a case against the FERC certificate—along with other separate challenges to three other federal permits—in federal court that winter.

What's more, Ernie Reed was fresh off a victory of his own. Connie Brennan, the most vocal opponent of the ACP on the county's five-member board of supervisors, had decided to retire. In November, Reed had been elected to take over her seat. He had decided to run in large part, he said, so he could carry on the pipeline fight from the perch of county government.[15]

But another recent and little-noticed vote helped explain why Reed was feeling, despite all the currents running against them, somewhat buoyed. If all the other legal challenges failed, it might give them one last line of defense to fall back on. And it was thanks to Vicki Wheaton.

When Wheaton had started lobbying to update Nelson's floodplain protections, Reed and Brennan were among the few who had encouraged her quest. For years, Wheaton had basically pushed for what the Federal Emergency Management Agency recommended: that the county voluntarily adopt higher standards restricting development in its flood-prone areas. If they did, incentives would kick in to make flood insurance cheaper for Nelson residents and business owners.

FEMA flood risk maps, model ordinance text, the arcana of flood insurance actuarial tables—this was stuff seemingly designed to put most people to sleep. But for Wheaton, the bloodless texts packed the punch of a suspense novel. She knew that those dry phrases held somebody's life or death in the balance. During every official meeting she attended, Wheaton described her promise to Tinker Bryant.

"It's because of Tinker that I'm here," Wheaton would tell them. "He asked me to do this, and you guys need to listen to me. He lost his family. I mean, how many people do we have to lose?"

Over the course of 2015 and 2016, the proposal was voted down or tabled by supervisors repeatedly. Wheaton kept pushing. The supervisors punted it to the planning commission, which chewed on it for several months before unanimously voting to recommend the higher standards for floodplain safety. In September 2017, the supervisors put the proposed ordinance on their agenda one more time.

As in any part of rural America, questions of cost and property rights were front and center. People didn't take kindly to being told what they couldn't do with their land in Nelson County—whether the dictates came from FEMA or Dominion Energy.

But—along with helping residents save money on flood insurance premiums and protect their property values—the reason to adopt the ordinance, Wheaton emphasized, was safety. Many homes and businesses were clustered along the Rockfish River and its tributaries, in the hollows and valley bottoms where past floods had wreaked the most havoc. As everyone there knew, the mountains of central Virginia have a special talent for grabbing hold of passing storms and wringing biblical quantities of rain out of them. Nelson's location made it the frequent site of "orographic lifting"—a phenomenon in which moisture-laden air coming up from the Gulf or Atlantic hit the Blue Ridge, rose, cooled, and dropped its entire liquid cargo on the hills below. In Nelson alone, Camille's rains had triggered nearly six thousand landslides. Most were debris flows: surging avalanches of trees, rocks, and mud that scoured valleys below with deadly force.[16]

Wheaton asked them to imagine what would happen if floods from a severe summer storm, let alone a Camille-type event, hit the buried Atlantic Coast Pipeline. If floodwaters and debris dislodged and ruptured the pipe, entire communities could be isolated. Wheaton and Connie Brennan had accordingly asked the county's planner to insert language in the ordinance text stating that natural gas was a "hazardous material."

Wheaton was a longtime volunteer at a retreat center in Nelson founded by a prominent leader of the Tibetan Bön Buddhist tradition. When the time came for the supervisors to vote on the proposal, she asked a master teacher from the center for some help. "What do you want me to do?" he asked her. "Just hold the space," she said. "I can do that," he said, then meditated and prayed in the back of the hearing room.

Then, to nearly everyone's surprise, the supervisors voted 3–2 to adopt the floodplain measure. For Vicki Wheaton, the vote was a "miracle"—and the fulfillment of a decades-old pledge.

Brennan and Reed congratulated her after the meeting. They shared her belief that it would make Nelson County safer. But they also saw that the ordinance would offer another tool to slow down the unwanted Atlantic Coast Pipeline. Dominion would have to apply for variances—exemptions to the new rules—for each of the dozens of streams and rivers it wanted to cross in Nelson County, one by one.

Like an undersized wrestler trying to get leverage on a much bigger, stronger opponent, little Nelson County had just positioned itself for a new hold.

Dominion Hears "No"

On March 1, Tom Farrell celebrated the long-awaited first shipment of liquefied natural gas from Dominion's Cove Point terminal, as the tanker ship *Gemmata* set out into the Atlantic with the first of 2.2 million metric tons of supercooled methane destined for Japan.[17]

The project, launched in 2011, was a major milestone on the United States' journey toward eventually becoming (in 2022) the world's largest exporter of natural gas: Cove Point was just the second major LNG export facility to come online since Cheniere's Sabine Pass terminal in Louisiana launched two years earlier.

But on the same day, a few hundred miles to the southwest, Dominion ran into something new: a headwind.

At the February meeting of the Augusta County Board of Zoning Appeals, the question of Dominion's pipe yard had been tabled yet again. Nancy Sorrells had rallied even more people to turn out in opposition to it. The board met again on the first day of March. In the interim, heavy rains had fallen across the county. Citizens went out to record video of knee-deep floodwaters rushing through the spot where Dominion wanted to store its pipes. Sorrells uploaded the footage to flash drives and hand-delivered them to each member of the board.[18]

At the March 1 meeting of the zoning board, its members voted 4–1 to deny Dominion a permit. As one would later say by way of explanation, "It's hard to support something nobody is in favor of."[19]

After three and a half years, the pipeline resistance in Augusta had its first small taste of victory. And the cumulative effect of all its piecemeal challenges was beginning to show: the ACP was falling behind schedule and over budget. In late February, Duke Energy CEO Lynn Good acknowledged as much when she told bank analysts that the projected cost of the project had increased by 30 percent to $6.5 billion.

As with the Nelson floodplain vote, outside of Augusta County, no one took much notice. But for Nancy Sorrells, it was an event of seismic significance. It was, to her knowledge, the first time that Dominion had been told "no" by any official body along its route.

"And it was by a local board of zoning appeals!"

Will Fenton's Pain Scale

On the morning of March 6, 2018, Will Fenton glanced down the hill and counted about twenty men with chainsaws fanning out through the oaks that stood thick on either side of Beech Grove Road. He watched with a sick feeling in his stomach as they set to work.

The week before, both the Fentons and the Wintergreen Property Owners Association had agreed to let ACP begin felling trees. The Fentons still hadn't negotiated an easement with Dominion, so the company asked the federal court of the Western District of Virginia to grant early access to their property so contractors could begin staging equipment and felling trees before a looming deadline imposed by regulators to protect migratory nesting birds.[20] The two sides came to an agreement just hours before the case was scheduled to be heard. Will Fenton thought the court would grant Dominion's request; he decided to save his energy for the eminent domain case. Soon after, he got a call from Joyce Burton: Would he like her to be there while the trees came down? The innkeeper said he would.

So, as the men revved up their saws, Fenton walked with Burton toward the edge of the easement. As a large tree fell and shook the earth, Fenton felt a strange, unfamiliar jolt of pain in his right side, followed by a wave of nausea. "It was a new pain, one that would come to reveal itself a month later, but for the time, I walked on and decided it was the trees' energy I was feeling," he recalled.

Fenton had cut down plenty of trees over the years. His email handle was "Wilhelm the Woodcutter." He worked with dead trees for a living. He had spent months felling, skidding, and stacking trees on his land—to clear the site and use them in building his inn. He milled them into boards and turned whole logs into the hand-hewn timber frame that spanned his church-like lobby. He even saved the small branches to carve into railings and door handles and whimsical owls. Some trees became tables, like the one where he and Greg Buppert had sat two and a half years earlier. He prized their grain, sweep, knots, and gnarls. "I didn't want to waste anything," Fenton said.

Now, as he watched a tangle of logs rise where that morning had stood a forest, Fenton was beside himself. "A constant crash of 100-year-old oaks and poplars shook the ground," he recalled. "It was so war-like and sickening."[21] Burton was beside him too. She had explained ahead of time that her role was just being present: "In Judaism when we sit shiva, we don't speak to you until you speak to us."[22]

All told, he reckoned the men dropped at least a hundred trees in six hours. "People at Wintergreen just drive by it to go up the mountain," said Burton. "It was an affront to their autonomy and privilege, not because they know those trees. Will knows the trees. Those trees have faces for him."

"It was a very deep moment from anyone to understand at least some of the pain," Fenton said. "Joyce Burton is an exceptional human being, in terms of knowing what it's like to be a human being."

His conversations with Burton had buoyed him, given him a perspective on the county-wide pipeline fight beyond his family's quiet war with Dominion's lawyers. And he respected those who were continuing the fight now that their own homes and businesses were no longer in the crosshairs.

Since 2015, Burton had contacted as many landowners on the route as she could, on foot, by Toyota Prius, by email and phone all over Nelson County. She had long ago quit her job as a physical therapist to work full-time on fighting the pipeline (though she was only paid by Friends of Nelson for fifteen hours a week). Farmers, military veterans, second-home owners, elderly widows, teachers, lawyers, electricians, entrepreneurs—she sat in their living rooms, phoned them after dinner, walked their land, saw where they had planned to build homes or gardens or barns. Many were scared, angry, confused, or overwhelmed. Some were battling terminal illnesses while they tried to line up eminent domain attorneys. Whenever people picked up the phone, she found that they had a lot to say. "Every conversation is about them needing to be heard, for the first half hour," she said.

And if they asked about her story, and how she landed in Nelson, she could tell them that she always knew she'd wind up in the mountains.

When she lived in New York City in the 1990s, she had been a "number-crunching type of desk geek"—working as a bookkeeper for a travel company and as a research analyst for Bankers Trust Company. "What became clear was that I wanted to do something that had more of an impact on people than sitting in a cubicle playing with numbers," she said. She had fallen in love with the Blue Ridge during childhood summer trips. And now, thanks to Dominion, she was *really* getting to know those mountains and its denizens, calling on neighbors in deep hollows, hiking their land, bushwhacking through thickets of laurel and redbuds and scrub oak.

Or watching those trees crash down, in a quiet act of solidarity. Will and Lilia had met Burton three years earlier at a fundraiser for the now defunct All Pain No Gain group. There were plenty of wealthy, connected people there, he recalled, except for them and Burton. "It turned out that the physical therapist was actually going to be the most influential person and not through connections at the country club, money, or political 'friends' but through determination and learning the law as she went," Fenton told me.

For three years, Burton had kept detailed logs and annotated maps to track the easements signed between Dominion and Nelson landowners. They ranged widely, she found, depending on people's financial means and inclination to push back—and whether they had effective lawyers helping them. "They put out a number to you, then come back with a number that's half again as much," she said. "People say, 'Great.' Then they pull it off the table and scare people into taking the lower number."

By early 2018, more than 80 percent of landowners, including hundreds of Nelsonians, along the ACP's whole route had signed easement agreements. And yet even as those easements were inked, opposition only deepened in Nelson County. It was a "myth," she said, that people who had made deals were okay with the pipeline. "People see the county as impacted, not just their own property. Many landowners are very passionately opposed, most are overwhelmed, and a lot are afraid to speak out."

In her view, many agreements were signed under duress, by landowners who worried that, if they didn't acquiesce, they would get a much worse deal down the road—that they would wind up with next to nothing *and* a pipeline in their yard. It often goes, she said, like this:

> From the day you get notice that they will survey your land without your permission, you are told that this will go to eminent domain. What kind of negotiating position does that put you in? Dominion has filed for "quicktake" [in some cases]. They are able to take your land without having even paid you the amount the court is going to decide when you go to court. They will show up with their appraisers, with a lowball offer. You have to hire an appraiser to get a better sense of what you're going to be losing. Your lawyer will get

one-third of anything Dominion offers you, and you pay the ap-
praiser. All you're going to get in court is money. If you want them to
not use pesticides or replace fences or to give you access to monitor
their activity, if you want twenty-four-hour notice before they start
blasting, you have to do that by signing an easement. And by the
time the court decision comes on eminent domain, the pipeline is
already in.[23]

Fenton and Burton watched the crews work for a while, then walked
back up to the inn, where they passed the storage room door that
Fenton had carved by hand—using trees from the land—depicting a
sly-looking dragon reaching its claw around to open the door handle.
Wilhelm the Woodcutter versus Dominion the Dragon.

In her view, the day's events were intended to cow other landowners
into falling in line. "Will Fenton was treated the way he was treated
because he was very public" in his opposition, she said. "They wanted
to make a lesson out of them."

The strange jab of pain Fenton felt earlier would turn out to be
a kidney stone, which he would pass a few weeks later on the same
day that Dominion had sent its hired appraisers to evaluate what they
thought Fenton's business was worth, in anticipation of the eminent
domain trial. ("While they snooped around, I was throwing up over
the deck," he recalled.)

The pain of the kidney stone soon faded. But reflecting on the
day—and his entire experience with the Atlantic Coast Pipeline—in
the months and years to come, Fenton would come up with a "scale for
suffering." It ran from 1 to 5. "The cutoff between 0 and 1 is passing a
kidney stone. So if you wouldn't trade some event for the kidney stone,
then it doesn't matter."

Hearing some of his guests' stories helped him calibrate the scale
and put things in perspective. There was the 80-year-old German man
whose apartment building was bombed during World War II, his entire street flattened, who survived for weeks eating only wild onions.
"That was a 4." There was the guest who had been in the Pentagon
on September 11 and barely survived as the hijacked plane crashed
through its outer rings. "That was a 4." There was the guest who had
told him about losing her daughter, her only child, from leukemia, and

that it was the first time she had told the story without breaking down. "That was a 5."[24]

The years-long battle with Dominion had been one of the more painful experiences of his life, when he added up all the stress, the time and money they had lost, the prospect of a fatal blow to their business—his dream.

"But on the scale that everyday people suffer, it comes in at 2," he said. "Anything less than twelve hours with a kidney stone should be forgotten."

Battle Hymn of the General Citizenry

On March 17, Joyce Burton and forty other Nelsonians gathered to hold a vigil of sorts over the tangle of trees below the Fenton Inn.

"I mean how does that make any sense?" asked Richard Averitt, a local landowner who had taken on a vocal role in fighting the pipeline, as he gestured toward the logged-over slope behind him, leading up toward the Fenton Inn and Reeds Gap.[25]

He and his wife Jill and their extended family had been "hit twice" by the pipeline: it was coming through his sister's land (their own home was a few hundred feet outside the pipeline right-of-way but well within its "incineration zone") and a commercial property they owned nearby. "None of this makes any sense," Averitt said. "And the only way we lose our rights is when we quit fighting for them."

Averitt pointed toward the 100-foot-wide strip of felled trees leading up toward Fortune Ridge. "And on that side of the road," he continued, anger rising in his voice, "that was nothing more than a show of force. There was no reason to cut that hill for another year. But they did that because they want us to quit. They want us to believe this is over with. But hell, it is not over with. This is the very beginning."

Fenton, too, saw the felling as an act of intimidation, a flex. Dominion would have to stop cutting trees soon due to the migratory bird restrictions. Construction wasn't slated to start elsewhere in Nelson County for another year; the company could have waited until they had all the permits they needed. To him, it was a statement: *This is happening; deal with it.* Trying to get him to tap out.

When it was his turn to speak, frustrations came tumbling out of the stocky innkeeper. "We've tried all the various avenues, we've been in all these different groups, people went to different congressmen—and find out they are owned by Dominion. . . . They pay both sides. It's not a Democrat versus Republican issue. It's a greed and corruption issue."[26]

Murmurs of assent came from his neighbors. They launched into a song set to the tune of "The Battle Hymn of the Republic":

No matter where you come from if you call this country home
the splendor of the mountains can be found wherever you roam,
Dominion wants to ruin it all, they'll blast right through the stone.
But we are Nelson strong.

"Seeing the carnage here is enough to make me, to make any of us, question the point of continuing the battle," Joyce Burton told the gathering. "But then I look at this group and I realize that what we just sang is true—together we are always stronger."

The sentiment of the song—much like *Waltons* creator Earl Hamner's equating Nelson County with "love"—was a bit corny and cliché. But, like most clichés, there was some truth to it. In the nearly four years since the pipeline had been announced, they had rallied together to demonstrate a new hyperlocal meaning for "full Nelson."[27] They had built the kind of bridges that nearly everyone, amid the disorienting maelstrom of America's accelerating polarization, claimed to yearn for. Everyone there could testify to it.

"We were able to build a coalition of people who work together even though their motivations may have been different," Burton told me later. "People felt like their neighbors had their back."

"It was the one time in the history I've lived in Nelson that I felt I was working with *everyone*," recalled Ron Enders. "Left, right, rich, poor, Black, white, we were all together. It was a wonderful experience."[28]

"It's awesome, in terms of the community it built," Wisteria Johnson said. "I realize most of the people I text with [now] are the folk I never knew and would not have come to know."[29]

In August 2017, Johnson, with great reluctance, had signed an easement through the Cove over to Dominion. Earlier that year, she had experienced heart trouble, including atrial fibrillation. She spent time in the hospital. When they ran tests, the doctors couldn't find anything physically wrong with her heart. They asked about sources of stress: "What's going on in your life?"

"Oh, honey, let me tell you," Johnson had replied, before describing her past three years of fears about the Atlantic Coast Pipeline. Her doctor agreed it could be a trigger for her symptoms. Her children, she said, were adamantly opposed to signing an easement. In a recent interview with the local newspaper, her eldest daughter had described Dominion's project as "a heist."

"[With] an act that heinous," C'ta DeLaurier said, "there really is not enough to repay what they've taken."[30]

On that, mother and daughter were in full agreement. But Wisteria and her sister Liz decided that the family needed some kind of resolution. Fighting a lawsuit from Dominion would be costly—and risky. Plus there was the specter of quicktake, a process in which a federal judge could grant ACP the power to claim their property and begin construction before any compensation had been decided. With it came the risk that they'd be rendered powerless to negotiate any conditions or restrictions on how Dominion operated in the Cove. Like many landowners, they worried about losing any leverage to press for small route changes. Once the matter went before a judge, it would be taken out of their hands.

"I decided to take the lead: instead of making the issue the enemy, if they wanted to blame somebody, blame me," she said, referring to her kids. "My sister agreed." It was a heartbreaking decision. "Change is the only constant. That's why we accepted the easement after a lot of soul searching. One tends to assume the worst part of life."

After they signed, the entire family continued to speak out against the project—including their matriarch. "I had to," Johnson said. "It was the principle of the thing."[31]

The mountains and streams needed a voice too. In all the talk about critical infrastructure in all the opinion articles and press releases and politicians' speeches since Tom Farrell's triumphal September 2014 press conference, there had been little mention of the mountains, the forests that held them together, and how together they filtered the waters that

Virginians depended on. People needed energy. But clean water was pretty critical infrastructure too. Nancy Sorrells liked to point out to state and federal decision-makers that no water flowed into Augusta County, only out: south to the James, the source of Richmond's water supply, or north to the Potomac, which supplied drinking water to the nation's capital. The Cove was like that on a smaller scale: the water in its spring-fed streams ran south to Dutch Creek, then the Rockfish River, then the James all the way to Richmond, where some drops of it flowed through the taps in Dominion's headquarters.

As the vigil drew to a close, it was Johnson's turn to speak:

I come from those who talk to the air, talk to the fire, talk to the waters. I talk to my mountains. And I apologize. I apologize for the upcoming surgery. I apologize to them for the abusive incision that will cut to their bellies. And then for the greedy people that will insert a tube with natural gas that not only will affect them, that will affect all that's around them. I look at the streams flowing so freely and pure. And they come from the top of the mountains where the water originates . . . and they go into other big creeks, and then into rivers, to water tables.

She sounded equally sorrowful, angry, and bemused. "And for the life of me," she continued, "I cannot understand why these greedy people don't understand that they're not only affecting poor little me up in Harris Cove, but they are affecting many more people. And even maybe their people, their children. But here I stand today to vow to continue to fight."

Then she leaned forward into the bullhorn and led the group in a chant: "NO PIPELINE! NO PIPELINE! NO PIPELINE!"

Part III

Path Dependence

Open-trench pipeline construction on a steep mountainside in the Dry
Branch area of Pocahontas County, West Virginia. This was the easternmost
extent of pipe installation for the ACP. (Pipeline Air Force/Allegheny–Blue
Ridge Alliance)

Chapter Eight

Rooftop to Rooftop

On a winter day in 2018, Sarah Francisco looked out the window of the Southern Environmental Law Center's office in downtown Charlottesville toward the nearby railroad tracks and saw train car after train car rolling by, laden with pipes heading west.

The sight was a gut check, as it had been for her friend Nancy Sorrells. Francisco knew those pipes were heading toward storage yards in West Virginia, where excavators and welders were waiting for them. Nearly four years into her organization's fight against the Atlantic Coast Pipeline, permit after permit was getting approved for the project. And while Francisco led SELC's Virginia office, this case also felt personal. She had grown up in an Augusta County farmhouse—where her parents still lived—just a few miles away from the ACP's path.

Her team of lawyers were feeling the pressure—perhaps none more so than Greg Buppert. The centerpiece of his strategy had long been to attack FERC's determination that the Atlantic Coast Pipeline was in the public interest—to challenge both the core premise that there was any demand to justify it *and* the commission's narrow approach to weighing its merits.[1]

From the outset, Buppert knew their challenge would be getting that case in front of federal judges before the pipeline was built—because of "tolling orders."

This was FERC's bland name for its longstanding practice of indefinitely postponing consideration of any challenges to a certificate until it held a "rehearing"—which it could also postpone indefinitely, according to its own opaque inclinations. Tolling orders effectively let FERC dodge legal challenges for as long as it liked; like an armadillo rolling up into an impervious ball, it could just wait them out. To Greg Buppert, it was "an egregiously unfair process that allowed pipelines to be built before communities and landowners can even go to court." To a federal judge who would later rebuke FERC for the practice, it was "Kafkaesque"—as in "having a nightmarishly complex, bizarre, or illogical quality."

Nightmarishly illogical or not, tolling orders posed an obstacle the SELC attorneys simply had to plan around. Greg Buppert couldn't launch his direct challenge on the most important permit of all—FERC's—until that agency denied a rehearing. That meant SELC needed to buy some time.

"Our strategy emerged from FERC not properly assessing the *need* for the project," Buppert said, "but we couldn't make that argument until it was mostly built." Why? Tolling orders.

This bureaucratic quagmire limited their options. "We knew we had to keep pipe out of the ground if we wanted a chance of winning," he said. "We needed construction to stop."[2]

That's why Sarah Francisco had asked D. J. Gerken to join the effort. He and his colleagues Amelia Burnette and Patrick Hunter in the Asheville office were tasked with studying the key permits issued by a bevy of federal agencies—the Forest Service, Park Service, Fish and Wildlife Service—for flaws and crafting arguments in response.

Gerken welcomed the challenge. One of SELC's top litigators, he had just wrapped up three grinding years of discovery, as part of an eight-year-long effort to hold Duke Energy and other companies accountable for cleaning up toxic coal ash waste produced from their power plants in North Carolina. That had been a "knockdown, dragout" litigation experience. This would be a sprint.[3]

"The pipeline companies have made these cases a race," Gerken said. "That's the industry strategy: build it before anyone can challenge it."[4]

His team's strategy: get into a courtroom as fast as possible. The three lawyers had found several weak spots to target in the agencies' analyses buttressing those federal permits. Snagging an early slot on the federal Fourth Circuit Court of Appeals' tight calendar to make their case would give them an outside shot at halting construction. If they missed, they might not get another chance.

Gerken got his wish, but precious little time to execute it. "Usually, the court of appeals is the punch line to years of work," he said. But on this case, they would arrive there in a matter of weeks. To make it onto the court's docket, he and his team agreed to a compressed timetable; they received 52,000 words of opponents' briefs on a Thursday and had until Monday to read through them and draft their own replies.

Gerken, Burnette, and Hunter handed the work off to each other, like a relay race, from Thursday afternoon to Monday morning. Hunter was a morning person, so he took the early shift. When his energy flagged, he did jumping jacks in the office to stay awake. Burnette had young children, so she took over in the afternoons and early evenings. Then Gerken, a night owl, handled the final leg. When he started getting sleepy, he took walks around the block to perk up.

"It was the craziest experience I've had as an attorney," said Gerken. Recent developments fueled their sense of urgency. District courts were ruling against landowners in eminent domain cases. Tree felling had begun in Virginia; construction was slated to begin soon in West Virginia. Once crews started laying pipe in the ground, the project would acquire unstoppable momentum.

In meetings, Gerken used a vivid metaphor to focus everyone's minds: "We're basically jumping from rooftop to rooftop, and we have to stick every landing or this pipeline will get built."

Two Cases, Twenty Minutes

The Lewis F. Powell Jr. building in downtown Richmond was familiar territory for D. J. Gerken. He had walked the halls of the country's oldest continuously operating federal courthouse—home to the US

Fourth Circuit Court of Appeals—many times. Gerken had clerked for the Fourth Circuit right after law school and had argued cases before it too.

Going before the Fourth Circuit—one of thirteen federal appellate courts that sit just below the Supreme Court—was always a humbling, high-stakes occasion. But on the morning of May 10, 2018, as he walked up the steps of the Powell building, Gerken felt a bit more adrenaline than usual. Normally he and his team would have had months to prepare. Normally, they would be arguing just one case. But Gerken was about to perform a high-wire act.

The court had consolidated into one action-packed session two separate cases: one targeting the National Park Service permit to cross the Blue Ridge Parkway, and the other aiming at the Fish and Wildlife Service's authorization for ACP's "incidental take" of a certain number of protected or endangered species during construction. Gerken's task was to convince the judges those agencies had failed to do their jobs—that their permits had fatal technical flaws. And he would have just twenty minutes to argue both cases.

The hulking, Italianate-style Powell building was in the heart of Richmond's power center. A few blocks away in one direction was Dominion's high-rise headquarters; a few blocks in the other direction sat the office of McGuireWoods, the law firm that frequently represented Dominion. Across the street was the State Capitol, sitting atop a long sloping lawn, where cadres of Dominion lobbyists could be found roaming the halls and chatting up lawmakers during legislative sessions. The Powell Courthouse was, in theory at least, a neutral venue, where any citizen or organization with standing could seek redress and stand equal to a Fortune 500 company before the law. All the same, Gerken knew from experience that they faced a structural disadvantage: federal judges did not like to second-guess agency experts.[5]

Once oral arguments got underway, Gerken launched his attack on the first permit. The Fish and Wildlife Service, he said, was not properly considering the risk the pipeline would pose to two species of endangered bats, freshwater crustaceans, a rare type of bumblebee, and a particularly vulnerable freshwater mussel known as the clubshell. As he made his case that FWS had failed to spell out, as required by law, the specific number of mussels and bees that the ACP would be allowed to wipe out, Judge James A. Wynn Jr. interjected.[6]

"It sounds macabre, but really this is a license, if you will, to kill and maim a certain number of species who we know will be killed."

"Absolutely, your Honor," Gerken replied, and without clearly set limits, "it becomes an unlimited license to kill these species."

The judges seemed receptive to his argument. Gerken, keeping a close eye on the clock—thirteen minutes had elapsed—pivoted to the next case. He went straight to the core of SELC's argument: the one-hundred-year-old Mineral Leasing Act prohibited pipelines from crossing lands in the National Park System without special permission from Congress. When the National Park Service issued a permit for the Atlantic Coast Pipeline to cross the Blue Ridge Parkway at Reeds Gap, just above the Fenton Inn, it had robbed Congress of its authority.

The statutes' provisions were arcane, the arguments technically dense, but Gerken had a very simple theory to explain these agencies' mistakes: haste borne of political pressure. Trump appointees had leaned on agency staffers to speed up their reviews so that Dominion could start building its pipeline. This led to slipshod work—to shortcuts that violated or misread the law.

Before the time was up, Judge Wynn had one more question. "I take it if you can't get this across the Appalachian Trail, this whole pipeline goes down the tubes, right?"

"Well, they are crossing the Appalachian Trail, your Honor," said Gerken. "Their theory is that because they're crossing on land managed by the Forest Service, they have authority to do that. That's at issue in another appeal pending before the court, in September we expect it to be heard."

With that, the arguments were gaveled to a close. As he gathered his papers, Gerken exhaled. They could catch their breath—for now. They'd be back in the Powell Building in five months' time to argue that the Forest Service permit—issued despite the warnings from veteran staff like Clyde Thompson and Kent Karriker—should be tossed out too.

Five days later, the Fourth Circuit threw out the Fish and Wildlife permit, deeming its ACP "license to kill" too vague and impossible to enforce. The court would issue a full ruling later that summer, but for now the upshot was clear: the agency would have to go back and redo its homework.

The SELC team had hit their first rooftop. Several more lay ahead.

Best in Class Revisited

The following month, as ACP construction got underway in West Virginia, a reminder of the stakes of Gerken's paper chase came along.

In the wee hours of June 7, 2018, the 36-inch TransCanada Leach Xpress Pipeline exploded near Moundsville, West Virginia, spitting an 83-foot-long section of pipe skyward. The fireball burned for hours, igniting half a million dollars' worth of methane—so brightly that people living nearby thought it was daylight. Federal investigators would later determine the cause: a landslide on a steep slope.[7]

Just a few weeks after the Leach Xpress exploded, the Nature Conservancy released a report on "best practices" for pipeline construction on steep slopes. The twenty-six-page document was produced in partnership with eight major gas pipeline companies, including Dominion and Southern (ACP), Williams (Constitution), and Enbridge (Dakota Access Pipeline). Another participant was the gas transmission subsidiary of EQT, the lead developer of the Mountain Valley Pipeline, which planned to cross terrain every bit as steep as ACP's.[8]

The report had grown out of conversations between the conservancy and pipeline developers in spring 2017, roughly around the time that Kent Karriker's letter about steep slopes had generated intense blowback from Dominion and brass at the Department of Agriculture. The Nature Conservancy presumably entered these discussions with the best of intentions: limiting damage in sensitive ecosystems. In the process, it also lent its implicit seal of approval to giant gas companies—who rushed to issue press releases trumpeting their partnership with the well-known environmental group.[9]

One of the companies participating in those early conversations was TransCanada, owner of the newly opened, newly exploded Leach Xpress, which was—like ACP—rated to move 1.5 billion cubic feet of gas per day. Just five months earlier, on the day the pipeline was put into service, TransCanada's CEO had said, "This is truly a best-in-class pipeline and we look forward to many years of safe, reliable and efficient operation on behalf of our customers."[10]

It wasn't the first West Virginia pipeline to go up in flames. In December 2012, a 20-inch Columbia Gas pipeline ruptured in Sissonville, sending flames a hundred feet high and melting a football-field-long section of Interstate 77. It was caused by a corroded pipe that had not been inspected for a quarter century. Remarkably, no one was killed, but five homes were destroyed. Nationwide, between 2010 and 2018, there were more than 5,500 accidents, 800 fires, 300 explosions, and 125 deaths due to pipeline failures: an oil and gas pipeline in the US exploded every 11 days and killed someone every 26 days.[11]

Inside a home, a leak usually comes with a whiff of a sulfurous odor, universally interpreted as a signal to shut off the gas line or call the gas company immediately. Methane is odorless; that rotten egg smell comes from a chemical called mercaptan, which utilities are required to add at the point of distribution.[12]

But if you lived next to a large-diameter gas pipeline, there was no mercaptan equivalent to alert you to the hidden dangers of corroding steel or moving earth. You just had to hope that "best in class" was more than a marketing tool.[13]

"Delusions of Invincibility"

From the earliest days of the pipeline fight, Lew Freeman had detected a familiar strain of confidence whenever he listened to Dominion's representatives. He had gotten a whiff of "snake oil" at the project's outset, but as the years wore on, he sensed another dynamic at play—a phenomenon he had seen enough, up close, that he had coined a name for it. One that sounded like it could be an entry in the *Diagnostic and Statistical Manual of Mental Disorders*: "delusions of invincibility."

As the head of the Allegheny–Blue Ridge Alliance, Freeman now spent much of his "retirement" running meetings with environmental lawyers and grassroots activists from throughout the region. But for decades—as a lobbyist for the American Petroleum Institute and the

National Association of Manufacturers, and then more than two decades as a vice president with the Society of the Plastics Industry—he had worked alongside both captains of industry and engineers.

"The energy industry is dominated by engineers," Freeman explained. "They're taught that they can solve any problem with engineering, with the right technology." If you start with that mindset, he said, "and then you add to it all this money that is at their disposal and, over the years, all of the favorable legislation and regulations, then they think they're invincible in one degree or another. In the face of natural obstacles, political obstacles—whatever the obstacle is."[14]

To his mind, the planning of the Atlantic Coast Pipeline took this to new heights of absurdity. One example was an exchange he had witnessed between a Dominion engineer and his own county's board of supervisors, in which the former pledged that, after they sheared off various Highland ridgetops for the pipeline right-of-way, "We're going to put it back the way it was." (Freeman, incredulous, had turned to a colleague sitting next to him and whispered, "What are they going to do, glue the rock back on?")

Another testament to that overweening confidence, though, lay just a dozen miles south of the house where Freeman and his wife lived on the verdant banks of Back Creek, near the West Virginia border. That's where Dominion, in its prior corporate avatar as VEPCO, had spent fifteen years and nearly $2 billion building a pumped hydroelectricity storage facility that has been described as the "biggest battery in the world." It was an impressive technical feat and a source of pride for Bath County, where locals referred to it simply as "The Project"—and proof of what utilities like Dominion could pull off if they set their employees' minds, and vast resources, to a task.[15]

And that faith in their own abilities—and the sheer power of money—was bolstered, Freeman speculated, by a sincere belief in their mission to drive economic growth, and in their sacred duty to keep the lights on.

"They really believe in what they're doing," he said, referring to the human beings occupying the corner offices at Dominion in Richmond and Duke in Charlotte. "You know, my environmental colleagues are always saying 'This is all deception.' Well, there is deception along the way. But it's deception backed up by a belief in what they're saying. Which creates this sense that 'We're doing God's work.'"

Can You Hit the Timeline?

Toward the end of a Dominion Energy quarterly earnings call on August 1, 2018, Steve the bank analyst finally raised the elephant in the room: Were the company's leaders worried about looming legal jeopardy for their flagship project?

"Could you just talk a little bit more about how you're managing things other than just the water crossings and conviction that you can hit the timeline?" he asked, alluding to a recent challenge to yet another ACP permit, issued by the Army Corps of Engineers.[16]

The financial gurus on the line seemed a bit nervous about all these delays. Diane Leopold sought to reassure Steve. The Forest Service had "conducted a very thorough and rigorous and very transparent review of our impacts and so we do believe and are confident that . . . the approval will be upheld and affirmed by the court," she said, referring to the case over ACP's special use permit scheduled to be argued soon.

Tom Farrell chimed in to make clear that he, too, was unconcerned: "The long and short of that, Steve, is that nothing's happened and we don't expect anything to happen that will take us off our schedule of late next year."

Steve surely took note, five days later, of the Fourth Circuit's decision tossing out ACP's National Park Service permit. The court also issued its full opinion explaining its May ruling vacating the Fish and Wildlife Service permit. "We conclude that both agency decisions are arbitrary and capricious," the judges wrote.[17]

D. J. Gerken and his team had landed on another rooftop. Four days later FERC ordered construction work to stop all along the 600-mile route; the chainsaws and excavators fell silent.

On the very same day, it denied a request for a rehearing on its approval of the Atlantic Coast Pipeline. With the "Kafkaesque" tolling order obstacle finally removed, Greg Buppert could take the step he had been plotting since 2014. On August 16, he filed another lawsuit in the Fourth Circuit to vacate the permit that mattered most, the one that declared the Atlantic Coast Pipeline to be in the best interests of the American people: FERC's certificate of public convenience and necessity.[18]

Donald Trump Goes to West Virginia

On the evening of August 21, 2018, Donald Trump entered the Charleston Civic Center to the soaring strains of John Denver's "Take Me Home, Country Roads," the beloved de facto anthem of West Virginia.

"What a great song," Trump said to a roaring crowd of ten thousand supporters in the arena, just 8 miles downstream from the site of George Washington's Burning Spring.

He had come to the Mountain State to campaign for the state's Republican attorney general, who was running to unseat incumbent Senator Joe Manchin III in the fall elections. It had already been an eventful day for the forty-fifth president: just a few hours before, his personal lawyer had pleaded guilty to campaign finance crimes and his campaign manager was convicted of fraud and other federal crimes. Trump made no mention of this legal peril but had much to say about power plants, climate accords, and carbon regulations.

Some of his biggest applause lines highlighted his efforts to undo his predecessor's climate and energy policies. "We're canceling Obama's illegal anti-coal destroying regulations, the so-called Clean Power Plan." He fulminated against the Paris climate agreement. "That was going to cost us hundreds of billions of dollars." He pledged to make it easier to dig up and burn fossil fuels. "I'm getting rid of some of these ridiculous rules and regulations, which are killing our companies, our states, and our jobs."[19]

Trump had indeed canceled Obama's Clean Power Plan, but the law required his administration to propose some kind of regulation of power plants' carbon pollution in its place. On that very same day (just a day after a 15-year-old student named Greta Thunberg first staged her lone climate strike protest outside of Sweden's parliament), his own Environmental Protection Agency had issued a new set of weaker rules that, according to the administration's own analysts, would likely *increase* overall carbon emissions from the electricity sector.[20]

A month later, Trump returned to West Virginia for another rally in the northern city of Wheeling, about 10 miles from the site of the June Leach XPress pipeline explosion. Again, he walked on stage as John Denver crooned over the loudspeakers, and as the crowd cheered: "USA! USA! USA!" And again, he reprised his assault on the EPA, the Paris climate agreement, and Senator Joe Manchin.

"We ended the coal crushing stream protection rule, which was killing your towns," he said. "So beautiful. The EPA, so-called, a killer. Clean power plants. It was a killer. It was costing this country a fortune. It was a total killer. Had such nice names, such a nice title. It put everybody out of business. And it took away our strength. It took away our wealth. And I withdrew the United States from the job-killing, very unfair, and very, very expensive Paris Climate Accord, another wonder."

Patrick Morrisey, Manchin's election opponent, took the stage. "Joe Manchin supported Hillary Clinton even after she made clear she wanted to take away our coal, our oil, and our gas jobs," he said to loud boos. "Shame on Joe Manchin. And that's why liberal Joe's got to go."[21]

This was an effective line of attack in West Virginia, and Joe Manchin knew it. He was leading in the polls, but the race was much closer than his last one. A veteran of the state's politics, Manchin knew he needed to defend his record on jobs and on coal—which retained a firm grip on his state's cultural identity, despite employing less than 1 percent of its adult population.

Manchin shared a core belief with his Republican adversaries that the primary threat to *both* industries was burdensome government regulation. But it didn't matter that Manchin was a vocal supporter of coal, gas—all the fossil fuels, really. Or that most of his wealth came from his ownership of a waste coal brokerage company, which his son still ran.[22] Or that he was the Senate's top recipient of contributions from the oil and gas industry and among the top beneficiaries of money from the electric utility industry. Or that Manchin loved John Denver's song too—at least well enough to name the yacht that served as his home in DC *Almost Heaven*. Or that he had won his first Senate campaign with the help of a television ad in which he shot a bullet through a copy of his own party's climate bill.[23] He was a Democrat, nevertheless.

All the same, when it came to West Virginia's fossil gas, Trump and Manchin were largely on the same page. He was an early and ardent supporter of the Atlantic Coast Pipeline (a Trump administration infrastructure priority) and of its twin at birth, the Mountain Valley Pipeline. Manchin wanted to make it easier to permit gas pipelines. Even as Trump attacked him at rallies in his own state, Manchin was cowriting—with West Virginia Republicans—a letter to FERC, urging it to lift its orders halting construction on both pipelines and to press other agencies "to quickly reconsider, correct and reissue the necessary permits for these projects."

"We got a lot of gas," Manchin would say later that fall at a Senate energy subcommittee hearing. "We are trying to get the pipeline through. We're trying."[24]

"Who's Running the Train Station?"

For Greg Buppert, D. J. Gerken, and their clients, September brought some dizzying regulatory and judicial whiplash.

As expected, the Fish and Wildlife Service and the National Park Service issued revised permits in mid-September, after the Fourth Circuit Court had sent them back to the drawing board. They looked nearly identical to the ones that had been thrown out, as far as Gerken could tell.

But FERC, citing those revised permits, gave a green light for construction to resume on September 17.

Then, just a week later, the court issued a halt to all construction in the national forest until the appeal of the Forest Service permit was decided.

And then, the next day, the Fourth Circuit stayed the Forest Service permit for crossing the Appalachian Trail *again*.

On September 28, Gerken found himself on the steps of the Powell Courthouse in downtown Richmond to argue before the Fourth Circuit yet again. After his May performance, it seemed almost luxurious to have the full twenty minutes for just one case. And he thought it was their strongest case yet.

Thanks to a Freedom of Information Act request, the Southern Environmental Law Center team had gained access to the complete record of correspondence between the Forest Service leadership and ACP LLC. They had read through every email sent by Clyde Thompson to Leslie Hartz at Dominion or superiors at USDA—every request for steep slope designs, every letter in which the Forest Service voiced skepticism about Dominion's ability to keep the pipeline on the mountain and the mountain on the mountain. In combing through that voluminous record, they had unearthed a striking story: the Forest Service had longstanding, grave concerns that very abruptly and inexplicably vanished in 2017. This is the story they would put before the court.

"Experts were shoved aside at the agency," Gerken told me, offering a blunt summary of their argument. "They were told to shut up. For years they asked for this information, and then they said they didn't need it."

In front of the Fourth Circuit's judges, Gerken attacked the Forest Service permit on multiple fronts, from violations of the National Environmental Policy Act to the end-run around seeking congressional approval to cross the Appalachian Trail. But the core argument he laid out was the same one Clyde Thompson had made to his own superiors: Dominion was proposing to do something on a scale that had never been done, but when asked to explain in detail how they would safely lay their pipe through this landslide-prone region, all they provided the Forest Service was a "cookbook of generalities."[25]

When the Department of Justice lawyer defending the Forest Service began his rebuttal, he didn't get far before the judges fired questions at him. Chief Judge Roger Gregory was particularly curious about the timeline of the Forest Service's decision-making.

What Gregory couldn't square was how the Forest Service had spent so long telling ACP that it hadn't proved it could safely build across steep mountain terrain, only to suddenly abandon its demands in July 2017. What explained that abrupt about-face? "Why did you lower the standards?" he asked.

The agency had required Atlantic "to abide by a robust set of mitigation measures," the government's counsel replied. "The Forest Service took its job here very seriously."

After more back and forth, Gregory kept pressing. The information in the Forest Service's possession hadn't really changed. Why the reversal? The reasoning was "clearly laid out in a year and a half of back and forth with Atlantic and FERC," came the reply. Judge Gregory had seen those documents too, apparently, and wasn't satisfied by this answer.

"But who's running the train station?" he asked, clearly exasperated by the evasive responses. "A private company? You represent the US government, correct?"

After more back and forth, Gregory demanded to know the moment that the agency's concerns disappeared. The government's attorney finally began to respond but wouldn't offer a date.

"When?" the judge repeated. The counsel began again, with another evasive response.

"*When?*" Gregory asked for the fifth time. The government's counsel finally conceded that it was in 2016, the year Trump was elected, that the Forest Service had begun its pivot leading to its approval.

Judge Gregory's question about *who* was running the train station had gone unanswered. But it seemed obvious enough that it was not Clyde Thompson and the Forest Service's experts.

Sticking the Landing

Tom Farrell had started the year off bullish. Back in January, he had predicted Dominion's pipeline would be operational in late 2019. But by late 2018, construction on his "energy superhighway" still had not begun in Virginia. And, thanks to the loss of key permits, it wasn't at all clear when it would get going. December brought even more cause for heartburn.

On December 7, the normally pliant State Corporation Commission of Virginia reprimanded Dominion for its pattern of overstating energy demand in the forecasts it submitted to regulators to justify its capital expenditures on gas power plants—and, for the first time ever, it rejected the company's long-term resource plan.[26]

On December 8, the Fourth Circuit ruled that the biological opinion issued by the US Fish and Wildlife Service for the Atlantic Coast Pipeline was flawed and therefore invalid. "In fast-tracking its decisions, the agency seems to have lost sight of its mandate under the Endangered Species Act," the judges wrote.

And then, on December 13, the Fourth Circuit Court struck again, throwing out ACP's special use permit from the Forest Service.[27]

"We trust the United States Forest Service to 'speak for the trees, for the trees have no tongues,'" the court's ruling concluded, quoting Dr. Seuss's famous children's book *The Lorax*, but the agency "abdicated its responsibility to preserve national forests."

This conclusion, the judges pointed out, was inescapable thanks to "the Forest Service's serious environmental concerns that were suddenly, and mysteriously, assuaged in time to meet a private pipeline company's deadlines."[28]

The court couldn't help noting that the Forest Service had cited "decades of slope stability" on a sister pipeline in the same corridor as the Leach Xpress—which had recently exploded *due to a landslide*—as reason not to be worried about the Atlantic Coast Pipeline's safety. "Perhaps nothing demonstrates the dangers of the Forest Service's insufficient analysis of landslide risks clearer."

The hits kept coming: the court also ruled that the Forest Service lacked the authority to grant a right-of-way across the Appalachian Trail. And in response to a separate court ruling, the Army Corps had suspended ACP's Clean Water Act permit for the entire length of the pipeline. It all added up to a resounding rebuke from the federal judiciary and a shocking setback for Dominion Energy.

"If I were Dominion, I'd be panicked," Greg Buppert told one reporter.[29]

With FERC's temporary work order, Dominion had lost a month's worth of construction time—a costly delay—and the latest rulings cast a shadow over its 2019 plans. In November, Duke Energy CEO Lynn Good acknowledged that the ACP's estimated cost had already risen 50 percent, to $7 billion.[30]

SELC's lawyers, meanwhile, congratulated each other for hitting every rooftop. But they saved some credit for Dominion, too, for refusing to budge from its chosen path. "It's hard to overestimate what a significant and persistent factor that arrogant route choice was at every turn," said Gerken.

The other gift, in his view, was that the Trump administration was working feverishly and overtly on behalf of Dominion's pipeline. "They thought it was Christmas, but it was a disaster for them," Gerken said, "firing, demoting, or shifting aside anyone at the agencies who looked at the facts, the people pointing out this was the worst place in the world to build a pipeline."

It was all brazen enough that, once they laid the evidence out, he said, the judges really had no choice but to throw out those permits. For Gerken, the decisions demonstrated how the system should work. "When political masters ignore the experts, that's what the courts are for. That's why we have judicial review."[31]

To Gerken's mind, the least noticed but most glaring example of regulators' failure to apply the laws of the land to the Atlantic Coast Pipeline was the case of the poor clubshell mussel. Earlier that year, the Fish and Wildlife Service had given Dominion permission to remove several dozen of the endangered mussels from Hackers Creek, a West Virginia stream that is one of just thirteen places on Earth where the species survives. Everyone agreed that pipeline construction upstream would dump a deadly amount of sediment into the mussels' habitat. So, the agency let Dominion's contractors relocate sixty-eight clubshells to a private hatchery. Every single one died.[32]

"That catastrophic blunder for me sums up the dereliction of every federal agency with respect to this project," Gerken said.

By the end of 2018, Keystone XL, Mountain Valley, and Atlantic Coast—the three biggest pipeline projects in the country—were all stalled due to successful legal challenges and sustained grassroots opposition. Senator Joe Manchin and much of the Republican Party complained loudly and bitterly that these legal tangles were keeping America from building much-needed infrastructure. They called for "permitting reform"—a shorthand for making it easier to build fossil fuel projects and making it harder to bring any kind of legal challenges against them.

But this rhetoric obscured a troubling fact: the question of whether these projects served the public interest had never been fully examined on the merits.

For three years, Greg Buppert and his colleagues had been building what Gerken described as "one of the best records for why a pipeline isn't necessary that's ever been brought to bear" in federal court. Gerken's team had achieved its mission: stopping the ACP freight train long enough so Buppert's team would have a chance to put a higher-stakes question before the federal courts. Were the tracks running in the direction the country needs to go, or was the gas building boom one long, disastrous detour?

Chapter Nine

The Limits of Disturbance

On a rain-soaked fall morning in 2018, a farmer named Dale Angle woke to find two 80-foot sections of steel pipe sitting in his cornfield in southwest Virginia. The next day, he answered his phone to find officials from the Mountain Valley Pipeline on the line with a request: Could they come onto his property to collect their pipes?

He told them he'd think it over. "I said I couldn't do it right now," he told a local reporter. "They've done destroyed enough of my property. I'm not going to let them do it again."

Angle had fought to deny MVP access to his land, but it had been seized through eminent domain. He complained that runoff from construction had been harming his farm operation for months. "They talk about soil and sediment and erosion control. All they do is dump it on the landowner," Angle said. "They haven't done any controlling."[1]

For those living in the path of the Atlantic Coast Pipeline farther north, Angle's muddy fields were a vision of a possible future to come. The two pipelines had been twins at birth, announced on the same day in 2014, approved by FERC on the same day in 2017, even originating in the same county in West Virginia. At 303 miles, the MVP was half

ACP's length, but they were both ambitious projects cutting through similarly difficult, ecologically sensitive, mountainous terrain.

Construction was further along on the MVP. Some landowners on its route were already taking steps that those in Nelson County had only contemplated, like the mother-and-daughter team who had sat in homemade tree stands on their own land for weeks, in defiance of police and chainsaw-wielding contractors milling around below, until a federal court order brought them down.[2] And the damage from MVP's construction so far had been worse than anyone had expected—bad enough that Virginia's attorney general had sued the Mountain Valley Pipeline for more than three hundred violations of state environmental regulations. Company officials blamed it all on "unforeseeable" weather and "unprecedented rains" that summer and fall.[3]

The pipes in Angle's fields had been sitting alongside an open trench. When the waters carried them off, one pipe traveled 1,000 feet before wedging against some trees. Both had floated well beyond the line of wooden stakes in the ground with the letters "L O D" scrawled on them. Those letters stand for "limits of disturbance"—a legal term of art used to mark out the legally permissible extent of the land that construction activity may directly alter, the idea being that any damage could be corralled within the invisible lines between them.

In the real world, of course, disturbance is not so easily contained.

The Accidental Activists

When Jill Averitt saw those stakes marked "L O D" in the woods near her own home, popping up like some new invasive species among the towering oaks, she made a point of imagining no disturbance at all.

It was her coping strategy: visualizing the Atlantic Coast Pipeline changing nothing. But by 2019, the unbuilt pipeline had seeped into nearly every corner of her life all the same. For over three years, the Averitts had been fighting to keep surveyors off their land and contesting the constitutionality of ACP's use of eminent domain in federal court. Now they were bracing for the possibility of "quicktake." Her husband Richard had a different daily visualization routine: picturing how it would all go down when the bulldozers and chainsaws came, and he would be arrested for standing in their way.[4]

Like many of their neighbors, the Averitts were accidental activists. They had moved to Nelson County in 2005 from North Carolina with plans to make a homestead for their extended clans. They had chosen their 135 acres carefully, settling on a spot that they felt confident would be safe from future development—whether it was highways, roads, or subdivisions. The plan was to build a family compound on adjacent properties: Richard, Jill, and their kids in one house, Richard's sister Dawn and the family she planned to have next door in another, and their parents spending part of the year in a smaller house nearby. "We were setting up for good," said Richard.

The dream of a family compound was also a kind of hedge against the unknown: Dawn had lived with HIV/AIDS since being diagnosed in 1988. In 2002, she and Richard had cofounded the Well Project, a nonprofit that worked to improve HIV prevention and treatment access for women around the world. She was healthy, but things could change. They wanted to maximize their time together, to draw the safety net of family tight.

Before long, the dream had come true. Jill's sister moved there too. Seven kids roamed freely in the woods between the homes that the extended family had built across four adjoining parcels. Then, in February 2015, they got the same letter that Wisteria Johnson and Will Fenton had received. They learned that the ACP would come within 150 feet of Dawn's house and straight through another commercial parcel they owned about a mile away. *You've got to be kidding me*, Richard thought.

"It was naïve, but we thought, 'There's no way they can just take your land. Surely this can't happen.'" Then came the FERC hearing at the high school in March 2015, when Nelsonians had three minutes to speak into the voice recorder—the one that produced a garbled transcript and widespread outrage. That was a turning point for the Averitts.

"We realized that they don't play fair," he said. "This was different than we thought. We all just felt we were screaming at the ocean."

So, they turned their focus to local elected officials instead. Thus began their education, as relative newcomers to Virginia, about the extent of Dominion's influence. As they researched the campaign contribution history of the company, they found its tentacles seemed to reach everywhere. "Every single one of the people we were talking to" took money from Dominion, Jill said. Richard started hounding county leaders, state legislators, and members of Congress. He called many out in public for accepting Dominion's contributions—which didn't make him many friends. "I was visibly angry at every public meeting," he said.

Richard has the high-energy, forthright, generally sunny disposition of the serial entrepreneur that he is—but he admits to an inability to mince his words. "I pushed the boundaries along the way to make sure I got a chance to say my piece," he acknowledged. "I was just built that way. I just wasn't afraid of these people. I have a kind of philosophical principle to my upbringing that says people in government work for us. That's the way it's supposed to work."

His relentlessness got him meetings with just about every politician he could think of: Senators Tim Kaine and Mark Warner, state senators, the governor. He even cornered the Republican candidate for governor in 2017 in the men's room at the Homestead Resort (owned by West Virginia's coal baron governor) to secure a meeting.

"I got to every single one of them," he said. "I pissed them off, but I never quit. [Some] said things like 'You can't stop Dominion in Virginia.' The things they said made your blood boil from a constitutional principled perspective."

That was the perspective that he initially brought to battling the pipeline: property rights. Richard's father had been a Marine Corps colonel during the Vietnam War and, later, a successful financial executive. Growing up, theirs was a conservative household, with a "don't draw a line in front of me" mentality, Richard said. But as time went on, their reasons for fighting the project spread beyond that narrow property rights lens, as they began linking arms with more of their neighbors.

The commercial land they owned nearby straddled Spruce Creek, a trout stream that rose on the mountain above near Reeds Gap—the same mountain facing the Fenton Inn. The Averitts had been planning to develop the 100-acre parcel, near a popular cidery and a brewery, into an eco-resort in 2014, hoping to create dozens of permanent jobs. The ACP right-of-way cut straight through the middle of the land.

In April 2017, they received a letter from Doyle Land Services on behalf of Dominion offering them $113,180 for the easement. Their response was to turn the grove into a pipeline fighters training camp instead.[5]

Throughout October 2018, they hosted hundreds of fellow pipeline resisters on the banks of Spruce Creek for a series of weekend workshops, trainings, and pep rallies. Where they had once envisioned a boutique hotel, now Greenpeace activists were giving trainings in direct action protests for retirees and gardeners and innkeepers and professors and farmers and entrepreneurs who had never contemplated chaining themselves to a piece of heavy machinery.

The Averitts were energized by the turnout. They decided to host more gatherings the following spring. There was another reason too. "It felt like any day the court would let them cut trees," Richard said.

He woke each morning wondering if it would be the day he went to jail. They were hearing that Dominion was preparing to appeal to the Supreme Court and lobbying Congress to pass a rider authorizing the ACP's crossing of the Appalachian Trail at Reeds Gap as a plan B. There was even speculation that maybe President Trump would try to force the whole project through by fiat. That sounded pretty unconstitutional, but then again, so did the entire venture to the Averitts. There was strength in numbers. If it came to that, the Spruce Creek camps would be a kind of dry run for the real thing: putting their bodies in front of the excavators.

CSI: Blue Ridge

At the end of March, as the Averitts prepared to host another camp at Spruce Creek, a handful of drone enthusiasts gathered down on the banks of the Rockfish River. On a wide, flat field just below the Averitts' land, where gliders took off to give tourists rides over the Blue Ridge, the group flew their drones and talked shop about how to get good images of open trenches and stream silt fences. They were there to practice maneuvering their unmanned aerial vehicles over the ACP route as volunteers for the Compliance Surveillance Initiative.[6]

Rick Webb and his Allegheny–Blue Ridge Alliance colleagues had launched CSI—named with a nod to the popular TV police procedural show, though Webb had initially and cheekily wanted to call it "Crime Scene Investigation"—to keep tabs on how well Dominion's construction matched its "Best in Class" pledges.

"The idea was to communicate to Dominion's board of directors they were facing a new level of public scrutiny," Webb said.

It was perhaps the most comprehensive and sophisticated citizen-led effort to watchdog the construction of a pipeline in real time that had ever been assembled. Volunteers monitored construction on foot where they could. For steep spots that couldn't be easily accessed, they had the Pipeline Air Force, a small cadre of drone operators and volunteer pilots in two-seater planes mounted with special cameras. If they found a possible violation—like sediment pouring into streams and drinking water sources—they would report it. Their team of digital mapping wizards would put their findings online for anyone to see, in a searchable tool with time, date, and location stamped on thousands of aerial photographs, all overlaid with Dominion's own construction documents for the entire route.

"They thought we were just hillbillies," Webb said with a laugh. "We're living in the modern age, folks. We have capabilities that only the CIA had thirty years ago."[7] On top of that, they even had a volunteer who *was* a former CIA image analyst helping to pore over their photos.

Earlier that month, Webb had presented what the CSI had unearthed so far to an ABRA workshop. The team had taken thousands of high-resolution snapshots. Webb walked the audience through images of muddy ponds alongside open trenches, sediment spilling into waterways, and excavation apparently underway before legally required erosion controls had been installed. They had submitted evidence of twenty-two violations to West Virginia environmental regulators, triggering inspections.[8]

"None of the environmental agencies have met their responsibilities," he told the gathering. The public's appointed guardians seemed to be asleep at the switch, so CSI was doing its work for them. "It's a case study of regulatory dysfunction," Webb concluded.[9]

The Ballad of Bob Orndorff

From Dominion's perspective, it was a case of regulatory overreach—and a source of consternation.

On public lands, the Atlantic Coast Pipeline remained stymied. About 39 miles of trees had been felled in Virginia. But progress was further along in West Virginia with 47 miles of construction activity and 23 miles of pipeline already laid. The Mountain State's physical topography was daunting, but it offered much friendlier political terrain.

So, while the company waited for its appeals to move through the courts and for federal agencies to revise their homework, a longtime Dominion lobbyist named Bob Orndorff traveled to Charleston with a proposal for state legislators: they should pass a formal resolution to condemn organizations—like ABRA and SELC—that opposed the Atlantic Coast Pipeline.

"I think it's important for the Legislature to stand up to these rogue environmental groups to say, 'You're going to impact our economy in West Virginia, you're going to impact job growth in West Virginia,'" Orndorff told the legislators. "Do a resolution supporting condemning them."[10]

He found a receptive audience. In early March, West Virginia delegates overwhelmingly approved House Resolution 11 on "recognizing the importance of the Atlantic Coast Pipeline." The resolution sang the praises of natural gas while calling out specific groups of citizens seeking redress under the law, accusing them of launching "attacks" and "assaults" on much-needed infrastructure.[11]

For four years, Bill Anderson—its lead sponsor and Republican chair of the energy committee—had refused to advance *another* proposed bill, sponsored by Barbara Fleischauer, a Democratic delegate. Her bill sought to expand the "limit of disturbance" around gas drilling operations, requiring a wider buffer zone from nearby homes. She pointed to constituents' experience of living next to wells so loud it was hard to sleep, breathing dust from nonstop truck traffic, watching their property values decline. Each year, she reintroduced her bill; each year it never made it out of the energy committee. In early 2019, she introduced it one more time, pushing to increase the LOD from 625 feet to 1,500 feet away from the nearest home. Fleischauer knew it would fail again. Nobody seemed interested. "You're the first person to ask me about it," she told one reporter.[12]

Anderson, the committee chair, explained his opposition by pointing out that "people in the community need to understand the needs of the industry, if we're going to have the benefits in terms of jobs."[13] It was one of the oldest of political tropes: the supposed trade-off between environmental protection and jobs. Sure, everyone wanted clean air and water. But people had to put food on the table, didn't they?

The familiar signs greeting anyone driving into the state read, "Welcome to Wild and Wonderful West Virginia."[14] But the imperatives of industry usually won out. Invoking jobs was the ultimate trump card in a state that ranked forty-seventh out of fifty in GDP per capita and suffered from steady population decline and a widespread sense among young people that economic opportunities mostly lay outside its borders.

The Atlantic Coast Pipeline had promised to generate thousands of jobs. Local leaders knew well enough that they wouldn't last. In April 2019, Brittany Moody, the engineer who had designed the original route in a little over a week, confirmed as much when she estimated the ACP would create four thousand temporary construction jobs but only a couple dozen permanent ones.[15] The shale boom had made fortunes for people like Aubrey McClendon and Toby Rice, the young CEO of fracking giant EQT, whose spinoff company Equitrans Midstream was behind the Mountain Valley Pipeline. But the boom offered an ephemeral economic sugar high to just about everyone else.[16]

The mayor of Marlinton, West Virginia, summed up the thinking of many peers when he welcomed the pipeline's path through his county all the same. "The Hoover Dam, Golden Gate Bridge and Alaskan Pipeline were all temporary jobs," he wrote in his weekly column in the local paper. "What are we going to do with this opportunity? Even if you see this project as a lemon, you should see the opportunity to 'make lemonade!'"[17] Temporary jobs were better than no jobs.

Against this background of economic stagnation, Dominion had been mounting a local charm offensive in the West Virginia counties where the pipeline would begin its 600-mile journey. Its charitable arm made donations to libraries, bookmobiles, outdoor education pro-grams, local civic groups, and fire departments. In Randolph County, its employees repaired roads washed out by flash floods, helped scour mud out of homes, and provided cleaning supplies, ice machines, and portable toilets. In Lewis County, Dominion employees helped en-large a school playground. In Pocahontas County, they donated $1,000 to support local library literacy programs and $1,500 to sponsor the county's famous "Roadkill Cook-off."

Bob Orndorff was a frequent guest at these events—and an even more familiar presence in the state capitol. It would later be revealed, in fact, that Orndorff had written the resolution recognizing the im-portance of his employer's pipeline himself. And that, a week before the vote, Orndorff had taken five Republican delegates out to dinner at an Italian restaurant. All five lawmakers cosponsored the resolution.

Orndorff saw nothing improper in either drafting the resolution or wining and dining lawmakers: it was standard practice. "I take delegates out to dinner all the time," he said. "I don't think there's a correlation between me feeding them and passing a resolution. It's relationship-building."

The relationship-building was strong enough that, when Orndorff retired from his post as Dominion's state policy director later that year, he was replaced by one of the delegates who cosponsored his resolution against "rogue" citizens groups.

But not everyone in West Virginia's capital was swayed by Dominion's largesse.

"Who are the real rogues?" asked the editorial board of the state's largest newspaper, the *Charleston Gazette-Mail*. Blaming environmen-talists, they contended, was "dishonest and simply wrong."

It is not a "rogue" action to hold companies and government agen-cies accountable to the minimal rules in place to protect quality of life. West Virginia has suffered enough of industry run amok. . . . These groups trying to protect their rights are made up of actual West Virginians who want to preserve what they have and avoid being steamrolled by big industry. Their government should be watching out for them, but it's not, so the only way to stand up for themselves is through the courts.[18]

Hung Up in the Mountains

On a Saturday morning in April 2019, several dozen Nelsonians drove onto the Averitts' grassy field near Spruce Creek.

Volunteers set up tarps for shade, a first aid station, a table with a water cooler. Another table was strewn with fact sheets tallying the economic and climate damage that would be wrought by the pipeline if it were ever built. A banner flapped from a simple plywood shelter with a message that captured the prevailing mood: "PROTECT AND DEFEND."

Once Richard Averitt stood up to welcome the assembled activists—most of retirement age, with a couple dozen millennials peppered among them, sitting in folding camp chairs—the vibe morphed from that of a weekend farmers' market into the charged focus of a rebel army outpost.

Averitt gave a summary of where they all stood. He pointed up toward the crest of the Blue Ridge, where—despite the tree felling exercise a year prior—Dominion was as thwarted in its crossing as John Lederer had been 350 years before.

There were only three ways, he said, that the ACP could get across the parkway and the Appalachian Trail. One: if the Supreme Court took up the case and ruled in their favor. Two: if Dominion succeeded in its efforts to lobby Congress to authorize the crossing. Three: if President Trump forced through all the approvals ACP needed by edict. "It's clearly illegal to do that," Averitt said. "But that doesn't seem to stop him." (That same week, Trump had issued two executive orders to promote fast-track reviews of pipelines and gas export terminals.[19])

Then he described how his own family's thinking about pipelines had evolved beyond their initial focus on eminent domain and property rights.

"Had Dominion started this project by saying 'We won't use eminent domain, we'll negotiate our way to the coast,' I probably wouldn't be in this fight today," Averitt admitted. "And I regret that, because I think that I now know enough to know there are many other reasons to not want this pipeline."[20]

Many of his neighbors nodded; they knew what he meant. Earlier that week, several of them had attended oral arguments in a federal courthouse in downtown Charlottesville, in the case of *Atlantic Coast Pipeline, LLC v. Nelson County Board of Supervisors*.

That case could be traced all the way back to Vicki Wheaton's long quest to fulfill her promise to Tinker Bryant. Citing the updated floodplain ordinance that she had spent years advocating, the Nelson zoning board had denied ACP's application for variances to cross 11 streams and floodplains back in December. Three days later, Nelson County became the first locality in the pipeline's path to be sued by ACP LLC.

Now, a federal judge was weighing in on whether a single county had the power to stop the pipeline in its tracks—and he appeared skeptical.

"Of all the different agencies approving the Atlantic Coast Pipeline, the Nelson board of zoning adjustment can say no?" Judge Norman Moon had scoffed at the hearing. "Why should one small dot on the map control the whole route?" After some more back and forth with the county's attorney, he posed the question again. "Why should Nelson County get the last word?"

"The federal government is holding them up, not Nelson County," she replied. "If those permits are not reinstated, they can't cross *any* floodplain." Almost as an aside, she added, "The process works, it has already made it a safer route."

The response from ACP's attorney was telling. "The question of safety is irrelevant, your Honor," he said, prompting audible gasps in the courtroom.[21]

The case—which basically pitted the federal Natural Gas Act of 1938 against the National Flood Insurance Act of 1968—would ultimately be decided in Dominion's favor. And despite Nelson's supervisors' defiant stand, the imperative of getting more gas to more burner tips would trump the imperative of protecting communities from the increasingly extreme weather fueled in part by all that burning.

So, on that April day on the banks of Spruce Creek, fresh off being called "one small dot on the map" whose safety was "irrelevant," the Nelsonians meeting on the Averitts' land—just a quarter mile distant from the spot where Camille's floodwaters had swept away two people sleeping in their homes on the banks of the Rockfish River[22]—were fired up. Their gathering was part strategy session, part pep talk, fueled by nearly half a decade's accumulated outrage.

Late in the afternoon, after a series of rain showers had passed through, Tom Hadwin rose to close out the day's agenda. "Okay, so here's the Atlantic Coast Pipeline," said the courtly former utility executive, pointing at the ACP route on a posterboard map. "We talked about how it's getting hung up coming from West Virginia through the mountains, for all the legal reasons that were discussed earlier," Hadwin continued. "Dominion sees that it's hung up. And they are *stunned* by this."

Several people cheered. "I've talked to people who worked at Dominion," Hadwin continued. "They said, 'We didn't expect any of this.'"

Like a general rallying his troops along a long battlefront, Hadwin exhorted everyone to focus on Buckingham County and communities farther southeast. Dominion, he said, wanted to start construction on that leg of the pipeline later that year. "It goes through African American communities, a lot of Native American communities, it's a rural area where energy companies typically like to go because there's not a lot of money to oppose them. We need to help them."

Joyce Burton asked Hadwin what he thought Dominion was going to do next.

"Investors are asking tough questions about this," he replied. "They are being hammered, telling investors it will all work out." Every day of delay brought rising costs and ratcheted up pressure from shareholders, he added.

"Dominion has been great at controlling the narrative," said Hadwin. "It's all about 'jobs and keeping the lights on.' Dominion has the best lobbyists. . . . They are determined. But Dominion is surprised that their playbook isn't working."

The Forever Fuel

"It's been a very frustrating process," Tom Farrell confessed to Greg the bank analyst a few weeks later on Dominion's quarterly earnings call.

The ACP needed its permits—and soon. But Farrell saw a path

forward: he suggested that Dominion would soon appeal the Fourth Circuit's ruling on the Forest Service permit to the Supreme Court. He was confident the court would take the case, thanks to an intervention from the Trump administration's solicitor general. (Bill Barr had recently resigned from Dominion Energy's board, after serving on it for nearly a decade, to become Trump's attorney general.) But in case that didn't pan out, he hinted at other options—a likely reference to congressional approval of the crossing at Reeds Gap.

But, as Tom Hadwin had observed, the delays were shaking the confidence of investors. A couple months earlier, Moody's Investors Service had rated the Atlantic Coast Pipeline "credit negative" due to the Fourth Circuit's rulings. Dominion had just added half a billion dollars to the estimated price tag of the project. Industry analysts were pointing out that these hikes would raise the price of ACP's gas well above the rates offered by existing pipelines. They suggested that, consequently, only one pipeline—the Mountain Valley Pipeline or the ACP—would get built, but likely not both.[23]

Another analyst followed up to ask Farrell if going through private lands to cross the Appalachian Trail was an option for ACP if the court decisions didn't go their way. And why didn't they consider that to begin with?

This second-guessing seemed to annoy the CEO. Farrell had a reputation as a disciplined leader with a temper—he was known to icily stare down messengers of unwelcome news in meetings—and a core belief that his company's noble service to society was generally underappreciated.[24]

His answer offered a glimpse of the consternation level in Dominion's C-suite. "As I've said, there are lots of alternatives. And we just don't think it's useful at this time to talk about them. I appreciate the frustration level. Believe me. One thing Greg said about how he thinks the investor community is as frustrated as we are, I'm not sure that that's a possibility."[25]

While they nervously eyed Dominion's pipeline permitting problems, Wall Street analysts were bullish on the company's other big gas venture: Cove Point. Just a few weeks earlier, Farrell had gone on CNBC to tell the colorful TV host Jim Cramer about the company's efforts to capitalize on surging foreign demand for American gas. He had good news: "We are sold out of LNG for twenty years to India and the Japanese."[26]

At least one commodities analyst writing for a popular financial website liked what he heard.

"Dominion offers a bullish trading pattern and sexy dividend," he wrote. In the old days, the analyst observed, gas demand peaked in the winter as people fired up their furnaces and slumped after March. But the sheer volume of Marcellus methane (coupled with ever warmer winters) had upended that traditional ebb-and-flow of the gas market: supply was now conjuring new sources of demand. Dominion, he added, was nicely positioned to profit twice over from that gusher of fossil gas: as both a consumer (in its power business) and an exporter (via Cove Point).[27]

Circa 2019, more than two hundred new gas-fired power plants were either planned or under construction around the country, with a combined capacity that was almost equal to the total amount of electricity generated in the state of Texas. Thousands of miles of new gas pipelines were planned for the Appalachian Basin alone—even though demand for heat and electricity was flat or declining in much of the country.[28] But the industry was banking that the new "bridge" might just be a tanker ship. A decade after Aubrey McClendon advised Cheniere's CEO to send gas in the other direction, liquefied natural gas exports had become the biggest source of projected long-term growth in demand for US natural gas. And all those new facilities would need pipelines to supply them.[29]

Since 2016, FERC had been flooded with new proposals for LNG terminals along the Gulf Coast—many of them right next to majority Black and low-income communities. New firms with blandly forward-looking names like Venture Global and NextDecade sought to replicate Cheniere's and Dominion's success. To deal with this surge of interest, FERC planned to open a new office in Houston dedicated solely to reviewing LNG applications.[30]

Cheap shale gas was now a geopolitical tool too. That May, as the Department of Energy granted approval for yet another new liquefied gas project in Texas, one senior official referred to LNG in the announcement as "freedom gas"; another said the move would allow "for molecules of U.S. freedom to be exported to the world."[31]

In the Trump era, gas executives seemed more emboldened than ever to stop pretending that the future belonged to renewables—or that gas would one day graciously cede the stage. Executives at the American Gas Association and American Petroleum Institute had been test-driving a more durable replacement for the "bridge" metaphor: "Natural gas is a foundation fuel for prosperity around the world."[32] The nation's top liquefied natural gas company had an even more grandiose vision.

"We want to make natural gas more than a bridge fuel," said Cheniere's CEO at an industry conference earlier in 2019, "to make sure that gas has a meaningful role not only today, not only in 20 years, but forever."[33]

Some executives seemed miffed that grassroots and environmental groups had taken their old metaphor too literally. That June, a Dominion senior vice president named Donald Raikes gave a speech at a shale gas industry conference aptly titled DUG East (for Developing Unconventional Gas) in Pittsburgh. He cued up a slide with an image of a long bridge twisting across a bay.

"I called my presentation A Bridge Too Far, because it's ironic that these same groups—these environmental groups that have made us public enemy number one—ten years ago, were singing the praises of this industry," said Raikes, sounding like a jilted lover. "They were singing the praises of this industry because they saw natural gas as a key—as a bridge to renewables. They saw us as a bridge to get coal out and bring natural gas in."[34]

Raikes tried to rally his audience—full of other major players in the Marcellus and Utica shales—to fight back against growing public suspicion that the costs of natural gas might outweigh its benefits. He quoted the French novelist Victor Hugo: "You have enemies? Why, it is the story of every man who has done a good deed or created a new idea." The good news, he continued, was that the industry had the "facts on our side." For example: "the rise and success of natural gas has brought dramatic benefits to the environment."

"The *environment*!" Raikes shouted for emphasis.

He then offered up the Atlantic Coast Pipeline as a prime example. It was at risk from a well-funded and sophisticated opposition that, he said, was misleading the public about the risks of the project. He shared a vignette about an unnamed candidate for public office in Virginia who had concerns about the pipeline.

"We went and met with them, went through the slide deck, showed them the route, talked about the benefits, talked about the reason," he said. "Showed them what the pipeline would look like. They said, 'Okay show me the pipeline.' We said, 'Well, this is the pipeline. They said, 'No show me the pipeline.' They were starting to get upset. Because they thought we were hiding something. They did not realize, because of that press, that the pipeline was actually underground."

"People aren't aware," Raikes concluded his tale ruefully. "We have to get the facts out."

A Question of Values

If anyone in rural Virginia might have been inclined to give Dominion the benefit of the doubt, the family of John Ed Purvis fit the bill.

"Our natural affiliation would have been with the people who are like, 'What are people making all this fuss about?'" said Martha Purvis Smith. "We would not have examined it like we did."

They had disdained protests against other pipelines. From afar, those projects seemed like the engines of economic bounty and energy independence that the industry always promised they would be. "Before the Atlantic Coast Pipeline," she added, "this is me with the Keystone Pipeline: 'What is wrong with those people? Why aren't they letting that through? All those jobs!'"

"I was too," said her sister Elizabeth, nodding.

"I now have a different perspective on the Keystone Pipeline, which I would have never had if it hadn't been for this [experience]," Martha said.

Yet few people ever notice. . . . They, however, had seen too much. As they learned more about what the pipeline might mean for their communities, it just didn't seem worth all the disturbance. Ever since her father first got his letter about the project in May 2014, Martha had settled on her own metaphor to describe the Atlantic Coast Pipeline: "The pipeline was like a bad person."

"Good people bear up over the years—you like them better over time," she elaborated. But prolonged and close exposure to certain people can be, let's face it, disillusioning. "If the longer you know someone, the less you like them, then you should pay attention to that."

"It was love bombing you in the beginning," she said of the ACP. "Taxes and jobs and 'this is gonna be great.' They made you feel like this was going to be the best thing ever. But the more you learned about it, the more you were like, 'No this is *terrible.*'" As time went on, they became convinced the whole thing was about profit—not keeping the lights on. "It just did not bear up under scrutiny at all."[35]

Martha and Elizabeth found their sympathies aligning with those landowners—Indigenous residents and white ranchers alike—who had fought Keystone XL, and with fellow Virginians fighting the Mountain Valley Pipeline farther south. And with central Virginia neighbors who they might otherwise never have encountered.

After the route shifted away from their land, the Purvis family stayed involved in the fight. Martha, a lawyer, volunteered to help advise those fighting in court to keep surveyors off their land. They went to meetings about Dominion's plans to site a compressor station in nearby Union Hill and came away impressed by the resolve of residents like John Laury, an outspoken ACP opponent whose ancestors had helped settle that community after Emancipation. Elizabeth went to Friends of Nelson meetings and reported back to her father, who was eager to hear the latest developments about rallies and court hearings, even as his health was failing.

In February 2019, John Ed passed away on his wedding anniversary. He had remained steadfastly opposed to the pipeline until the end.

David and Judy Matthews, who lived above Davis Creek, had gone to school with the Purvis children. David's father Curtis, a well-known local banjo player and logger, had known John Ed well. Dominion's tactics in Nelson County had moved the Matthewses to reconsider some long-held views about energy and politics too.

Judy couldn't help thinking about that night at the high school for the FERC meeting in March 2015, watching the older generation—people like John Ed Purvis and Wisteria Johnson—forced to get up and share their fears for their children and the land. "To the point where they literally broke down and cried, they couldn't get their words out," she recalled. It infuriated her.

After seven months of sleepless nights and negotiations, the Matthewses had signed an easement in 2016. "We got pretty close to fair compensation," David said, for the easement. But they felt that Dominion had taken advantage of some of their neighbors. "Some people got almost nothing." Judy didn't bear her employer of over thirty years any ill will. "But I have a lot of lost respect," she said. "It was totally unethical."[36]

Meanwhile, some of their more liberal neighbors rose in their estimation. Whenever Joyce Burton called to ask if she could bring soil scientists or reporters onto their land, to see the right-of-way on the steep slopes of Roberts Mountain above, the Matthewses didn't hesitate. "We rolled out the red carpet for them," David said. With Judy still working for Dominion, it was a way, they said, to quietly help the cause. David observed with a laugh that he and Burton were likely on opposite ends of the political spectrum, but she would always be welcome at their home.

"Joyce Burton is directly responsible for me becoming more sympathetic to the Mountain Valley Pipeline people," he added, because it showed they weren't just being NIMBYs. He was impressed that many Friends of Nelson members fought so hard, even though the pipeline wasn't coming through their land. His thinking changed in other ways too; initially, environmental impacts weren't much on his radar.

"But when I started realizing the terrain they were going through and what could happen to it, and Judy's fear of living near the blast zone, I got a lot more environmentally friendly in my thought processes." David, who had narrowly escaped Camille's floodwaters as a ten-year-old boy, had a confident prediction if a similar event ever hit the buried pipeline: "That thing is going to fold up like an accordion."

But few in Nelson County had seen Dominion's methods as up close and personal as Will and Lilia Fenton. Throughout the first half of 2019, they remained locked in a legal battle with Dominion over how to measure the value of what they had built up on the mountain—and how to reckon the costs of the drilling-related disturbance to come.

Dominion sent appraisers and subpoenaed receipts from every aspect of their business, along with building permits and zoning records. Will sat through three depositions, the first almost eight hours long. (To get in the right frame of mind, he ate the breakfast he used to eat before weightlifting competitions.) The last one was on April 9, the day after the hearing in ACP's lawsuit against Nelson County over the floodplain issue. To prepare for that one, Fenton attended those arguments, so he could get a sense of the layout of the building where his own trial would happen. (He also prepped by watching a scene in the film *The Last Samurai* where Tom Cruise gets whacked again and again with a wooden sword and keeps getting up.)[37]

In various motions and hearings leading up to the trial, Dominion's lawyers had argued that round-the-clock drilling and truck hauling would have minimal effects on the Fentons' business. The two sides jousted over which testimony from expert witnesses—on nighttime light pollution, on noise and vibration levels, on hotel valuations and appraisals—should be admitted for jurors to see. The thing that galled Fenton most was being told that his business had little value.

"Our business did well from the very beginning," Fenton told me. "Each day, people would come here, hand me money, tell me my work is amazing, say such nice things. I couldn't enjoy it. I was going to depositions telling me this place is worthless."[38]

At a key hearing in June, Dominion's lawyers argued before presiding judge Norman Moon that, in weighing fair compensation, jurors shouldn't be allowed to consider future plans for the inn. "What it is zoned for is a bed and breakfast, but they don't even meet that," the McGuireWoods attorney said. "It's a transient lodging facility," he added.[39]

Dominion's attorney asked for more time to depose Fenton yet again. Under questioning by Judge Moon, the Fentons' attorney admitted that he hadn't formally notified Dominion's lawyers earlier that winter that Fenton was putting together a valuation on the inn as part of the "discovery" process before the trial. Judge Moon called that

move "misleading" and then decided on the spot not to admit *any* of
Will Fenton's testimony. He would not be allowed to speak to the value
of what he had built—his life's dream.

The hearing continued, as the two sides hashed out details for the
next week's trial and whether the jury should get a chance to view
the spot Dominion sought to condemn, and the Fenton Inn too. Will
Fenton listened as the two sides sparred over these logistics. And it
began to dawn on him that none of it mattered. If he couldn't speak to
the full value of his property and business both now and in the future,
then their case had already collapsed.

The Fentons decided to settle. Two days later, the trial was canceled.
After four years of fighting, Dominion could keep throwing money
and their lawyers' time at it. The Fentons could not. They tapped out.

That was painful enough. But on top of all the legal expenses,
Fenton dwelled on what he might have done with all the time he had
poured into the fight. All the late nights, meetings, letters and phone
calls with all the different government agencies, all the depositions and
court hearings. He couldn't tally up the hours, but he figured that, in all
that time, he could have built a 3,000-square-foot home by himself.[40]

In October, the settlement was finalized. ACP LLC dropped its
suit against Fenton Family Holdings LLC. And that month the
Fentons got more bad news: the US Supreme Court had agreed to
hear Dominion's appeal, thus raising the odds they could cross Reeds
Gap—and start drilling right next door—without special permission
from Congress.

"I never had hope," Fenton said. "I just decided to fight to the end.
I worried hope would leave or be broken. I knew determination would
not be taken. Even if we lost, the fight was worth it."[41]

The Activated Virginians

Early on, one of Richard Averitt's close friends, a lawyer, had given him
some advice that he thought about often in the ensuing years.

"Practically speaking, you have very little chance of beating this
thing," the friend told him. "That doesn't mean you shouldn't fight. If
you decide to fight, you have to decide you're going all the way to the

mat. Every day you'll feel like you're just pissing in the ocean. Because you'll never, ever see a crack until the day they quit. You'll never know if you're winning or not. Until the day they shut it down."[42]

By the fall of 2019, the Averitts were one of just two families in Nelson County who refused to negotiate. They had the financial means to press on—but also the determination. Will Fenton admired them not just for carrying on their own fight but for their unflagging conviction that, whatever happened to individual landowners, they could all still prevail in the larger fight. Whenever he ran into Jill at Friends of Nelson events, she never seemed to waver in her faith that the pipeline would never be built, that the land between and beyond the LOD stakes would remain intact.

Yet Jill Averitt, too, thought about the time cost and how hard it was to measure. About their kids' school events and soccer games they had missed while going to pipeline meetings and hearings—about having to defend the family's dream of having time together, with Richard's sister Dawn and her kids, instead of *enjoying* that time. But they had gained something, too, from the disturbance. A wider sense of community—friends and neighbors they might not have encountered, like Joyce Burton—and a new sense of purpose.

As he waited for the quicktake and the cops and the bulldozers, Richard Averitt's coping mechanism was to hold two possible futures at once.

"One is, I know intellectually, the odds of us winning are really small. But I also know, intellectually and emotionally, that at some point, someone will beat a pipeline, and turn the tide of this. And if that's true, then why not here? Why not now? Why can't we be those people and do what it takes?"

To that end, even as the Averitts fought the use of eminent domain in court, they had decided to go on offense—to play "the long game."

A few years earlier, they had gotten involved in a citizen-led effort to pressure candidates in the 2017 elections to reject contributions from Dominion or Virginia's other major utility, Appalachian Power. In that year's voting, thirteen of those candidates won their races for the House of Delegates; several had campaigned loudly on promises to rein in Dominion's influence. ("It was so easy to build a coalition against them," said the movement's founder, citing widespread frustration with the pipeline as a key factor in their success.)[43]

There had long been calls from some quarters in Richmond for tougher oversight of Dominion and tighter curbs on the company's political activities—efforts that always foundered on the shoals of expediency. Some of the new delegates promised to introduce legislation to ban political contributions from regulated monopolies.

Just a few weeks before that 2017 election, in his presentation to fellow gas executives in Arizona, Bruce McKay had lamented the "politicization" of the gas pipeline approval process—a complaint that seemed to be saying, in effect, *Very few people used to notice this stuff.*

In 2018, a new organization called Clean Virginia was launched by a wealthy investment manager and Democratic donor named Michael Bills. The group steadily built out a list of candidates who pledged not to take any contributions from Dominion. One clear outcome of the pipeline fight, said Cassady Craighill, Clean Virginia's communications director at the time, was a more energized and educated electorate. For example, she noted, ordinary citizens were even starting to attend public utility commission hearings on the rates Dominion wanted to charge them—something that never used to happen. "The fact that ACP was a thinly veiled profit grab from day one," she said, "activated a lot of people in Virginia."[44]

In trying to push its pipe through Virginia's mountains, Dominion seemed to have triggered a disturbance that spilled over the boundaries of its chosen route, all the way back to Richmond, and right into its own backyard.

Chapter Ten

The Gas Light Company

The distance from Buckingham County to downtown Richmond is about 80 miles—just an hour and a half's drive on most days. But soon after Chad Oba, Ella Rose, Ada Washington, and John Laury pulled onto Interstate 64, they encountered the worst traffic jam they'd ever seen. By the time they finally pulled up outside the Lewis F. Powell Jr. Courthouse, oral arguments in their case—which would determine whether Dominion Energy would be permitted to build a 58,000-horsepower compressor station on a site just 150 feet from Ella Rose's front door—had already begun.

Oba dropped off her companions and went in search of a place to park. As her friend drove away, Ella Rose took a moment to collect herself. Then she and her two neighbors from the community of Union Hill—founded by formerly enslaved Black Virginians right after Emancipation in 1865—climbed the courthouse steps. Across the street, with its classical façade and stately columns, loomed the State Capitol, home to the General Assembly, the nation's oldest elected legislative body, and, from 1861 to 1865, the capitol of the Confederacy. The courthouse had a similarly checkered history. As the three visitors made their way up to the fourth-floor courtroom where their case,

Friends of Buckingham v. State Air Pollution Control, was being heard by the Fourth Circuit Court of Appeals, they passed chambers that had once served as the war planning room for Confederate leaders and the office of their president, Jefferson Davis.[1]

When Rose and her neighbors tried to enter the courtroom, security guards wouldn't let them in at first, until they discovered that someone had been saving seats for them. The three quickly made their way to the front row.

Their grassroots organization, Friends of Buckingham, was challenging the state's decision to grant an air quality permit for Dominion's proposed compressor station. The group's attorneys— from the Southern Environmental Law Center and the Chesapeake Bay Foundation—were already arguing that Dominion and the Commonwealth of Virginia had failed to fully study the risks posed to them and other residents of Union Hill by the facility's four gas-fired turbines, which would burn 24 hours a day, 365 days a year. The Atlantic Coast Pipeline would need three of those facilities to push methane onward through its 600-mile length: one near its start in West Virginia; one in North Carolina; and one in the middle. For the latter, Dominion chose a spot in the geographic heart of Virginia, in the rolling Piedmont of Buckingham County, whose residents' per capita income was roughly half the state average.[2]

Union Hill was an unincorporated, majority Black community of about a hundred households arrayed in a triangle around two Baptist churches. In January 2019, Virginia's Department of Environmental Quality, acting on the recommendation of the state's air pollution control board, had approved the "suitability" of Dominion's compressor site—squarely in the middle of Union Hill.[3]

That decision had brought Ella Rose and her neighbors to this session of the Fourth Circuit. When Rose sat down, Judge James Wynn Jr. turned toward her.

"And he just fixed his eyes on me when I sat down," she recalled.

Years later, this moment would stand out for Ella Rose.[4] In her view, Dominion had spent years effectively maintaining that her community did not really exist, and the state had more or less agreed. But here, in the heart of Virginia's power center, after five years of fighting for recognition, Ella Rose could not help noticing that a federal judge seemed to be signaling that he *saw* her.

Another unforgettable moment came thirty minutes into the proceedings. The state's attorney rose to rebut the argument that Virginia had failed to adequately study whether Rose's community would suffer "disproportionate harm" from breathing the compressor's pollution.

Ever since the 1980s, when grassroots campaigns and research studies revealed that toxic waste and polluting facilities were disproportionately sited near communities of color across America, the environmental justice movement had turned a moral cause into a practical policy imperative. The federal government was now required to consider environmental justice in its analysis of pipeline siting; Virginia had its own guidelines too. But none of the relevant authorities had designated Union Hill as an "environmental justice community" or studied whether Ella Rose and her neighbors would bear a heavier burden than other county residents.

Chief Judge Roger Gregory seemed incredulous at this. If the state hadn't even bothered to study the difference between what people would inhale in Union Hill and the air breathed by their mostly white neighbors in another part of the county, he mused aloud, then how could it claim to be satisfying the demands of justice?[5]

"We're not just talking about a legal argument," he said, "we're talking about people who breathe and live in communities. I'm asking you now, do you concede that 84 to 85 percent of the people who live in the 1.1 [mile] band of the compressor are people of color, predominantly African Americans? Do you concede that?"

"Your Honor, I have no reason to doubt the validity of the door-to-door study, so yes I would concede that," the state's counsel replied, referring to a household survey that Friends of Buckingham had conducted to show authorities who really lived in Union Hill.

For the casual observer, this moment passed quickly. But the concession was freighted with significance.[6] The state and Dominion had repeatedly asserted that minorities made up less than 40 percent of the community. After years of effectively denying the existence of this overwhelmingly Black community, they had finally been *compelled* to see them.

The Best Laid Plans

Ella Rose had simply wanted to retire in peace.

She had been working almost her whole life. After a long career in food service in the Washington, DC area, at downtown restaurants and then a bustling military base, she was ready to go back to the quiet Virginia countryside of her youth.

Rose and her older sister Merneice had planned to live together in retirement. ("We were peas in a pod.") In 1998, they bought a one-story gray-sided house, surrounded by greenery, just 8 miles from Wingina, the Nelson County hamlet where they were born and raised with their five siblings. But her sister died soon after, and Rose kept working for another decade.[7]

In 2012, she finally moved to the house in Buckingham just across the street from her older brother, who had retired there after serving in the US Navy for thirty years. Rose hadn't married or had children. Her retirement to-do list was short but quite full: see all the national parks; finish visiting all fifty states; spend time with family; and attend St. Hebron's, the congregation of her childhood and the oldest Black church in that part of Virginia.[8]

She had two years to enjoy it before her sister-in-law called with some news: Dominion Energy was planning to build a pipeline nearby.

To someone driving past Ella Rose's home on Route 56, through surrounding tracts of pines and pastures and cornfields, it might seem like a lonely, empty stretch of Virginia. To Dominion's planners, it met all the criteria: mostly rural, near a major road, and right next to the Transco Pipeline. Connecting to Transco meant that ACP's gas could be shipped onward to other customers and end users, including, perhaps, the Cove Point LNG export terminal that the company owned.

But to Ella Rose and her neighbors, it was home. A home that had been hard won, on ground that held a long, painful history.

Buckingham is one of Virginia's dozen or more "burned counties"—places where historical records had been consumed in mysterious fires. On February 23, 1869, the county courthouse burned to the ground. Congress was on the verge of passing the Fifteenth Amendment, prohibiting the denial of a citizen's right to vote "on account of race, color, or previous condition of servitude." The House and Senate had agreed to resolve the versions they had passed just the day before. As the building, designed by Thomas Jefferson in 1822, went up in flames, all its contents—records dating back to 1761, birth and death certificates, land surveys and deeds—were lost too. Arson by aggrieved plantation owners was one suspected but never proven cause.[9]

That event has confounded local historians ever since. In the years after the Civil War, the loss of the records made it more difficult for Black citizens to prove their ownership of land and claim their newly enshrined civil rights. Centuries later, it made it hard to locate and identify the gravesites of those who lived and worked and died before 1869.[10] What survived were some documents in families' possessions and oral histories passed down for generations—stories about ancestors who started businesses and farmed and built homes not far from the plantations where they were once forced to labor.

In August 2015, Dominion spent $2.5 million—more than ten times the area's going rate—to purchase a 68.5-acre wooded parcel in Union Hill.[11] The sellers were a group of absentee owners, including descendants of the original slaveholding families of the Variety Shade plantation, the largest tobacco operation in the county, which dated back to 1798.[12]

The company had already bought another property a few miles south for $225,000, which seemed to meet all the criteria: it was near the Transco Pipeline on a well-maintained road. That parcel was twice as large, mostly wooded, and more sparsely populated than the Variety Shade site.[13]

But Dominion ultimately chose the land next to Ella Rose, in the heart of a community founded by formerly enslaved Virginians immediately after the Civil War, and explained the choice by simply saying it was more "suitable." (Presumably for technical and financial reasons: in its environmental impact statement, FERC had noted that Dominion's other site "would require additional pipeline and would increase the construction footprint of ACP."[14])

Ella Rose had a different theory.

"I was annoyed because they knew this was a predominantly Black neighborhood," she said, and because Dominion "wasn't expecting anyone to fight or say anything."

The Yogis and the Baptists

When Chad Oba first learned about the compressor station, her first thought was concern for her husband. The home they had lived in since 1984 was equidistant from the potential sites Dominion was considering. Oba worked full-time as a mental health counselor, supporting families around the county. But her husband, a stone sculptor and landscaper, worked mostly outdoors. She worried about what he'd be breathing all day.[15]

In the fall of 2014, Oba, who is white, began knocking on the doors of her neighbors, most of whom were Black, to see if they had heard about the project. Ella Rose wasn't at home that day, but the two women met soon after at the Union Hill Baptist Church, when Rose attended an information meeting about the pipeline and found Oba sitting at a table out front with a sign-up sheet.

Oba had also, meanwhile, reached out to some friends who lived a few miles down the road, in another spiritual community that seemed a world apart. Yogaville was an ashram founded by Swami Satchidananda, a yoga master from India who had become famous in the US for opening the Woodstock music festival in 1969 with a "prayer of peace and love." In 1980, he chose 600 rolling acres on the banks of the James River as the site for an ashram dedicated to interfaith understanding—his teaching centered on the idea that many different paths could lead to the same truth. Over time, Yogaville adherents bought land and built houses nearby, and a community sprang up around the ashram and the lotus-shaped shrine at its center.

In the fall of 2014, Oba and a core group of residents from both Yogaville and Union Hill formed Friends of Buckingham. While they shared the concerns of other groups along the ACP's route—about water contamination, landslides, property rights, and fossil fuel dependence—they decided that their organization's focal point would instead be the compressor station.

Other Union Hill residents soon became outspoken members of Friends of Buckingham too. John and Ruby Laury had moved back to the area in 2003 after years of living in California. They tended cattle and grew hay on their 98 acres, a mile from the compressor site.

John, an air force veteran, was preceded by five generations of Laurys in Union Hill; he wondered if his own ancestors might be buried in unmarked graves on the Variety Shade land sold to Dominion.[16]

The Union Hill Baptist Church became the group's de facto headquarters. The church's pastor, Reverend Paul Wilson, had agreed to host that initial information meeting. It would be the first of many, and the beginning of a years-long partnership between the Baptists and the yogis. The two communities hadn't had much interaction prior to the pipeline's announcement. But Pastor Wilson took the unprecedented step of welcoming the Yogaville-ians into his church for strategy meetings that sometimes became joint prayer sessions.[17] Some memorable interfaith scenes ensued. Each meeting started and ended with a prayer led by Wilson. At one point, though, a well-known vocalist was invited to come and perform some Hindu devotional songs. "Everybody was chanting, the church was rocking, it was amazing," Oba recalled, laughing. "Pastor Paul got up and was dancing with his wife. 'This is fine,' he said, 'but I'm a Baptist.'"

Like their neighbors next door in Nelson County, the Friends of Buckingham tried pushing on various doors to see which might open. "We kind of did everything all at once," said Oba. "Whatever popped up in our face that day—respond, respond, respond." They joined the Allegheny–Blue Ridge Alliance and called in to the weekly phone meetings led by Lew Freeman. They went to Richmond for meetings of the State Air Pollution Control Board and State Water Control Board, and they went to Richmond for protests and rallies outside of Dominion's headquarters and the governor's mansion. They pressed Dominion and the county government for details about emergency planning, in the event of a rupture or leak. (Some locals remembered quite well the huge explosion on the Transco gas pipeline that had destroyed two homes in Appomattox, just 20 miles south, back in 2008.) They set up their own well water testing and air monitoring programs in eight homes around the compressor site—to establish a baseline against which future pollution could be measured.[18]

One of the group's biggest concerns were "blowdowns"—periodic events in which operators intentionally vent gas to relieve pressure or perform scheduled maintenance. Blowdowns could take hours, during which noise levels would approach that of a jet taking off. Nobody in the community knew how often that would happen, or what other gases and chemicals would be released into the air along with the vented methane. So, they invited people from other parts of the country who lived next to compressor stations to come and speak about what it was like.

The more they learned, the more they worried about the health and safety risks of living in the facility's shadow: studies of blowdowns in other communities had documented releases of toxic gases like benzene, formaldehyde, and hexane into the surrounding air.

"We became one big family," Oba said wryly, "who don't want to be poisoned to death."

"I Wasn't Going to Leave"

Ella Rose's first thought had been about the noise. One of her great pleasures was watching turkeys, deer, and the occasional bear amble through her yard. She feared the incessant noise would scare away her wild neighbors.[19] And it would, of course, be hard to live with day after day. The noise could wear you down, sap your spirit.

As she learned more, she began to worry about dust from the truck traffic during construction, about breathing in pollutants from the compressor turbines, about her water. Like everyone in that part of Buckingham, she relied on a well. How would she know if it was contaminated?

At first, Rose had some reluctance about speaking out all these fears. She had never been an activist. She wasn't keen on drawing attention to herself. But beyond her concerns about pollution and noise and safety, there was a principle at stake.

"My mother passed away when I was seven," she said. "My father worked for the railroad for forty-odd years. And we were on our own, you know, we had to help each other. That's why I didn't want Dominion to run me from my property. Because that's my brother over there"—she pointed across the street—"and we always looked out for each other."

As she saw it, she had saved for decades to buy this house, near her family, near her childhood home, in the beloved countryside of her youth. Why should *she* have to move?

"It's my home," she said. "I wasn't going to leave."

Sitting in Rose's living room, across from a mantle laden with pictures of her sisters and nieces and nephews and her brother in his navy uniform, Oba looked over at her friend and smiled as she recalled the early days of their relationship.

"Ella repeatedly said to me," Oba said, "'When somebody tells me I can't do something it makes me want to do it.'"

"I know!" Rose laughed. "When they bully me, that makes me stronger, makes me want to fight harder."[20]

That was another source of energy to draw on: wherever she went, Oba was by her side. They lived a mile apart, were separated in age by just a few years, but their paths hadn't crossed until Dominion came knocking. In the course of their joint travels, attending hearing after hearing and rally after rally together, they became close. They took a trip to Boston for a conference and took an extra day to stay with Oba's daughter, who lived nearby. On one of those drives, they discovered that, in their teenage years, they had shared a neighborhood before: Oba grew up near Hartford, Connecticut, not far from a tobacco farm where Rose spent each summer for several years working to save money for school expenses. Oba's siblings had worked on the same farm, as part of the same program.

As the months and years went on, and the protests and meetings and interfaith rallies and official hearings came and went, getting behind a microphone and in front of large crowds became easier. As she spoke out, Rose discovered that support could emerge from surprising corners: "If you help yourself, someone else will fall in and help you."

In the summer of 2016, Dominion applied for a special use permit to build the compressor station, setting in motion a series of hearings by county officials. By then, the Friends of Buckingham had been organizing intensively for nearly two years. But when those hearings were announced, Rose said, "I had to get busy."

She wasn't alone. At the planning commission meeting that September, so many speakers signed up they had to schedule another one.

At the next one in October, about one hundred people turned out again.

And then in December, when the board of supervisors held another meeting to discuss the compressor proposal, more than 150 people turned out.

Pastor Paul Wilson spoke about Dominion's projection that their cash-strapped county stood to gain $8.7 million in tax revenue over its first eight years from hosting the compressor station. "Every county, city, town and state needs money," he said. "I need money, my church needs money. But I sure wouldn't sell my soul to gain the whole world, just for money. So I would like to suggest to you that you be careful of who you go to bed with."[21]

When Ella Rose came to the microphone, she described her fears for her health and water and safety. This, she explained, was not her plan for retirement. When she finished, her neighbors rose and gave her a standing ovation. That display of support, she said, "gave me an incentive to continue to fight."

A few weeks later, in January 2017, the Buckingham board of supervisors held one final meeting on the issue. As she waited for her PowerPoint to appear on the screen, Dominion corporate communications manager Carla Piccard told the packed room that her company operated 106 compressor stations across its vast natural gas storage and transmission system spanning six states. "The Buckingham Station will probably be one of if not *the* best station within the system for a number of reasons," she said.

The main reasons: "Best in Class design . . . and environmental controls" to reduce noise and air pollution. Piccard added that they would only perform a full blowdown once every five years.[22] In sum, Buckingham residents had nothing to worry about. *Very few people ever notice.*

After the presentation, nearly every one of the ninety-five people who rose to speak voiced opposition to the permit. They articulated their various concerns about health, property values, water, and environmental justice in granular detail. After a few hours, one supervisor asked wearily, "Does anybody have anything new? We've basically heard the same thing over and over and over."

Ernie Reed had driven across the James River for the meeting. After reminding the supervisors that they could defer their decision until federal regulators completed their various analyses and they had more information to work with, he offered something that no one had yet said: he thanked Dominion for expanding his circle of neighbors. "Before the two and a half years that this has gone on, I probably had a handful of friends in Nelson County," he said. "And now I have dozens of them and I'm very grateful to each and every one of them because they are some of the best people I know."

Then Ella Rose stood and faced the supervisors. "It is disheartening to know that everything I have worked for all my life, which was to own my own home and live in peace the rest of my life, will be taken away from me if I am forced to live with a large, noisy, polluting compressor station nearby," she told them. "Our lives should not be sacrificed. Our lives count and are dependent on you to make a decision that favors life and not financial interests. Most especially Dominion's financial interest. Thank you."

At nearly 11:00 p.m., after five hours, the board voted 5–0 to approve the permit.[23] Two members had abstained: one because he owned land "pertaining to the pipeline" and another because he worked for Dominion Energy.[24]

Canal Place

Later that year, in August 2017, Dominion unveiled the name for the 20-story, million-square-foot, $120 million gleaming new office tower it was building in downtown Richmond, selected from a thousand proposals submitted by its employees: Canal Place.

The choice was a nod to the location—just a stone's throw from the old James River and Kanawha Canal—but also to the company's origin story.[25] Dominion's corporate progenitor was the canal-building Upper Appomattox Company, germinated in 1787 with a charter from the General Assembly, and with George Washington and James Madison among its original trustees.[26]

The company's official corporate history, *Dominion's First Century: A Legacy of Service*, proudly points to the firm's Upper Appomattox origins as evidence of its long place of prominence at the heart of Virginia's political and economic journey.[27] The book makes no mention of the fact that the very first act of the Appomattox company was to force enslaved Black people to dig the canal on the eponymous river.[28] Instead, there is plenty of text painting Dominion's evolution as a story of technological progress, sweeping energy transitions, and shrewd financial decision-making.

But it was also a story that—like so much of the state's infrastructure and history—was inextricably tied to the exploitation and marginalization of Black Virginians.

Dominion's *other* distant corporate ancestor was the City Gas Light Company of Norfolk—one of dozens of urban gas light companies created in nineteenth-century America.[29] Before "natural gas" became widely available, for decades these ventures turned coal and tar into "town gas" used in streetlights and homes and businesses. This is the industry that gave us the 1944 film *Gaslight*, about a woman in Victorian England whose scheming husband dims the lights in their home to convince her she's going mad—that she's not seeing what's right in front of her eyes.

Fighting "Erasure"

When Lakshmi Fjord read through Dominion's filing to the Federal Energy Regulatory Commission in September 2015, she was alarmed by what she saw as "the erasure" of Union Hill. She decided to reach out to Greg Buppert at the Southern Environmental Law Center with her concerns. Fjord had a dual perspective on this question. She had been a longtime resident of Buckingham County—having moved there as one of Yogaville's earliest members—and was an anthropologist with deep expertise in conducting participatory field research.

Fjord knew that FERC required pipeline applicants to submit "cultural resources amendments" to address any historic or other cultural resources that might be disturbed by a proposed project.[30] ACP LLC had submitted some information about ancient Monacan burial sites and settlements along the James River in Nelson County—but almost nothing about Buckingham's history. And in its final review before approving the pipeline, FERC likewise said nothing about the historic or cultural resources of the compressor station site or the surrounding community. There were, FERC concluded, no environmental justice concerns involved—nothing to see here.[31]

Chad Oba had been combing through some of those documents too. And to her, the numbers in them didn't add up. FERC's analysis, based on 2013 census data, had claimed that minorities made up just 31 percent of the local population near the compressor site. Virginia's environmental regulators, meanwhile, had pointed to estimates that the minority population around the compressor station was "in the range of 37 to 39%." Dominion had cited yet another study, which claimed that Black residents made up an even lower share of the population in the immediate area: just 22 to 25 percent compared to the countywide average of 34 percent. On top of that, they claimed that only a few dozen households were occupied full-time during the week.[32]

To Oba, the intent behind citing those numbers was clear enough: implying that Union Hill wasn't a real community, that there weren't all that many people around to be exposed to any pollution the compressor station might release, that environmental justice shouldn't enter the equation at all.

"They said, 'Nobody lives there,'" said Oba. "I've lived here for thirty-five years. I knew that this was a predominantly Black neighborhood."[33]

Many residents knew their ancestors were Freedmen and Freedwomen who founded Union Hill soon after Emancipation. Cora Perkins, for instance, who lived 1,500 feet from the compressor site, was a descendant of Caesar Perkins, one of the earliest settlers.[34] He was born enslaved in 1839 and was elected to the House of Delegates in 1869. As a Virginia delegate, he voted to ratify the Fourteenth and Fifteenth Amendments.[35]

Friends of Buckingham decided to do the painstaking work of documenting this history—and documenting exactly who lived around the compressor site—themselves. Fjord, a visiting scholar at the University of Virginia, led the design of the survey. Over the course of two intensive phases in 2016 and 2018, the organization's volunteers—Black and white—knocked on every door they could. With those who agreed to participate, they went through dozens of questions, about who lived there, where they worked, their family history, and medical conditions they suffered from.

They ultimately reached more than 75 percent of households—an unusually high response rate for field surveys. And when Fjord and her colleagues sat down to analyze the data, they found that 84 percent of the 199 Union Hill residents were people of color; most were African American. About 63 percent reported that they were descendants of formerly enslaved people from nearby plantations, such as Variety Shade, who had settled in the area after Emancipation.[36]

The study confirmed that there were there far more people (two hundred) living full-time near the compressor site than Dominion or state agencies had claimed (thirty). It revealed that they all relied on private wells for water, connected to the same aquifer. And in keeping with national data showing that Black Americans suffered from higher rates of respiratory and cardiovascular illness, the study found that thirty-five of those households had reported preexisting medical conditions such as asthma, chronic bronchitis, and heart disease.

The survey made one thing blindingly clear: Union Hill was the very definition of an "environmental justice community."

And in May 2018, Virginia's Advisory Council on Environmental Justice agreed, when it came to visit Union Hill for a fact-finding mission and listed the compressor station at the top of its statewide list of areas posing environmental justice concerns. "That was very big for us," said Oba.

The advisory council would later recommend that regulators deny the air permit and form an emergency task force to ensure nonwhite and poor Virginians weren't bearing a heavier burden of the pipeline's impacts. Though it had a mandate to advise state agencies on "integrating environmental justice considerations throughout the Commonwealth's programs," the council's recommendations were nonbinding. And after its members issued a strongly worded statement calling on Governor Ralph Northam to halt permitting for both the ACP and MVP, his office informed them that their mandate had technically expired. He thanked them for their service.

The governor had a very different reaction to another gas compressor station earlier that same year, when Dominion had proposed building a similar facility on land that happened to lie just across the Potomac River from Mount Vernon.

The Mount Vernon Ladies' Association, the nonprofit that managed the estate of the nation's first president, quickly launched a media campaign to block the project. The group circulated a petition, which soon garnered twenty thousand signatures, and posted ear-rattling audio of what a compressor blowdown event sounds like. The National Trust for Historic Preservation soon put the estate on its annual list of the country's "most endangered historical sites"—entirely thanks to the threat that Dominion's project posed to its viewshed.[37]

Three hundred enslaved people had once labored there in George Washington's tobacco fields and gristmills. But in 2018, no one lived at Mount Vernon. It was a popular tourist destination that served as an occasional backdrop for exclusive events and dignitaries' visits. A couple months earlier, President Trump had landed in a helicopter on its lawn and hosted the president of France and his wife for a private dinner.

"This development is going to destroy the unique and special experience of walking in the footsteps of our Founding Father, of being inspired by the extraordinary view that he so enjoyed," Mount Vernon's president and CEO said. "Can you imagine that view with a compressor station and smokestacks?"

Governor Northam swiftly pledged to look into the matter. "If it's going to impact their view, if it's going to contribute to environmental detriment, then it's something I'm concerned about," he said.

After a few weeks of this pushback, after previously insisting that relocation was not an option, Dominion agreed to find a less objectionable site for the compressor station.[38]

Folks in Union Hill took note of the alacrity with which Dominion accommodated Mount Vernon's demands. Several state lawmakers noticed, too, and wrote to Northam to ask why Union Hill didn't deserve the same consideration.

But in Buckingham County, Dominion took a very different tack. Earlier that year, the company hired Basil Gooden, a former state agricultural secretary who had grown up in Union Hill and was a member of Paul Wilson's congregation, as a liaison to the community.[39]

At one point, Rose said, Gooden came to her home and made her an informal offer for her home and acre of land, but she sent Dominion's emissary on his way. "My whole intention—that wasn't money, nor fame," she said. "I was trying to keep my property. It took me twenty years to pay for this place. I just want to keep my home."

Dominion's outreach soon generated tensions within Union Hill. Throughout 2018, overtures by Gooden and Carlos Brown, a Dominion vice president who came to meet with residents after the environmental justice advisory panel took up their cause, swayed some community residents. Some felt that Friends of Buckingham was too dogmatic in its opposition. A familiar question was aired at meetings and to reporters: If it was going to be built, why not get some benefit out of it?[40] The project, after all, seemed inevitable.

"They were throwing big figures around and offers of community buildings that Dominion would build for us," Oba said. "They were saying, 'You have to have a plan B because this is gonna happen.' But it essentially divided this community."

Tense moments ensued at meetings in the local churches. Questions flew about who really had the community's best interests at heart. At one point, during one particularly charged gathering, Ella Rose tried to lighten the mood. "As Dolly Parton would say, 'It's enough to drive you crazy if you let it,'" she interjected, getting laughs out of folks on both sides.[41]

Rose and Oba understood those folks' point of view. It was a natural reaction, to make the best of a bad situation. It was the same perspective that John Ed Purvis had heard from his own supervisor next door in Nelson: *This thing is gonna get built, so you might as well try to get the best deal you can.* But Rose and Oba had noticed something else at work, too, during the past four years: those who had moved away—like Rose herself or John and Ruby Laury, who had lived in California for years—and then moved back later in life seemed more inclined to speak out. Those who had grown up in the area and never left seemed more resigned, they observed, even if they didn't want the compressor station. It was hard not to wonder if the sheer weight of Virginia's history didn't have something to do with it.[42]

At the end of July 2018, DEQ published a draft air permit. Over the ensuing forty-day public comment period, the agency received more than 5,600 comments—most in opposition to the permit. Many raised concerns about how the compressor station would impact the Black residents of Union Hill. At a hearing in November dedicated to the air permit application, more than eighty citizens spoke in opposition. To everyone's surprise, the board voted to delay a decision until their next meeting.

Chad Oba found herself buoyed by the vote and by some board members' probing questions. She couldn't help hoping they would deny the permit.[43]

Then, five days later, Governor Northam removed two members of the air board—the two who were most outspoken about their concerns over siting the compressor station in Union Hill. It felt like a rug had been pulled out from under her.[44]

That same week, Dominion had presented a $5 million "community investment package" to finance a community center and purchase ambulances and other emergency service equipment, among other projects, in Union Hill. "We have a profound respect for this community and its history, and we're investing in their future," said spokesman Aaron Ruby.

An Ugly History

Ryan Emanuel had already been tracking Dominion's pipeline for years when the Southern Environmental Law Center asked him to weigh in on the environmental justice implications of building a compressor station in Union Hill, ahead of the air board's final vote in January.

He had a professional perspective on the project—as a veteran environmental scientist and professor at North Carolina State University, who would later be named to EPA's science advisory board and its Environmental Justice Science Committee—and a personal one: he was a citizen of the Lumbee Tribe, the largest Native American tribe east of the Mississippi. The ACP's final leg was slated to run right through the center of Lumbee territory in Robeson County, North Carolina.

In July 2017, Emanuel had authored an article in *Science*, in which he argued that the Atlantic Coast Pipeline was a prime example of flawed environmental justice analysis in action. He noted that the project's route crossed the territories of four different Native American tribes. A full quarter of North Carolina's entire Indigenous population lived in census tracts along the route.[45] But just as they had seen no majority Black community in Union Hill, state and federal regulators hadn't really *seen* the Indigenous communities in the path of the Atlantic Coast Pipeline. "There is no other energy project currently under federal review that stands to impact as many American Indians," Emanuel wrote in his own formal comments to FERC. And yet FERC had found "no evidence" that the ACP would disproportionately impose a higher share of "adverse environmental or socioeconomic impacts on any racial, ethnic, or socioeconomic group."

In his comments for the air board, Emanuel praised Fjord's door-to-door study for providing data "that is unquestionably superior to preliminary statistical estimates."

"These results suggest that the compressor station would place a disproportionately high and adverse burden on the surrounding community," Emanuel wrote. "If the Air Board fails to account for the results of this survey or other fieldwork in its decision on the compressor station, I believe that the decision will be ill-informed and could perpetuate the ugly history of environmental injustice that exists in Virginia and North Carolina."[46]

On January 9, several hundred people turned out for the final air board meeting at a hotel in a Richmond suburb. Outside were police in riot gear. Inside, two dozen state troopers were spread around the perimeter of the room. Dominion executives sat in two reserved rows at the front of the room.

In their presentations, Dominion representatives rehashed their Best-in-Class promises that air emissions would be 50 to 80 percent lower than those from any other compressor station in Virginia. Later, the DEQ's air director would say that the facility would "set a new national standard that all future compressor stations will have to meet across the country." The word "stringent" was used a lot.

Those arguments proved persuasive. When it was the board members' turn to explain how they stood on the matter, one argued that

because the emissions would be under EPA limits, there was no reason to be concerned about "disproportionate" effects on Union Hill.
"The region needs the energy; the state needs the energy," said another
board member, William Ferguson, explaining his support for the project. "How much is Dominion paying you?" a woman shouted from the
crowd. (Ferguson happened to be vice president of a real estate firm
that represented Smithfield Foods, which had just a couple months
earlier announced a $250 million partnership with Dominion Energy
to develop "renewable natural gas" sourced from hog manure lagoons in
North Carolina—a novel form of methane that Tom Farrell predicted
would "inevitably" make its way into the Atlantic Coast Pipeline.[47])

As the board voted unanimously to approve the permit, Chad Oba
stood next to Ella Rose, holding her hand. Her other hand covered her
heart. (She looked stricken enough that a friend would later tell her she
thought Oba was having a heart attack.[48]) People cried out "Shame!
Shame!" from their seats.[49]

The troopers immediately began herding everyone out of the
room—including Greg Buppert, who had been sitting up front and
who was already mentally planning his next steps: review the document that had just been approved, consult with clients in Union Hill,
craft a strong argument in response. If his clients wanted to challenge
the fresh permit in federal court, he reckoned they had about thirty
days to do so. The clock was ticking.

Earlier that week, in a bit of timing that consultants might describe
as "bad optics," Governor Ralph Northam had attended a fundraiser
hosted by Dominion executives for his political action committee. (Dominion was its leading donor.)[50] A pediatric neurologist and
former army officer known for his low-key approach to governing,
Northam had remained studiously silent on the compressor station.
He had pledged to let the permitting process unfold without any inter-
ference, but critics had called foul after he removed the two air board
members before the key vote.

Soon Northam had bigger problems on his hand. A few weeks
later, on February 2, an online blog post revealed photos of Northam
in his medical school 1984 yearbook wearing blackface and standing
next to someone wearing a Ku Klux Klan hood and robes. Northam

admitted the figure in blackface was him, then denied it, then admitted to wearing blackface on other occasions, then refused to resign despite mounting calls from within his own party to do so. The scandal threw Virginia's political establishment into crisis and dominated national news cycles.[51]

Amid campaigns to remove Confederate statues from public spaces around the state—and in the wake of the deadly Unite the Right white supremacist rally in Charlottesville in August 2017—the scandal added fuel to a resurgent conversation about Virginia's failure to fully reckon with its ugly history of racism and its still-reverberating effects.

Holy Ground

A few weeks later, on February 19, 2019, Rev. William Barber II—one of the country's most prominent civil rights activists—came to Union Hill, accompanied by former vice president Al Gore. Their visit, with reporters from national news outlets in tow, was the culmination of five years of fighting and many months of planning by the Friends of Buckingham and their allies.

The two men were there to headline a rally decrying the "environmental racism" behind Dominion's compressor station plans and the state's support for them. Before the evening's main event, Barber and Gore went on a listening tour of Union Hill.

The first stop was Ella Rose's house. From her front yard, she pointed out where the compressor station would be built.

"How far from here?" the former vice president asked.

"A hundred and fifty feet," she replied.

"A hundred and fifty feet?" Gore said. He shook his head in disbelief. "Well, you wouldn't be able to hear yourself think."

"I know. And it's only maybe two city blocks from my well."

As he stood on Rose's front porch, Reverend Barber said that Governor Northam needed to demonstrate his sincerity about addressing entrenched racism and Virginia's troubled history by listening more to people like Ella Rose and less to the lobbyists of Dominion Energy.

"All the stuff that he has said—wanting forgiveness, wanting this, wanting to apologize—is suspect until he faces these kinds of systemic problems," he said.[52]

Reverend Barber had come to national prominence as the leader of the Poor People's Campaign, an anti-poverty campaign that crisscrossed the country in 2018, inspired by the movement of the same name launched by Dr. Martin Luther King Jr. in the months before his assassination. That evening, nearly a thousand people filled the seats and spilled out the aisles and doors of the gymnasium of Buckingham County Middle School. The mood was rapturous and raucous. Ella Rose sat near the stage, flanked by friends and neighbors, wearing a blue jacket and one of her blue church hats. The event had the feeling of a spiritual revival, with people clasping hands and raising their arms as Reverend Barber came to the podium to praise the courage of Union Hill's residents and to pillory Dominion.

Barber mused aloud as to why these projects always seemed to wind up in poor, minority communities. "Yes, it's environmental racism, but it's also something deeper," he intoned. "It's 'Locally undesirable environmental land uses.' It's a term called LULUs."

"Really, they use it in court," he said to incredulous laughter and shouts. "In other words, where they think they can put it and get away with it. Hazardous waste facilities. Solid waste disposal sites. Contaminated industrial sites. And now pipelines and compressors."

"They are disproportionately placed in poor communities and Black communities," he continued, his voice rising, "because they think they are LULUs. But if they thought they were going to get away with it in Union Hill, they are out of luck. This ain't no LULU, this is holy ground!"

People rose out of their seats, whistling and cheering.

"This is where the slaves were buried, who believed in freedom!" Barber thundered. "And the ancestors are calling us."[53]

When it was his turn to speak, the former vice president and longtime climate advocate excoriated Northam for removing the two most outspoken members of the air board—"a favor for Dominion"—and railed against the entire pipeline venture—"a reckless, racist rip-off" and potentially "the single largest increase in global warming pollution from the state of Virginia, ever."

"We're here to say to Union Hill, you are not standing alone," Gore said. "We are standing with you."

For Ella Rose, as memorable as it had been to hear a thousand people cheering in support of her cause, and to hear the Reverend Barber and former vice president call out her name as a leader of the fight, the part of the day she will never forget came just before the two men left her home that morning. Barber and Gore were on a tight schedule, but on their way out the door, the reverend offered to bless Rose's home. Barber walked around her living room and kitchen, singing a hymn.

"I had an out-of-body experience," she recalled, laughing and shaking her head at the memory. "I was levitating!"

Overpowered

As the residents of Union Hill got louder and louder, and their cause generated more and more attention, the end of an era came and went without any fanfare at all, in an unincorporated community known as Bremo Bluff about 30 miles east.

That's where, earlier that spring, Dominion Energy had quietly closed down its 254-megawatt gas-fired power plant sitting on the banks of the James River.

A nineteenth-century plantation built by an early investor in the James River and Kanawha Canal Company had once dominated Bremo Bluff. It had been a waypoint and wharf for the flat-bottomed batteaux that plied the river. Then during the Civil War, the plantation became a refuge for the wife of General Robert E. Lee, while he was off fighting the Union Army to defend Virginia's slaveholding "way of life."

A century later, it was mostly known as the site of Dominion's longest-operating power plant. Bremo Bluff first started cranking out electricity in 1931, burning through mountains of coal until 2014, when the company announced plans to convert two of its units to run on gas.

The plant was an exemplar of the company's ballyhooed coal-to-gas switch. But when it closed for good in 2019, after just four years of operation, it wound up exemplifying the risks of those investments instead.

Meanwhile, Virginia's regulators were finally calling out Dominion for years of overstating energy demand. In December 2018, for the first time ever, the State Corporation Commission had rejected the company's long-range resource plan because the utility hadn't investigated lower-cost alternatives like expanding energy efficiency programs and battery storage pilots. The commission voiced its "considerable doubt regarding the accuracy and reasonableness of the Company's load forecast for use to predict future energy and peak load requirements." Such forecasts were a key justification for massive investments like the ACP and for the eight new gas-fired power plants that Dominion had planned to build in Virginia by 2033.[54]

In 2018, Dominion admitted those gas plants probably wouldn't be built. It had no plans to purchase more combined-cycle gas power units from manufacturers like General Electric, a Dominion spokesman acknowledged, because "solar is very cheap."[55]

But its plan still called for major investments in new gas peaker plants—which can be ramped up and down quickly to respond to peaks in demand—to "maintain reliability." When I spoke with Dominion spokesperson Aaron Ruby in November 2019, this theme came up again and again.

"For the foreseeable future, natural gas is an essential partner with renewables for building a low-carbon future," said Ruby. "Renewables are inherently intermittent. We have an obligation to deliver reliability for our customers. I think the need for ACP is even stronger today than when we announced it five years ago. The infrastructure that's serving Virginia and North Carolina today is very congested. It's not keeping up with peak demand. As more renewables come online and natural gas peaking facilities come online, demand for natural gas is only going to grow."

Just a few weeks after we spoke, on December 2, 2019, a multipart, in-depth investigation by S&P Global, a market research and energy industry news firm, found that utilities across the US had inflated their demand projections to justify an unprecedented gas power plant building spree over the previous decade.

"Between 2008 and Aug. 1, 2019, a period of essentially flat demand, the U.S. added 120,498 MW of natural gas–fired capacity to its generation fleet, including nearly 26,000 MW in 2018 and 2019 alone," the piece's authors observed.[56] They singled out Dominion Energy as the poster child for an industry that couldn't resist hyping demand so it could build lucrative but largely unnecessary gas power plants.

The very next day after this exposé was published, Dominion suspended without explanation a request for proposals to build 1,500 megawatts of new peak generation capacity (most likely gas-powered) that it had announced just the month before.[57]

By the end of 2019, the original justification for the Atlantic Coast Pipeline—the claim that there was an insatiable hunger for gas in coastal population centers—seemed more suspect than ever. Financial titan Warren Buffett's adage seemed increasingly apt: "Only when the tide goes out do you discover who's been swimming naked."

Actions Speak Louder

In 2011 Ernest Moniz of MIT had foretold a bright future for natural gas, extending into the twenty-first century. "(G)iven the large amounts of natural gas available in the U.S. at moderate cost, natural gas can indeed play an important role over the next couple of decades (together with demand management) in economically advancing a clean energy system," he assured senators on the Energy and Natural Resources Committee.[58]

A decade later, the switch from coal to gas had indeed reduced US utilities' carbon dioxide emissions. Nationwide power plant emissions had gone down by 23 percent. But not in Virginia. In 2019, Virginia's total carbon dioxide emissions from generating electricity were actually *higher* than they had been in 2009. The reason? Dominion had built so much gas that it was wiping out the gains from closing coal plants.[59]

But growing emissions from gas threatened to swamp those gains on a national scale too. Gas was the fastest-growing source of carbon dioxide globally—growing so fast that its emissions had eclipsed reductions from the falling use of coal.[60]

And those numbers didn't even include the warming impact of methane leaks. The science had advanced on that front too. By the end of the decade, energy experts were warning that, when you took all those emissions into account, "we should be very hesitant of investing in new infrastructure with a long life."

That was the verdict of Jessika Trancik, an affiliated researcher at MIT's Energy Initiative—the program that Ernest Moniz had once led. Trancik's modeling studies had found that methane leaks would have to be reduced by as much as 90 percent to justify any further expansion of natural gas infrastructure from a carbon-saving perspective instead of investing in low-carbon electricity sources like solar and wind.[61]

In 2011, Moniz had told Congress that "the bridge must have a suitable landing point." The chart he presented showed natural gas use starting to ramp down around 2045. But by December 2019, a chorus of energy scholars was saying the world couldn't afford to wait any longer. Investments in natural gas were *slowing down* the transition to a clean energy system, and building new gas plants or pipelines would make the task of phasing out fossil fuels more prolonged and difficult.

"It has served as a bridge," Trancik told one reporter. "But we're kind of nearing the end of the bridge."[62]

Wall Street seemed to agree. That same month, a prominent financial industry analyst, who had sat through his fair share of Tom Farrell's quarterly earnings calls, predicted that the Atlantic Coast Pipeline would not get built. "We believe this project will not move forward due to legal risks," Stephen Byrd of Morgan Stanley wrote in a report.[63]

But he had a friendly suggestion as to what they should build instead: a whole lot of renewable energy. Byrd and his colleagues laid out in detail how Duke, Dominion, and other big utilities could generate higher returns by switching from coal to wind and solar and skipping the new gas-fired generation they had planned. It would benefit customers, shareholders, and the environment, the author noted, as well as their bottom line.[64]

Around the same time, Chaz Teplin, Mark Dyson, and fellow researchers at the Rocky Mountain Institute published a modeling analysis of eighty-eight proposed gas-fired power plants across the US. They found that building "clean energy portfolios"—which they defined as "an optimized combination of wind, solar, storage and demand-side management"—was already cheaper than building 90 percent of those gas plants. Doing so would save utility customers $29 billion and avoid 100 million tons per year of carbon emissions.[65]

Teplin and his colleagues at RMI sometimes worked closely with utilities like Duke Energy. He sympathized with the daunting task they faced: decarbonizing power systems even as they kept them running twenty-four hours a day, seven days a week. But he took a dim view of their reluctance to embrace mature clean energy technologies in favor of the familiar but polluting path of burning more methane. Less than 10 percent of electricity generated in the Southeast, Dominion and Duke's neighborhood, came from renewables—far below the national average. "It you look at any utility's portfolio," Teplin said, "if wind and solar is not making up more than 10 percent, they have an opportunity to save tons of money by integrating those things." He took issue with the arithmetic behind the emissions reduction plans in their glossy reports.

"Do we believe in climate change and acknowledge the costs of that are high?" Teplin said. "If we start from there, then expanded use of fossil gas is simply incompatible with that. The math just does not work. Period. There's just no way. Yes, it's cleaner than coal. Maybe half the carbon, maybe a quarter if you count all the methane leaks. But we need to be close to zero by 2030. Half is not zero. It's not even close to zero."[66]

Soon after those analyses were published, Dominion quashed any hopes that it would seize the opportunities they laid out. In its 2019 annual report, Dominion did not mention its recent gas power plant cancellations or the brutal climate math around methane emissions. The report's title was *Embracing Change,* but one thing that apparently hadn't changed was Dominion's appetite for more gas. In his "letter to investors," Tom Farrell doubled down on his career-defining bet on methane.

"Gas is essential to reduce greenhouse gas emissions," he wrote. "Our net zero commitment does not affect our investment in the approximately $8 billion Atlantic Coast Pipeline (ACP). This 600-mile pipeline is needed as much today as it was in late-summer 2014, when it was announced."[67]

Back then, Farrell had pledged to "work closely with landowners and other stakeholders to find the best possible route, one that minimizes the impact on natural, cultural and historic resources." Five years later, Dominion's corporate communications team seemed determined to double down on that rhetoric, too, as though the intervening years of grassroots fury had never happened. The report touted the company's environmental and community outreach plans under the heading "Actions Speak Louder®": "We say what we mean, and we mean what we say. . . . Our vision in this new decade is to build a clean and sustainable energy future for our customers, communities, employees, shareholders—and the Earth. It means protecting the environment, and combatting climate change. It means improving the way we interact with our customers and partnering with our communities to make them more vibrant."

Not a Box to Be Checked

The compressor station air permit had been the last key approval that ACP needed in Virginia.

In January 2020, almost exactly a year after the air control board had approved it, the Fourth Circuit Court of Appeals tossed it out.

In a blistering rebuke, the court concluded that the state agencies had paid the briefest lip service to environmental justice and then waved away its demands. They had failed to examine the likelihood that siting the compressor in Union Hill would place a disproportionate burden on the community's residents. They had ignored the carefully documented demographic evidence presented by the Friends of Buckingham.

"The Board rejected the idea of disproportionate impact on the basis that air quality standards were met . . . (b)ut environmental justice is not merely a box to be checked," the judges wrote.[68]

Greg Buppert had been fighting the Atlantic Coast Pipeline on multiple fronts since 2014. In one sense, what he saw take place in Union Hill was part of a pattern. "It's the same story again and again," he said. "Dominion tried to force a pipeline compressor station into a community where it didn't belong, just like it has tried to force the pipeline through a national park, national forests, and steep mountains."[69]

But Union Hill also stood apart. To Buppert, what his clients in Buckingham faced was perhaps the most egregious instance of that larger pattern. "ACP made the decision to deny that the community exists," he told me. "For four years since the compressor was proposed, the company is *still* saying there is no environmental justice community in Union Hill, that the demographics are just like everywhere else. That's a choice with consequences."[70]

The first call Buppert made upon learning of the court's ruling was to Chad Oba. She then promptly called her friend Ella Rose.

"We won!" Oba shouted.

The two women started screaming in each other's ears. Oba couldn't stop jumping up and down in her kitchen. Rose apologized for shouting into the phone.[71]

"It's something to scream about," her friend said, "go right ahead."

Part IV

Sea Change

A wind turbine 27 miles off the Atlantic Coast, part of a pilot for Dominion Energy's Coastal Virginia Offshore Wind project. The installation of the pilot project's two turbines was announced one week before the cancellation of the Atlantic Coast Pipeline in 2020. Upon completion in 2026, the project's 176 turbines will supply enough clean electricity to power 660,000 homes. (Sarah Vogelsong/*Virginia Mercury*)

Chapter Eleven

The New Dominion

A day after the Fourth Circuit tossed out the state's air permit for the compressor station in Union Hill, Virginia's 161st General Assembly was gaveled into session.

The new Democratic majority wasted little time in putting forward a flurry of bills on the very first day—including the Virginia Clean Economy Act. The proposed law would require Dominion and the state's other major power utility to make huge new investments in wind, solar, and battery storage, close almost all of their coal power plants by 2024, expand energy efficiency programs, and boost funding for renewable energy in historically marginalized communities.

The day after the previous fall's election—in which Democrats had gained control of the General Assembly for the first time in twenty-six years—Dominion spokesman Aaron Ruby had deflected my questions about what the historic outcome would mean for the company's fortunes. He noted that they would work constructively with whoever was in control.[1] But by any sober reckoning, the outcome was a blow to Dominion. Virginians had chosen new lawmakers who had not only promised to push a comprehensive clean energy bill early in the new session, but who had campaigned explicitly on their plans to reform the cozy, backslapping relationship that prevailed between Dominion and many delegates and senators. Many victorious candidates had signed Clean Virginia's pledge to reject the utility's money.

Did the push to build the Atlantic Coast Pipeline, in the face of widespread opposition around the state, help trigger that outcome? While the pipeline wasn't the only factor, it certainly seemed to aggravate a wide swath of Virginians.

"Anti-Dominion sentiment is pretty high," Lee Francis, deputy director of the Virginia League of Conservation Voters, told me in 2020. "The ACP is one example. They've been screwing over Virginians for years. The latest estimate is that they've over-earned half a billion dollars since 2015. That's our money."[2] (In 2020, the State Corporation Commission would conclude that Dominion had overcharged ratepayers to the tune of $502 million above authorized earnings between 2017 and 2019.[3]) "Their overreach has put them into hot water."

Polling by the League of Conservation Voters during the 2019 campaign had found that the broad messages of climate action and "holding corporate polluters accountable" resonated with many voters. For decades Dominion had been every Virginia politician's best friend—an unparalleled source of campaign contributions. But for a growing number, Francis said, having Dominion in your corner was no longer a clear advantage. "More lawmakers are realizing they are a liability and not a friend," he said. "There's a larger sea change that's happened."[4]

On February 11, the Virginia House and Senate passed their own separate versions of the Clean Economy Act. Dominion Energy—the state's largest single emitter of greenhouse gases—was now facing the prospect of a legally mandated timetable to wring the carbon out of its portfolio. It would have to produce 100 percent of its electricity from renewable sources by 2045.[5] The nation's oldest continuously operating legislative body had formally approved an expiration date for natural gas.

In a move that struck few observers as a coincidence, on the same day as the House and Senate votes, Dominion announced that it would achieve "net-zero emissions" by mid-century. The pledge improved on a previous voluntary commitment to reduce carbon dioxide from its power plants by 80 percent between 2005 and 2050.[6]

"Our mandate is to provide reliable and affordable energy—safely," said CEO Tom Farrell in a statement. "We do that every day, all year long. But we recognize that we must also continue to be a leader in combatting climate change."

Through the gauzy promises and splashy press releases, the contours of the story were clear enough: Dominion's hand had been forced. By the time Governor Northam signed the Clean Economy Act into law in April, Americans' attention was wholly focused on the fast-spreading COVID-19 pandemic. But for climate advocates and energy analysts, it was nevertheless a landmark event: Virginia became just the ninth US state or territory to legally mandate the transition to 100 percent clean electricity. And the very first in the American South.[7]

Pipe Dreams Die Hard

A month later, a hole was punched into Richmond's skyline when Dominion's old office tower at One James River Plaza collapsed into a cloud of dust in a controlled demolition right next to the gleaming new 20-story headquarters that had risen at 600 Canal Place. Spectators hooted and hollered from a safe distance. Crews soon combed through the wreckage for steel and concrete to be salvaged.

Energy analysts were meanwhile combing through the latest "integrated resource plan" that Dominion had filed with regulators, detailing what the company sought to build over the next fifteen years. As expected, it called for major new investments in solar, offshore wind, and battery storage. But Dominion also wanted to bring nearly 10,000 megawatts of gas-fired generation online through 2045 and add 970 megawatts of new gas-fired peaker plants, to boot. The two original sponsors of the Clean Economy Act, Senator Jennifer McClellan and Delegate Rip Sullivan, struggled to see how those plans lined up with the new law's requirements, calling them "tantamount to quitting the game before the first pitch is thrown."[8]

That gas build-out was also increasingly at odds with independent analysts' arithmetic. A few weeks later, a team of researchers at UC Berkeley and Energy Innovation released a study showing that the US electricity system could be made 90 percent carbon free by 2035 while lowering electricity rates by 10 percent—all without building a single new gas power plant.[9]

"You don't need to build new natural gas plants for any reliability or dependability reasons," Dr. Amol Phadke, a lead author of the study, told me.[10] Thanks to George Mitchell, Aubrey McClendon, Tom Farrell, Tom Fanning, Lynn Good, and a host of other energy CEOs, the United States had by far the biggest gas power plant fleet in the world. "There's enough existing gas, and cheap storage available," Phadke said, noting that gas generation would instead need to *decrease* by 70 percent. "If we are to decarbonize, we don't need the new [plants]. Ideally, they shouldn't be built."

But there were no signs that Dominion or its ACP partners were preparing to move away from their fossil gas fixation. In May, Duke's CEO expressed confidence that crews would resume felling trees for the pipeline by November.[11] The same week, Tom Farrell pledged that it would have gas flowing through it in 2022.

Greg Buppert and D. J. Gerken had been hearing from their contacts at federal agencies, meanwhile, that the "pedal was down" on reissuing the permits they had gotten tossed out. And they were bracing for the Supreme Court's ruling, expected any day now, in *United States Forest Service v. Cowpasture River Preservation Association*—the case that had sprouted from the seed of an idea first planted when Buppert sat down at Will Fenton's table a half decade earlier to pore over old Park Service maps just below Reeds Gap.[12]

The decision came down on June 15: in a 7–2 vote, the Supreme Court overruled the Fourth Circuit's decision vacating the permit for ACP to cross the Appalachian Trail.[13] Media outlets speculated that, with it, the momentum had shifted back in Dominion's favor.

But Buppert didn't have time to stew about it. In mid-June, ACP LLC asked the Federal Energy Regulatory Commission for a two-year extension of its certificate, which was due to expire in October. Buppert and colleagues like Mark Sabath, who had been toiling in the ACP trenches alongside him for more than half a decade, now had just two weeks to finish compiling all the reasons why, in their view, FERC should not extend that deadline. The project still lacked eight other critical permits. Buppert's legal challenge to the FERC certificate was still pending in the DC Circuit Court of Appeals; if FERC granted the extension, they were prepared to go to court to keep fighting that too. But for now, they focused on explaining why Dominion's problems were of the company's own making—and how the demand case that FERC relied on when it greenlit the project in 2017 had all but collapsed.

On July 1, a clutch of protestors stood on the sidewalk in front of Dominion's Charlottesville office, waving their American flags and "NO PIPELINE" and "HONK FOR CLEAN ENERGY NOW" signs, just as they had nearly every other Wednesday for the past five years. On July 2—exactly six years after he first started looking into Dominion's then unnamed pipeline—Greg Buppert and his team put all the relevant facts and all their best arguments into the official Docket # CP15-554-009 of the Federal Energy Regulatory Commission, in the form of a mammoth 5,500-page filing that basically told the agency: *Enough already.*[14]

Then he took a break to enjoy the long Fourth of July weekend at the foot of the Blue Ridge Mountains with his family.

Cancellation Day

That Sunday afternoon, Buppert was working on a project in his backyard when his phone rang. It was D. J. Gerken. "I just got the craziest call," Gerken said.

While they were on the phone, *another* SELC colleague was trying to call Buppert at the same time. Will Cleveland, who worked on utility regulation issues in Richmond, had heard the same wild news as Gerken: Dominion had been calling around that morning to let state officials know that it was canceling the Atlantic Coast Pipeline.

Buppert's first reaction was incredulity. For six years, the pipeline had consumed nearly all his work life, a couple vacations, most of his waking hours, and not a few of his nights too. In that, he was far from alone: since they took on their first grassroots clients in 2014, dozens of SELC staffers had collectively logged more than forty thousand total hours of attorney time and $1.6 million in expenses in fighting ACP.[15] And Buppert was still waiting for the DC Circuit to hear the case he had filed two years earlier, challenging the entire methodology that the federal government used to determine whether gas pipelines were in the public interest.

"I just found it very hard to believe that this was happening," he said. So, he and Gerken made some of their own calls to confirm the rumor.

It checked out: Dominion was finally abandoning its pipe dreams.

A giddy game of telephone reverberated across the mountains of Virginia. Buppert called Chad Oba in Buckingham County.

Oba almost fell on the floor when she heard the news. When she recovered her composure, she called Ella Rose. "Have you heard?" she said.

"Heard what, the thunder?" Rose replied. There was an electrical storm happening outside.[16]

"No, no, the pipeline! We won, Ella, we won!"

"Oh Hallelujah!" Rose cried out.

Buppert then called Lew Freeman in Highland County: "Are you sitting down? Dominion's canceled the pipeline."

After six years of compiling weekly updates, leading weekly strategy sessions, and shepherding a coalition of fifty-some grassroots and environmental groups across western Virginia, Freeman was equally incredulous that it was all over.

"Are you kidding me?" he said.[17]

Meanwhile, elsewhere in Highland County, Anne Adams, publisher of the *Recorder*—which had been the first media outlet to break the news of Dominion's pipeline plans back in May 2014 and covered it tirelessly ever since, in hundreds of detailed articles—had caught wind of the cancellation. Her first phone call was to Rick Webb (just a few minutes before Buppert called him).

"Well, you did it," Adams told him. Webb didn't believe her at first either.

"What are you talking about? Are you serious?" he replied.

"Are you working on pipeline stuff right this minute?"

"Yeah."

"Put it down, put it away," she said. "You're done."

Then Adams went back to work herself, pulling together one more pipeline piece for the July 9 issue of the *Recorder* with the headline: "Ordinary Citizens Become Extraordinary":

They drove to Richmond, or Washington, to attend hearings or stand in protest outside the General Assembly and the now-leveled company headquarters. They wrote letters; they sat in trees; they hosted meetings; they wrote songs and made documentaries; they made phone calls and signs and websites. They put thousands of their own dollars behind the organizations that joined forces for legal battles and research. They pushed their elected leaders. They demanded details. They demanded fairness. They demanded information, justification, and truth. And they never gave up.[18]

Nancy Sorrells was visiting her brother in North Carolina that weekend. While her family had gone boating out on a lake, she had stayed back to do pipeline-related work. She was taking a quick nap when her phone rang. It was Kate Wolford, a longtime ACP-fighting colleague from Augusta County. She had just talked to Greg Buppert: "He said Dominion's pulled the plug on the pipeline."[19]

This is a dream, thought Sorrells, still waking up.

"I think it's true," Wolford said. A few minutes later Buppert called Sorrells to confirm the news. "There's a press release coming out," he told her.

"You're kidding. Are you kidding?"

She had been working for so long toward this outcome, that once it happened, her first thought was the exact same as Buppert's had been: *Now what am I going to do?*

Joyce Burton checked her email that afternoon and found a message from a Nelson landowner with a link to a news story and the subject line: "Not sure if this is true???"

She read the article and took a moment to shout at the top of her lungs: "Oh my God, it's canceled!"

Then she began furiously calling and texting dozens of landowners to deliver the news. "Some of them were literally sobbing, saying they can't believe the mountains are safe," she recalled.[20]

When Burton called Wisteria Johnson, the matriarch of Harris Cove simply cried out.

"Mama screamed like a banshee!" her daughter Deanna, who was walking into the house at that moment, recalled.

"I didn't believe it at first," Johnson told me a few days later. "I'm still waiting for the monster to raise its ugly head. I'm 69 years old, and I'm not used to things being what they appear to be. We've been struggling to hold on to this land in so many ways in my lifetime." She was flooded with relief—and gratitude. "All of these things that have sustained the mountains and streams and the people down through the generations can remain intact, until there's another threat. For now, we breathe easy."[21]

"The End of New Pipelines?"

"Is This the End of New Pipelines?" wondered the *New York Times* in a story headline a few days after the ACP's demise.

To be fair, it had been a pretty rough stretch for large, controversial fossil fuel pipelines in the United States of America. The day after ACP's cancellation, the Supreme Court ruled against the Trump administration's motion to overturn a lower court ruling halting construction on the Keystone XL pipeline. After a decade of controversy and protests, that project's future seemed more uncertain than ever. On the same day, a federal judge ordered the Dakota Access Pipeline to be shut down and drained of oil while a more rigorous review of its environmental and safety risks was conducted.[22]

Kelcy Warren, the billionaire CEO of Energy Transfer, owner of Dakota Access and several Marcellus pipelines, had famously said the quiet part out loud back in 2015 by declaring that "the pipeline business will overbuild until the end of time." Now, just weeks after hosting a fundraiser at his Dallas home for Donald Trump, he declared that his company would refuse to comply with the court's order.[23]

Despite Warren's defiance, his peers wondered aloud if the pipeline party was finally over. The CEO of Con Edison, one of the nation's largest utilities, said his company would no longer invest in long-haul gas pipelines and was considering selling its stake of the Mountain Valley Pipeline, which continued to be held up by legal challenges and ferocious opposition in southwest Virginia.

"We made those investments five to seven years ago, and at that time we—and frankly many others—viewed natural gas as having a fairly large role in the transition to the clean energy economy," he said. "That view has largely changed, and natural gas, while it can provide emissions reductions, is no longer . . . part of the longer-term view."[24]

At the northern end of the Marcellus, the Holleran family was planting new maple trees. They would take forty years to grow big enough to be tapped but were likely to stand for generations because the Constitution Pipeline had finally been canceled in March by its group of owners—which included Duke Energy.

The zeitgeist seemed to have shifted. Maybe the gas building boom was over. Maybe the prospect of an actual carbon-free energy system— forever being kicked down the road by gas industry leaders—was finally on the doorstep.

On the same day as the ACP cancellation, Dominion quietly announced it was selling more than 7,700 miles of gas pipelines, 900 billion cubic feet of gas storage assets, and a share in its Cove Point LNG terminal in Maryland to Warren Buffett's Berkshire Hathaway Energy.[25]

In one fell swoop, Dominion offloaded a huge part of its natural gas business. It still retained local gas distribution networks in half a dozen states. But the move seemed to be a concession in all but words that Dominion's bets on methane as the fuel of the future hadn't panned out—that it was time to cut its losses and move on.

Buffett, for his part, had declined to purchase Dominion's 53 percent stake in the Atlantic Coast Pipeline, including all its easements. Presumably, the legendary investor saw no path to bringing ACP back from the dead.

The ACP Autopsy

Who killed the Atlantic Coast Pipeline?

It depends on who you ask. Postmortem analyses proffered a range of theories, suspects, heroes, and culprits.[26] Excessive red tape and hostile judges. A Trump administration that ran roughshod over the law, pressuring thinly staffed agencies into issuing shoddy permits that were vulnerable to legal attack. Dominion's "delusions of invincibility" (per Lew Freeman) and an "arrogant route choice" from which it refused to budge (per SELC's lawyers).[27] Broad, deep, and determined opposition from a citizenry that wanted clean energy instead of more fossil gas infrastructure (per both grassroots opponents *and* Dominion's leaders, though the latter never worded it quite that way).

"To state the obvious, permitting for gas transmission and storage has become increasingly litigious, uncertain and costly," Tom Farrell remarked to investment analysts in a call the day after the cancellation.[28]

The official statements from Dominion, Duke, and the Trump administration made it sound like they were the underdogs, outgunned by an all-powerful set of interest groups.[29] "The well-funded, obstructionist environmental lobby has successfully killed the Atlantic Coast Pipeline," complained Trump's secretary of energy.

But to anyone who knew anything about the extent of Dominion's power in Virginia, or Duke's in North Carolina—or about the political influence of well-funded trade groups like the Edison Electric Institute and American Gas Association, on the one hand, relative to that of SELC and ABRA's members, on the other—the idea that the political playing field was tilted *against* the Atlantic Coast Pipeline strained credulity.[30]

It was true, however, that the project's opponents had stalled it long enough to raise costs to the breaking point for its owners. Immobilized in a pincer-like "full nelson" applied by SELC and other legal advocates in federal courts on one side and the relentless pressure of the "general citizenry" in the court of public opinion on the other, Dominion had been forced to tap out.

All parties seemed to agree, whether it was cause for lament or celebration, that the "death by a thousand cuts" strategy that Nancy Sorrells had articulated way back in 2014, with grassroots groups dogging the project on multiple fronts, had won the day.

For her part, Sorrells had a succinct account of what happened: "We know the power of the people with the law behind them can win."[31]

Back to the Future

At the end of July, Dominion announced a leadership shakeup.

After fifteen years in the role, Tom Farrell would step down as CEO in October; he would continue to serve as executive chairman of the board. Bob Blue, a longtime executive vice president, would take over as CEO, and Diane Leopold, the former gas operations leader, would become sole chief operating officer.[32]

Farrell's tenure had been defined by his bets on fossil gas. Dominion had been forced to write off a $2.8 billion loss with the ACP's demise. Analysts wondered: With his longtime deputy Blue now taking control, would Dominion keep its foot down on the gas pedal?

Farrell, for one, did not seem chastened. Dominion and Duke had planned to convert more coal plants to gas, he told analysts later that summer, but the death of the ACP had foiled those plans. "That need will now go unmet," he lamented.

For years, the project's backers had suggested that without the Atlantic Coast Pipeline's "affordable, reliable natural gas," homes in coastal Hampton Roads might freeze for lack of heating fuel, industries would relocate en masse, and the world's largest naval base at Norfolk would have to ration fuel.[33] But since its cancellation, the lights had stayed on. Electricity prices didn't skyrocket. Virginia's economy kept growing at the same pace. The US Navy kept patrolling the Atlantic.

What did change rather abruptly was Dominion's public messaging. Suddenly, Dominion's leaders were talking up a very different reason for gazing toward the Atlantic coast—27 miles off the coast, to be exact.

That's where the company planned to build a 176-turbine offshore wind project. It would be the largest and first of its kind in the country. Dominion hoped to finish it by late 2026. There was even a symmetry to the price tag: nearly $8 billion.

The company's public relations machine switched gears from gas to gigawatts of wind power with a speed that was head-spinning to the weary citizens who had fought the ACP tooth and nail for six years. On September 20, 2020, Dominion took out full-page ads in the *New York Times* and the *Washington Post*. Set against a photo of a wind turbine rising from the sea, in bold letters was the caption: "A cleaner energy future is on the horizon."

"While our commitment to cleaner energy has made us a national leader in sustainability, it is our commitment to future generations that inspires us every day," the ad copy read, just above the firm's tagline: "*Actions Speak Louder.*"

Bob Burnley, the former Dominion consultant and onetime head of Virginia's Department of Environmental Quality, had taken his employers at their word when they said the pipeline's gas was desperately needed to sustain the region's economy. His expertise, after all, was environmental regulation and water quality, not energy demand. But when it was canceled, he sounded almost relieved.

"I don't think not having that pipeline hurts us in any way," Burnley told me. "Environmentally, I'm glad the thing wasn't built. Those things are pretty much forever once they go in the ground. And the fragmentation of forests that take place and some other environmental impacts are hard to overlook. From that aspect, we're probably better off without it."

"And it may have contributed to some of this push for renewables as well," he added, noting that Dominion's leaders were "smart, practical . . . very politically astute. I would not be surprised if they came to the conclusion one day, with the CEA, 'Maybe we're going in the wrong direction on this.'"[34]

By D. J. Gerken's lights, Dominion had stuck a finger in the shifting political and financial winds and finally made—albeit very late in the game—the smart call.

"Divesting gas is as much a concession to reality as anything else," he said, referring to the binding terms of the new Clean Economy Act. The company's leaders were merely responding to the incentives of the prevailing system. The role of SELC, as he saw it, was to change those incentives.

"This job makes one cynical," he continued. "Having wrangled with these utilities, I don't consider them good or evil or misguided or the like. They are just wild animals that eat profit. At any given moment they could turn on a dime, where money is to be made."[35]

"All of the Above" vs. "Existential Threat"

In November 2020, during the same week that Dominion finalized the sale of its gas transmission and storage assets to Berkshire Hathaway, Joe Biden was elected forty-sixth president of the United States.

During his long tenure as a senator and his eight years as the forty-seventh vice president, Biden wasn't a particularly outspoken voice on climate and energy issues—he was more of a foreign policy guy. But during his presidential campaign, Biden had made climate action a central plank of his pitch to voters.

He repeatedly called climate change an "existential threat to humanity." He vowed to rejoin the Paris climate agreement. He pledged to rebuild the battered EPA, which had lost thousands of employees—who had either quit or been purged—under Trump. He promised to ban fracking on federal lands. He acknowledged that the country couldn't wean itself off fossil fuels overnight but said that speeding the transition to clean energy was a moral imperative.

"It's the number one issue facing humanity," Biden said, referring to climate change. "And it's the number one issue for me."[36]

But he was also wary of alienating vocal gas-friendly unions in Rust Belt swing states or spooking the powerful oil and gas and utility industries. More than anything, Biden wanted to project himself as a steady hand, the clear choice for those Americans who—after four years of Trump-induced chaos—desperately wanted a return to normalcy.

Normalcy favored the status quo, however. And the status quo was drenched in methane.

A decade after the failure of the cap-and-trade climate bill in Congress (the one that Senator Joe Manchin shot with a deer rifle), the US government had still not passed any significant legislation to reduce the nation's climate-warming pollution. Virginia now had its Clean Economy Act, but a national clean electricity mandate had proved elusive.

Biden's answer to this stasis was the most ambitious climate plan ever put forward by a presidential candidate. He proposed policies to speed up the widespread electrification of systems in homes, business, and factories that run on fossil fuels and to power them with renewable energy instead. He called for $2 trillion in investments in clean energy infrastructure, including 500,000 electric vehicle charging stations and 1.5 million new energy-efficient homes.

The centerpiece of his plan: eliminating all carbon emissions from the power sector by 2035 and achieving net zero emissions across the entire economy by 2050. The logical implication of these targets was clear: utilities would need to start taking carbon-emitting infrastructure offline, starting now. While Biden didn't say this part out loud, his proposed net-zero commitment meant no new gas-fired power plants (or quickly retiring the ones that did get built) and phasing out many existing ones (or retrofitting them with unproven and expensive carbon capture systems) over the next decade.

And if there weren't any new gas power plants being built, there would be little need for new gas pipelines to supply them.

No one was going to "ban fracking," as Republicans kept accusing him of wanting to do. Under Biden's plan, the country would keep burning methane for years to come, but begin the serious work of phasing it out without delay. In late 2020, however, the US was *still* in a gas infrastructure building frenzy. More than 230 new gas-fired power plants were currently planned or under construction nationwide. Dozens of new pipelines were planned or being built to supply those power plants or new LNG terminals.

Biden himself shied away from calling his plan what it really was: a nation finally pledging to move on from its old flame, natural gas, two and a half centuries after George Washington was seduced by the Burning Spring.

Instead, Biden repeatedly called natural gas a "transitional fuel," echoing the language of the gas industry itself. To climate and energy advocates, this generated some serious cognitive dissonance. Politically, it paid off. When Pennsylvania—the second-largest gas producing state, and an epicenter for the Marcellus Shale boom—was called for Biden on November 7, he clinched the presidency.

Post-election, after the waves of relief had washed over them and receded, climate advocates started getting nervous. Battles loomed ahead and gas—as the fastest growing source of carbon emissions worldwide—would be at the center of them. Biden was vocal about his bold climate targets, but his policy team was notably quiet on the subject of the fastest-growing fossil fuel: natural gas.[37]

In Richmond, despite climate-concerned Democrats' recent takeover of the state legislature, there were signs that Dominion's old playbook was still very much in effect.[38]

In Washington, similar concerns tempered the hopes of climate hawks. Some were alarmed by rumors that Ernest Moniz, the academic godfather of the "bridge fuel" narrative, was a leading contender for his old job as secretary of energy.[39] Moniz was on the board of Southern Company, the erstwhile ACP partner, and kept pushing vigorously for more gas production and for outfitting gas plants with still-unproven carbon capture technology.

Climate advocates feared his appointment would augur a return to an "all of the above" energy strategy, with methane, once again, front and center. A decade after President Obama's full-throated endorsement of natural gas, would President Biden declare definitively that the "bridge" had been crossed? Or would his administration extend the gas bridge even deeper into dangerous territory for the climate?[40]

Chapter Twelve

Pipes vs. Wires

On a late July day in 2022, in a lot off Route 48 near Buckhannon, West Virginia, workers navigated forklifts between two giant stacks of metal that represented divergent possible futures for the nation's energy system.[1]

On one side, shrink-wrapped in plastic, lay dozens of sleek, tapered, 130-foot-long wind turbine blades. On the other, lined up in a row, sat 40-foot-long, 42-inch-wide, 1,500-pound sections of coated white steel pipe.

The blades were destined for nearby Laurel Mountain, to upgrade a decade-old project where sixty-one massive turbines, with rotor diameters nearly a football field in length, were generating 260,000 megawatt-hours of carbon-free electricity a year—enough to power a city of sixty thousand. The pipes—originally purchased for the Atlantic Coast Pipeline—were waiting to be loaded onto rail cars and shipped south, to be repurposed for a gas pipeline project in Texas.

Does the future belong to molecules of methane or megawatt-hours of clean electricity?

Despite ACP's demise, and the shudder it sent through the gas industry, that future remained very much up for grabs. While the blades and pipes were being sorted for their onward journeys, a couple hundred miles to the east two veteran politicians named Joe were hashing out a deal that would profoundly influence whether the nation's energy trajectory swung toward pipes or wires—or "all of the above."

For pundits, journalists, policy wonks, and climate advocates, that month had been a roller coaster ride. On July 14, Senator Joe Manchin had announced that he would not support President Joe Biden's flagship legislation, the Build Back Better Act, and its slate of clean energy provisions. The bill had been held up for over a year in grinding negotiations, with Manchin whipsawing White House staff and congressional Democratic leaders back and forth as he changed his mind again and again.

On his first day in office, Biden had signed an executive order rejoining the Paris climate agreement. In April 2021, he made official his administration's goal of cutting US net greenhouse gas emissions in half by 2030. The key to pulling that off would be cleaning up the nation's power sector. That, in turn, hinged largely on how far and how fast big utilities would go in building renewable energy and storage and transmission lines and retiring fossil fuel plants.[2] Clean energy was broadly popular with the public. Polls showed that a solid majority of Americans—including Republican voters—wanted the government to do more to counter climate change and wanted companies to speed up adoption of renewable energy.[3]

But the West Virginia senator was not yet on board. And as the swing vote of the party's slim Senate majority, he had plenty of leverage.

Manchin had come out against the bill in December 2021. Its social safety net provisions were too generous, its clean energy mandates and incentives too aggressive for his taste. "I've tried everything humanly possible," he said in a Fox News interview announcing his decision. "I can't get there. This is a no."[4] Blindsided fellow Democrats accused him of breaking pledges to continue talking. Once tempers cooled, they coaxed Manchin back into negotiations and made steady progress through the spring.

Then, in mid-July, Manchin shocked members of both parties by bailing on the talks again.[5] Democratic leaders took the gloves off this time, in rage and disappointment. "This is bullshit," tweeted Senator

Tina Smith of Minnesota, a key architect of a clean electricity standard that Manchin had quashed the previous fall. Senator Martin Heinrich of New Mexico proposed removing Manchin from his post as chair of the Energy and Natural Resources Committee.[6] "It seems odd that Manchin would choose as his legacy to be the one man who single-handedly doomed humanity," said John Podesta, a veteran Democratic operative, former Obama aide, and future Biden advisor.[7] News outlets ran pieces reminding readers that the West Virginia senator who had killed the biggest piece of federal climate policy in history was the top recipient of oil and gas money in Congress—and had made his own millions trading coal.[8]

This backlash apparently stung Manchin enough to trigger some second thoughts. A few days later, he and Senate Majority Leader Chuck Schumer agreed to hold secret talks, to see if some pared-down version of the bill could be revived. On July 27 they announced a break-through. The bill had been whittled down from its $2.2 trillion start-ing point to $375 billion in climate and clean energy incentives. The new version was all carrots and no sticks: there were no mandates or penalties to compel utilities to choose clean energy, but it was loaded with tax credits, rebates, and other enticements to prod them to build more wind and solar and to help businesses and consumers adopt clean technologies like heat pumps and electric vehicles. Energy experts es-timated that these measures would reduce US carbon emissions by 40 percent by 2030—close to the president's target of a 50 percent cut.[9]

When President Biden signed the result—the Inflation Reduction Act—into law on August 16, 2022, and then handed the pen to Manchin with a meaningful look, it was a watershed moment.[10] Without a sin-gle Republican vote, the Democrats had passed the most far-reaching piece of carbon-cutting legislation in history. And they had taken a huge step toward accelerating the clean energy transition.

But to some climate advocates' consternation, the law also included provisions to boost fossil fuel production. Industry lobbyists had se-cured a tit-for-tat measure: before the government could lease any ar-eas for offshore wind projects, it would first have to hold auctions for offshore oil and gas leases.[11] And there was another bill coming due.

Manchin had extracted a key concession. The White House had

promised its support for legislation to "streamline" the permitting of energy infrastructure—including gas pipelines. Manchin also sought to push the Mountain Valley Pipeline, ACP's surviving twin, over the finish line via legislative blunt force—by forbidding any further judicial review in what he saw as a hostile Fourth Circuit Court of Appeals. The MVP had been limping along for years, hamstrung by its loss of key permits and tenacious opposition from communities in its path. Democratic leadership threw it a lifeline by promising to bring Manchin's measure up for a vote.[12]

They could not afford to lose Manchin's swing vote on the IRA, and any number of other issues. To keep him on board, they would have to make it easier to build pipes too.

The View from Cooperative Way

In August 2020, a month after ACP's cancellation, a new energy infrastructure project was announced in Nelson County.

Appalachian Power (APCo), Virginia's other big utility, was embarking on a multiyear effort to upgrade high-voltage transmission lines. The project would involve building two new electrical substations and replacing aging equipment—some dating back to the 1940s—so they could carry much higher voltages.

One substation would be built in Shipman, not far from the Purvises. Another would be in Schuyler, the birthplace of *The Waltons* creator. The upgraded lines would run between them, just south of Harris Cove. Hundred-foot-tall steel poles would be erected to connect the substations to an existing transmission line—a key part of the network that fed power to the local electric cooperative, which provided electricity to nearly forty thousand homes and businesses across fourteen counties, including two-thirds of all Nelson residents.[13]

When APCo held a virtual open house to share these plans and seek feedback, the reaction was starkly different from the one that greeted Dominion's 2014 pipeline charm offensive. The lack of pushback might be explained by the fact that the cooperative is a universally beloved institution in Nelson County.

The Central Virginia Electric Cooperative's main office sits at the end of a street called Cooperative Way south of Lovingston, next to the bucolic grounds of a popular brewery with a striking view of the Blue Ridge beyond—not unlike the one that must have caused John Lederer's companions to kneel in reverence in 1669. Today that view is clustered with transmission lines and an electric substation. Nobody seems to mind this sight, though, as they sip their Full Nelson Pale Ales: in Nelson County, people know just how precious those power lines are.

In the 1930s, when John Ed Purvis was born, only one in ten residents of central Virginia had electricity in their homes.[14] Thomas Edison had switched on the first grid in Manhattan in 1882, but half a century later most Nelsonians kept their milk cool in springhouses instead of refrigerators. Wisteria Johnson's grandparents still lit their home with kerosene and candles—just as most rural Americans did, even as urban-dwellers enjoyed the smoke-free light of electric bulbs.[15]

The reason for this disparity was simple: big power companies didn't see much financial sense in putting up lines to places like Harris Cove. They assumed that the smattering of farmsteads out in the hill country were too remote, their residents too benighted, to justify the expense.

President Franklin D. Roosevelt saw this as both an injustice in need of remedy and an opportunity to unleash bottled-up economic energy at the height of the Great Depression. In 1935, he launched the Rural Electrification Administration as a flagship program of the New Deal. A year later he secured $100 million from Congress to expand electricity access to rural Americans. If big utilities didn't want to connect 90 percent of America, the REA would finance it. The new agency issued loans to citizens who wanted to literally take power into their own hands.[16]

On September 22, 1937, a group of local citizens held a meeting at Lovingston High School and organized themselves into the Central Virginia Electric Cooperative. Four hundred members signed up at that first meeting, each paying a $5 fee to supplement the $100,000 federal loan to build 129 miles of lines and two substations. Within a year, power was flowing through its first line to a store in Afton.[17]

The co-op's wires soon transformed daily life in Nelson County, illuminating farmhouses and powering mills and other labor-saving devices. Demand was huge: by the summer of 1940, advertising with the tagline "Electricity is your best bargain," the cooperative had over 1,400 members. Nelsonians clamored for the lines. Treated poles were hard to come by during the war years. So, they cut logs, brought them to Norfolk to be cured so they wouldn't rot, brought them back, then dug the holes, set the poles by hand, and then pulled the wires between them with teams of horses.[18] "The wires which tied the homes of rural people together also seemed to unite their spirits," wrote Clyde Ellis, a leader of the national rural electric cooperative movement through the 1940s and 1950s.

The big utilities watched all this unfold and realized that rural Virginians represented a vast potential market, what with all the new appliances and machines they were buying. They built "spite lines" to skim off the easiest-to-reach big farms and businesses whose regular payments could help subsidize bringing electricity to poorer residents. Early on, VEPCO (Dominion's corporate forerunner) and APCo made life hard for the fledgling cooperative, charging it high whole-sale rates for power and cutting off supply from time to time. VEPCO raced to put up lines into other new cooperatives' service areas north of Richmond to deny them revenue they needed to be financially solvent.[19] But eventually, after their service territories were settled, the utilities pursued other avenues for growth: persuading customers to buy more electricity. From 1955 to 1969, VEPCO focused its marketing on what it called the "all-electric living concept."[20]

By 2020, that vision had finally gone mainstream. There was an emerging consensus among energy and climate experts that meeting the nation's climate targets requires transforming the economy to run on clean electricity instead of fossil fuels. This new vision could be summed up in two words: "electrify everything." Think heating buildings with highly efficient heat pumps instead of gas furnaces and charging cars with a plug instead of filling up at the pump.

Much of that heavy lifting—making big investments to build wind, solar, storage, and transmission lines—will be done by the investor-owned utilities that provide electricity to three out of four Americans. In any plausible pathway to zeroing out greenhouse gas emissions by

2050, companies like Dominion, Duke, and Southern will be key play-ers. But half a century after going all in on an electrified future, those utilities' perspective had flipped: "electrifying everything" was now viewed as an existential threat rather than an opportunity. They owned wires, but plenty of pipes too. And they were determined to protect those lucrative assets.[21]

In 2019, cities in California began adopting ordinances to restrict gas connections in new homes and businesses, with the aims of sav-ing homeowners money, improving air quality, and meeting their own climate action goals. By the end of 2020, more than forty cities and counties in California had adopted similar measures. Soon, cities in Massachusetts and Maryland were considering similar steps.[22]

For gas utilities, this trend posed a dire threat. After all, if millions of homeowners tore out their gas furnaces and stoves, and if homebuild-ers stopped putting in new gas lines, there wouldn't be much need for all the storage tanks, compressors, gas line mains, and interstate pipe-lines that they had on their balance sheets.[23]

Dominion Energy, for example, still owned half a dozen gas utilities across seven states. Member-funded trade groups like the American Gas Association—whose board chair in 2020 was Dominion executive Diane Leopold—launched advertising campaigns against these "gas bans" around the country, claiming that the ordinances would "elimi-nate consumer choice."[24]

In a 2020 webinar, Dominion executive Donald Raikes described the growing movement of electric-only ordinances moving outward from California not as a glowing opportunity (as his 1960s-era prede-cessors might have) but in terms that made it sound like a deadly new coronavirus variant that must be contained. "Unless we do something about it, they will spread," he warned.[25]

Rural electric cooperatives operated according to a strikingly differ-ent paradigm than the one that governed the Dominions and Dukes. They had no distant shareholders to pay dividends to, no stock price to track, no investment bank analysts to court. They had to navigate the same complex challenges—shifts in technology, the imperatives of re-ducing carbon pollution, financial recessions, supply chain constraints, the duty to keep the lights on come hell or high water—but their decision-making was guided by a simple mandate: they did whatever their members wanted. The customers owned the company.

That logic dictated some of CVEC's new wire-based investments: laying 4,500 miles of fiber-optic cable to deliver high-speed internet to rural residents. When it first piloted this venture, the cooperative projected that, without outside support, it might break even after seven years. But it was still worth doing, it reckoned, because internet access was as critical and neglected a piece of infrastructure for rural Americans today as electricity was seventy years ago.[26] Like roads, phone, and power lines before it, fiber-optic cable was the kind of infrastructure that Nelsonians actually wanted in their backyards—as Wisteria Johnson would say, "the good stuff."

The co-op was investing in new solar arrays and battery storage, too, and helping members who wanted to add their own rooftop solar to the grid. It launched a community solar program for those who didn't have a good spot to install solar panels on their own property. It was also busy upgrading its own transmission lines—installing new towers way up on the mountain near Wintergreen, not far from Reeds Gap—to keep up with new voltage requirements. To keep the lights on, but also to prepare for the future of rising electricity demand that the co-op's leaders saw on the near horizon. A future in which more and more people would turn to electricity to fuel their cars, heat their homes, and power their daily lives.

At a recent annual meeting, CEO Gary Wood explained the co-op's plans for the near future—more transmission upgrades, more solar arrays—and then took questions. "I don't have any questions," one member said. "I just want to say thank you very much. I've been receiving your service for the last twenty-six years. . . . Thank you for what you do."

"The reason we're here is for the members," Wood replied with a shrug.[27]

That "We" Energy

On a warm, muggy summer evening at the foot of the Blue Ridge, more than a hundred people gathered in a field next to the Rockfish Valley

Community Center. Nearby, kids did tricks in the skate park, where a sign read "NO PIPELINE, YES HALFPIPE." Other signs large and small were all around, reading "OUR COMMUNITY WON." A large stage was set up, under which hung a sign with the words: "One Down One to Go STOP the MVP."

The scene buzzed with pent-up energy—after a year of living under pandemic-era social distancing, and a year spent unable to thank each other in person, the people of Nelson County were finally convening to celebrate their victory over the Atlantic Coast Pipeline.

Joyce Burton scurried about, clad in her old blue NO PIPELINE T-shirt—now modified with a sharpie to show a box with a check mark underneath the phrase. She tacked up the banner with two hundred names on it that she had held up in front of FERC's office six years prior. She greeted landowners as if they were old friends—even a few she was meeting for the first time in the flesh, after years of emails and phone calls.

Wisteria Johnson and her family sat under a tent, handing out postcards that read: "Thank you for your commitment to helping save the mountains and streams of Nelson County." As folks walked past, they explained the idea behind them: write a thank-you note to another person you admire for their efforts to stop the pipeline, and then go up and hand it to them. Everyone turned toward the stage as Marion Kanour, the Episcopal priest who had been active in the pipeline resistance, came up to read an opening benediction. She asked everyone to remember John Ed Purvis and other friends and neighbors who were no longer with them. Then, to rousing cheers, Ernie Reed read an official resolution passed by him and his fellow county supervisors, designating July 5, 2021, "a commemorative date to celebrate the accomplishment."

Richard Averitt, the emcee, introduced Wisteria Johnson as the next speaker. She described the headwaters and wild creatures that remained undisturbed thanks to their efforts. "Our mountains, our lovely steep slopes are unscarred, you guys! Praise my god, when heavy rains come, nature still has something to protect itself, and perhaps us."[28]

"I'm a landowner that belongs to a grateful club, thanks to all of you for your faith, belief, and perseverance," she said.

A local candidate for Congress from Augusta County exhorted people to keep calling elected officials to oppose the Mountain Valley Pipeline. Musicians came up to sing an original composition with the refrain "No Dominion over Me." Then Joyce Burton climbed onstage, clutching a copy of the July 9, 2020, edition of the *Nelson County Times* newspaper with the giant headline on the front page announcing the pipeline's cancellation.

"Right now, I'm feeling really grateful for all the ways we connected," she told her neighbors. "I'm feeling like we showed up for each other. And we shored each other up. We refused to give up. And damn it, eventually ACP bled out from those thousand cuts. And we are a stronger community for that."

But, she added, the job wasn't over. She described her ongoing work to get Dominion to restore the easements they had purchased from Nelson landowners. "Landowners, even though you signed, the vast majority didn't sign because they wanted this, or the money, but because they wanted to avoid going to court and paying lawyers and appraisers. The couple landowners who got taken to court went through unbelievable hell."

When Richard Averitt invited anyone up for an "open mic gratitude fest," Will Fenton's stocky frame soon materialized behind the microphone. "I'd like to thank Joyce Burton," said the innkeeper, "Jill Averitt, and Greg Buppert—the man who went into the lion's den and kicked ass. Let's keep that kind of 'We' energy together."

Then Nancy Sorrells came up to talk about her friend Ann Schages, who had fought to get Dominion to move a pipeline access road a few dozen feet away her home while she was terminally ill, and persevered until the company agreed. Sorrells got to tell Schages she had won that small fight on her deathbed, but never got to tell her that they had won the larger fight.

"We did something that nobody in this country has done before," Sorrells concluded.

When he first started looking into it back in 2014, Greg Buppert hadn't been able to find a single case where citizens had stopped a large methane gas pipeline. Now, as he climbed onto the stage—in shorts and baseball cap, no briefcase—he was surrounded by the people who had pulled it off. "It was SELC's privilege and honor to represent Friends of Nelson and fourteen other organizations," his colleague Sarah Francisco said, standing next to him. "We stopped a project that would have resulted in 30 million tons of greenhouse gases every year," Buppert added to cheers.

Richard Averitt spoke last. "I want to thank each of you who were not landowners," he said. "You weren't fighting for yourself, your own property, your own family the way we were. I entered this fight in a naïve way. Many of you taught me about environmental justice, and the environmental damage of fracking. Beyond just property rights, you taught me to think about stewardship versus ownership."

As clouds piled high over the Blue Ridge, local musicians led the audience in a modified version of Woody Guthrie's "This Land Is Your Land." The celebrants drew tight together for a group photo. "Maybe we'll mail it to our friends at Dominion and let 'em know we won," Averitt shouted, "and don't come in our county again."

"We Have a Huge Methane Problem, Folks"

There is one federal agency that has authority over both pipes and wires.

And six years after Nelson County visited its headquarters, five years after Megan Holleran invited its commissioners to eat some pancakes, four years after Cheryl LaFleur aired her concerns that it was permitting projects without fully studying the need for them, there were signs that the Federal Energy Regulatory Commission was finally listening to its critics.

After a forty-year delay, FERC had finally created an Office of Public Participation in early 2021, soon after new chair Richard Glick took office. The "situation," as LaFleur once labeled it, seemed to have the upper hand.

Throughout the preceding year, Congressman Jamie Raskin had led a series of hearings and investigations into how sharply the playing field was tilted against landowners and toward pipeline developers. Richard Averitt spoke to Raskin for his investigation and described his and his neighbors' experience with calm, cold fury. The process, he said, "is wildly imbalanced."

Thanks to tolling orders, Averitt explained, "we were held in limbo for a year or so while they were going around and more or less coercing citizens in the community into signing easement agreements by telling them 'We're going to get your land through eminent domain anyway so we either get it through quicktake or you sign a deal with us.' The stress that puts people under is extraordinary. So most people settled."[29]

"By the time FERC lets challenges go forward, the pipe is usually in the ground," he added. "And landowners have lost any power to compel the company to move it away from cemeteries, building sites, or the like."

In December 2020, at a hearing releasing all his findings, Raskin cited the tale of the Hollerans in Pennsylvania. He described how the Constitution Pipeline cut most of their sugar maple trees down and then promptly abandoned the project.

"FERC is an accomplice to the destruction of the Hollerans' family maple syrup business," Raskin said, and then described landowners who had abandoned their own businesses and building plans because they were in the ACP's corridor. "These are Americans who have rights to their property, and their rights are being demolished."[30]

Giving landowners more of a voice was just one of the changes that weary pipeline fighters sought from FERC. In July, Ella Rose had driven north from Union Hill to Washington, DC, to testify to a different congressional subcommittee about another reform: a meaningful commitment to environmental justice. She described how she had spoken up over and over, for five years, to state and federal regulators about her concerns about the compressor station being sited in her community—but felt "largely ignored" by FERC and other agencies.

On top of those demands, a chorus of federal judges, lawmakers, and independent analysts alike had long called on FERC to overhaul the way it counted the likely climate impacts of projects it reviewed.

All of these demands finally bore fruit on February 17, 2022, when FERC issued long-awaited updates to its gas pipeline review policies, for the first time since 1999, in a 3–2 vote led by chairman Richard Glick.[31] The new guidelines directed FERC to take climate change impacts, landowner concerns, and environmental justice—issues that those fighting the Atlantic Coast Pipeline had highlighted for years—into account when it reviewed new pipeline projects. It seemed like the commission was finally going to take its role as one of the federal government's key climate actors—and as a steward of the public interest—seriously.

Meanwhile, in the halls of power—at big media and finance events, on cable news shows, in all the places where elites signaled to each other the boundaries of conventional wisdom—the gas brand seemed to be on the wane. A decade after Robert Howarth's research had suggested methane leaks would make the gas build-out a "bridge to nowhere," there was at last some focus at the highest levels of government on the urgency of plugging those leaks and tackling methane more broadly. And thanks to the relentless grassroots pressure, more decision-makers were coming to share Cheryl LaFleur's concerns that the federal government might be abetting the gas industry's chronic overbuilding habit.

This, of course, was an existential threat to the gas industry. Soon after the ACP was canceled, and just months before the 2020 election, Duke and Southern Company helped set up a front group called "Natural Allies for a Clean Energy Future." Pipeline companies like Williams, LNG giant Cheniere, and Marcellus fracking heavyweight EQT, whose spinoff subsidiary owned the Mountain Valley Pipeline, were also key funders. Natural Allies' mission was to shore up the beleaguered gas brand—to "protect the social license to operate."[32]

Republicans were already firmly on board. GOP state legislators were busy passing "preemption laws" (i.e., bans on local gas bans) in dozens of states, criminalizing pipeline protests in nineteen states,[33] and even introducing bills to certify methane as "clean" energy in states like Tennessee and Ohio.[34]

So, Natural Allies set its sights on "opinion leaders and influencers" in the Democratic Party. To that end, Natural Allies signed up former Democratic senators Mary Landrieu and Heidi Heitkamp as ambassadors to make sure their party's leaders kept using the same "clean natural gas" songbook that everyone had been singing for over the past decade.[35]

They seemed to have their work cut out for them. Their former

Senate colleague John Kerry, the new US climate envoy, had captured the zeitgeist when he told the World Economic Forum, days after President Biden was inaugurated in January 2021: "If we build out a huge infrastructure for gas now and continue to use it as the bridge fuel . . . we're gonna be stuck with stranded assets in 10 or 20 or 30 years. Gas is primarily methane, and we have a huge methane problem, folks."[36]

Molecules of Freedom, Redux

A week after FERC's pipeline permitting reforms were announced, Russian president Vladimir Putin sent his army into Ukraine. His brutal invasion shifted the discourse around methane almost overnight.

Suddenly, America's abundant shale gas wasn't just the key to energy independence—the longstanding shibboleth favored by politicians on the left and right—but to global security. Producing more gas was essential to shoring up allies in Europe who relied heavily on Russia's gas, to stiffen their spines in the fight. Nobody was calling them "freedom molecules" anymore, but methane had been elevated to a tool of statecraft all the same.

Senator Joe Manchin wasted no time seizing this opportunity. He hauled Chairman Glick before his committee and assailed FERC's new pipeline policy. The war in Ukraine demanded that they make it *easier* to build gas pipelines and export terminals, Manchin said, whereas the new policy amounted to a "short-sighted attack on fossil fuel resources."

Federal judges had ruled that FERC must examine pipelines' downstream carbon emissions, but for Manchin this was a bridge too far. "In my view, there is an effort underway by some to inflict death by a thousand cuts on the fossil fuels that have made our energy reliable and affordable while also providing us countless products and a vast strategic advantage over our adversaries and to the benefit of our allies and trade partners," Manchin said. He didn't name the late Atlantic Coast Pipeline, but it was clear that it was on his mind. "We sit on an ocean of energy in West Virginia with nearly 214 trillion cubic feet of untapped natural gas in the Appalachian Basin."

"But we can't get our abundant natural gas out of West Virginia with the roadblocks being placed in the way of these project developers," he added.

The gas industry, meanwhile, had its talking points ready. Russia's disastrous war on Ukraine proved a boon for the companies developing new gas export terminals: many that had been desperate for financing saw their prospects revived overnight. They pressed their advantage. Just a day after Putin's invasion began, a trade group called LNG Allies wrote to Biden calling for immediate approval of proposed gas export facilities and more pressure on FERC to *speed up* its pipeline permitting. "Policies such as pausing leasing on federal lands, preventing new pipeline infrastructure, and discouraging investments across the hydrocarbon value chain hamper U.S. production," it wrote, "thereby driving up prices and making the world more reliant on energy from nations such as Russia."[37]

FERC's new policy didn't stand a chance against this coordinated assault and its invocation of patriotic duty. In late March, the commission retracted the changes and said it would seek further input "from all stakeholders." One former GOP-appointed commissioner described it as a "complete and total retreat."[38] The old pipeline procedures would stay in place. There would be no increased scrutiny of climate impacts or environmental justice populations, no heightened outreach or consideration for landowners like the Hollerans, the Averitts, or Ella Rose, no overhaul of the way regulators assessed economic need for projects beyond the narrow focus on precedent agreements.

The Biden administration stayed silent on FERC's reversal. But it soon made its own announcement: the US would act quickly to boost exports of liquefied natural gas to European allies to help them wean themselves off Russian gas.

Energy experts worried that those investments risked locking in polluting infrastructure, even as reducing gas demand—through energy efficiency and wider adoption of heat pumps, for example—could help achieve the desired outcomes.

Exasperated climate advocates quickly pressed the White House for an explanation.[39] How would the administration reconcile boosting exports of methane to 50 billion cubic feet by 2030, with *another* recent announcement it had made? The one in which the United States led more than one hundred countries at the recent United Nations climate meeting in Glasgow, in pledging to *cut* their methane emissions by 30 percent by 2030?[40]

The MVP'S MVP

Throughout the fall of 2022, Joe Manchin tried repeatedly to get his favorite project, the beleaguered Mountain Valley Pipeline, across the finish line.

As the price for his Inflation Reduction Act vote, President Biden, Senate Majority Leader Schumer, and Speaker of the House Nancy Pelosi had promised him a vote on his proposed legislation to fast-track permitting for pipelines and other fossil fuel infrastructure. Manchin's bill would also authorize all remaining permits that the MVP needed and bar the Fourth Circuit Court of Appeals from reviewing them further—the legislative equivalent of overturning the Scrabble board in a fit of pique when you're losing a game fair and square.[41]

Fellow senators pointed out that Manchin's measure would enshrine into law a dangerous precedent by bulldozing a path for MVP through the normal judicial process. Senator Tim Kaine of Virginia refused to vote for it. "If the MVP owners are unhappy with a court ruling, they should do what other litigants do and appeal," he said. "Allowing them to fundamentally change federal law to achieve their goal would surely encourage other wealthy people and companies to try the same. I won't participate in opening that door to abuse and even corruption."[42]

Undeterred, Manchin pursued a series of maneuvers to attach the measure to "must-pass" bills that had nothing to do with energy. First, he tried in September to have the language attached to a continuing resolution to fund the federal government—but withdrew it because he didn't have enough votes. He tried again in December—with Democratic leadership's support—to attach the MVP provision to another "must-pass" vehicle: the annual defense authorization bill. Again, Kaine spoke out against it, environmental groups rallied to oppose it, and again, the measure was withdrawn for lack of votes. Manchin tried one more time to add it to a must-pass budget bill right before Christmas. That failed too.

But the fourth time was the charm. The following spring, Biden and GOP leaders were locked in tough negotiations to hammer out a deal to raise the nation's debt ceiling. If they missed the early June deadline, the United States would default on its debts.

With time winding down, a last-minute maneuver finally secured Manchin's prize. Buried on page ninety-five of the ninety-nine-page proposed bill—apparently inserted late in the negotiations, to most lawmakers' surprise—was a section authorizing the completion of the Mountain Valley Pipeline: "The Congress hereby finds and declares that the timely completion of construction and operation of the Mountain Valley Pipeline is required in the national interest."[43]

Thanks to Manchin's last-minute intervention (and with an assist from industry lobbyists), it seemed that the Mountain Valley Pipeline would be spared the fate of its twin, the Atlantic Coast Pipeline.[44]

Still, the deal had to come up for a vote.

Gaslighting's Greatest Hits

On June 1, 2023, the ghost of the Atlantic Coast Pipeline was haunting the US Senate.

Late that morning, senators began debating legislation to raise the country's debt ceiling. The treasury secretary warned the US would default by the following week if no action was taken. The global economy would be thrown into a tailspin. It was the hardest of deadlines.

Senator Tim Kaine had proposed an amendment stripping the MVP provision—which, of course, had nothing to do with the debt ceiling—from the bill. A dozen other proposed amendments had to be addressed too. At the outset of a long day, Joe Manchin took the podium to persuade his colleagues to reject them and to make his case for the Mountain Valley Pipeline get-out-of-jail-free card.

He opened by citing the cautionary tale of the Atlantic Coast Pipeline. He lamented how long it took, how litigation tied it up in knots, how it got so expensive that Dominion had to pull the plug on it. He mentioned Duke Energy's claim that MVP would save its customers millions of dollars. "They were counting on ACP to get them the product. That didn't happen. Now they're counting on MVP." He claimed that no project had "ever been more scrutinized" than MVP. "Everybody had a good look at this thing."

He reminded everyone how patient he had been through all the long negotiations. "We have tried everything humanly possible, we really have," he said. "I just couldn't believe we couldn't get this to work after what happened to the previous lines they were trying to build."

Throughout his floor speech, Manchin worked his way through the greatest hits in the gas industry's public relations catalogue: energy independence, energy security, keeping the lights on, helping low-income households with high energy bills heat their homes.[45]

"It is basically 'all of the above.' It is wind, solar. It is coal. It is gas. It is everything that gives the reliability that, when you turn that switch on, you are going to have lights."

He lambasted federal agencies for overly stringent reviews and wistfully observed that American gas could spread freedom but for all the red tape keeping it bottled up. He conceded that the energy transition was underway, that "there will be a transition into new technology that will replace an awful lot of what we're talking about, but we're a long way away from that."[46]

"There are so many benefits from two billion cubic feet a day," he said, repeating the number like a mantra. "Two billion. Two billion cubic feet a day will go through this line, helping America be energy independent."

It was a virtuosic performance, compressing decades' worth of industry talking points into a few adrenalized minutes on the Senate floor.

Behind it all loomed the premise that America desperately needed the gas that MVP would provide—the same "fact" that had gone unquestioned during the 2020 Supreme Court oral arguments when Chief Justice Roberts worried aloud that the Appalachian Trail would become an "impermeable barrier" to the Atlantic Coast Pipeline and others like it.

Manchin closed his speech by emphasizing the inevitability of it all—how the project was on its way to completion anyway, regardless of the opposition. White House officials, eager to spin the outcome of the negotiations as a thoroughgoing "win," had been quick to defend the MVP provision. "This pipeline was going to happen anyway," one person close to the negotiations told a reporter, "so all this really does . . . is just codifies something that was going to happen."[47] (To the victorious grassroots veterans of the ACP fight, this must have sounded familiar: they had been hearing that project was inevitable from day one.)

And if none of that was persuasive, Manchin had a final trump card to play. His provision was now securely on board a legislative train that had to leave the station. "Everyone deserves to have their say," he said, in a nod toward Kaine, his colleague from Virginia. "I agree. But we've come down to the reality . . . that this piece of legislation that we have before us has to pass. The Mountain Valley Pipeline is in that piece of legislation."

After twelve hours of debate, all ten amendments, including Kaine's proposal to strip MVP out, were defeated. By midnight, the Senate had voted to approve the deal, thus averting a default, by a vote of 63–36. The bill had its critics, who said it rewarded irresponsible GOP hostage-taking, and plenty of cheerleaders, who praised the pragmatic Democratic leadership for being the adults in the room. The latter reminded the public, with rhetorical pats on the head, that's how the art of compromise works. The Washington press corps swooned over a bipartisan victory for Biden. Some even ventured that it was a "win" for the climate.

The very next day, MVP's owners—who had become leading donors to both Manchin and Chuck Schumer[48]—predicted that their pipeline would be complete by the end of 2023. Those living in Mountain Valley's path, who had fought it for nearly a decade, watching as its construction caused severe erosion and triggered over five hundred recorded violations of water quality and other regulations, saw it as a terrible betrayal. But many legal experts worried that it also set a perilous precedent and warned that it wouldn't be the last time the tactic was pursued to shield fossil fuel projects from judicial review or scientific scrutiny, if they happen to be deemed by their developers and political allies to be in the "national interest."[49]

But the gaslighting went even further. Now codified into federal law was the claim that "the Mountain Valley Pipeline will . . . reduce carbon emissions and facilitate the energy transition."

The law of the land now proclaimed that the pumping, piping, and burning of more fossil fuels was indeed—after all the years of accumulating science, and common sense, to the contrary—a *solution* to a global crisis primarily caused by the burning of fossil fuels.

Taken together, by one estimate, the MVP would generate yearly emissions equal to 89 million metric tons of carbon dioxide, equivalent to what's produced by twenty-six coal plants.[50] Other estimates were lower: the government pegged it at 40 million tons. Regardless, analysts didn't dispute that building the pipeline would result in more climate-warming carbon and methane heading skyward for as long as it operated.

Meanwhile, new research drawing on sophisticated satellite monitoring programs revealed that some pipelines were "super-emitters," leaking methane at rates far higher than government estimates. "No one expects that pipelines are sometimes wide open, pouring gas into the atmosphere," said the lead author.[51]

Another new study summed up lifecycle emissions across the entire gas supply chain and concluded that a leak rate as low as 0.2 percent rendered gas as bad for the climate as coal.[52] (Leak rates as high as 9 percent had been observed in the Permian Basin, the nation's largest shale play.) "It can't be considered a good bridge, or substitute," said the lead author.[53]

And yet the construction of a giant methane delivery device was now officially deemed to be in the "national interest."

The bridge had not only been extended but officially relabeled as a destination.

And for the political party that had first embraced the industry's "bridge fuel" slogan way back in 2008, the "all of the above" energy vision was alive and well.

"We Will Win"

And yet some people stubbornly refuse to be gaslit.

A week later, hundreds of protestors—some who had been fighting the Mountain Valley Pipeline for nearly a decade—gathered in front of the White House, chanting and carrying signs pillorying the "MVP dirty deal."[54]

The rest of the city was quiet. The Washington Nationals baseball team had canceled its game and the National Zoo was closed, as smoke streaming south from hundreds of unprecedented early season wildfires in Canada triggered the highest levels of fine particulate pollution ever measured in the capital's skies. The haze was so thick that the Washington Monument wasn't visible from the Senate side of the Capitol, where some lawmakers gathered to demand that President Biden declare a "climate emergency" and deploy broader powers to reduce emissions.

But Chad Oba was there, along with several other Friends of Buckingham members, in Lafayette Park—where American citizens have gathered for decades to air their grievances in front of the "People's House." They were surrounded by fellow protestors, Black and white and brown, millennials and Gen Z and retirees—most of them wearing masks to keep from inhaling soot that had, just a few days before, been boreal forest. Some were in rocking chairs, the signature protest tool of Third Act, a new movement to channel the energy and experience of people 60 and older to press for climate action.[55]

Justin Pearson, a charismatic young state legislator from Tennessee wearing a dark suit and sneakers, paced in front of them. Gripping a bullhorn and borrowing the cadence of the civil rights preachers he grew up idolizing, Pearson exhorted the protestors to keep fighting.[56]

"It's hard to breathe here today because of the pollution that's in the air, but we've still got breath in our bodies," he said. "Which means we've still got fight left. We've got to use that fire to keep on believing in the future that we know is possible."

A rising voice for environmental justice, Pearson knew a thing or two about defeating pipelines. When he was 25, Pearson had cofounded an organization dedicated to fighting an oil pipeline slated to go through an aquifer, wetlands, and mostly Black neighborhoods in his hometown of Memphis. The Southern Environmental Law Center sued on the group's behalf to overturn a key federal permit, and to challenge the use of eminent domain to take Black-owned lands. In July 2021, the company behind the pipeline threw in the towel.

"We gotta tell Joe Manchin, we will never quit," Pearson shouted. "We gotta tell Joe Biden we will never quit. We gotta tell the Mountain Valley Pipeline developers we will never quit. And because we will never quit, we know we will win."

"This movement is not rooted in money," Pearson continued, "it's rooted in love of place. It's rooted in love of people from West Virginia to Virginia to North Carolina to Memphis, Tennessee, to California to Nebraska. And a movement that's rooted in love will always win."

Epilogue

Pass It On

Wisteria Johnson near the boulder where her ancestors ground corn in
Harris Cove. (Jonathan Mingle)

The next month was the hottest in recorded history.

For much of July 2023, a "heat dome" settled over the
American Southwest and refused to budge. Residents of
Phoenix suffered through thirty-one consecutive days over 110 de-
grees. Smoke from those record-setting Canadian wildfires reached
Chicago, leading to the worst air quality ever recorded in the city, just
weeks after doing the same to New York, Washington, and much of the
East Coast. Torrential rains sent record-smashing floodwaters surging

through communities from Vermont to Spain to northern India to southern Japan to China.[1] A road in New York's Hudson Valley collapsed after 8 inches of rain fell in three hours—a "once in a thousand year" event, experts called it, using a label that now seems obsolete. Temperatures topped 100 degrees in ocean waters along Florida's coast. Scientists warned that this was not some "new normal" but just the beginning of a quickening slide into chaos that wouldn't end until humanity kicked its fossil fuel habit and brought net greenhouse gas emissions down to zero.

Toward the end of the hottest month in over 120,000 years,[2] the lawyers of the Southern Environmental Law Center were back in rooftop-to-rooftop mode. Once again, they were preparing to file briefs in the US Supreme Court arguing that a large methane gas pipeline cutting through Appalachia didn't deserve exemption from the laws of the land. The déjà vu went even further: at issue was a decision by the Fourth Circuit Court of Appeals.

SELC attorneys had filed a motion in June arguing that the special protections for the Mountain Valley Pipeline that Joe Manchin had jammed into the debt ceiling legislation were unconstitutional. On July 10 the Fourth Circuit ordered a halt to pipeline construction in Virginia's Jefferson National Forest; a few days later, the MVP's owners made an emergency appeal to the Supreme Court. Two weeks later, the court sided with the pipeline and, though it didn't explain its reasoning, cleared the way for construction to continue.[3]

SELC's new executive director D. J. Gerken, who had taken the helm the previous fall, pledged to continue to fight alongside local activists who had been working for nearly a decade to stop the project. "We stand by our argument that the MVP rider—Congress's reckless attempt to bless a single gas pipeline—violates the separation of powers and is unconstitutional," he said.[4]

Meanwhile, as Congress was encroaching on the judiciary's turf, candidates who wanted to take control of the *other* branch of government were testing out their messages to voters. With campaigns for the 2024 presidential election already well underway, conservative think tanks were preparing a plan called Project 2025, offering any Republican who might win in 2024 a playbook for unraveling the federal government's climate change programs. The nearly one-thousand-page document called for repealing the Inflation Reduction Act, making it harder to build renewable energy and easier to drill for fossil fuels on public lands, and dismantling efforts to limit pollution from power plants. When asked if they had any other ideas for how to slow down climate change, a key participant in Project 2025 could only suggest that Americans should produce and burn more natural gas.[5]

That was Republicans' climate action plan: less renewable energy, more methane.[6]

Democrats, meanwhile, planned to run on Biden's signature legislative achievements, including the Inflation Reduction Act, a climate bill in all but name. They continued unveiling other more incremental steps to curb warming too. In July, the White House announced a new interagency task force to improve detection of methane leaks.[7] Soon, this unit would have some new places to go hunting: two new LNG export terminals on the Gulf Coast and another one in Alaska, recently approved by . . . the Biden administration. (And FERC, of course.)

The cognitive dissonance didn't stop there. Data from the government's own National Oceanic and Atmospheric Administration suggested those methane hunters might want to hurry up. NOAA kept diligently reporting both carbon dioxide and methane levels in the atmosphere, based on samples of air collected from all over the planet. The latest methane number, 1.92 parts per million, had been notched after a record increase over the previous year. Earth had not seen methane concentrations that high since at least 800,000 years ago, or carbon dioxide levels that high since 3 million years ago.

In midsummer, amid all the floods and heat waves and wildfire smoke, a group of the world's leading methane researchers published a paper with a stark warning: this might be as good as it gets on planet Earth for a very long time.

When they looked at ice core records of Earth's past climates, today's methane trends looked disconcertingly similar to what happened during global-scale shifts from ice ages to sweltering "interglacial" periods that lasted tens of thousands of years. The rapid spike in methane levels possibly signaled that the planet was shifting into a new climate regime.[8] In decades past, oil and gas were the biggest driver

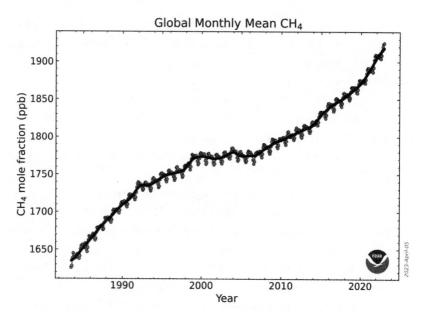

Globally averaged, monthly mean abundance of methane in the atmosphere (as of April 5, 2023). (NOAA Global Monitoring Laboratory)

of methane emissions, but scientists were seeing signs that natural sources of methane—especially tropical wetlands—seemed to be taking over.[9] Feedback loops were threatening to kick into gear. As the world warmed, bacteria in thawing permafrost and warming wetlands turned organic matter into more methane, which in turn led to more thawing and warming and more methane. It was as though, like an anchor leg runner in a relay race, those natural methane sources were grabbing the baton from humanity's fossil fuel emissions and saying, *Thanks for the push, we'll take it from here.*

At the summer's outset, the United Nations secretary-general had stated plainly that continued reliance on fossil fuels was "incompatible with human survival."[10] At its end, on September 8, the first official UN report card on progress toward the Paris climate agreement warned that "there is a rapidly narrowing window" to reduce emissions to meet nations' agreed-upon goals for maintaining a livable climate.[11] Just the day before, on September 7, separate storms turned the streets of Athens and Hong Kong into raging rivers. Villages in Greece were submerged after nearly 30 inches of rain fell in 24 hours. In Hong Kong, over 31 inches were reported in 12 hours, the most since record-keeping began there 140 years ago.[12] Camille-scale events, happening simultaneously, on opposite sides of the world.

And with them, a mounting sense among scientists and citizens alike that humanity was on the cusp of changes that could render our climatic "home place"—the relatively stable climate that allowed organized societies to develop and flourish—into something unrecognizable.

At the end of August, shattering rains had also fallen on a cluster of towns in Kanawha County, West Virginia—exactly 250 years after George Washington first took a shine to the tract of land that encompassed them. Seven inches fell overnight, in just a few hours. Mudslides closed the main road near the stream that flowed down from what was once known as the Burning Spring. "It came out of nowhere, so fast . . . it was scary, especially with three young kids," said one local, calling it the worst flooding she had ever seen.[13]

In Washington's day—long before it came to be known as "natural gas" and before a nineteenth-century German chemist gave it the name "methane"—the vapors rising out of the Burning Spring were called "marsh gas." In folk legends of that time, "will-o'-the-wisp" was the name given to the flickering, flame-like orb of light that sometimes appeared at night near a marsh. The phenomenon lured unsuspecting travelers off their intended path; mistaking it for a candle in a window, they wandered into dangerous bogs. There were countless tales of such deadly detours.

What might have happened if the warnings of scientists like Robert Howarth had been heeded, just as the gas boom was picking up steam? How much further along on the energy transition might the US and the world be? What if giant utilities like Dominion and Duke and Southern had embraced clean energy with the same get-it-done-come-hell-or-high-water attitude they brought to getting more lucrative gas infrastructure built? It's impossible to know. It's hard not to wonder.

What might have happened, on the other hand, if ordinary people hadn't stood in its way? If they had simply accepted Dominion's pipe-line—and the power behind it—as inevitable? If the ACP hadn't, like some latter-day John Lederer, gotten hung up in the mountains of Virginia?

For one, Dominion would likely not have sold all of its gas distri-bution utilities, from Ohio to Utah to North Carolina, to a Canadian pipeline company—which is exactly what it did in early September 2023. With that sale, Dominion off-loaded "approximately 78,000 miles of natural gas distribution, transmission, gathering, and storage pipelines." Earlier in the summer, it had sold its remaining 50 percent stake in Cove Point LNG to Berkshire Hathaway. Just three years ear-lier, Dominion's leaders had still insisted that their gas holdings had a bright future. Now, CEO Bob Blue had ditched the pipes. His firm, he said, would focus on seizing the grand opportunity of widespread electrification.[14]

One of America's biggest energy companies was now on a markedly different trajectory: all in on offshore wind instead of an Appalachian pipeline, all in on wires instead of piping methane into homes. Dominion had been forced to confront the set of hard choices about how to power the future that its leaders had been trying to put off for years.

But even as it divested from pipes, Dominion clung to its plans to fuel that electric future with . . . more methane. In June, the company had announced it would build a new 1,000-megawatt gas peaker plant on the James River. The "Chesterfield Energy Reliability Center" was intended, as the name suggested, to help meet surging demand from, say, air-conditioning use during heat waves like the one that struck Virginia that summer.[15] Dominion's new leaders apparently saw a prof-itably electric future—just one that wasn't necessarily carbon free, at least not for a good long while.[16]

※

For the citizens who had fought tooth and nail to muscle Dominion Energy onto a cleaner path, the post-ACP era didn't bring much rest and relaxation. There was still much to do.

In September 2022, Chad Oba and Ella Rose traveled to a rally in DC to protest alongside activists from around the country against Joe Manchin's first attempt to force his MVP rider through Congress. Back home in Buckingham, they faced a new threat: a Canadian corporation planning to develop a large gold mine just a few miles from Union Hill. The Friends of Buckingham had barely caught their breath after ACP's cancellation before gearing up for this new fight. Just four days after the MPV rally, Oba and Rose both commented at a hearing in support of a ban on gold mining in the county. The two friends had been talking about taking a road trip together for years. At the end of August 2023, they finally hit the road. The two septuagenarians spent a day soaking in the famous thermal pools of Warm Springs, Virginia—and then drove an hour south to attend *another* rally against the Mountain Valley Pipeline.

Tom Hadwin, whose plans to write a few letters to the editor turned into years of working six- and seven-day weeks to fight the ACP, likewise didn't find much free time after its defeat. He immediately began working to persuade Virginia's decision-makers that they didn't need two other smaller planned gas pipelines, *or* a large proposed gas power plant planned for a majority-minority community south of Richmond. Then he turned his sights on the MVP, arguing in a series of detailed comments to FERC that there was no demand for that project's gas either.

Ron Enders kept neglecting his half-dug pond. In October 2022, he completed a seventy-eight-page "Pipeline Fighters Guide" intended to help other communities hit the ground running, learning from their missteps and successes in Nelson County. In another room of their Nelson County farmhouse, meanwhile, Ellen Bouton was deep in her own project of preserving lessons: she had spent two years assembling the *Records of the Western and Central Virginia Resistance to the Atlantic Coast Pipeline*. By the time she and Ron drove to Richmond to deliver it to the Library of Virginia, where it would be permanently housed, the archive contained over 300 gigabytes, 14,700 digital files, and four large boxes of paper documents (as well as a reusable ACP promotional grocery bag that she used to store three preserved protest banners.)

Richard and Jill Averitt kept working on various fronts to reform what they saw as a broken gas pipeline permitting process. As Richard participated in Rep. Jamie Raskin's investigation to reform FERC, he lobbied other officials to reform the Natural Gas Act. Jill led the development of a detailed toolkit, as part of a project with the Pipeline Rights and Property Center: the "Landowners Rapid Response Guide" included a series of videos, links, and resources to help landowners organize quickly and effectively in response to proposed pipelines.

Lew Freeman was looking forward, finally, to more time for his passions of acting, opera, and chamber music after six years of leading the Allegheny–Blue Ridge Alliance, guiding weekly meetings, and producing (along with his colleague Dan Shaffer) more than three hundred weekly updates for the coalition's fifty-plus members. But first he spent nearly a year compiling a thorough chronology of the ACP fight, including all the key legal moments. Then, in June 2022, he handed the reins of ABRA over to its new executive director: Rick Webb.

Webb's own "un-retirement" continued: building on the success of the citizen-led monitoring programs developed during the ACP fight, he and colleagues launched a program called the Conservation Hub, focused on sharing information with the public about environmental risks and public lands management in the central Appalachian region and keeping tabs on proposed projects like commercial timber harvests and coal mining activities in and around the Monongahela. The brook trout on Benson's Run would have to keep waiting.

Nancy Sorrells remained active with the Alliance for the Shenandoah Valley, which had been formed from a merger with the group she helped launch in 2014 to fight the ACP—the Augusta County Alliance—and three other nonprofits. She went back to her work as a publisher, historian, and writer. She still held on to the flyer that Dominion sent her in 2014, along with another motivational tool: a copy of a children's book about David and Goliath that she had found in a store's giveaway bin a few years later.

With the ACP's cancellation, Will and Lilia Fenton could focus on being innkeepers for the first time, planning for future events and building projects—and then Putin launched his wider invasion of Lilia's native Ukraine. ("Pipeline, Pandemic, Putin, it is like getting pounded by waves and barely getting a breath in before the next crisis," Will observed.) Fenton had been reflecting on what he had learned from the experience and marveling that a group of people could, "even when poorly funded and chaotically coordinated, stop the most politically and financially powerful force in the state of Virginia." And while he gave special credit to Greg Buppert and Joyce Burton, he thought there were at least a dozen people of whom it could be said, "If you remove them, you get a pipeline."

Buppert and Burton both enjoyed hiking in Virginia's mountains, but neither found themselves with a lot of freed-up time to hit the trails. Buppert had been named leader of a new SELC team focused on curtailing methane gas use around the region. After the ACP, they were part of a successful effort that led to cancellation of a 1,600-megawatt gas power plant in a majority Black community in eastern Virginia.

Joyce Burton's work wasn't finished either. She spent two and a half years working with the Niskanen Center, a DC think tank, and later with Senator Tim Kaine's office, to press Dominion to return all Nelson County pipeline easements to landowners. She wanted each of them to be free and clear of restrictions on what they could build or farm or otherwise do on their land. In late 2022, Dominion agreed to start releasing the easements.

Wisteria Johnson was among the first batch to have their easements returned, in October 2022. The same week, her daughter Deanna's family finally began work on the house in the Cove that they had put on hold eight years earlier. Johnson had since experienced more heart problems, but with the clouds of the pipeline and the easement lifted, she was finally enjoying some relief—for the mountains, and for her children and grandchildren, who would inherit the land in unfragmented form.

In the evenings, in the home where Wisteria and Liz were raised, under the lights powered by the lines brought by the cooperative when they were children, the sisters talked about the future. They were making plans to help their children not just keep the farm going and their land "in one piece," but to share in and spread its intangible benefits. "We were given a gift," she said. "Our relatives held on to it down through the years. That's what we want to pass on to the children. So they can pass it on to their children. So they can come up with a model, so even *their* great-grandchildren can hold on to it—for *their* sanity."

Johnson had put together a book about ancestors who lived in the Cove for far-flung relatives and nearby descendants—those she hopes will enjoy its shelter for years to come. The Cove could at times feel like an isolated place, she said, but generations had depended on its mountains, fields, and waters for survival and nourishment and re-newal during difficult times.

"When I go out there, I feel nothing but love," she said. "I hear my relatives, my ancestors. I hear it in the wind."[17]

Her book ends with a poem she wrote to capture what it's like to listen to that breeze whispering through the hollow, to feel the warmth of the sun and the roughness of the boulder where her great-grand-mother ground corn. Wisteria Johnson wanted future generations to feel it too. Handing down the land intact—a home place that is whole, vibrant, and beloved—was a task without end.

The poem's final words were her message to those in the here and now: *Now pass it on.*

Acknowledgments

"Everybody thinks the fight against the Atlantic Coast Pipeline began around their kitchen table," Rick Webb told me with a laugh.

It's funny because it's true. And they are right: across Virginia's mountains, citizens made parallel, nearly simultaneous decisions to organize and oppose the project. I'm grateful to many of them for inviting me to sit at their tables and for sharing their stories. I want to acknowledge the many other actors—from West Virginia down through North Carolina—who undertook similar efforts against daunting odds, and whose stories were beyond the scope of this book.

I'm indebted to the energy, climate, legal, and utility experts who patiently tutored me about methane measurements, natural gas regulations, and the recondite ways of FERC and public utility commissions (among other obscure topics). Some are mentioned in these pages; many are not; all were generous with their insights. A lot of those conversations took place during my year as an Alicia Patterson Foundation Fellow reporting on the future of natural gas. I'm deeply grateful for the foundation's support; my fellowship proved to be not only an anchor during that first disorienting pandemic year but a launchpad for this project. Some of the reporting in this book has also appeared in other forms in the *New York Times*, the *New York Review of Books*, *Undark Magazine*, and *Yale Environment 360*.

In piecing together events across the six years of the ACP struggle (especially ones I wasn't there to witness) I relied on the reporting of several journalists and outlets in particular: Anne Adams and John Bruce of the *Recorder*; Gregory Schneider of the *Washington Post*; Michael Martz of the *Richmond Times-Dispatch*; Robert Zullo of the *Times-Dispatch* and later the *Virginia Mercury*; Sarah Vogelsong of the *Virginia Mercury*; and Emily Brown of the *News and Advance*. I'm grateful to Joyce Burton for connecting me with landowners along the ACP route, and to Woody Greenberg and Ron Enders for sharing the more than two dozen oral history interviews they conducted for their *Lessons Learned* video series, which also proved quite helpful. Lew Freeman's detailed chronicle of the six-year ACP fight from ABRA's perspective was another valuable resource. I'm also indebted to Ellen Bouton, who gave me access to the extensive archive of records related to the grassroots movement against ACP that she assembled for the Library of Virginia. Future writers and researchers should start there in looking for stories and angles that I've missed or overlooked.

A while back, Emily Turner of Island Press reached out to ask if I had another book in me. Years later, her thoughtful and incisive edits—along with her gift for reconciling the sometimes divergent interests of reader and writer—ensured that it was as accessible as a book about regulatory wrangling over a gas pipeline could possibly be. Whenever I reached out, Minh Lê was there to give me a lift, in the form of a pep talk, a few deft line edits, or forehead-slap-inducing good advice (as in, "Why didn't I think of that?"). My parents James and Barbara Mingle offered unending encouragement and sharp editorial input, as well as food, shelter, and childcare during many reporting trips to Virginia. Jock and Lorni Cochran, my in-laws, provided similarly essential support during many long stretches of writing back in Vermont. My sister Christina and brother-in-law Jeff also offered both culinary and moral support at critical junctures, along with my nephews Timothy and Reid. One day, the latter opened my eyes to some oft-overlooked Blue Ridge denizens: while hiking up on Reeds Gap (or is it Reids Gap?), he pointed out twenty-five different species of birds, including several migrating warblers. It was a helpful reminder that, while Reeds Gap won't be a byway for molecules of methane, it remains a crossing for a whole host of creatures, whether they are "come-heres" or "from-heres." Back at home, my wise and shaggy writing coach, Po, daily sought to teach me about the problem-solving power of taking him for a walk in the woods. (And he was right every time.)

My daughters Quinn and Vivien provided the most essential ingredient of all: the motivation to write this book. (And occasionally counterbalanced that by serving as the most delightful distractions.) And when I was lost in the narrative wilderness, Quinn was there to get me back on track with a handy compass: "It's about people working together to change things."

Liza Cochran—my favorite writer, my essential reader, whose genius for helping others understand the value of their work is its own form of renewable energy—made this, as she makes all things, possible.

Liza and I sat around the table with Wisteria Johnson and her family one spring day in Harris Cove. As I asked questions and listened and scribbled in my notebook, I was awestruck anew by the leap of faith required to share one's deepest fears, fondest hopes, struggles, regrets, and triumphs not just with a stranger, but with a stranger who plans to write it all down. I am profoundly thankful to all who entrusted me with their stories in the course of my reporting for this book. Any errors of fact or interpretation in its pages are mine and mine alone.

Notes

To avoid overwhelming the reader with endnotes, I have limited citations for quotations to cases that require additional context. Where not explicitly indicated, all direct quotations from individuals are either based on my own reporting or from sources cited in the following notes.

Note to Reader

1. Cheryl LaFleur, interview, June 16, 2020.

2. Karine Lacroix, Matthew Goldberg, Abel Gustafson, Seth Rosenthal, and Anthony Leiserowitz, "Should It Be Called 'Natural Gas' or 'Methane'?" Yale Program on Climate Change Communication, December 1, 2020, https://climatecommuni cation.yale.edu/publications/should-it-be-called-natural-gas-or-methane/.

3. US Energy Information Administration, "Natural Gas Explained," December 27, 2022, https://www.eia.gov/energyexplained/natural-gas/.

4. Christopher Castaneda, "Manufactured and Natural Gas Industry," EH.Net Encyclopedia, edited by Robert Whaples, September 3, 2001, http://eh.net/encyclo pedia/manufactured-and-natural-gas-industry/.

Prologue

1. Dominion Energy, "Dominion, Duke Energy, Piedmont Natural Gas and AGL Resources Form Joint Venture to Own Proposed Atlantic Coast Pipeline," news release, September 2, 2014, https://news.dominionenergy.com/2014-09-02-Dominion -Duke-Energy-Piedmont-Natural-Gas-and-AGL-Resources-Form-Joint-Venture -to-Own-Proposed-Atlantic-Coast-Pipeline.

2. Nancy Sorrells, interview, August 30 and 31, 2021.

3. Bobby Whitescarver, "I Spent a Night in Line Awaiting 'Equal Justice' on a D.C. Sidewalk," *News Leader* (Staunton, VA), February 27, 2020, https://www.newsleader .com/story/opinion/columnists/2020/02/27/dominion-acts-if-its-deep-pockets-all -matters-justice/4893663002/.

4. Nancy Sorrells, email communication with author, September 3, 2023; Nancy Sorrells, photograph, *Friends of Nelson Records of the Western and Central Virginia Resistance to the Atlantic Coast Pipeline, 2014–2022*, Accession 53723, Organization Records Collections, the Library of Virginia, Richmond, Virginia.

5. Thomas F. Farrell II, "Powering Virginia's Future with Clean, Affordable, and Reliable Energy," *Richmond Times-Dispatch*, October 20, 2018, https://richmond.com /opinion/their-opinion/guest-columnists/thomas-f-farrell-column-powering-vir ginia-s-future-with-clean/article_c2185eb5-959c-5738-aecc-204f3edbd45d.html.

6. Bob Stuart and Rachael Smith, "ACP: Dominion Puts Price Tag on Pipeline Connections," *Daily Progress* (Charlottesville, VA), May 3, 2015, https://dailyprogress .com/archives/acp-dominion-puts-price-tag-on-pipeline-connections/article_7a753 956-f13a-11e4-83f2-3ffeed7e9fce.html.

7. Martha M. Hamilton, "Natural Gas, Nuclear Backers See Opportunity in 'Greenhouse' Concern," *Washington Post*, July 22, 1988, https://www.washingtonpost .com/archive/business/1988/07/22/natural-gas-nuclear-backers-see-opportunity-in -greenhouse-concern/b7c3ad3f-280f-439c-8041-3cf3fc99d999/.

8. R. B. Jackson, P. Friedlingstein, R. M. Andrew, J. G. Canadell, C. Le Quéré, and G. P. Peters, "Persistent Fossil Fuel Growth Threatens the Paris Agreement and Planetary Health," *Environmental Research Letters* 14, no. 12 (2019): 121001. https://doi .org/10.1088/1748-9326/ab57b3.

9. Natural gas is about 90 percent methane, on average, along with a bit of benzene, hexane, odorants, and other trace gases mixed in.

10. David Boeri, "In Mass., Many Small Gas Leaks Add Up to Big Consequences for the Environment," WBUR, February 29, 2016, https://www.wbur.org/morning edition/2016/02/29/massachusetts-gas-leaks.

11. Jonathan Mingle, "The Methane Detectives: On the Trail of a Global Warming Mystery," *Undark Magazine*, May 13, 2019, https://undark.org/2019/05/13/methane -global-warming-climate-change-mystery/.

12. Robert McSweeney, "Scientists Concerned by 'Record High' Global Methane Emissions," Carbon Brief, July 14, 2020, https://www.carbonbrief.org/scientists-con cerned-by-record-high-global-methane-emissions/; Hiroko Tabuchi, "Halting the Vast Release of Methane Is Critical for Climate, U.N. Says," *New York Times*, April 24, 2021, https://www.nytimes.com/2021/04/24/climate/methane-leaks-united-nations .html.

13. Damian Carrington, "Revealed: 1,000 Super-Emitting Methane Leaks Risk Triggering Climate Tipping Points," *Guardian* (US edition), March 6, 2023, https:// www.theguardian.com/environment/2023/mar/06/revealed-1000-super-emitting -methane-leaks-risk-triggering-climate-tipping-points.

14. In 1981, the American Gas Association took out a full-page advertisement in the *Wall Street Journal*, with a picture of the little blue flame at the top and the headline "The Promise of Methane: Vast Supplies of Future Energy." The body of the ad's text began: "Methane: Most people know it as natural gas." Within a few years, scientists began pointing out that methane was a potent greenhouse gas. By the end of that de- cade, the industry had read the room: henceforth it stopped talking about "methane" and stuck to "natural gas" instead.

15. Transcript of oral argument, United States Forest Service v. Cowpasture River Preservation Association (18-1584), Oyez, https://www.oyez.org/cases/2019/18-1584.

16. Greg Buppert, email communication, May 5, 2023.

17. Greg Buppert, interview, July 9, 2020.

18. U.S. Forest Serv. v. Cowpasture River Pres. Ass'n, 140 S. Ct. 1837, 1850 (2020).

19. Greg Buppert, interview, April 29, 2021.

Chapter One

1. Sir William Talbot, trans., *The Discoveries of John Lederer* (London, 1672), 8–10, posted online by University of North Carolina, Research Laboratories of Archaeology, http://rla.unc.edu/archives/accounts/lederer/lederertext.html.

2. Michael P. Branch and Daniel J. Philippon, *The Height of Our Mountains: Nature*

Writing from Virginia's Blue Ridge Mountains and Shenandoah Valley (Baltimore: Johns Hopkins University Press, 1998), 54–57.

3. "Monacan Indian Nation," *Encyclopedia Virginia*, Virginia Foundation for the Humanities, December 7, 2020, https://encyclopediavirginia.org/entries/monacan-in dian-nation.

4. Danielle Moretti-Langholtz and Angela L. Daniel, "A Seventeenth Century Chronology Drawn from Colonial Records with Contemporary Native Perspectives," chapter 7 in *A Study of Virginia Indians and Jamestown: The First Century*, ed. Danielle Moretti-Langholtz (Williamsburg, VA: Colonial National Historical Park, 2005), https://www.nps.gov/parkhistory/online_books/jame1/moretti-langholtz/chap7.htm.

5. Nicole DeSarno, "The Kanawha Tracts," in *The Digital Encyclopedia of George Washington*, ed. Anne Fertig and Alexandra Montgomery, Mount Vernon Ladies' Association, https://www.mountvernon.org/library/digitalhistory/digital-encyclopedia/arti cle/the-kanawha-tracts/.

6. Gerald S. Ratliff, "Burning Springs," e-WV: The West Virginia Encyclopedia, last revised October 18, 2023. https://www.wvencyclopedia.org/articles/725.

7. In this—as in his warnings that partisan factions would become vehicles "by which cunning, ambitious, and unprincipled men will be enabled to subvert the power of the people" and threaten "the very engines which have lifted them to unjust dominion"—the father of the country would prove to be prescient. In the early nineteenth century, that stretch of the Kanawha River became the site of the earliest industrial use of natural gas in the United States. Naturally occurring salt deposits were also located along the river. Workers had used wood and then coal to boil the brine into salt. In 1841, while drilling for brine, a local entrepreneur struck gas instead; he built wooden pipelines to use it in his saltworks. So, the Burning Spring also spurred the development of gas pipeline technology while prefiguring two centuries of resource extraction in West Virginia to benefit distant financial interests.

8. Emily Brown, "Pipeline Architects with Project since Inception Work through Obstacles, Criticism," *News and Advance* (Lynchburg, VA), December 27, 2017, https:// newsadvance.com/nelson_county_times/news/pipeline-architects-with-project-since -inception-work-through-obstacles-criticism/article_baf944e0-0682-586d-82e2-79 4afocbddce.html.

9. John Funk, "Shale Gas Is Invigorating the U.S. Economy and Will Make America an Arsenal of Energy, Says Dominion Chief Executive," *Cleveland Plain Dealer*, June 27, 2014, https://www.cleveland.com/business/2014/06/shale_gas_is_invi gorating_the.html.

10. US Geological Service, "USGS Estimates 214 Trillion Cubic Feet of Natural Gas in Appalachian Basin Formations," October 3, 2019, https://www.usgs.gov/news /national-news-release/usgs-estimates-214-trillion-cubic-feet-natural-gas-appalachi an-basin.

11. Douglas Martin, "George Mitchell, a Pioneer in Hydraulic Fracturing, Dies at 94," *New York Times*, July 26, 2013, https://www.nytimes.com/2013/07/27/business /george-mitchell-a-pioneer-in-hydraulic-fracturing-dies-at-94.html.

12. Bethany Mclean, *Saudi America: The Truth about Fracking and How It's Changing the World* (New York: Columbia Global Reports, 2018).

13. Duncan Adams, "Debate about Overbuilding Raises Questions about Pipeline Projects," *Roanoke Times*, May 15, 2016, https://roanoke.com/business/debate-over-overbuilding-raises-questions-about-pipeline-projects/article_8f5c9cec-447f-521e-b580-c9869e746723.html.

14. "Dominion Resources Broadens its Reach," *POWER Magazine*, May 1, 2016, https://www.powermag.com/dominion-resources-broadens-reach/.

15. Martha Purvis Smith and Elizabeth Purvis Shepard, interview, April 28, 2023.

16. Older Nelson residents were familiar with eminent domain thanks to the Blue Ridge Parkway, which meanders along the county's western edge. During the 1920s and 1930s, the federal government invoked it to move landowners, some forcibly, and clear mountaintop farms to make way for the new road. Most locals welcomed the project, some resented it, but it was open to everyone. Today the Blue Ridge Parkway is perennially the most visited unit in the National Park System.

17. Martha Purvis Smith and Elizabeth Purvis Shepard interview, Friends of Nelson Lessons Learned Video Series, April 21, 2022, https://youtu.be/rmEFTz6TJys?si=ohsA8Nv3lJKiMbQO.

18. Marcie Gates, "Purvis vs. Pipeline," *Blue Ridge Life Magazine*, April 2015.

19. Elizabeth Purvis Shepard, letter to the editor, *Nelson County Times*, January 1, 2015.

20. Smith and Shepard, interview.

21. Rick Webb, interviews, September 4, 2021 and August 18, 2021.

22. Rick Webb, "The Shenandoah Watershed Study and the Virginia Trout Stream Sensitivity Study: 35 Years of Watershed Research and Monitoring," presentation, January 5, 2014, SWAS-VTSSS Program Department of Environmental Sciences, University of Virginia, https://swas.evsc.virginia.edu/POST/assets/docs/SWAS_VTSSS_20140105.pdf.

23. Fariss Samarrai, "Longtime Trout Stream Researcher Rick Webb Retires," *UVA Today*, February 6, 2014, https://news.virginia.edu/content/longtime-trout-stream-researcher-rick-webb-retires.

24. Webb, interview, August 18, 2021.

25. US Department of Transportation, Pipeline and Hazardous Materials Safety Administration, "Phases of Pipeline Construction: An Overview," https://www.phmsa.dot.gov/pipeline/pipeline-construction/phases-pipeline-construction-overview.

26. Webb, interview, September 4, 2021.

27. Anne Adams, "Proposed Pipeline Would Run through Highland," *Recorder* (VA), May 22, 2014, https://www.therecorderonline.com/articles/proposed-pipeline-would-run-through-highland/. That summer a Dominion spokesperson promised to answer all of Anne Adams's questions, so she sent along a three-page memo full of them. Over the ensuing years, the company never responded. "That document became somewhat of a joke," she said, in the *Recorder*'s office over the course of the pipeline fight. Anne Adams, interview, August 30, 2021.

28. "Dominion Resources Is Increasing Its Natural Gas Operations," Yahoo Finance, December 25, 2014, https://www.yahoo.com/finance/news/dominion-resources-increasing-natural-gas-174902468.html.

29. Heidi Tyline King, *Dominion's First Century: A Legacy of Service* (Hasbrouck Heights, NJ: CorporateHistory.net, 2010), 11.

30. Jeff Thomas, *The Virginia Way: Democracy and Power after 2016* (Charleston, SC: History Press, 2019).

31. Rachel Weiner, "McAuliffe Raises More than $1 Million for Inaugural Celebration in Virginia," *Washington Post*, January 10, 2014, https://www.washington post.com/local/virginia-politics/mcauliffe-raises-more-than-1-million-for-inaugural -celebration-in-virginia/2014/01/10/583f966c-798e-11e3-af7f-13bf0e9965f6_story.html. Dominion was also one of the biggest donors to former Governor Terry McAuliffe, giving $50,000 to his inaugural committee alone in 2013.

32. Michael Martz, "A Man of Influence, Dominion Energy Chairman and CEO's Reach Is Long in State, Regional Affairs," *Richmond Times-Dispatch*, October 13, 2017, https://richmond.com/a-man-of-influence-dominion-energy-chairman-and-ceos -reach-is-long-in-state-regional/article_5485772a-ae9c-11e7-8a7d-eb84b48e60e5.html.

33. Kevin Conner, "The Power behind the Pipelines: Atlantic Coast Pipeline," Public Accountability Initiative, June 1, 2017, https://public-accountability.org/report /the-power-behind-the-pipelines-atlantic-coast-pipeline/.

34. Patrick Wilson, "Lobbyists Take Changes to Gift Law in Stride," *Virginian-Pilot* (Norfolk), May 11, 2015, https://www.pilotonline.com/2015/05/11/lobbyists-take -changes-to-gifts-law-in-stride/.

35. Senate Joint Resolution No. 323, 2015 session, https://lis.virginia.gov/cgi-bin/le gp604.exe?151+ful+SJ323ER.

36. Southern Environmental Law Center, "In the Path of the Pipeline: The Harris Family," video, July 18, 2017, https://youtu.be/E6g3CmL_imo?si=4FMvBcwIOaz4 YUqT.

37. Department of Energy, "Fossil Energy Study Guide: Natural Gas," February 2014, https://www.energy.gov/sites/prod/files/2014/02/f8/HS_NatGas_Studyguide _draft2.pdf.

38. "President Barack Obama's State of the Union Address," White House Office of the Press Secretary, January 28, 2014, https://obamawhitehouse.archives.gov/the -press-office/2014/01/28/president-barack-obamas-state-union-address.

39. John M. Broder, "Obama Affirms Climate Change Goals," *New York Times*, November 18, 2008, https://www.nytimes.com/2008/11/19/us/politics/19climate.html.

40. Valerie Richardson, "Obama Takes Credit for U.S. Oil-and-Gas Boom: 'That Was Me, People,'" Associated Press, November 28, 2018, https://apnews.com/article /business-5dfbc1aa17701ae219239caadobfefb2.

41. "Remarks by the President on American-Made Energy Cushing Pipe Yard, Cushing, Oklahoma," White House Office of the Press Secretary, March 22, 2012, https://obamawhitehouse.archives.gov/the-press-office/2012/03/22/remarks-presi dent-american-made-energy.

42. Dan Berman and Reid J. Epstein, "Obama's Options on Keystone," Politico, January 31, 2014, https://www.politico.com/story/2014/01/barack-obama-keystone-op tions-102956.

43. "Transcript and Audio: Second Presidential Debate," NPR, October 16, 2012, https://www.npr.org/2012/10/16/163050988/transcript-obama-romney-2nd-presiden tial-debate.

44. Cheryl LaFleur, interview, June 16, 2020.

45. Brad Plumer, "Obama Says Fracking Can Be a 'Bridge' to a Clean-Energy

Future. It's Not That Simple," *Washington Post*, January 29, 2014, https://www.washing
tonpost.com/news/wonk/wp/2014/01/29/obama-says-fracking-offers-a-bridge-to
-a-clean-energy-future-its-not-that-simple/.

46. Beth Gardiner, "Is Natural Gas Good, or Just Less Bad?" *New York Times*,
February 22, 2011, https://www.nytimes.com/2011/02/21/business/energy-environment
/21iht-renogas21.html.

47. Bill McKibben, "The Methane beneath Our Feet," *New York Review of Books*,
April 1, 2013, https://www.nybooks.com/online/2013/04/01/gas-leaks-methane-bene
ath-our-feet/.

48. Robert W. Howarth, Renee Santoro, and Anthony Ingraffea, "Methane and
the Greenhouse-Gas Footprint of Natural Gas from Shale Formations: A Letter,"
Climatic Change 106, no. 4 (2011): 679–90, https://doi.org/10.1007/s10584-011-0061-5.

49. Robert W. Howarth, "A Bridge to Nowhere: Methane Emissions and the
Greenhouse Gas Footprint of Natural Gas," *Energy Science and Engineering* 2, no. 2
(2014): 47–60, https://doi.org/10.1002/ese3.35.

50. Adam R. Brandt, G. A. Heath, E. A. Kort, F. O'Sullivan, G. Pétron, S. M.
Jordaan, P. Tans, et al., "Methane Leaks from North American Natural Gas Systems,"
Science 343, no. 6172 (2014): 733–35, https://doi.org/10.1126/science.1247045.

51. Ramón A. Alvarez, Daniel Zavala-Araiza, David R. Lyon, David T. Allen,
Zachary R. Barkley, Adam R. Brandt, Kenneth J. Davis, et al., "Assessment of Methane
Emissions from the U.S. Oil and Gas Supply Chain," *Science* 361, 186–188 (2018), https://
doi.org/10.1126/science.aar7204.

52. Haewon McJeon, Jae Edmonds, Nico Bauer, Leon Clarke, Brian Fisher, Brian
P. Flannery, Jérôme Hilaire, et al., "Limited Impact on Decadal-Scale Climate Change
from Increased Use of Natural Gas," *Nature* 514-2 no. 7523 (2014): 482–85.

53. Massachusetts Institute of Technology, *The Future of Natural Gas: An Inter-
disciplinary MIT Study* (Cambridge, MA: MIT Energy Initiative, 2011), https://energy
.mit.edu/wp-content/uploads/2011/06/MITEI-The-Future-of-Natural-Gas.pdf.

54. Kevin Connor and Robert Galbraith, "Industry Partner or Industry Puppet?
How MIT's Influential Study of Fracking Was Authored, Funded, and Released
by Oil and Gas Industry Insiders," Public Accountability Initiative, March 20, 2013,
https://public-accountability.org/report/industry-partner-or-industry-puppet/.

55. "Testimony of Ernest J. Moniz, MIT Energy Initiative Massachusetts Institute
of Technology before the United States Senate Committee on Energy and Natural
Resources," July 19, 2011, https://www.energy.senate.gov/services/files/42C2523F-B0
96-189B-6A12-925E1F9D1481.

56. Annie Snider, "FERC Quorum A-Coming?" Politico, August 3, 2017, https://
www.politico.com/tipsheets/morning-energy/2017/08/03/ferc-quorum-a-coming-22
1678.

57. Charles K. Ebinger, "President Obama, This Is Your Energy Moment," Brookings, February 12, 2014, https://www.brookings.edu/articles/president-obama-this-is
-your-energy-moment/.

Chapter Two

1. John Bruce, "Pipeline Decision Due within 60 days," *Recorder* (VA), August 7,
2014,   https://www.therecorderonline.com/articles/pipeline-decision-due-within-60
-days/.

2. Rick Webb, interview, August 18, 2021.

3. After the meeting, Webb approached Moody's colleague Bill Scarpinato, Dominion's environmental management lead for the project, and told him: "You're not going to build this pipeline, so you might as well quit."

4. Lew Freeman, interview, August 30, 2021.

5. Graelyn Brashear, "Hundreds Turn Out to Hear Nelson Supes Grill Dominion on Pipeline," *C-Ville Weekly*, August 13, 2014, https://www.c-ville.com/hundreds-turn -hear-nelson-supes-grill-dominion-pipeline/.

6. Minutes of the Nelson County Board of Supervisors Meeting, Nelson County Middle School, Lovingston, Virginia, August 12, 2014.

7. Minutes of the Augusta County Board of Supervisors Meeting, August 13, 2014, Government Center, Verona, Virginia.

8. Nancy Sorrells, interviews, August 30 and 31, 2021.

9. In the ensuing years, the unified opposition to the project in her politically conservative county would continue to surprise Sorrells. People "who I know are die-hard Republicans," she said, would regularly come up to her on the streets of Staunton, unsolicited, and tell her: "Keep up the fight. You're not going to win. But it's the right thing to do and we're behind you."

10. "Residents All Revved Up, but Unlikely to Win," *News Leader* (Staunton, VA), August 14, 2014, https://www.newsleader.com/story/opinion/editorials/2014/08/14/do minion-proposal-seems-like-done-deal/14064537/.

11. Anne Adams, "Concerns about Pipeline Strong," *Recorder* (VA), August 21, 2014, https://www.therecorderonline.com/articles/concerns-about-pipeline-strong/.

12. Buppert was no stranger to fighting large energy companies. In 2010, as an attorney at Defenders of Wildlife, Buppert led a team that sued oil giant BP in federal court over its Deepwater Horizon explosion and well blowout, which leaked oil for months. They sought to force BP to set up a fund to rehabilitate the degraded coasts and wildlife habitat across the region. He worked with SELC attorneys on that case; by 2013, he'd join the organization.

13. Greg Buppert, interview, September 19, 2023.

14. Dominion Energy, "Dominion, Duke Energy, Piedmont Natural Gas and AGL Resources Form Joint Venture to Own Proposed Atlantic Coast Pipeline," news release, September 2, 2014, https://news.dominionenergy.com/2014-09-02-Dominion -Duke-Energy-Piedmont-Natural-Gas-and-AGL-Resources-Form-Joint-Venture -to-Own-Proposed-Atlantic-Coast-Pipeline.

15. Dominion Energy, "Gov. McAuliffe Atlantic Coast Pipeline," press conference, video, September 2, 2014, https://youtu.be/FMn16nJx7OU?si=mA9H1wTQ7H -TnZcT.

16. Mark Leibovich, "Terry McAuliffe and the Other Green Party," *New York Times Magazine*, July 19, 2012, https://www.nytimes.com/2012/07/22/magazine/terry-mcau liffe-and-the-other-green-party.html.

17. Dominion Energy, "Atlantic Coast Pipeline—Tom Farrell," press conference, video, September 2, 2014, https://youtu.be/ATOjj8UCr5M?si=8Xc5sToUVhfO CAjA.

18. Peter Bacque, "Dominion Resources Pipeline Project a 'Game Changer' for Virginia's Economy, Governor Says," *Richmond Times-Dispatch*, September 2, 2014, https://richmond.com/business/dominion-resources-pipeline-project-a-game-chan

ger-for-virginia-s-economy-governor-says/article_3a9b68a0-3290-11e4-a404-0017 a43b2370.html.

19. Dominion Energy, "Dominion to Present at Barclays Capital 2014 CEO Energy-Power Conference," news release, August 27, 2014, https://news.dominionen ergy.com/2014-08-27-Dominion-To-Present-At-Barclays-Capital-2014-CEO-Energy -Power-Conference.

20. Dominion Resources presentation, Barclays Capital CEO Energy-Power Conference, September 3, 2014.

21. Dominion presentation, Barclays conference, September 3, 2014.

22. Richard Zeits, "Dominion Resources: A New 2 Bcf/D Pipeline for Marcellus and Utica Gas," Seeking Alpha, September 5, 2014, https://seekingalpha.com/article /2474265-dominion-resources-a-new-2-bcf-d-pipeline-for-marcellus-and-utica-gas.

23. Katharine Tweed, "U.S. Electricity Demand Flat since 2007," IEEE Spectrum, February 6, 2015, https://spectrum.ieee.org/us-electricity-demand-flat-since-2007.

Chapter Three

1. Vicki Wheaton, interview, September 2, 2021.

2. Stefan Bechtel, *Roar of the Heavens* (New York: Citadel Press, 2006), 5.

3. Wheaton, interview.

4. Lynn Coffey, "Frank George 'Tinker' Bryant Jr.: Third Generation Roseland Rural Route Carrier," *Virginia Humanities: Backroads*, https://nelsonhistorical.org/up load/files/Humanities_Backroads/Tinker_Bryant.pdf.

5. Coffey, "Frank George 'Tinker' Bryant Jr."; Bechtel, *Roar of the Heavens*, 169–70; Paige S. Simpson and Jerry H. Simpson Jr., *Torn Land* (Lynchburg, VA: J. P. Bell Company, 1970), 151–52.

6. Vicki Wheaton interview, Friends of Nelson: Lessons Learned Video Series, April 21, 2022, https://youtu.be/kZ9VrqiFkvk?si=0jJTcaqkjnpzngqq.

7. Wheaton, interview.

8. Connie Brennan, interview, April 25, 2022.

9. "Dominion Continues to Frustrate and Obfuscate Nelsonians at Open House," *Blue Virginia* (blog), September 17, 2014, https://bluevirginia.us/2014/09/dominion -continues-to-frustrate-and-obfuscate-nelsonians-at-open-house.

10. Michael Martz, "Dominion Gas Pipeline Faces Mountain of Opposition in Western Virginia," *Daily Progress* (Charlottesville, VA), January 3, 2015, https://daily progress.com/news/local/dominion-gas-pipeline-faces-mountain-of-opposition-in -western-virginia/article_54cfb258-93ac-11e4-a2e1-2b487cfcedra.html.

11. Marilyn Shifflett, "Free Nelson Responds to Governor McAuliffe's Radio Remarks on Proposed Pipeline," *Augusta (VA) Free Press*, March 31, 2015, https://au gustafreepress.com/news/free-nelson-responds-to-governor-mcauliffes-radio-re marks-on-proposed-pipeline/. The governor's slip led some to wonder if Dominion chose to go through areas like Highland and Nelson because it would entail less regulation—federal pipeline classifications, which dictated safety requirements, were correlated to the number of structures per mile along their routes—or because the company's leaders thought they might have an easier time farther away from the intense spotlight it might encounter in more affluent communities like Charlottesville.

12. Jim Grevem, "Nelson County in Hollywood," The Uncommon Wealth: Voices

from the Library of Virginia, November 12, 2014, https://uncommonwealth.virginia memory.com/blog/2014/11/12/nelson-county-in-hollywood/.

13. According to Enders and Bouton, the community's founding group had bought the farm from a certain Mrs. Shannon, whose late husband was a retired FBI agent. "One of the three, I think, that tracked down Bonnie and Clyde," said Enders. "Ultra-conservative. When the electric cooperative came through with the power lines, he thought it was a communist conspiracy! He was up in arms." The neighbors all called it Shannon Farm, so that's what the newcomers called it too. Enders noted with relish that the commune continues to bear the "ultra-conservative" Mr. Shannon's name.

14. Ron Enders and Ellen Bouton, interview, April 29, 2021.

15. Erin O'Hare, "After Inhabiting Virginia Land for 10,000 Years, the Monacan Indian Nation Finally Receives Federal Recognition," *C-Ville Weekly*, March 9, 2018, https://www.c-ville.com/inhabiting-virginia-land-10000-years-monacan-indian -nation-finally-recevies-federal-recognition/.

16. Martha Purvis Smith and Elizabeth Purvis Shepard interview, Friends of Nelson Lessons Learned Video Series, April 21, 2022, https://youtu.be/rmEFTz6T Jys?si=nA1C-ps9iasyJb-3.

17. Enders and Bouton, interview.

18. Kathy Plunket Versluys, *Friends of Nelson Records of the Western and Central Virginia Resistance to the Atlantic Coast Pipeline*, 2014–2022, Accession 53723, Organization Records Collections, the Library of Virginia, Richmond, Virginia, video.

19. June 8, 2014, meeting at Memorial Library, Lovingston, Virginia, Kathy Plunket Versluys, *Friends of Nelson Records of the Western and Central Virginia Resistance to the Atlantic Coast Pipeline*, 2014–2022, Accession 53723, Organization Records Collections, the Library of Virginia, Richmond, Virginia, video. Ernie Reed also reminded everyone present of some relevant history: "Nelson County has got a history of saying no to things like this and being very successful at it." In 1988 the US Air Force wanted to build a powerful 300-foot radio tower in the middle of Nelson County, as part of its Ground Wave Emergency Network to maintain communications during a nuclear attack. A grassroots coalition emerged quickly to push back; Reed himself had been a key player in that effort. Through public awareness campaigns and pressure on elected officials, they forced military brass to come and hold public meetings. The ensuing scrutiny from the media and policymakers revealed that the project's planners hadn't thoroughly studied the fundamental need for the project or its potential risks. Soon the air force canceled the program nationwide; soon after that, the Soviet Union collapsed and the Cold War ended. The moral of that story, according to Reed, was that it wasn't enough to push an unwanted and unnecessary project onto some *other* county. "Solidarity . . . will be extremely important," he predicted.

20. Friends of Nelson Official Documents, Meeting Minutes of June 29, 2014, *Friends of Nelson Records of the Western and Central Virginia Resistance to the Atlantic Coast Pipeline*, 2014–2022, Accession 53723, Organization Records Collections, the Library of Virginia, Richmond, Virginia.

21. Ron Enders, "A Pipeline Fighters' Guide," October 2022, http://friendsofnelson .com/wp-content/uploads/2022/10/A-Pipeline-Fighters-Guide-v1.pdf.

22. Martha Purvis Smith and Elizabeth Purvis Shephard interview, Friends of

Nelson: Lessons Learned Video Series, April 21, 2022, https://youtu.be/rmEFTz6T
Jys?si=96sXUKezsDodq6vI.

Chapter Four
1. National Press Club, "Transcript: Luncheon with FERC Chairman Cheryl
LaFleur," January 27, 2015, https://www.press.org/sites/default/files/20150127_lafleur
.pdf.
2. Nancy Sorrells, interview, August 30, 2021; Connie Brennan, interview, April 22,
2022.
3. National Press Club, "Transcript."
4. Susan Tierney, "Natural Gas Pipeline Certification: Policy Considerations
for a Changing Industry," Analysis Group, November 6, 2017, https://www.analysis
group.com/uploadedfiles/content/insights/publishing/ag_ferc_natural_gas_pipeline
_certification.pdf.
5. Joyce Burton, interview, October 8, 2021.
6. "Agenda for Jan. 25, 2015 All Pain, No Gain Gathering," *Friends of Nelson Records
of the Western and Central Virginia Resistance to the Atlantic Coast Pipeline*, 2014–2022,
Accession 53723, Organization Records Collections, the Library of Virginia, Richmond,
Virginia.
7. Elana Schor, "Pipeline Politics: Virginia's Keystone?" Politico, May 3, 2015, https://
www.politico.com/story/2015/05/virginia-keystone-pipeline-natural-gas-117578.
8. Rick Webb, email communication, January 31, 2022.
9. Rachael Smith, "Dominion Resources to Drop Lawsuits against 14 Nelson
County Landowners," *News and Advance* (Lynchburg, VA), January 19, 2015, https://
newsadvance.com/news/local/dominion-resources-to-drop-lawsuits-against-14-nel
son-county-landowners/article_412b591a-a0a8-11e4-8ce5-ab73027ee7e1.html.
10. Ron Enders, interview, April 29, 2021.
11. Rachael Smith, "Dominion Identifies Alternative Routes for Planned Atlantic
Coast Pipeline," *News and Advance* (Lynchburg, VA)/*Nelson County Times*, February
23, 2015, https://newsadvance.com/nelson_county_times/updated-dominion-identifi
es-alternative-routes-for-planned-atlantic-coast-pipeline/article_2872268e-bbb4-11
e4-bf8c-efd18d61e423.html. The resort's owner, West Virginia coal baron and future
governor Jim Justice, had just announced he was selling it; the timing of the proposed
new route announcement right after that sale raised some eyebrows around the county.
12. Elizabeth Purvis Shepard, interview, April 28, 2023.
13. Minutes of the Nelson County Board of Supervisors Meeting, August 12, 2014.
14. Wisteria Johnson, interview, July 8, 2020; Wisteria Johnson and Elizabeth
Miles, interview, April 30, 2021.
15. Emily Brown, "Family on Pipeline Route Fights ACP to Preserve Its History,"
News and Advance (Lynchburg, VA), July 19, 2017, https://newsadvance.com/nelson
_county_times/news/family-on-pipeline-route-fights-acp-to-preserve-its-history/ar
ticle_1463165d-dad8-5f11-bdcf-7beeba63d73f.html.
16. Deanna Mitchelson, interview, July 8, 2020.
17. Michael Martz, "Alternative Pipeline Routes Create New Heartaches in Nelson
County," March 15, 2015, *Richmond Times-Dispatch*, https://richmond.com/news

/virginia/alternative-pipeline-routes-create-new-heartaches-in-nelson-county/article
_24227ab1-308a-5402-bd5d-9dc1995b537a.html.

18. National Park Service, "Edward Alfred Pollard," https://www.nps.gov/people
/edward-alfred-pollard.htm.

19. C'ta DeLaurier, interview, April 19, 2022.

20. Martz, "Alternative Pipeline Routes."

21. Brad Horn, "A Country's Need for Natural Gas, a Woman's Beloved Farmland,
a Pipeline that Tore a County Apart," *Washington Post*, June 9, 2016, https://www
.washingtonpost.com/sf/style/2016/06/09/one-womans-fight-to-save-her-land-from
-a-pipeline-that-tore-a-region-apart/.

22. Kody Leibowitz, "Nelson County Crowds Restless at Times during Packed
Pipeline Meeting," WSET ABC 13 News, March 18, 2015, https://wset.com/archive
/nelson-county-crowds-restless-at-times-during-packed-pipeline-meeting.

23. Will Fenton, interview, June 10, 2021.

24. "What's Next from ACP? ACP Officials Outline Their Construction Plans at
Wintergreen," Wintergreen Property Owners Association, May 1, 2018, https://www
.wtgpoa.org/news-updates/2014/1/1/whats-next. The Virginia project manager for
ACP told Wintergreen property owners to expect construction activity and heavy
truck traffic for about a year. "I'm not going to pretend it's not going to be messy and
disruptive for the people at Wintergreen," he said. "It's going to be uncomfortable.
You're going to know we are there. It's not going to be subtle."

25. Will Fenton, email communication, May 30, 2021.

26. Federal Energy Regulatory Commission, "Transcript of 3/18/15 Technical
Conference Held in Lovingston, VA re the Supply Header Project et al under PF15-5
et al.," https://elibrary.ferc.gov/eLibrary/idmws/file_list.asp?accession_num=20150521
-4008.

27. John Ed Purvis, public comment, FERC Scoping Meeting, Nelson County,
March 18, 2015.

28. Michael Martz, "With Hurricane Camille in Mind, Nelson County Worries
about Potential Steep Price for Pipeline," *Richmond Times-Dispatch*, August 16, 2019,
https://richmond.com/weather/plus/with-hurricane-camille-in-mind-nelson-county
-worries-about-potential-steep-price-for-pipeline/article_1ef86333-2299-5c1a-aa20
-26919c4d6ae.html.

29. Wisteria Johnson, public comment, FERC Scoping Meeting, Nelson County,
March 18, 2015.

30. Senator Richard Blumenthal, "Blumenthal Calls on Federal Energy Regulatory
Commission to Fully Fund Office of Public Participation, Give Consumers a Voice
in Ratemaking Decisions," press release, April 18, 2016. https://www.blumenthal.sena
te.gov/newsroom/press/release/blumenthal-calls-on-federal-energy-regulatory-com
mission-to-fully-fund-office-of-public-participation-give-consumers-a-voice-in-rate
making-decisions.

31. "FERC's Works Matters," *American Gas: The Monthly Magazine of the American
Gas Association*, April 2015, 28–31.

32. Michael Tabony, public comment, FERC Scoping Meeting, Nelson County,
March 18, 2015.

33. Webb also noted that FERC's contention that any given pipeline's emissions were "less than significant" could be said about any individual coal mine, power plant, pipeline, or oil platform. "If they are dismissed on the basis that, well, it's a tiny fraction of global emissions—that's true of almost every project, so you would never do anything about climate change." Romany Webb, interview, December 16, 2020; Romany Webb, *Climate Change, FERC, and Natural Gas Pipelines: The Legal Basis for Considering Greenhouse Gas Emissions Under Section 7 of the Natural Gas Act*, Sabin Center for Climate Change Law, Columbia Law School, June 2019, https://ssrn.com/abstract=3402520.

34. Rachael Smith, "Errors Rife throughout FERC Meeting Transcripts, Pipeline Meeting Speakers Say," June 10, 2015, *Nelson County Times*, https://dailyprogress.com/news/local/errors-rife-throughout-ferc-meeting-transcripts-pipeline-meeting-speakers-say/article_3624ce72-0fb9-11e5-b684-cb16d2286deo.html.

35. Friends of Nelson, "FERC DOES NOT WORK," May 22, 2015, https://friendsofnelson.com/ferc-does-not-work/.

36. Joyce Burton, email communication, March 27, 2022.

37. Connie Brennan, interview, April 25, 2022.

38. Wisteria Johnson, interview, September 3, 2021.

39. Andrew Gantt, public comment, FERC Scoping Meeting, Nelson County, March 18, 2015.

40. Rachael Smith, "Owner of Historic Wingina Property Is Epitome of Pipeline Opposition," *News and Advance* (Lynchburg, VA), January 21, 2015, https://newsadvance.com/nelson_county_times/news/owner-of-historic-wingina-property-is-epitome-of-pipeline-opposition/article_1d165b8e-a1b5-11e4-afo4-8750d4e07378.html.

41. Andrew Gantt, email communications, August 5 and 6, 2021.

42. Rhamonia Woodson, correspondence to Federal Energy Regulatory Commission, "Cultural Attachment to Land in Wingina, Nelson County, VA," May 31, 2016.

43. Connie Brennan, interview, April 25, 2022.

44. Helen Kimble, interview, May 27, 2021.

45. Joanna Salidis, interview, June 1, 2021.

46. Will Fenton, interview, September 1, 2021; Will Fenton, email, May 22, 2021.

47. Statement of Greg Buppert, Senior Attorney, Southern Environmental Law Center, Before the Subcomm. on Energy and Mineral Resources of the H. Comm. on Natural Resources, on H.R. 2295, 114th Cong., May 20, 2015.

48. Will Fenton, interview, June 10, 2021.

49. Greg Buppert, interview, September 19, 2023.

50. Michael Godfrey, letter to the editor, *News Leader* (Staunton, VA), August 26, 2014, https://www.newsleader.com/story/opinion/readers/2014/08/26/valley-can-still-win-pipeline-fight-dominion/14647105/.

Chapter Five

1. Steven Mufson and Brady Dennis, "Trump Victory Reverses U.S. Energy and Environmental Priorities," *Washington Post*, November 11, 2016, https://www.washingtonpost.com/news/energy-environment/wp/2016/11/09/trump-victory-reverses-u-s-energy-and-environmental-priorities/.

2. Darius Dixon, "Trump Team's Demands Fuel Fear of Energy Department 'Witch Hunt,'" Politico, December 9, 2016, https://www.politico.com/blogs/donald -trump-administration/2016/12/trump-transition-wants-names-of-energy-depart ment-staff-who-worked-on-climate-232424.

3. Kent Karriker, interview, August 16, 2021.

4. Clyde Thompson, US Forest Service, email to Glenn Casamassa, US Forest Service, December 20, 2016, 2:07 p.m.

5. Clyde Thompson, interview, August 16, 2021.

6. Clyde Thompson, letter to Kimberly D. Bose, secretary, Federal Energy Regulatory Commission, Subject: Comments Regarding Soils Surveys Conducted to Date, OEP/DG2E/Gas 4 Atlantic Coast Pipeline, LLC, Docket No. PF15-554, November 5, 2015.

7. Dominion's approach also seemed to run counter to industry best practice. In April 2016, the gas pipeline industry's trade association (INGAA) produced its own report on the risks of building in "steep and rugged terrain," with a focus on lessons learned from West Virginia. The report was rather technical but its two main conclusions seemed like common sense: one, select a route that minimizes the crossing of this kind of terrain; two, identify and study specific hazards such as slide-prone slopes *before* the design and construction phases. See *Mitigation of Land Movement in Steep and Rugged Terrain for Pipeline Projects: Lessons Learned from Constructing Pipelines in West Virginia* (Washington, DC: INGAA Foundation Inc., April 2016), https://ingaa .org/wp-content/uploads/2016/05/28629.pdf.

8. H. Thomas Speaks Jr., US Forest Service, letter to Kimberly D. Bose, FERC, 1, Dkt. No. PF15-6, September 17, 2015, eLibrary No. 20150917-5134.

9. Kathleen Atkinson, US Forest Service, letter to Leslie Hartz, ACP, 1, Dkt. No. CP15-554, January 19, 2016, eLibrary No. 20160121-5029.

10. US Forest Service, Comments on the Draft EIS for Proposed ACP Project 13, Dkt. No. CP15-554, April 6, 2017, eLibrary No. 20170406-5532.

11. Andrew Young, *Landslides and the ACP: An In-Depth Examination of the Threat Landslides Pose to the Atlantic Coast Pipeline* (Monterey, VA: Allegheny–Blue Ridge Alliance, June 2020), https://www.abralliance.org/wp-content/uploads/2020/06/Land slides-and-the-ACP-June-2020.pdf.

12. Richard Pérez-Peña, "West Virginia Floods Cause 23 Deaths and Vast Wreckage," *New York Times*, June 24, 2016, https://www.nytimes.com/2016/06/25/us /west-virginia-floods.html.

13. National Oceanic and Atmospheric Administration, "'Thousand-Year' Down-pour Led to Deadly West Virginia Floods," July 8, 2016, https://www.climate.gov/news -features/event-tracker/thousand-year-downpour-led-deadly-west-virginia-floods.

14. Federal Emergency Management Agency, *Understanding Flood Dangers in Central West Virginia: Lessons Learned from the June 2016 Flood* (Washington, DC: FEMA, July 2018), https://www.fema.gov/sites/default/files/documents/Region_III _WV_FloodReport.pdf.

15. James Bruggers, "Appalachia's Strip-Mined Mountains Face a Growing Climate Risk: Flooding," Inside Climate News, November 21, 2019, https://insideclimatenews .org/news/21112019/appalachia-mountains-flood-risk-climate-change-coal-mining -west-virginia-extreme-rainfall-runoff-analysis/.

16. Michon Scott, "Prepare for More Downpours: Heavy Rain Has Increased across Most of the United States, and Is Likely to Increase Further," NOAA News feature, July 10, 2019, https://www.climate.gov/news-features/featured-images/prepare-more-downpours-heavy-rain-has-increased-across-most-united-o.

17. Clyde Thompson, forest supervisor, Monongahela National Forest, letter to Kimberly D. Bose, secretary, Federal Energy Regulatory Commission, Subject: Forest Service Analysis of Landslide Data from a Recent Flood Event on the Monongahela National Forest, December 23, 2016.

18. Clyde Thompson, interview, August 16, 2021.

19. Rick Webb kept a close watch on all the regulatory reviews as they unfolded. As far as he could tell, the climate lens was never used. "It was never applied to any decision-making point." Rick Webb, interview, September 4, 2021.

20. Blackburn Consulting Services LLC, *Report: Analysis and Field Verification of Soil and Geologic Concerns with the Atlantic Coast Pipeline (ACP) in Nelson County, VA* (Berryville, VA: Blackburn Consulting Services, March 2017), http://friendsofnelson.com/wp-content/uploads/2020/05/Final-Steep-Slope-Report-March-2017.pdf.

21. Friends of Wintergreen, "New Geology Studies Show Building the Atlantic Coast Pipeline in the Steep Mountains by Wintergreen (VA) Is Risky," news release, March 14, 2017, https://www.einnews.com/pr_news/371029235/new-geology-studies-show-building-the-atlantic-coast-pipeline-in-the-steep-mountains-by-wintergreen-va-is-risky. In another submission, this expert geologist, Dr. Mervin Bartholomew, used more direct language: "I am concerned because I know that high rainfall events like Camille will happen again and again!"

22. Federal Energy Regulatory Commission, Draft Environmental Impact Statement for the Atlantic Coast Pipeline, LLC, Dominion Transmission Inc. and Atlantic and Piedmont Natural Gas. Co. Inc. (CP15-554-000, -001; CP15-555-000; and CP15-556-000), issued December 30, 2016, https://www.ferc.gov/draft-environmental-impact-statement-atlantic-coast-pipeline-llc-dominion-transmission-inc-and.

23. Jacob D. Hileman, Mario Angst, Tyler A. Scott, and Emma Sundström, "Recycled Text and Risk Communication in Natural Gas Pipeline Environmental Impact Assessments," *Energy Policy* 156 (September 2021), https://doi.org/10.1016/j.enpol.2021.112379.

24. Clyde Thompson, forest supervisor, Monongahela National Forest, letter to Kimberly D. Bose, secretary, Federal Energy Regulatory Commission, Subject: Request for Site-Specific Design of Stabilization Measures in Selected High-Hazard Portions of the Route of the Proposed Atlantic Coast Pipeline Project in the Monongahela National Forest and George Washington National Forest, October 24, 2016.

25. Glenn Casamassa, US Forest Service, email to Kathleen Atkinson, US Forest Service, December 27, 2016, 12:56 p.m.

26. Kent Karriker, interview, August 16, 2021.

27. Jon Swaine, "Donald Trump's Team Defends 'Alternative Facts' after Widespread Protests," *Guardian*, January 23, 2017, https://www.theguardian.com/us-news/2017/jan/22/donald-trump-kellyanne-conway-inauguration-alternative-facts.

28. Karen Tumulty and Juliet Eilperin, "Trump Pressured Park Service to Find Proof for His Claims about Inauguration Crowd," *Washington Post*, January 26, 2017,

https://www.washingtonpost.com/politics/trump-pressured-park-service-to-back-up
-his-claims-about-inauguration-crowd/2017/01/26/12a38cb8-e3fc-11e6-ba11-63c4
b4fb5a63_story.html.

29. Georgina Gustin, "USDA Staff Were Coached Not to Say 'Climate Change,'
Emails Show," Inside Climate News, August 7, 2017, https://insideclimatenews.org
/news/07082017/usda-trump-ban-words-climate-change-agriculture-conservation
-email/.

30. Bill Holland, "Atlantic Coast Gas Pipeline Named on Trump Priority Infrastructure List," S&P Global Market Intelligencer, January 25, 2017, https://www
.spglobal.com/marketintelligence/en/news-insights/trending/U13EI41elXxigQ3jMa
mM3A2.

31. Mike Soraghan, "How Trump's 'Energy Dominance' Backfired on an $8B
Pipeline," E&E News, July 7, 2020, https://subscriber.politicopro.com/article/eenews
/1063518775.

32. Statement of Diane Leopold, president and CEO of Dominion Resources,
before the Senate Committee on Energy and Natural Resources on "Opportunities to
Improve American Energy Infrastructure," 115th Congress, March 14, 2017.

33. Clyde Thompson, letter to Kimberly D. Bose, secretary, FERC, Subject:
Reiteration of Previous Information Requests and Discussions Regarding Steep Slope
Sites on the Monongahela National Forest and George Washington National Forest,
OEP/DG2E/Gas 4 Atlantic Coast Pipeline, LLC, Docket Nos. CP15-554-000 and
-001, May 14, 2017.

34. Leslie Hartz, letter to Clyde Thompson, May 17, 2017.

35. Diane Leopold, remarks at ACP Project Update and Executive Press Briefing,
April 27, 2017.

36. Clyde Thompson, interview, August 16, 2021.

Chapter Six

1. Agenda, AGA State Affairs Committee Meeting, October 8–11, 2017, Scottsdale,
Arizona, https://www.desmog.com/wp-content/uploads/files/state_affairs_committ
ee_meeting_draft_agenda_updated.pdf.

2. Ryan Maye Handy, "Natural Gas Surpasses Coal as Fuel for Power Production,"
Houston Chronicle, January 16, 2017, https://www.houstonchronicle.com/business/arti
cle/Natural-gas-surpasses-coal-as-fuel-for-power-10861176.php.

3. US Energy Information Administration, "Today in Energy: The United States
Exported More Natural Gas than It Imported in 2017," March 19, 2018, https://www
.eia.gov/todayinenergy/detail.php?id=35392.

4. Seeking Alpha, "Dominion Energy (D) Q2 2017 Results-Earnings Call
Transcript," August 2, 2017, https://seekingalpha.com/article/4093699-dominion-ener
gy-d-q2-2017-results-earnings-call-transcript.

5. Gregory S. Schneider, "'Campaign to Elect a Pipeline': VA's Most Powerful
Company Ran Multi-Front Fight," *Washington Post*, November 29, 2017, https://
www.washingtonpost.com/local/virginia-politics/campaign-to-elect-a-pipeline-vas
-most-powerful-company-runs-multi-front-fight/2017/11/28/2d1209ce-cf03-11e7
-9d3a-bcbe2af58c3a_story.html.

6. Bill McKibben, "Beyond Keystone: Why Climate Movement Must Keep Heat On," Yale Environment 360, November 10, 2015, https://e360.yale.edu/features/beyond_keystone_why_climate_movement_must_keep_heat_on.

7. Gregory S. Schneider, "Dominion Letter Shows Why Staying Neutral on Pipeline Project Could Help Northam," *Washington Post*, May 16, 2017, https://www.washingtonpost.com/local/virginia-politics/dominion-letter-shows-why-staying-neutral-on-pipeline-project-could-help-northam/2017/05/16/1e60fb40-3a63-11e7-9e48-c4f199710b69_story.html.

8. Itai Vardi, "Virginia Won't Say Whether Its Official Spoke at Gas Industry Panel on Curbing Pipeline Protesters," DeSmog, December 1, 2017, https://www.desmog.com/2017/12/01/virginia-hayes-framme-gas-industry-panel-dominion-pipeline-protesters/.

9. Martha M. Hamilton, "Natural Gas, Nuclear Backers See Opportunity in 'Greenhouse' Concern," *Washington Post*, July 22, 1988, https://www.washingtonpost.com/archive/business/1988/07/22/natural-gas-nuclear-backers-see-opportunity-in-greenhouse-concern/b7c3ad3f-280f-439c-8041-3cf3fc99d999/.

10. Judy and David Matthews, interview, April 25, 2022.

11. David Pomerantz, "Front Group Paid by Dominion Releases Shady Poll Showing Support for Dominion's Atlantic Coast Pipeline," Energy and Policy Institute, May 22, 2017, https://energyandpolicy.org/front-group-cea-releases-poll-showing-support-dominion-atlantic-coast-pipeline/.

12. Chesapeake Climate Action Network, "Six Hundred Virginians 'March on the Mansion' to Tell Gov. McAuliffe: Put People over Polluters on Pipelines, Coal Ash, and Climate Action," news release, July 23, 2016, https://chesapeakeclimate.org/six-hundred-virginians-march-on-the-mansion-to-tell-gov-mcauliffe-put-people-over-polluters-on-pipelines-coal-ash-and-climate-action/.

13. Eric Lipton, "Hard-Nosed Advice from Veteran Lobbyist: 'Win Ugly or Lose Pretty,'" *New York Times*, October 30, 2014, https://www.nytimes.com/2014/10/31/us/politics/pr-executives-western-energy-alliance-speech-taped.html.

14. Rick Berman, "Big Green Radicals: Exposing Environmental Groups," presentation to Western Energy Alliance Annual Meeting, Colorado Springs, Colorado, June 25, 2014.

15. CBS News, "Guards Accused of Unleashing Dogs, Pepper-Spraying Oil Pipeline Protesters," September 5, 2016, https://www.cbsnews.com/news/dakota-access-pipeline-protest-turns-violent-in-north-dakota/.

16. Alleen Brown, Will Parrish, and Alice Speri, "Leaked Documents Reveal Counterterrorism Tactics Used at Standing Rock to 'Defeat Pipeline Insurgencies,'" Intercept, May 27, 2017, https://theintercept.com/2017/05/27/leaked-documents-reveal-security-firms-counterterrorism-tactics-at-standing-rock-to-defeat-pipeline-insurgencies/.

17. Eamon Javers, "Oil Executive: Military-Style 'Psy Ops' Experience Applied," CNBC, November 8, 2011, https://www.cnbc.com/id/45208498.

18. Sharon Wilson, "Fracking Season Is upon Us. Have You Been Inoculated?" EarthWorks blog, December 6, 2011, https://earthworks.org/blog/fracking_season_is_upon_us_have_you_been_inoculated/.

19. Brendan DeMelle, "Gas Fracking Industry Using Military Psychological Warfare Tactics and Personnel in U.S. Communities," DeSmog, November 9, 2011,

https://www.desmog.com/2011/11/09/gas-fracking-industry-using-military-psycholo
gical-warfare-tactics-and-personnel-u-s-communities/.

20. Jeff Brady, "How Gas Utilities Used Tobacco Tactics to Avoid Gas Stove
Regulations," NPR, October 17, 2023, https://www.npr.org/2023/10/17/1183551603
/gas-stove-utility-tobacco; Rebecca John, "Burning Questions: A History of the Gas
Industry's Campaign to Manufacture Controversy over the Health Risks of Gas
Stove Emissions," Climate Investigation Center, October 2023, https://climateinvest
igations.org/wp-content/uploads/2023/10/Burning-Questions_Climate-Investigatio
ns-Center.pdf. The martial rhetoric is far from new: in the 1960s, gas utilities created a marketing campaign called "Operation Attack" to boost gas cooking appliance
sales, which were being overtaken by electric ranges. As for the "long-range public
relations programs" that Hill and Knowlton counseled, they proved wildly successful:
five decades would pass before federal regulators pledged to review the robust science
on the health risks posed by gas stoves, and before the American Gas Association's
efforts to cast doubt on that science came to light. For more on the deep history
of Hill and Knowlton's cross-pollinating work on behalf of the tobacco, oil and gas,
and other powerful industries, see Amy Westervelt, "John Hill and the Tobacco-Oil-
Plastic Triangle," *Drilled* (podcast), season 3, episode 7, February 2020, https://drilled
.media/podcasts/drilled/3/drilleds03-e07.

21. Allan M. Brandt, "Inventing Conflicts of Interest: A History of Tobacco
Industry Tactics," *American Journal of Public Health* 102, no. 1 (2012): 63–71, https://
doi.org/10.2105/ajph.2011.300292; Sam Meredith, "'Profoundly Disturbing': The PR
Firm for the COP27 Climate Summit Has a Long History with Big Oil," CNBC,
November 16, 2022, https://www.cnbc.com/2022/11/16/cop27-egypts-pick-to-run-pr
-at-the-uns-climate-talks-criticized.html.

22. DeMelle, "Gas Fracking Industry Using Military Psychological Warfare."

23. Patrick Field and Lawrence Susskind, *Dealing with an Angry Public: The Mutual
Gains Approach to Resolving Disputes* (New York: Free Press, 2010).

24. Megan Holleran, interview, December 4, 2020.

25. "Filmmaker Josh Fox and Six Others Arrested at Pancake-Cooking Action
at FERC," Beyond Extreme Energy, March 25, 2016, https://beyondextremeenergy
.org/2016/03/24/filmmaker-josh-fox-and-six-others-arrested-at-pancake-cooking
-action-at-ferc/.

26. Joseph Spector, "DEC Rejects Constitution Pipeline," *Press and Sun-Bulletin*
(Binghamton, NY), April 22, 2016, https://www.pressconnects.com/story/news/local
/new-york/2016/04/22/dec-reject-constitution-pipeline-permit/83401098/.

27. Jacob Pramuk, "Police: McClendon Crashed Traveling at 'High Rate of Speed,'"
March 2, 2016, https://www.cnbc.com/2016/03/02/ex-chesapeake-ceo-mcclendon
-dies-in-car-wreck-day-after-indictment.html.

28. Bethany Mclean, *Saudi America: The Truth about Fracking and How It's Changing
the World* (New York: Columbia Global Reports, 2018), 27–28.

29. Bryan Gruley, Joe Carroll, and Asjylyn Loder, "The Incredible Rise and Final
Hours of Fracking King Aubrey McClendon," *Bloomberg Businessweek*, March 10, 2016,
https://www.bloomberg.com/features/2016-aubrey-mcclendon/.

30. David Whitford, "Meet Mr. Gas: Aubrey McClendon," *Fortune Magazine*,
March 12, 2008.

31. Jeff Goodell, "The Big Fracking Bubble: The Scam behind Aubrey McClendon's Gas Boom," *Rolling Stone*, March 1, 2012, https://www.rollingstone.com/politics/poli tics-news/the-big-fracking-bubble-the-scam-behind-aubrey-mcclendons-gas-boom -231551/.

32. Ian Urbina, "Insiders Sound an Alarm amid a Natural Gas Rush," *New York Times*, June 25, 2011, https://www.nytimes.com/2011/06/26/us/26gas.html.

33. John Shiffman, Anna Driver, and Brian Grow, "Special Report: The Lavish and Leveraged Life of Aubrey McClendon," Reuters, June 7, 2012, https://www.reuters .com/article/us-chesapeake-mcclendon-profile-idUSBRE8560IB20120607.

34. Robert Frank, "Aubrey McClendon's Wine Sells for $8.4 Million," CNBC, September 19, 2016, https://www.cnbc.com/2016/09/19/aubrey-mcclendons-wine-sells -for-84-million.html.

35. Edward McAllister, "Chesapeake Chief Opposes Exporting US Natural Gas," Reuters, November 16, 2011, https://www.reuters.com/article/natgas-export-chesa peake-idCNN1E7AF1L720111116.

36. Gregory Zuckerman, *The Frackers: The Outrageous Inside Story of the New Energy Revolution* (London: Portfolio Penguin, 2014), 313.

37. Bryan Walsh, "Exclusive: How the Sierra Club Took Millions from the Natural Gas Industry—and Why They Stopped [UPDATE]," *Time Magazine*, February 2, 2012, https://science.time.com/2012/02/02/exclusive-how-the-sierra-club-took-mil lions-from-the-natural-gas-industry-and-why-they-stopped/.

38. Josh Fox et al., *Gasland: Can You Light Your Water On Fire?* (New York: Docurama Films, 2010).

39. Ben Casselman, "Sierra Club's Pro-Gas Dilemma," *Wall Street Journal* (Eastern Ed.), December 22, 2009, https://www.wsj.com/articles/SB126135534799299475.

40. Alexander C. Kaufman, "Natural Gas Industry Brings a Fake Grassroots Group to Eastern Pipeline Fights," HuffPost, June 12, 2017, https://www.huffpost.com/entry /natural-gas-pipeline-your-energy-virginia_n_593afeb1e4b0240268793e8d?ly8=.

41. DeSmog, "Your Energy America," https://www.desmog.com/your-energy-ame rica/.

42. Pomerantz, "Front Group Paid by Dominion Releases Shady Poll."

43. Peter Galuszka, "An Energy Group Is Fronting a Pro-Pipeline Campaign in Virginia," *Washington Post*, June 12, 2017, https://www.washingtonpost.com/blogs /all-opinions-are-local/wp/2017/06/12/an-energy-group-is-fronting-a-pro-pipeline -campaign-in-virginia/.

44. Schneider, "'Campaign to Elect a Pipeline.'"

45. Tom Hadwin, interview, September 15, 2020.

46. Hadwin, interview.

47. Thomas Hadwin, letter to the editor, *News Leader* (Staunton, VA), April 23, 2018, https://www.newsleader.com/story/opinion/readers/2018/04/23/virginians-save-billi ons-without-atlantic-coast-pipeline/543349002/; Thomas Hadwin, "To Understand Pipeline Economics, Follow the Money," Power to the People VA, September 5, 2017, https://powerforthepeopleva.com/2017/09/05/to-understand-pipeline-economics -follow-the-money/.

48. Tom Hadwin, remarks, Spruce Creek Camp, Friends of Nelson, April 13, 2019.

49. Hadwin, interview, August 31, 2021.

50. Ivy Main and Seth Heald, "Inside the Minds of Dominion's Leaders, Vacant

Space Where Climate Thinking Should Be," Power for the People VA, May 19, 2016, https://powerforthepeopleva.com/2016/05/19/inside-the-minds-of-dominions-lead ers-vacant-space-where-climate-thinking-should-be/.

51. Dominion Resources, "2017 Proxy Statement to the United States Securities and Exchange Commission, SCHEDULE 14A, Proxy Statement Pursuant to Section 14(a) of the Securities Exchange Act of 1934," March 3, 2017, https://www.sec.gov/Ar chives/edgar/data/715957/000119312517089312/d340312ddef14a.htm.

52. Ceres, *Benchmarking Utility Clean Energy Deployment: 2016* (Boston, MA: Ceres, June 27, 2016), https://www.ceres.org/resources/reports/2016-clean-energy-utility -benchmarking-report.

53. American Council for an Energy-Efficient Economy, *Research Report: The 2017 Utility Energy Efficiency Scorecard* (Washington, DC: ACEEE, June 13, 2017), https:// www.aceee.org/research-report/u1707.

54. Dominion Energy, "2017 Summary Annual Report," 2018, https://www.domin ionenergy.com/library/domcom/media/investors/sec-filings-andreports/summary-an nual-report/annual-2017/dom-annual-2017-full.pdf.

55. Rod Kuckro, "Dominion CEO Charts the Company's Low-Carbon Future," E&E News, July 10, 2017, https://subscriber.politicopro.com/article/eenews/2017/07 /10/dominion-ceo-charts-the-companys-low-carbon-future-056738.

56. Thomas Farrell, remarks at National Governors Association Winter Meeting, C-SPAN, video, February 23, 2008, https://www.c-span.org/video/?204153-2/states -energy-resources.

57. Lazard, "Lazard Releases Annual Levelized Cost of Energy and Levelized Cost of Storage Study," news release, November 2, 2017, https://www.lazard.com/news-an nouncements/lazard-releases-annual-levelized-cost-of-energy-and-levelized-cost-of -storage-study/.

58. Eileen Claussen and Thomas Farrell II, "Natural Gas Can Benefit the Economy and the Climate," *Richmond Times-Dispatch*, June 24, 2013, https://richmond.com/opin ion/their-opinion/columnists-blogs/guest-columnists/claussen-and-farrell-natural -gas-can-benefit-the-economy-and/article_676ac42e-23d9-521a-9791-2eb71314f4 8a.html.

59. Alexander C. Kaufman, "Virginia's Energy Kingpin Could Finally Face a Reckon ing over Race," HuffPost, July 23, 2020, https://www.huffpost.com/entry/dominion -energy-thomas-farrell-pipeline-confederacy_n_5f188364c5b6296fbf3cc73c. When he made these claims, Farrell sometimes sounded like the weary, put-upon parent of know-it-all adolescents. He often framed Dominion and its peers as victims of their own success. They were so good at their jobs, he once suggested, that they had "helped create a 'take it for granted' mindset among the American public," who "had little un derstanding of what it actually takes to produce and deliver power on a massive scale."

60. Kuckro, "Dominion CEO Charts the Company's Low-Carbon Future."

61. Farrell's numbers were less about what was technically feasible than a statement of preference. Independent energy analysts tended to agree that firms like Dominion and Duke could bring much more solar and wind and storage online before running into problems around reliability or intermittency.

62. "President Trump Announces U.S. Withdrawal from the Paris Climate Accord," June 1, 2017, https://trumpwhitehouse.archives.gov/articles/president-trump-announ ces-u-s-withdrawal-paris-climate-accord/.

63. "Remarks by President Trump at the Unleashing American Energy Event," June 29, 2017, https://trumpwhitehouse.archives.gov/briefings-statements/remarks -president-trump-unleashing-american-energy-event/.

64. Thomas Farrell II remarks at Global Energy Institute, video, July 10, 2017, https://youtu.be/ya9iRzS6BiU?si=N39u2wQk3AL7iGrB.

65. Matthew J. Belvedere, "Like the New EPA Chief, Southern Company's CEO Doesn't See CO2 as Main Reason for Climate Change," CNBC, March 28, 2017, https://www.cnbc.com/2017/03/28/like-the-new-epa-chief-southern-companys-ceo -doesnt-see-co2-as-main-reason-for-climate-change.html. In addition to flouting the laws of physics, Fanning's statement was an odd claim coming from the head of a company that had spent seven years and $7 billion building a power plant designed to showcase the promise of so-called "clean coal" technology, using systems to capture carbon dioxide emissions. If carbon emissions weren't something to worry about, why spend so much trying to store them underground? The technology never worked as intended, and after mounting costs and scandals related to concealment of those problems, Southern would shut it down later in 2017.

66. David Anderson, "Report: Southern Company Knew," Energy and Policy Institute, June 2022, https://energyandpolicy.org/wp-content/uploads/2022/06/Sou thern-Company-Knew-Report-2022.pdf. Oil and gas companies like ExxonMobil have earned much more scrutiny for hiding what they've known about how their activities would worsen climate change for decades, but utilities have skeletons buried in their closets too: Southern Company's own in-house experts discussed the risks that its fossil fuel burning would contribute to global warming as early as the 1960s.

67. Emily L. Williams, Sydney A. Bartone, Emma K. Swanson, and Leah C. Stokes, "The American Electric Utility Industry's Role in Promoting Climate Denial, Doubt, and Delay," *Environmental Research Letters* 17, no. 9 (2022): 094026, https://doi.org/10 .1088/1748-9326/ac8ab3; Leah Stokes, *Short Circuiting Policy: Interest Groups and the Battle Over Clean Energy and Climate Policy in the American States* (New York: Oxford University Press, 2020).

68. Chris Mooney and Brady Dennis, "Extreme Hurricanes and Wildfires Made 2017 the Most Costly U.S. Disaster Year on Record," *Washington Post*, January 8, 2018, https://www.washingtonpost.com/news/energy-environment/wp/2018/01/08/hur ricanes-wildfires-made-2017-the-most-costly-u-s-disaster-year-on-record/.

69. Charlie Peete Rose, "Charlie Rose Talks to ExxonMobil's Rex Tillerson," Bloomberg, March 7, 2013, https://www.bloomberg.com/news/articles/2013-03-07/charlie -rose-talks-to-exxonmobils-rex-tillerson.

70. Tom Hadwin, interview, August 31, 2021.

71. Tom Hadwin, remarks at Spruce Creek Camp, Friends of Nelson, April 13, 2019.

72. That 15 percent rate of return that FERC guaranteed to Dominion would get baked into the price of gas bought by . . . Dominion. (Its subsidiary power utility was a primary customer of its subsidiary ACP LLC.) That price premium would then, in turn, get folded into the monthly bills paid by Dominion's electric utility customers.

73. Testimony of Thomas Hadwin before the State Corporation Commission, Commonwealth of Virginia, Case No. PUE-2016-00049, Application of Virginia Electric and Power Company, Integrated Resource Filing, October 5, 2016.

74. Thomas Ritchie, *Fourteenth Annual Report of the Board of Public Works to the*

General Assembly of Virginia (Richmond: Samuel Shepherd and Company, 1830), 407–8. Crozet gained fame for designing the tunnel and supervising its construction; the tunnel itself was hacked through the Blue Ridge by enslaved Black and poor Irish laborers, dozens of whom died during the decade it took to make it.

75. Charles A. Grymes, "Second-Worst Decision of the State of Virginia?" Virginia Places, http://www.virginiaplaces.org/transportation/secondworst.html.

76. Oil Change International, "New Analysis: Mountain Valley and Atlantic Coast Pipelines Are Climate Disasters," news release, February 15, 2017, https://priceofoil.org/2017/02/15/new-analysis-mountain-valley-and-atlantic-coast-pipelines-are-climate-disasters/. Note that this number combined both carbon dioxide (from extraction, processing, and combustion of the gas) and methane (from leaks across the supply chain and pipeline operation).

77. Federal Energy Regulatory Commission, "Final Environmental Impact Statement—Atlantic Coast Pipeline and Supply Header Project," July 21, 2017, https://www.ferc.gov/final-environmental-impact-statement-atlantic-coast-pipeline-and-supply-header-project.

78. In one ruling on a pipeline in Tennessee, Cheryl LaFleur performed her own back-of-the-envelope calculation of its likely impact on upstream and downstream emissions, just to demonstrate to her fellow commissioners how feasible it was. "If one commissioner can do it, I have full faith that the full brain trust of statisticians and climatologists available to FERC can develop a test that works for this," said Gillian Giannetti, an energy law expert at the Natural Resources Defense Council. "FERC needs to stop playing this game of intellectual shuffleboard when it comes to climate emissions, that is no longer tolerable." Gillian Giannetti, interview, November 11, 2020.

79. Sierra Club v. Fed. Energy Regulatory Comm'n, 867 F.3d 1357 (D.C. Cir. 2017), www.cadc.uscourts.gov/internet/opinions.nsf/2747D72C97BE12E285258184004D1D5F/$file/16-1329-1689670.pdf.

80. Robert Zullo, "Dominion Fails in Attempt to Bar Testimony on Pipeline's Potential $2.3 Billion Hit on Ratepayers," *Richmond Times-Dispatch*, March 12, 2018, https://richmond.com/news/virginia/government-politics/dominion-fails-in-attempt-to-bar-testimony-on-pipeline-s/article_fd1b3914-fd12-569e-9c58-77c82a0ab032.html.

81. Southern Environmental Law Center, "Dominion Doesn't Deny Preparing to Charge Customers $2B for Pipeline Construction," news release, September 27, 2017, https://www.southernenvironment.org/news/dominion-doesnt-deny-preparing-to-charge-customers-2b-for-pipeline-construc/.

82. Sarah Rankin, "Disputed East Coast Pipeline Likely to Expand," Associated Press, September 29, 2017, https://www.apnews.com/d9e1216747d642abb025dedb0043462f.

83. FERC, "Commissioner Cheryl A. LaFleur Statement: Dissent on Order Issuing Certificates and Granting Abandonment Authority (Mountain Valley Pipeline and Atlantic Coast Pipeline), Docket Nos. CP15-554-000 CP16-10-000," October 13, 2017, https://www.ferc.gov/news-events/news/commissioner-cheryl-lafleur-dissent-order-issuing-certificates-and-granting.

84. Greg Buppert, interview, September 19, 2023.

85. Hannah Northey, "FERC Isn't Responsible for Gauging Projects' Impact on

Warming—LaFleur," E&E News, November 17, 2014, https://subscriber.politicopro
.com/article/eenews/1060009034.

86. Gillian Giannetti, interview, November 11, 2020.

87. Cheryl LaFleur, interview, June 16, 2020.

88. Lorne Stockman, "Bank of America Leads Finance for Atlantic Coast Pipeline,"
Oil Change International, April 18, 2018, https://priceofoil.org/2018/04/18/bank-of
-america-leads-finance-for-atlantic-coast-pipeline/.

89. Tom Hadwin, interview, August 31, 2021.

90. "Edited Transcript, Q3 Duke Energy Corporation Earnings Call," November 3, 2017, https://s201.q4cdn.com/583395453/files/doc_events/2017/11/03/3q2017earn
ingscall.pdf.

91. Virginia Public Access Project, "Ralph Northam: Donations from Dominion
Energy," https://www.vpap.org/candidates/67038/donor/120206/.

Chapter Seven

1. Motley Fool, "Dominion Energy Inc. (D) Q4 2017 Earnings Conference Call
Transcript," January 29, 2018, https://www.nasdaq.com/articles/dominion-energy-inc
-d-q4-2017-earnings-conference-call-transcript-2018-01-29.

2. Dominion Energy, "Dominion Energy Fires Up Greensville County Power
Station," news release, December 10, 2018, https://news.dominionenergy.com/2018
-12-10-Dominion-Energy-Fires-Up-Greensville-County-Power-Station.

3. Emily Brown, "Atlantic Coast Pipeline Files Eminent-Domain Suit against
Nelson County Family," *News and Advance* (Lynchburg, VA), February 9, 2018, https://
newsadvance.com/news/local/atlantic-coast-pipeline-files-eminent-domain-suit
-against-nelson-county-family/article_62efc37c-0db2-11e8-b840-2fee32999ddf.html.

4. Will Fenton, interview, June 10, 2021; Tate Mikkelsen, "Atlantic Coast Pipeline
to Put $58 Million Back into Environment," *Rockbridge Report*, February 15, 2018,
https://rockbridgereport.academic.wlu.edu/2018/02/15/atlantic-coast-pipeline-put
-58-million-back-environment/.

5. Fenton, interview; Will Fenton, email communication, May 22, 2021.

6. Will Fenton, letter to Nathaniel J. Davis Sr., deputy secretary, Federal Energy
Regulatory Commission, RE: Docket Nos. CP15-555-000 & CP15-554-000 & CP15-
554-001 Atlantic Coast Pipeline Comments and requests of Fenton Inn (intervenor),
March 27, 2017.

7. Thomas Gerbasi, "Minotauro Nogueira and the Art of Never Giving Up,"
Ultimate Fighting Championship, October 11, 2012, https://www.ufc.com/news/mino
tauro-nogueira-and-art-never-giving.

8. Will Fenton, email communication, October 12, 2022.

9. Palmer's lead attorney, Henry "Hank" Howell III, made the case that the ACP
was not a public utility and as such did not enjoy constitutional protections for taking
private property. A specialist in eminent domain law, he had signed on to represent
dozens of Nelson landowners, including Wisteria Johnson and Liz Miles. In addition
to being a practicing attorney, he was an outspoken advocate for eminent domain
reform. Challenging Dominion Energy, it turned out, was something of a family tradition for Howell. He was the son of the late lieutenant governor Henry Howell, who

had campaigned in 1969—the summer of Camille—for the Democratic nomination for governor. The elder Howell's slogan back then was "Keep the Big Boys Honest"— and his primary target was VEPCO, as Dominion was known before the 1980s. "You guys have done the best to motivate a grassroots movement than anyone could have imagined through this pipeline," Howell said of Dominion's leadership. "And I've been at it since the sixties, through my father fighting that power. This is very, very different than anything before. It's a tipping point." Hank Howell, interview, December 3, 2020.

10. "Virginia Supreme Court Sides with Pipeline in Survey Lawsuit," Associated Press, July 13, 2017. https://apnews.com/article/cf695ee19ef04cda83bf59d060a6688d. In a forty-three-page report that he submitted to FERC, Rick Webb had analyzed the horizontal directional drilling planned for Reeds Gap in minute detail. He argued that the agency failed to analyze the environmental impacts of the site work involved to create a temporary tower of cranes "necessary to suspend the pipe for approximately 2,000 feet at heights approaching 200 feet above the sloping mountainside."

11. Leslie Hartz, Dominion Transmission Inc., email to Clyde Thompson, US Forest Service, January 26, 2016.

12. Nancy Sorrells, interview, August 30, 2021.

13. Minutes of Augusta County Board of Zoning Appeals Meeting, January 4, 2018, https://www.co.augusta.va.us/home/showdocument?id=11135.

14. Gabe Cavallaro, "Augusta County Residents Pack Meeting to Oppose Pipeline Storage Yard in Churchville," *News Leader* (Staunton, VA), January 4, 2018.

15. Ernie Reed, interview, August 11, 2021.

16. Dr. Anne Carter Witt, "Landslides Associated with Hurricane Camille: 1969," presentation to Friends of Nelson Public Meeting, Lovingston, VA, June 30, 2019, http://friendsofnelson.com/wp-content/uploads/2019/07/Landslides-ACP.pdf.

17. Dominion Energy, "First LNG Commissioning Cargo Departs from Dominion Energy Cove Point Terminal," news release, March 2, 2018, https://news.dominion energy.com/2018-03-02-First-LNG-Commissioning-Cargo-Departs-From-Domini on-Energy-Cove-Point-Terminal.

18. Sorrells, interview.

19. Laura Peters, "Zoning Board Nixes Permit Request for Dominion Storage Yard," *News Leader* (Staunton, VA), March 1, 2018, https://www.newsleader.com/sto ry/news/local/2018/03/01/zoning-board-nixes-permit-request-dominion-storage-yard /384761002/; Robert Whitescarver, "Time for Dominion to Cut Its Losses on the Atlantic Coast Pipeline," *News Leader* (Staunton, VA), February 12, 2019, https://www .newsleader.com/story/opinion/columnists/2019/02/12/time-dominion-cut-its-los ses-atlantic-coast-pipeline/2848848002/.

20. Emily Brown, "Nelson Couple Grants 'Immediate Access' for Atlantic Coast Pipeline," *News and Advance* (Lynchburg, VA), February 27, 2018, https://newsadvance .com/news/local/nelson-couple-grants-immediate-access-for-atlantic-coast-pipeline /article_b9faeda6-1c0b-11e8-9d34-3bf4b38eb0a4.html.

21. Will Fenton, email communication, July 16, 2021.

22. Joyce Burton, interview, October 8, 2021.

23. Joyce Burton, interview, March 18, 2019.

24. Will Fenton, email communication, September 2, 2021.

25. Ken Wyner, video of March 17, 2018 "Remember and Recommit Action," Friends of Nelson, *Records of the Western and Central Virginia Resistance to the Atlantic Coast Pipeline.*

26. Wyner, video.

27. For some, the phrase "Full Nelson" has taken on yet another meaning: it's the popular flagship pale ale produced by Afton-based Blue Mountain Brewery, which supported Friends of Nelson's efforts from the beginning, hosting fundraisers and other events. See Mason Adams, "Craft Brewers Join the Fight against Natural Gas Pipelines," Grist, October 22, 2014, https://grist.org/climate-energy/craft-brewers -join-the-fight-against-natural-gas-pipelines/.

28. Ron Enders, interview, September 2, 2021; Martha Purvis Smith and Elizabeth Purvis Shepard interview, Friends of Nelson Lessons Learned Video Series, April 21, 2022, https://youtu.be/rmEFTz6TJys?si=nA1C-ps9iasyJb-3.

29. Wisteria Johnson, interview, July 8, 2020.

30. Emily Brown, "Family on Pipeline Route Fights ACP to Preserve Its History," *News and Advance* (Lynchburg, VA), July 19, 2017, https://newsadvance.com/nelson _county_times/news/family-on-pipeline-route-fights-acp-to-preserve-its-history/ar ticle_1463165d-dad8-5f11-bdcf-7beeba63d73f.html.

31. Wisteria Johnson, interview, August 3, 2023.

Chapter Eight

1. "Nancy Sorrells and Sarah Francisco," StoryCorps Archive, June 8, 2021, https:// archive.storycorps.org/interviews/nancy-sorrells-and-sarah-francisco/.

2. Greg Buppert, interview, April 29, 2021.

3. D. J. Gerken, interview, August 23, 2021.

4. D. J. Gerken, interview, July 9, 2020.

5. D. J. Gerken, interview, August 23, 2021.

6. Oral arguments before the US Fourth Circuit Court of Appeals, Case No. 18-1082, Sierra Club vs. National Park Service, May 10, 2018, https://www.ca4.uscourts .gov/OAarchive/mp3/18-1082-20180510.mp3.

7. Mike Soraghan, "Landslides, Explosions Spark Fear in Pipeline Country," E&E News, June 4, 2019, https://www.eenews.net/articles/landslides-explosions-spark-fear -in-pipeline-country/.

8. Dominion Energy, Kinder Morgan, UGI Energy Services, Enbridge, NiSource, EQT Midstream Partners, Southern Company Gas, and Williams, *Improving Steep-Slope Pipeline Construction to Reduce Impacts to Natural Resources* (Arlington, VA: Nature Conservancy, July 2018), https://www.conservationgateway.org/Documents /ImprovingSteepSlopePipelineConstructionReport.pdf.

9. Williams Companies, "Williams Collaborates in Effort to Reduce Pipeline Construction Impacts," news release, July 16, 2018, https://www.williams.com/2018 /07/16/williams-collaborates-in-effort-to-reduce-pipeline-construction-impacts/.

10. TC Energy, "Leach Xpress Project Placed into Service," news release, January 2, 2018, https://www.tcenergy.com/announcements/2018/2018-01-02leach-xpress -project-placed-into-service-mountaineer-xpress-gulf-xpress-receive-ferc-certificates/.

11. Matt Kelso, "Pipeline Incidents Continue to Impact Residents," FracTracker

Alliance, December 7, 2018, https://www.fractracker.org/2018/12/pipeline-incidents
-impact-residents/.

12. The reason we equate that distinctive aroma with danger can be traced back to
March 18, 1937. On that day, a spark from an electric sander ignited gas that had been
leaking, unnoticed, underneath an elementary school in New London, Texas. The gas
was piped in for heating from nearby oil fields to save money; local drillers at the time
considered it an annoying byproduct. The resulting explosion killed almost three hundred students and teachers. The tragedy triggered new requirements that utilities add
mercaptan to gas lines to prevent similar accidents.

13. For most of us, the thought that gas poses any risks begins and ends with that
rotten egg smell. But researchers have found serious risks at both ends of the gas
line. At the household end, decades of studies reveal a clear link between gas stove
use and childhood asthma. Gas appliances can produce levels of nitrogen dioxide
and other respiratory irritants inside homes that would be illegal outdoors. In 2022,
a peer-reviewed study estimated that nearly 13 percent of childhood asthma in the
US was attributable to gas stoves, comparable to the risk from chronic secondhand
cigarette smoke exposure. Taylor Gruenwald, Brady A. Seals, Luke D. Knibbs, and
H. D. Hosgood, III, "Population Attributable Fraction of Gas Stoves and Childhood
Asthma in the United States," *International Journal of Environmental Research and
Public Health* 20, no. 1 (2022): 75, https://doi.org/10.3390/ijerph20010075. Researchers
have found high levels of benzene and other toxics leaking into unventilated spaces
even when gas stoves were turned *off.* Drew R. Michanowicz, Archana Dayalu, Curtis
L. Nordgaard, Jonathan J. Buonocore, Molly W. Fairchild, Robert Ackley, Jessica E.
Schiff, et al., "Home Is Where the Pipeline Ends: Characterization of Volatile Organic
Compounds Present in Natural Gas at the Point of the Residential End User,"
Environmental Science and Technology 56, no. 14 (2022): 10258–68, https://doi.org/10.10
21/acs.est.1c08298. And at the production end of the line, researchers at the University
of Pittsburgh have found that people living near fracking wells during gas extraction are
much more likely to have severe asthma events than those living farther away. Another
study by the same team found that children living with a mile of a fracked well were
five to seven times more likely to develop lymphoma than kids living more than five
miles away. Marc Levy, "A Pennsylvania Study Suggests Links between Fracking and
Asthma, Lymphoma in Children," Associated Press, August 16, 2023, https://apnews
.com/article/fracking-pennsylvania-health-environment-research-79dd7cfb9b3799e6
28b0c3667f30dcc4.

14. Lew Freeman, interview, August 30, 2021.

15. "The Project: A Look Back at How the World's Largest Pumped Storage
Station Came to Back Creek . . . and Changed Everything," *Recorder* (VA), commemorative edition, December 23, 2010.

16. Motley Fool, "Dominion Energy, Inc. (D) Q2 2018 Earnings Conference Call
Transcript," August 1, 2018, https://www.fool.com/earnings/call-transcripts/2018/08
/01/dominion-energy-inc-d-q2-2018-earnings-conference.aspx.

17. Sierra Club v. U.S. Dep't of the Interior, 899 F.3d 260 (4th Cir. 2018).

18. Robert Zullo, "New Atlantic Coast Pipeline Suit Takes Aim at FERC Approval,
which Underpins the Whole Project," *Virginia Mercury*, August 16, 2018, https://www

.virginiamercury.com/blog-va/after-a-string-of-successful-legal-challenges-to-the-at
lantic-coast-pipeline-new-suit-takes-aim-at-ferc-approval/.

19. Transcript of Donald J. Trump's Speech in Charleston, West Virginia, Factbase,
August 21, 2018, https://factba.se/transcript/donald-trump-speech-maga-rally-charleston-
wv-august-21-2018; Linda Qui and John Schwartz, "Trump's False Claims about Coal,
the Environment, and West Virginia," *New York Times*, August 21, 2018, https://
www.nytimes.com/2018/08/21/us/politics/trump-fact-check-west-virginia-rally.html.

20. Eric Niiler, "Trump's New Power Plan Comes with a Deadly Price," *Wired*,
August 22, 2018, https://www.wired.com/story/trump-new-power-plan-air-pollution
-deaths/.

21. Transcript of Donald J. Trump's Speech in Wheeling, West Virginia, Factbase,
September 29, 2018, https://factba.se/transcript/donald-trump-speech-maga-rally
-wheeling-wv-september-29-2018.

22. Christopher Flavelle and Julie Tate, "How Joe Manchin Aided Coal, and
Earned Millions," *New York Times*, March 27, 2022, https://www.nytimes.com/2022
/03/27/climate/manchin-coal-climate-conflicts.html.

23. Meredith Shiner, "Manchin Takes Shot at Dem Bill," Politico, October 11, 2010,
https://www.politico.com/story/2010/10/manchin-takes-shot-at-dem-bill-043399.

24. Jeremy Dillon, "Manchin's Focus on Pipelines May Equal His Love of Coal,"
E&E News, January 18, 2019, https://www.eenews.net/articles/manchins-focus-on
-pipelines-may-equal-his-love-of-coal/.

25. Oral arguments before the U.S. Fourth Circuit Court of Appeals, Case No.
18-1144, Cowpasture River Preservation v. Forest Service, September 28, 2018, https://
www.ca4.uscourts.gov/OAarchive/mp3/18-1144-20180928.mp3.

26. Gavin Bade, "In First, Virginia Regulators Reject Dominion Integrated
Resource Plan," Utility Dive, December 10, 2018, https://www.utilitydive.com/news
/in-first-virginia-regulators-reject-dominion-integrated-resource-plan/543988/.

27. Gregory S. Schneider, "Federal Appeals Court Rejects Permits for Atlantic
Coast Pipeline." *Washington Post*, December 13, 2018, https://www.washingtonpost
.com/local/virginia-politics/federal-appeals-court-rejects-permits-for-atlantic-coast
-pipeline/2018/12/13/d1c845da-fef7-11e8-83c0-b06139e540e5_story.html.

28. *Cowpasture River Pres. Ass'n v. Forest Serv.*, 911 F.3d 150 (4th Cir. 2018).

29. Robert Zullo, "'If I Were Dominion I'd Be Panicked': Federal Court Vacates
Another Atlantic Coast Pipeline Permit," *Virginia Mercury*, December 13, 2018,
https://www.virginiamercury.com/2018/12/13/if-i-were-dominion-id-be-panicked
-federal-court-vacates-another-atlantic-coast-pipeline-permit/.

30. Robert Zullo, "Atlantic Coast Pipeline Cost Estimates Surge to $7 Billion,"
Virginia Mercury, November 20, 2018, https://www.virginiamercury.com/blog-va/acp
-cost-estimates-surge-to-more-than-7-billion/.

31. D. J. Gerken, interview, July 9, 2020.

32. US Fish and Wildlife Service, "Five-Year Review: Summary and Evaluation:
Clubshell (*Pleurobema clava*)," report, 2019.

Chapter Nine

1. Laurence Hammack, "Flood Carries a Piece of the Mountain Valley Pipeline
into the Hands of Opposing Landowner," *Roanoke Times*, October 12, 2018, https://

roanoke.com/news/local/flood-carries-a-piece-of-the-mountain-valley-pipeline-in
to-the-hands-of-opposing-landowner/article_2f9eb2e6-71b4-566c-bce5-659ad31f2
dea.html.

2. Mason Adams, "'This Land Is My Heart': A Mother and Daughter's 34-Day
Stand against the Mountain Valley Pipeline," *Belt Magazine*, May 17, 2018, https://belt
mag.com/tree-sits-against-mountain-valley-pipeline/.

3. Sarah Vogelsong, "Mountain Valley Pipeline Agrees to Pay Virginia $2.15
Million for Environmental Violations," *Virginia Mercury*, October 11, 2019, https://
www.virginiamercury.com/blog-va/mountain-valley-pipeline-agrees-to-pay
-virginia-2-15-million-for-environmental-violations/.

4. Richard and Jill Averitt, interview, September 2, 2021.

5. Michael Martz, "Nelson Family Invites Public to Camp along Atlantic Coast
Pipeline's Path," *Richmond Times-Dispatch*, October 4, 2018, https://richmond.com
/news/local/government-politics/nelson-county-family-invites-public-to-pitch
-tents-in-pipelines-path-through-proposed-resort/article_be08c6ee-d906-58f2
-8ca0-d529b66d15fc.html.

6. Richard Chumney, "Environmental Activists Fight Atlantic Coast Pipeline from
the Sky," *News and Advance* (Lynchburg, VA), March 30, 2019, https://newsadvance
.com/news/local/environmental-activists-fight-atlantic-coast-pipeline-from-the-sky
/article_e8572448-0129-50e8-9f51-5ab74a613ea5.html.

7. Rick Webb, interview, September 4, 2021.

8. Daniel Shaffer, "CSI Program Shows Results, ACP Construction Violations
Cited," Allegheny–Blue Ridge Alliance, January 25, 2019, https://www.abralliance.org
/2019/01/25/csi-program-shows-results-acp-construction-violations-cited/.

9. Rick Webb, email communication, August 7, 2023; Rick Webb, "Construction of
the ACP across the Central Appalachians: A Case Study in Regulatory Dysfunction,"
presentation to ABRA, March 27, 2019.

10. Kate Mishkin, "A Resolution Condemning Pipeline Challengers Passed Easily
in the WV House. A Pipeline Lobbyist Wrote It," ProPublica/*Charleston Gazette-
Mail*, July 11, 2019, https://www.propublica.org/article/dominion-energy-lobbyist
-wrote-west-virginia-pipeline-resolution.

11. House Resolution 11, 84th Leg., 1st Sess. (W.V. 2019).

12. Kate Mishkin, "Residents Say Natural Gas Production Is Marring West
Virginia. And the Legislature Isn't Doing Anything About It," ProPublica/*Charleston
Gazette-Mail*, March 6, 2019, https://www.propublica.org/article/fracking-natural-gas
-harms-west-virginia.

13. Mishkin, "Residents Say Natural Gas Production Is Marring West Virginia."

14. In 2006, when he was governor, Joe Manchin put up new signs that read "Open
for Business"—but West Virginians didn't seem to like them very much. He soon
proposed replacing them with the "Wild and Wonderful" signs that used to welcome
drivers since the 1970s. "'Wild Wonderful West Virginia' Slogan Has History Dating
to 1969," *West Virginian Times*, September 20, 2007, https://www.timeswv.com/news
/wild-wonderful-west-virginia-slogan-has-history-dating-to-1969/article_45980471
-9fa8-5ab9-9c58-4edaoabe54d7.html.

15. Student Reporting Labs, "Can West Virginia's Pipeline Jobs Keep Youth in
the State?" PBS NewsHour, April 7, 2019, https://www.pbs.org/newshour/show/can

-west-virginias-pipeline-jobs-keep-youth-in-the-state. By 2019 researchers had over a decade of data suggesting the promises of gas-fueled economic revival had been a mirage. One 2019 report from the Institute for Energy Economics and Financial Analysis found that permanent jobs in the drilling sector itself had *declined* over the decade. Another report from the Ohio River Valley Institute found that, between 2008 and 2019, the highest-producing gas counties in Pennsylvania, Ohio, and West Virginia had actually lost jobs and shrunk in population, even as there were statewide gains in both categories, and that about 90 percent of wealth generated by fracking had left the region.

16. Fracking companies had left those communities something more durable, though: thousands of abandoned wells. It is estimated that Pennsylvania alone has 200,000 orphaned wells. West Virginia has at least 10,000 documented and likely many more. There are at least 3 million abandoned oil and gas wells around the country, according to the EPA. Many have changed hands several times, typically sold from big operators to smaller fly-by-night drillers as they decline in production over time. Most are quietly leaking methane. Exactly how much is unknown.

17. Sam Felton Jr., "Marlinton Mayor's Corner," *Pocahontas Times*, August 1, 2018, https://pocahontastimes.com/marlinton-mayors-corner-76/.

18. Editorial Board, "Who Are the Real Rogues?" *Charleston Gazette-Mail*, January 10, 2019, https://www.wvgazettemail.com/opinion/editorial/gazette-editorial-who-are-the-real-rogues/article_e535fd93-26f6-583b-8988-02d6aa589d3f.html.

19. Cat Schuknecht, "Trump Signs Executive Orders in Push to Make It Easier to Build Oil and Gas Pipelines," NPR, April 11, 2019, https://www.npr.org/2019/04/11/712121425/trump-signs-executive-orders-in-push-to-make-it-easier-to-build-oil-and-gas-pipe.

20. Richard Averitt, remarks, Spruce Creek Camp, Friends of Nelson event, April 13, 2019.

21. Author notes from attending hearing in case of *Atlantic Coast Pipeline, LLC v. Nelson County Board of Supervisors*, in United States District Court for the Western District of Virginia, Charlottesville, VA, April 8, 2013.

22. Rockfish Valley Foundation, "Camille Historic Marker Dedication," August 19, 2008, https://www.rockfishvalley.org/august-19-2008-at-2-pm-dedication-of-hurricane-camille-marker/.

23. Michael Martz, "4th Circuit Decision Prompts Wall Street Concern over Pipeline," *Richmond Times-Dispatch*, March 4, 2019, https://richmond.com/news/local/government-politics/4th-circuit-decision-prompts-wall-street-concern-over-pipeline/article_ee339c15-c39c-5885-a95a-918a8229fff1.html.

24. Michael Martz, "A Man of Influence, Dominion Energy Chairman and CEO's Reach Is Long in State, Regional Affairs," *Richmond Times-Dispatch*, October 13, 2017, https://richmond.com/a-man-of-influence-dominion-energy-chairman-and-ceos-reach-is-long-in-state-regional/article_5485772a-ae9c-11e7-8a7d-eb84b48e60e5.html.

25. Motley Fool, "Dominion Energy, Inc. (D) Q1 2019 Earnings Call Transcript," May 3, 2019, https://www.fool.com/earnings/call-transcripts/2019/05/03/dominion-energy-inc-d-q1-2019-earnings-call-transc.aspx.

26. "Dominion Energy CEO: Making the Switch from Coal to Natural Gas," *Mad Money with Jim Cramer*, aired on CNBC, April 3, 2019, https://www.cnbc.com/video

/2019/04/03/dominion-energy-ceo-making-the-switch-from-coal-to-natural-gas.html.

27. Andrew Hecht, "Natural Gas Is Holding," Seeking Alpha, April 15, 2019, https://seekingalpha.com/article/4254234-natural-gas-is-holding.

28. Stephanie Tsao and Richard Martin, "Overpowered: Why a US Gas-Building Spree Continues Despite Electricity Glut," December 2, 2019, S&P Global Market Intelligence, https://www.spglobal.com/marketintelligence/en/news-insights/latest-news-headlines/overpowered-why-a-us-gas-building-spree-continues-despite-electricity-glut-54188928.

29. "This whole LNG story is just a dream," Kingsmill Bond, a chartered financial analyst and senior strategist at Rocky Mountain Institute, told me in 2020. Whereas natural gas prices are notoriously volatile, the price of renewables keeps moving in one direction only: down. Before long, nearly all marginal growth in demand would be going to renewables, he argued, which is why exports won't save the US natural gas industry, why the tanker ship won't be the new "bridge," and why investors should think carefully before loaning LNG developers $20 billion to build what could soon be stranded assets. "LNG is pretty expensive stuff. . . . People look at India and say, 'Wow, India will go from 5 percent [gas consumption] to 40 percent.' Why would it, when it's so expensive?"

30. Federal Energy Regulatory Commission, "FERC Reorganizes to Create New LNG Division, Open Houston Regional Office," news release, July 23, 2019, https://www.ferc.gov/news-events/news/ferc-reorganizes-create-new-lng-division-open-houston-regional-office.

31. Emily S. Rueb, "'Freedom Gas,' the Next American Export," *New York Times*, May 29, 2019, https://www.nytimes.com/2019/05/29/us/freedom-gas-energy-department.html.

32. Jessica Lutz, "Don't Call It a Bridge Fuel," American Petroleum Institute, June 27, 2018, https://www.api.org/news-policy-and-issues/blog/2018/06/27/dont-call-natural-gas-a-bridge-fuel.

33. Nicholas Kusnetz, "Energy Execs' Tone on Climate Changing, but They Still See a Long Fossil Future," Inside Climate News, March 18, 2019, https://insideclimatenews.org/news/18032019/energy-oil-gas-industry-climate-change-ceraweek-shell-bp/.

34. Sharon Kelly, "'We Can't Sit on the Sidelines and Be Climate Deniers,' Dominion VP Warns Natural Gas Industry," DeSmog, July 16, 2019, https://www.desmog.com/2019/07/16/dugeast-climate-deniers-dominion-raikes-natural-gas/.

35. Elizabeth Purvis Shepard and Martha Purvis Smith, interview, April 28, 2023.

36. Judy and David Matthews, interview, April 25, 2022.

37. Will Fenton, email communication, October 12, 2022.

38. Will Fenton, interview, June 10, 2021.

39. Transcript of Motions Hearing before the Honorable Norman K. Moon, US Senior District Judge, Western District of Virginia in *Atlantic Coast Pipeline, LLC v. Fenton Family Holdings, LLC*, June 19, 2019. "Transient lodging facility" is an odd formulation, when you think about it, because aren't all hotels lodging for transients?

40. Will Fenton, email communication, September 8, 2021.

41. Will Fenton, email communication, May 22, 2021.

42. Richard and Jill Averitt, interview, September 2, 2021.

43. Will Driscoll, "How Activate Virginia Persuaded 76 Candidates to Sign the 'No Dominion $' Pledge—A Model for Other States," Blue Virginia, November 22, 2017, https://bluevirginia.us/2017/11/how-activate-virginia-persuaded-76-candidates-to-sign-a-no-dominion-pledge-a-model-for-other-states.

44. Cassady Craighill, interview, September 14, 2020.

Chapter Ten

1. Richard K. Perkins, "A Brief History of the Lewis F. Powell, Jr. United States Courthouse, 1858–2012," Office of the Circuit Executive: United States Court of Appeals for the Fourth Circuit, 2012, https://www.ca4.uscourts.gov/docs/pdfs/Brief HistoryofPowellCourthouse.pdf. When the courthouse was completed in 1858, the interior was illuminated by the young technology of gas lights. Extensive remodeling between 1910 and 1913 added a fourth floor and repurposed the third-floor rooms that had once been taken over by the Confederates (and that had hosted the abortive trial of Jefferson Davis for treason in 1867) into multiple courtrooms and offices. At that time, electric wiring and lights were installed and the old gas lines were abandoned in place.

2. US Census Bureau, "Quick Facts: Buckingham County, Virginia," https://www.census.gov/quickfacts/fact/table/buckinghamcountyvirginia,VA/SBO050217.

3. Mechelle Hankerson, "Air Board Unanimously Approves Buckingham Compressor Permit," *Virginia Mercury*, January 8, 2019, https://www.virginiamercury.com/2019/01/08/air-board-unanimously-approves-buckingham-compressor-permit/.

4. Ella Rose, interview, April 28, 2023.

5. Oral arguments before the US Fourth Circuit Court of Appeals, Case No. 19-1152, Friends of Buckingham v. State Air Pollution Control Board, October 29, 2019, https://www.ca4.uscourts.gov/OAarchive/mp3/19-1152-20191029.mp3.

6. Michael Martz, "Under Questioning by 4th Circuit at Pipeline Hearing, State Concedes Union Hill's Racial Status," *Richmond Times-Dispatch*, October 29, 2019, https://richmond.com/news/virginia/plus/under-questioning-by-th-circuit-at-pipe line-hearing-state-concedes/article_2f37c452-6238-595f-bce0-be4e70583850.html.

7. Elizabeth McGowan, "Rural Virginia Activist, 75, Vows to 'Keep on Fighting' Atlantic Coast Pipeline," Energy News Network, August 20, 2019, https://energy news.us/2019/08/20/rural-virginia-activist-75-vows-to-keep-on-fighting-atlantic -coast-pipeline/.

8. Ella Rose, interview, April 28, 2023.

9. Brandon Shillingford, "For Black Virginians, Fight against White Supremacy Continues," VPM, March 1, 2021, https://www.vpm.org/news/2021-03-01/for-black -virginians-fight-against-white-supremacy-continues.

10. Staff report, "A Grave Project," *Farmville (VA) Herald*, March 11, 2014, https://www.farmvilleherald.com/2014/03/a-grave-project/.

11. Jordan Miles, "Property for Compressor Station Purchased for $2.5 Million," *Farmville (VA) Herald*, August 26, 2015, https://www.farmvilleherald.com/2015/08/property-for-compressor-station-purchased-for-2-5-million/.

12. Variety Shade Landowners of Virginia, "Variety Shade History," https://vslva .org/variety-shade-history/.

13. Jordan Miles, "Potential Compressor Station Property Purchased by Pipeline Venture," *Farmville (VA) Herald*, July 20, 2015, https://www.farmvilleherald.com/2015/07/potential-compressor-station-property-purchased-by-pipeline-venture/.

14. Federal Energy Regulatory Commission, Draft Environmental Impact Statement, Atlantic Coast Pipeline and Supply Header Project, Volume I, December 2016, https://www.ferc.gov/sites/default/files/2020-05/volume-I_0.pdf.

15. Chad Oba, interview, April 28, 2023.

16. Cat McCue, "History, Health at Stake in Buckingham County," *Front Porch Blog*, Appalachian Voices, June 4, 2018, https://appvoices.org/2018/06/04/history-health-at-stake-in-buckingham-county/.

17. Gregory S. Schneider, "The Baptists and the Yogis Join to Fight a Pipeline," *Washington Post*, August 18, 2018, https://www.washingtonpost.com/local/virginia-politics/the-baptists-and-the-yogis-join-together-to-fight-a-pipeline/2018/08/18/9eb54816-9fe6-11e8-83d2-70203b8d7b44_story.html. After Wilson was arrested protesting in front of the governor's mansion in October 2016, he performed his court-mandated community service at Yogaville for five days. "I had the most amazing experience. It's really a spiritual place," he told one reporter.

18. Oba, interview.

19. Samantha Willis, "State Board Will Decide Permit for Buckingham Compressor Station, Focus of Virginia's Biggest Environmental Justice Debate," *Virginia Mercury*, November 8, 2018, https://www.virginiamercury.com/2018/11/08/state-board-will-decide-permit-for-buckingham-compressor-station-virginias-biggest-environmental-justice-debate/.

20. Ella Rose, interview, April 28, 2023.

21. Jordy Yager, "Opposition to Pipeline Voiced Again in Buckingham," WMRA News, December 13, 2016, https://www.wmra.org/wmra-news/2016-12-13/opposition-to-pipeline-voiced-again-in-buckingham.

22. Minutes of Buckingham County Board of Supervisors Meeting, January 5, 2017.

23. Robert Zullo, "Buckingham Approves Compressor Station for Dominion Pipeline," *Richmond Times-Dispatch*, January 5, 2017, https://richmond.com/business/buckingham-approves-compressor-station-for-dominion-pipeline-over-opposition-from-residents/article_b406a13b-0259-56f1-add8-b8b3da1e1e28.html.

24. Zullo, "Buckingham Approves Compressor Station."

25. Robert Zullo, "Dominion's New Office Tower in Downtown Richmond Gets a New Name," *Richmond Times-Dispatch*, August 15, 2017, https://richmond.com/business/dominions-new-office-tower-in-downtown-richmond-gets-a-name/article_add88885-c359-56c8-96e4-03589b912784.html.

26. Across the street was an open space known as Kanawha Plaza—another allusion to those canal days. George Washington had been one of the earliest cheerleaders for the idea of linking the Kanawha River in what is now West Virginia (where his Burning Spring property lay) with the James River as a conduit for commerce.

27. Heidi Tyline King, *Dominion's First Century: A Legacy of Service* (Hasbrouck Heights, NJ: CorporateHistory.net, 2010), 11.

28. Thomas Ritchie, *Fourteenth Annual Report of the Board of Public Works to the General Assembly of Virginia* (Richmond: Samuel Shepherd and Company, 1830), 317. In the section of this report devoted to the Upper Appomattox Company, it is noted

that, prior to some hired work done in 1830, "all our works were executed by slaves, purchased by the company, which, in this country, we find much cheaper than to hire labourers."

29. Dominion's modern incarnation took shape on June 29, 1909, when the Virginia Railway and Power Company was created from the merger of three different electric streetcar lines in Richmond, under the ownership of Frank Jay Gould, a casino magnate and son of the infamous robber baron Jay Gould. Two years later, VR&P acquired the Norfolk gas light company, marking the company's earliest venture into the gas distribution business. In 1925, a New York–based syndicate purchased VR&P and renamed it the Virginia Electric and Power Company—or VEPCO, as it would be known for the next sixty years. The streetcar industry faded, but the gas and electricity distribution businesses boomed. After World War II, VEPCO bought up smaller power companies and became Virginia's biggest electricity provider. Many modern utility holding companies emerged from these twisting paths through the past century's major infrastructure and energy transitions: town gas to natural gas, horses to trolley cars, gas lights to electric lights. Southern Company, a partner in the Atlantic Coast Pipeline and owner of major monopoly gas and electric utilities in the southeast, followed a similar path: its origins go back to the Atlanta Gas Light Company, formed in 1856.

30. Southern Environmental Law Center, "Union Hill's Historic Value Recognized in Unanimous Decision against Atlantic Coast Pipeline," news release, February 1, 2021, https://www.southernenvironment.org/news/union-hill-makes-historyagain/.

31. Author's notes of Lakshmi Fjord presentation at Spruce Creek Camp, Friends of Nelson workshop, April 13, 2019.

32. Friends Buckingham v. State Air Pollution Control Bd., 947 F.3d 68 (4th Cir. 2020).

33. Chad Oba, interview, April 28, 2023.

34. Lisa Goff, "In Path of Pipeline, Descendants of Freedmen Fight to Preserve Historic Virginia," Platform, June 27, 2019, https://www.platformspace.net/home/in-path-of-pipeline-descendants-of-freedmen-fight-to-preserve-historic-virginia.

35. Dustin Robinette and *Dictionary of Virginia Biography*, "Caesar Perkins (1839–1910)," *Encyclopedia Virginia*, Virginia Humanities, December 7, 2020.

36. Lakshmi Fjord, "Union Hill Community Household Study Site and Methods Report: A Community Participatory Action Research Project; Part II: Households: Demographics, Health, Land Use, Family Heritage," Department of Anthropology, University of Virginia, December 14, 2018.

37. Rachel Sadon, "Mount Vernon Named One of the Country's Most Endangered Historic Sites as It Fights a Natural Gas Project," DCist, June 27, 2018, https://dcist.com/story/18/06/27/mount-vernon-named-one-of-the-count/.

38. Teo Armus, "Dominion May Move the Compressor It Planned to Build across from Mount Vernon," July 3, 2018, *Washington Post*, https://www.washingtonpost.com/local/md-politics/dominion-says-it-will-seek-new-site-for-planned-natural-gas-facility/2018/07/03/ddaa82a6-7ec7-11e8-bb6b-c1cb691f1402_story.html.

39. Robert Zullo, "In Buckingham's Union Hill, a Center of Resistance for the Atlantic Coast Pipeline, Dominion Brings in a Ringer," *Virginia Mercury*, August

2, 2018, https://www.virginiamercury.com/2018/08/02/in-buckinghams-union-hill-a
-center-of-resistance-for-the-atlantic-coast-pipeline-dominion-brings-in-a-ringer/.

40. Gregory S. Schneider, "Big Company, Big Dollars, Small Community: Dominion Deal Sparks Dissent in Community Facing Gas Project," *Washington Post*, December 9, 2018, https://www.washingtonpost.com/local/virginia-politics/domin ion-deal-sparks-dissent-in-community-facing-pipeline-project/2018/12/09/050e5f 52-f99d-11e8-863c-9e2f864d47e7_story.html.

41. Erik Ortiz, "How Money Stokes Divide of Historic Black Community in Virginia Pipeline Battle," NBC News, December 7, 2018, https://www.nbcnews.com /news/us-news/how-money-stokes-divide-historic-black-community-virginia-pipe line-battle-n943236.

42. Ella Rose and Chad Oba, interviews, April 28, 2023.

43. Gregory S. Schneider, "Virginia Regulators Balk at Voting on Pipeline Permit Affecting Historic African American Community," *Washington Post*, November 9, 2018, https://www.washingtonpost.com/local/virginia-politics/virginia-regulators -balk-at-voting-on-pipeline-permit-affecting-historic-african-american-commu nity/2018/11/09/bf1929d6-e444-11e8-b759-3d88a5ce9e19_story.html.

44. Gregory S. Schneider, "Former Board Members Challenge State Data ahead of Key Vote on Pipeline Facility," *Washington Post*, January 7, 2019, https://www.washingt onpost.com/local/virginia-politics/former-board-members-challenge-state-data -ahead-of-key-vote-on-pipeline-facility/2019/01/07/4a49852a-1288-11e9-b6ad-9cfd62 dbb0a8_story.html. Two days before the air board was scheduled to vote on the per-mit, the two former members who Northam had removed claimed that Dominion and state regulators had presented incomplete and misleading information to them. "The record Dominion prepared was based on a not-very-serious look at the neighbors," one warned. "It's a historic free-Black community. There are churches and cemeteries and people who live there—none of which shows up in the analysis they presented."

45. Ryan E. Emanuel, "Flawed Environmental Justice Analyses," *Science* 357, no. 6348 (2017): 260. https://doi.org/10.1126/science.aao2684.

46. Ryan E. Emanuel, comments to Virginia Air Pollution Control Board, *On the Demographics and Site Suitability for Buckingham Natural Gas Compressor Station*, January 4, 2019.

47. Itai Vardi, "Virginia Air Board Member Who Approved a Controversial Atlantic Coast Pipeline Permit Has Links to a Dominion Gas Partner," DeSmog, January 16, 2019, https://www.desmog.com/2019/01/16/virginia-air-board-william-fer guson-atlantic-coast-pipeline-union-hill-dominion/.

48. Chad Oba, interview, September 11, 2023.

49. Denise Lavoie, "Hissing, Shouts of 'Shame' as Pipeline Station Gets Permit," Associated Press, January 8, 2019, https://apnews.com/1b76ccabf70544618d2fbcd83aec b34d.

50. Virginia Public Access Project, "The Way Ahead: Top Donors," https://www.vp ap.org/committees/318122/top_donors/?start_year=2019&end_year=2019.

51. Caroline Kelly, "Virginia Governor Apologizes for 'Racist and Offensive' Costume in Photo Showing People in Blackface and KKK Garb," CNN, February 2, 2019, https://www.cnn.com/2019/02/01/politics/northam-blackface-photo/index.html.

52. Gregory S. Schneider, "Al Gore, Civil Rights Leader William Barber Call on Northam to Seek Forgiveness through Action," *Washington Post*, February 20, 2019, https://www.washingtonpost.com/local/virginia-politics/al-gore-civil-rights-leader -william-barber-call-on-northam-to-seek-forgiveness-through-action/2019/02/20 /13c85666-347a-11e9-854a-7a14d7fec96a_story.html.

53. Reverend William Barber II and Al Gore remarks, Moral Call for Ecological Justice in Buckingham event, February 19, 2019, video, https://www.facebook.com /watch/?v=2113974475384696.

54. Cathy Kunkel, "Atlantic Coast Pipeline Risk Is Being Borne Not by Dominion and Duke, but by Their Customers," Institute for Energy Economics and Financial Analysis, September 8, 2017, https://ieefa.org/resources/ieefa-update-atlantic-coast -pipeline-risk-being-borne-not-dominion-and-duke-their.

55. Alwyn Scott, "General Electric's Power Unit Fights for Growth as Wind, Solar Gain," Reuters, May 24, 2018, https://www.reuters.com/article/us-ge-renewables/gen eral-electrics-power-unit-fights-for-growth-as-wind-solar-gain-idUSKCN1IP0LE.

56. Richard Martin and Darren Sweeney, "Overpowered: In Virginia, Dominion Faces Challenges to Its Reign," S&P Global Market Intelligence, December 4, 2019, https://www.spglobal.com/marketintelligence/en/news-insights/latest-news-head lines/overpowered-in-virginia-dominion-faces-challenges-to-its-reign-54171542.

57. Robert Walton, "Dominion Suspends Plan to Add 1.5 GW of Peaking Capacity as Virginia Faces Gas Glut," Utility Dive, December 5, 2019, https://www.utilitydive .com/news/dominion-suspends-plan-to-add-15-gw-of-peaking-capacity-as-virginia -faces/568489/.

58. "Testimony of Ernest J. Moniz, MIT Energy Initiative Massachusetts Institute of Technology before the United States Senate Committee on Energy and Natural Resources," July 19, 2011, https://www.energy.senate.gov/services/files/42C2523F-B0 96-189B-6A12-925E1F9D1481.

59. Benjamin Storrow, "Coal Plants Disappear in VA. But CO2 Is Rising," E&E News, May 20, 2020, https://www.eenews.net/articles/coal-plants-disappear-in-va -but-co2-is-rising/.

60. Nicholas Kusnetz, "Natural Gas Rush Drives a Global Rise in Fossil Fuel Emissions," Inside Climate News, December 4, 2019, https://insideclimatenews.org /news/04122019/fossil-fuel-emissions-2019-natural-gas-bridge-oil-coal-climate -change/.

61. Magdalena M. Klemun and Jessika E. Trancik, "Timelines for Mitigating the Methane Impacts of Using Natural Gas for Carbon Dioxide Abatement," *Environmental Research Letters* 14, no. 12 (2019): 124069, https://doi.org/10.1088/1748 -9326/ab2577.

62. Nicholas Kusnetz, "Is Natural Gas Really Helping the U.S. Cut Emissions?" Inside Climate News, January 30, 2020, https://insideclimatenews.org/news/300120 20/natural-gas-methane-carbon-emissions/.

63. Darren Sweeney, "Morgan Stanley: $64B Capex Upside for Utilities Replacing Coal with Renewables," S&P Global Market Intelligence, February 18, 2020, https:// www.spglobal.com/marketintelligence/en/news-insights/latest-news-headlines /morgan-stanley-64b-capex-upside-for-utilities-replacing-coal-with-renewables-569 87725.

64. Joe Smyth, "Financial Analysts Expect Decarbonization Will Benefit Utility Ratepayers and Shareholders," Energy and Policy Institute, January 10, 2020, https://energyandpolicy.org/financial-analysts-expect-decarbonization-will-benefit-utility-ratepayers-and-shareholders/.

65. Mark Dyson, Charles Teplin, Alex Engel, and Grant Glazer, "Report: The Growing Market for Clean Energy Portfolios," Rocky Mountain Institute, 2019, https://rmi.org/insight/clean-energy-portfolios-pipelines-and-plants/.

66. Chaz Teplin, interview, December 8, 2020.

67. Dominion Energy, *Embracing Change: 2019 Summary Annual Report* (Richmond, VA: Dominion Energy, 2020), https://s2.q4cdn.com/510812146/files/doc_financials/2019/ar/DE_2019SAR_Final_032320.pdf.

68. Friends Buckingham v. State Air Pollution Control Bd., 947 F.3d 68 (4th Cir. 2020). The judges went even further, rebuking the air board, DEQ, and ACP LLC for citing a state doctrine "that does not exist" as justification for its failure to even consider using non-polluting electric motors to power its compressors instead of gas-fired turbines.

69. Robert Walton, "4th Circuit Nixes Key Permit for Dominion's Atlantic Coast Pipeline, Citing Environmental Justice Concerns," Utility Dive, January 8, 2020, https://www.utilitydive.com/news/4th-circuit-nixes-key-permit-for-dominions-atlantic-coast-pipeline-citing/570005/.

70. Greg Buppert, interview, July 9, 2020.

71. Elizabeth McGowan, "In Virginia, Anti-Pipeline Activists Feel 'Justice Was Served' with Court Ruling," Energy News Network, January 15, 2020, https://energynews.us/2020/01/15/in-virginia-anti-pipeline-activists-feel-justice-was-served-with-court-ruling/.

Chapter Eleven

1. Aaron Ruby, interview, November 6, 2019.

2. Lee Francis, interview, September 9, 2020.

3. Kate Andrew, "SCC: Dominion Overcharged Customers by $502M in 2017–19," *Virginia Business*, August 18, 2020, https://www.virginiabusiness.com/article/scc-report-dominion-overcharged-customers-by-502m-in-2017-19/.

4. Francis, interview.

5. Sarah Rankin and Alan Suderman, "Virginia Lawmakers Pass Major Renewable Energy Legislation," Associated Press, February 11, 2020, https://apnews.com/article/cddda59df1d16ec02435f1a3e8e898a7.

6. Dominion Energy, "Dominion Energy Sets New Goal of Net Zero Emissions by 2050," news release, February 11, 2020, https://news.dominionenergy.com/2020-02-11-Dominion-Energy-Sets-New-Goal-of-Net-Zero-Emissions-by-2050. The company's targets on methane were less ambitious: cutting 80 percent of emissions from 2010 levels by 2040 and using "renewable natural gas" generated from landfills and livestock manure to cancel out remaining fossil methane emissions. That same day, another announcement drew less attention: Dominion would buy Southern Company's 5 percent stake in the Atlantic Coast Pipeline, which it projected would be finished by the end of 2022.

7. David Roberts, "Virginia Becomes the First State in the South to Target 100%

Clean Power," Vox, April 13, 2020, https://www.vox.com/energy-and-environment/20 20/3/12/21172836/virginia-renewable-energy-100-percent-clean.

8. Sarah Vogelsong, "Despite Clean Economy Act, Dominion Forecasts a Strong Role for Natural Gas in Virginia," *Virginia Mercury*, May 8, 2020, https://www.vir giniamercury.com/2020/05/08/despite-clean-economy-act-dominion-forecasts-a -strong-role-for-natural-gas-in-virginia/.

9. Amol A. Phadke, Umed Paliwal, Nikit Abhyankar, Taylor McNair, Ben Paulos, David Wooley, and Ric O'Connell, "2035 Report: Plummeting Solar, Wind, and Battery Costs Can Accelerate Our Clean Energy Future," June 2020, https://www.20 35report.com/electricity/.

10. Amol Phadke, interview, July 30, 2020. Dominion and other firms regularly warned that because the sun doesn't always shine and the wind doesn't always blow, installing more renewables without new gas plants to back them up would lead to outages. But a series of extreme weather events would soon reveal that overreliance on gas had made the grid *less* reliable in some regions. During a deep freeze in Texas in 2021, key points in the gas delivery system froze up and gas power plants failed to run, leading to prolonged and deadly power outages. Jeff St. John, "Natural Gas Is the Pillar of the US Electric Grid. It's Also Unreliable," Canary Media, July 5, 2023, https:// www.canarymedia.com/articles/fossil-fuels/natural-gas-is-the-pillar-of-the-us-elec tric-grid-its-also-unreliable.

11. AlphaStreet, "Duke Energy Corp Q1 2020 Earnings Call Transcript," May 12, 2020, https://news.alphastreet.com/duke-energy-corp-nyse-duk-q1-2020-earnings -call-transcript/.

12. Greg Buppert and D. J. Gerken, interviews, July 9, 2020.

13. U.S. Forest Serv. v. Cowpasture River Pres. Ass'n, 140 S. Ct. 1837, 1850 (2020).

14. Southern Environmental Law Center, "Atlantic Coast Pipeline Confronts Its Expiration Date," press release, July 2, 2020, https://www.southernenvironment.org /press-release/atlantic-coast-pipeline-confronts-its-expiration-date/.

15. Jeff Gleason, director's letter, Southern Environmental Law Center, September 2020, https://legacy.uploads.southernenvironment.org/words_docs/Directors_Letter _0920_F.pdf.

16. Chad Oba and Ella Rose, interview, April 28, 2023.

17. Lew Freeman, interview, August 30, 2021.

18. Anne Adams, interview, August 30, 2021; Anne Adams, "Ordinary Citizens Become Extraordinary," *Recorder* (VA), July 9, 2020, https://www.therecorderonline .com/articles/ordinary-citizens-become-extraordinary/.

19. Nancy Sorrells, interview, August 31, 2021.

20. Joyce Burton, interview, July 6, 2020.

21. Wisteria Johnson, interview, July 8, 2020.

22. Hiroko Tabuchi and Brad Plumer, "Is This the End of New Pipelines?" *New York Times*, July 8, 2020, https://www.nytimes.com/2020/07/08/climate/dakota-access -keystone-atlantic-pipelines.html.

23. Michelle Lewis, "Dakota Access Pipeline's Owner Defies Courts, Refuses to Shut Down," Electrek, July 9, 2020, https://electrek.co/2020/07/09/dakota-access -pipeline-energy-transfer-defies-courts-refuses-to-shut-down/.

24. Allison Good, "ConEd May Sell Pipeline Stakes as It Reconsiders Gas

Transmission Investments," S&P Global Market Intelligence, August 26, 2020, https://www.spglobal.com/marketintelligence/en/news-insights/latest-news-head lines/coned-may-sell-pipeline-stakes-as-it-reconsiders-gas-transmission-invest ments-60093361.

25. Dominion Energy, "Dominion Energy Agrees to Sell Gas Transmission, Storage Assets to Berkshire Hathaway Energy—Strategic Repositioning toward 'Pure-Play' State-Regulated, Sustainability-Focused Utility Operations," news release, July 5, 2020, https://news.dominionenergy.com/2020-07-05-Dominion-Energy-Agre es-to-Sell-Gas-Transmission-Storage-Assets-to-Berkshire-Hathaway-Energy-Stra tegic-Repositioning-Toward-Pure-Play-State-Regulated-Sustainability-Focused-Uti lity-Operations.

26. Sarah Vogelsong, "What Sank the Atlantic Coast Pipeline? It Wasn't Just Environmentalism," *Virginia Mercury*, July 8, 2020, https://www.virginiamercury.com /2020/07/08/what-sank-the-atlantic-coast-pipeline-it-wasnt-just-environmentalism/.

27. Jonathan Mingle, "How Overreach by Trump Administration Derailed Big Pipeline Projects," Yale Environment 360, July 15, 2020, https://e360.yale.edu/features /how-overreach-by-trump-administration-derailed-big-pipeline-projects.

28. Darren Sweeney, "Dominion Points to ESG as Key Factor in Decision to Off-Load Gas Assets," S&P Global Market Intelligence, July 10, 2020, https://www.sp global.com/marketintelligence/en/news-insights/latest-news-headlines/dominion -points-to-esg-as-key-factor-in-decision-to-off-load-gas-assets-59346029.

29. Dominion Energy, "Dominion Energy and Duke Energy Cancel the Atlantic Coast Pipeline," July 5, 2020, https://news.dominionenergy.com/2020-07-05-Domini on-Energy-and-Duke-Energy-Cancel-the-Atlantic-Coast-Pipeline.

30. It's worth noting that, for many years, the Edison Electric Institute and the American Gas Association have undertaken influence and advertising campaigns to forestall climate action and policies—and that these activities are partly funded by cap tive ratepayers, who finance the annual dues paid by Dominion, Duke, and Southern and other member companies to these utility trade associations.

31. "Nancy Sorrells and Sarah Francisco," StoryCorps Archive, June 8, 2021, https:// archive.storycorps.org/interviews/nancy-sorrells-and-sarah-francisco/.

32. Richard Foster, "Dominion Taps New CEO, Rearranges Top Leadership," *Virginia Business*, July 31, 2020, https://www.virginiabusiness.com/article/dominion -taps-new-ceo-rearranges-top-leadership/. Tom Farrell would retire from his role as chairman of Dominion Energy on April 1, 2021. He died the next day, after a long and private battle with cancer. Praise poured in from all corners: his Dominion colleagues, Virginia politicians, fellow utility executives, the leaders of education and arts institu tions on whose boards he had long served. Governor Ralph Northam said that "his quiet, calm work made Virginia better." Most news reports mentioned the failed ACP a few paragraphs in.

33. Frank Wagner, "Hampton Roads Urgently Needs the Atlantic Coast Pipeline," *Richmond Times-Dispatch*, January 9, 2019, https://roanoke.com/opinion/commenta ry/wagner-hampton-roads-urgently-needs-the-atlantic-coast-pipeline/article_dcf0f4 2d-8b75-5d43-9833-7aeff28508c4.html.

34. Bob Burnley, interview, December 8, 2022.

35. D. J. Gerken, interview, July 9, 2020.

36. Emma Newburger, "Joe Biden Calls Climate Change the 'Number One Issue Facing Humanity'," CNBC, October 24, 2020, https://www.cnbc.com/2020/10/24/joe -biden-climate-change-is-number-one-issue-facing-humanity.html.

37. Sammy Roth, "The 'War on Coal' Is Over. The Next Climate Battle Has Just Begun," *Los Angeles Times*, November 17, 2020, https://www.latimes.com/business/sto ry/2020-11-17/climate-change-gas-biden-moniz.

38. Patrick Wilson, "Inside the Utility Company Lobbying Blitz That Will Hike Electric Bills," ProPublica and *Richmond Times-Dispatch*, October 9, 2020. https://www .propublica.org/article/inside-the-utility-company-lobbying-blitz-that-will-hike -electric-bills. Tom Hadwin thought the company had played its hand with the new legislature well: the CEA would ensure that Dominion would have a monopoly on wind power in Virginia for decades. He worried that ratepayers would pay needlessly higher rates due to the lack of competition in building the project. Dominion had mounted a well-documented lobbying effort to make sure it didn't bear the full risks of the new offshore wind project if costs proved higher than predicted, and that those costs would be passed on to ratepayers. The company had pivoted from pipes to wires—but seemed to be using the same playbook: engineering its own very lucrative incentive structure. But for Will Cleveland, the SELC senior attorney who had worked for months to help hammer out the new law's terms, and his colleagues, there was some consolation: at least Dominion was getting handsomely rewarded for building clean energy instead of planet-warming methane gas projects. In fall 2022, Dominion agreed to a more balanced risk-sharing arrangement, after pressure from state regulators, Walmart (a huge customer), and groups like the Sierra Club and Appalachian Voices. Ethan Howland, "Dominion Settles with Walmart, Others on Potential Cost Overruns for $9.8B Offshore Wind Project," Utility Dive, October 31, 2022, https://www.utilitydive.com/news/dominion -virginia-scc-cost-overrun-offshore-wind/635343/.

39. Rachel Frazin, "Progressives Urge Biden away from Including Obama Energy Secretary in Administration," *The Hill*, November 16, 2020, https://thehill.com/policy /energy-environment/526217-progressives-urge-biden-away-from-including-obama -energy-secretary/.

40. Claudia Kemfert, Fabian Prager, Isabell Braunger, Franziska M. Hoffart, and Hanna Brauers, "The Expansion of Natural Gas Infrastructure Puts Energy Transitions at Risk," *Nature Energy* 7 (2022): 582–87, https://doi.org/10.1038/s41560-022-01060-3.

Chapter Twelve

1. Brad Johnson, "Lot Holds Windmill Parts, Pipe Joints," *Inter-Mountain* (Elkins, WV), July 30, 2022, https://www.theintermountain.com/news/local-news/2022/07 /energy-storage/.

2. To hit its climate goals, the US will need a lot more wires. Jesse Jenkins, an energy engineer at Princeton, and his team of researchers have calculated that the US needs to build 75,000 miles of new high-voltage transmission lines by 2035—a rate of con-struction that is more than double the pace of transmission additions since 2013. "For my entire lifetime, we've been coasting off infrastructure investments made between the New Deal and the 1970s, be it the rural electrification and hydropower dams of the 1930s, or the Eisenhower interstate highway system, or the nation's aging fleet of nuclear power plants and transportation hubs," he has written. "Most people alive

today haven't experienced the kind of building boom we must embark upon." Jesse D. Jenkins, "What 'Electrify Everything' Actually Looks Like," *Mother Jones*, May/June 2023, https://www.motherjones.com/environment/2023/04/electrify-everything-scope-data/.

3. Alec Tyson, Cary Funk, and Brian Kennedy, "Americans Largely Favor U.S. Taking Steps to Become Carbon Neutral by 2050," Pew Research Center, March 1, 2022, https://www.pewresearch.org/science/2022/03/01/americans-largely-favor-u-s-taking-steps-to-become-carbon-neutral-by-2050/.

4. Arnie Seipel and Joe Hernandez, "Joe Manchin Says He Won't Support President Biden's Build Back Better Plan," NPR, December 19, 2021, https://www.npr.org/2021/12/19/1065636709/joe-manchin-says-he-cannot-support-bidens-build-back-better-plan.

5. Tony Romm and Jeff Stein, "Manchin Says He Won't Support New Climate Spending or Tax Hikes on Wealthy," *Washington Post*, July 15, 2022, https://www.washingtonpost.com/us-policy/2022/07/14/manchin-climate-tax-bbb/.

6. Eli Stokols, "How the Climate Movement Learned to Win in Washington," Politico, April 2, 2023, https://www.politico.com/news/2023/04/02/climate-politics-change-00088107.

7. Coral Davenport and Lisa Friedman, "How One Senator Doomed the Democrats' Climate Plan," *New York Times*, July 15, 2022, https://www.nytimes.com/2022/07/15/climate/manchin-climate-change-democrats.html.

8. Fredreka Schouten, "Joe Manchin, Who Just Torpedoed Democrats' Climate Agenda, Has Long Ties to Coal Industry," CNN, July 15, 2022, https://www.cnn.com/2022/07/15/politics/joe-manchin-coal-financial-interests-climate/index.html.

9. The White House, "Fact Sheet: How the Inflation Reduction Act Builds a Better Future for Young Americans," August 16, 2022, https://www.whitehouse.gov/briefing-room/statements-releases/2022/08/16/fact-sheet-how-the-inflation-reduction-act-builds-a-better-future-for-young-americans/.

10. Juliet Grable, "A People's History of the Inflation Reduction Act," *Sierra Magazine*, December 22, 2022, https://www.sierraclub.org/sierra/people-s-history-inflation-reduction-act. Twelve years after the demise of the Waxman-Markey cap-and-trade bill, sustained and focused grassroots organizing—partly fueled by energy generated from pipeline fights like Keystone and Dakota Access—had helped create the conditions that led to the historic passage of the IRA.

11. The law also included generous subsidies for companies to install carbon capture and sequestration systems and for producing hydrogen fuels. These were two of the gas industry's favored—but expensive and yet to be deployed at commercial scale—decarbonization solutions. A growing chorus of experts warned they could just as easily slow the energy transition down and prolong the lifespan of fossil fuel infrastructure, depending on how they were defined and regulated. Hydrogen can be made from clean electricity, but today most hydrogen is made from fossil methane—making many independent researchers wary that utilities' hydrogen pilot programs were simply rationales for protecting their networks of pipes.

12. Coral Davenport and Brad Plumer, "Debt Deal Includes a Green Light for a Contentious Pipeline," *New York Times*, May 30, 2023, https://www.nytimes.com/2023/05/30/climate/mountain-valley-pipe.html.

13. Appalachian Power, "Fact Sheet: Central Virginia Transmission Reliability Project: Shipman to Schuyler," August 3, 2020, https://www.aeptransmission.com/vir ginia/Shipman-Schuyler/docs/Shipman-Schuyler_Factsheet_V8.pdf.

14. Nelson County Historical Society, "Cuttin' on the Lights: Rural Electrification," Exhibit of the Oakland Museum, Lovingston, Virginia, https://nelsonhistorical.org /cpage.php?pt=17.

15. Wisteria Johnson, interview, August 3, 2023.

16. Richard A. Pence, ed., *The Next Greatest Thing* (Washington, DC: National Rural Electric Cooperative Association, 1984), 15.

17. Central Virginia Electric Cooperative, "The History of CVEC," https://www .mycvec.com/history.

18. Paul Saunders, *Heartbeats of Nelson* (Piney River, VA: Saunders Publishing, 2007).

19. George H. Gilliam and William G. Thomas III, "The Story of Rural Electrification," *The Ground Beneath Our Feet: A Documentary Film Series and Website about Virginia's History after the Civil War*, https://www.vahistory.org/electrification .html.

20. Richard Hirsh, *Technology and Transformation in the American Electric Utility Industry* (Cambridge: Cambridge University Press, 1989), 219, note 34. The wider in- dustry also lobbied hard for "electrifying everything." The major trade association rep- resenting the industry, the Edison Electric Institute, launched a marketing campaign in 1971 called "The Electric Climate," which included print advertisements to promote electric heating, such as one that beckoned: "Come live in the electric climate. The air is so clean there."

21. In 2020, for instance, Dominion lobbyists worked quietly to help kill proposals to transition to 100 percent clean energy by some towns in Ohio—where it owned a large gas distribution utility. Kathiann M. Kowalski, "Utilities, Gas Industry Coordinate to Oppose Ohio Village's Clean Energy Goal," Energy News Network, May 6, 2020, https://energynews.us/2020/05/06/utilities-gas-industry-coordinate-to-oppose-ohio -villages-clean-energy-goal/.

22. Jonathan Mingle, "To Cut Carbon Emissions, a Movement Grows to 'Electrify Everything,'" Yale Environment 360, April 14, 2020, https://e360.yale.edu/features/to -cut-carbon-emissions-a-movement-grows-to-electrify-everything.

23. Trade groups like the AGA launched advertising campaigns against these "gas bans" around the country, claiming that they would "eliminate consumer choice." In dozens of states, Republican lawmakers began putting forward bills that would block local governments from implementing what they called "gas bans." In 2020, Arizona, Louisiana, Oklahoma, and Tennessee adopted such laws; the following year, over a dozen more states passed similar measures. Many of them were drafted by indus- try lobbyists or based on friendly suggestions provided by their gas utilities. "I didn't dream this up," said the state legislator who introduced one such bill, which became law in Utah in 2021. "I became aware of it, frankly, from my local natural gas supplier, Dominion." Jeff Brady and Dan Charles, "As Cities Grapple with Climate Change, Utilities Fight to Stay in Business," NPR, February 22, 2021, https://www.npr.org/20 21/02/22/967439914/as-cities-grapple-with-climate-change-gas-utilities-fight-to -stay-in-business.

24. Dominion, Duke, and other utility companies pay membership dues to trade groups like the American Gas Association and the Edison Electric Institute. The former spends part of its roughly $30 million in annual revenue on public relations campaigns to downplay the climate impacts of natural gas and to push for policies that would slow down the transition to electrification; the latter has a $90 million budget, which it uses in part to fight state laws expanding rooftop solar and federal carbon-reduction policies that it doesn't like. Much of that money comes from captive ratepayers: millions of Americans pay fees on their monthly utility bills that subsidize trade associations' anti–clean energy activities. In other words, these customers are helping to pay for influence campaigns that run directly counter to their own stated preferences—and interests. See David Anderson, Matt Kasper, and David Pomerantz, "Paying for Utility Politics: How Utility Ratepayers Are Forced to Fund the Edison Electric Institute and Other Political Organizations," Energy and Policy Institute, May 2017, https://energyandpolicy.org/wp-content/uploads/2017/05/Ratepayers-fun ding-Edison-Electric-Institute-and-other-organizations.pdf.

25. Sammy Roth, "Boiling Point: In the West, Opposing Natural Gas Is Tricky—Even for a Democrat with Climate Cred," *Los Angeles Times*, November 26, 2020, https://www.latimes.com/environment/newsletter/2020-11-26/in-the-west-oppos ing-natural-gas-is-tricky-even-for-a-democrat-with-climate-cred-boiling-point.

26. Melissa Gay (communications and member services manager, CVEC), interview, September 7, 2021.

27. Annual Meeting, CVEC, June 22, 2022, https://www.facebook.com/watch/?v= 360803972830317.

28. Video of Friends of Nelson, July 10, 2021 Celebration, *Records of the Western and Central Virginia Resistance to the Atlantic Coast Pipeline.*

29. Richard Averitt, U.S. House of Representatives, Civil Rights and Civil Liberties Subcommittee, "Taking Your Land for Natural Gas Pipelines: FERC Undermines Property Rights, April 28, 2020, YouTube video, https://youtu.be/gY4E2JarHoU?si= PS-4DqxCnhcO3bnb.

30. House Hearing, 116th Congress, Civil Rights and Civil Liberties Subcommittee Hearing, "Pipelines Over People: How FERC Tramples Landowner Rights in Natural Gas Projects," December 9, 2020, https://www.congress.gov/event/116th-congress /house-event/LC65797/text?s=1&r=13.

31. Federal Energy Regulatory Commission, "FERC Updates Policies to Guide Natural Gas Project Certifications," news release February 17, 2022, https://www .ferc.gov/news-events/news/ferc-updates-policies-guide-natural-gas-project-certifi cations. Glick was a vocal proponent of both making pipeline reviews more stringent *and* making it easier to build transmission lines.

32. Energy and Policy Institute, "Natural Allies for a Clean Energy Future," https:// energyandpolicy.org/natural-allies-for-a-clean-energy-future/.

33. Naveena Sadasivam, "Welcome to Utah, Where Pipeline Protests Could Now Get You at Least Five Years in Prison," Grist, March 21, 2023, https://grist.org/protest /utah-critical-infrastructure-law-felony/.

34. Arielle Samuelson and Emily Atkin, "Climate Misinformation Is Becoming Law," HEATED Newsletter, May 11, 2023, https://heated.world/p/climate-misinfor mation-is-becoming.

35. Rachel Frazin, "Democratic Ex-Senators Join Pro-Gas Organization," *The Hill*, January 26, 2022. https://thehill.com/policy/energy-environment/591506-democratic -ex-senators-join-pro-gas-organization/.

36. Michael Tobin, "Kerry Warns of Stranded Asset Risk from Natural Gas Build-out," Bloomberg News, January 27, 2021, https://news.bloomberglaw.com/environ ment-and-energy/kerry-warns-of-stranded-asset-risk-from-natural-gas-buildout.

37. LNG Allies, "Joint Letter to President Biden on Energy Security," February 25, 2022, https://lngallies.com/energy-security/.

38. Miranda Willson, "FERC Retreats on Gas Policies as Chair Pursues Clarity," E&E News, March 25, 2022, https://www.eenews.net/articles/ferc-retreats-on-gas -policies-as-chair-pursues-clarity/.

39. Anna Phillips and Tyler Pager, "A Top Energy Regulator Is in Turmoil over Climate Rules," *Washington Post*, April 27, 2022, https://www.washingtonpost.com /climate-environment/2022/04/27/top-energy-regulator-is-turmoil-over-climate -rules/.

40. Jonathan Mingle, "How U.S. Gas Exports to Europe Could Lock in Future Emissions," Yale Environment 360, April 21, 2022, https://e360.yale.edu/features/how -u.s.-gas-exports-to-europe-could-lock-in-future-emissions.

41. Jonathan Mingle, "Congress Is Turning Climate Gaslighting into Law," *New York Times*, June 1, 2023, https://www.nytimes.com/2023/06/01/opinion/debt-ceiling -mountain-valley-pipeline-joe-manchin.html.

42. Senator Tim Kaine, "Kaine Statement on Vote to Exempt the Mountain Valley Pipeline from Normal Permitting Rules," press release, September 27, 2022, https:// www.kaine.senate.gov/press-releases/kaine-statement-on-vote-to-exempt-the-moun tain-valley-pipeline-from-normal-permitting-rules.

43. H.R.3746, Fiscal Responsibility Act of 2023, Public Law 118-5, 118th Congress, https://www.congress.gov/bill/118th-congress/house-bill/3746/text.

44. Maxine Joselow, "How a Fossil Fuel Pipeline Helped Grease the Debt Ceiling Deal," *Washington Post*, May 31, 2023, https://www.washingtonpost.com/climate-envi ronment/2023/05/31/debt-deal-mountain-valley-pipeline/.

45. Meanwhile, analysts at IEEFA and elsewhere were pointing out that gas was a commodity with volatile prices—and surging LNG exports were driving up the price of natural gas at home for US consumers.

46. 118 Cong. Record S1880 (daily ed. June 1, 2023) (statement of Senator Manchin), https://www.congress.gov/118/crec/2023/06/01/169/95/CREC-2023-06-01.pdf.

47. Emma Dumain, "Debt Limit Deal Would Complete Mountain Valley Pipeline," E&E News, May 28, 2023, https://www.eenews.net/articles/debt-limit-deal-would -complete-mountain-valley-pipeline/.

48. Hiroko Tabuchi, "Manchin's Donors Include Pipeline Giants That Win in His Climate Deal," *New York Times*, August 7, 2022, https://www.nytimes.com/2022/08/07 /climate/manchin-schumer-pipeline-political-funding.html.

49. Mingle, "Congress Is Turning Climate Gaslighting Into Law."

50. Lorne Stockman, "The Mountain Valley Pipeline: Greenhouse Gas Emissions Briefing," Oil Change International, February 15, 2017, https://priceofoil.org/2017/02 /15/mountain-valley-pipeline-greenhouse-gas-emissions-briefing/.

51. Dan Charles, "A Satellite Finds Massive Methane Leaks from Gas Pipelines,"

NPR, February 3, 2022, https://www.npr.org/2022/02/03/1077392791/a-satellite -finds-massive-methane-leaks-from-gas-pipelines.

52. Deborah Gordon, Frances Reuland, Daniel J. Jacob, John R. Worden, Drew Shindell, and Mark Dyson, "Evaluating Net Life-Cycle Greenhouse Gas Emissions Intensities from Gas and Coal at Varying Methane Leakage Rates," *Environmental Research Letters* 18, no. 8 (2023): 084008. https://doi.org/10.1088/1748-9326/ace3db.

53. Hiroko Tabuchi, "Leaks Can Make Natural Gas as Bad for the Climate as Coal, a Study Says," *New York Times*, July 13, 2023, https://www.nytimes.com/2023/07/13" /climate/natural-gas-leaks-coal-climate-change.html.

54. Ellie Silverman, "Climate Advocates Protest Mountain Valley Pipeline outside White House," *Washington Post*, June 8, 2023, https://www.washingtonpost.com/dc -md-va/2023/06/08/mountain-valley-pipeline-protest-white-house-debt-ceiling-ap palachia/.

55. Cara Buckley, "A 'Rocking Chair Rebellion': Seniors Call on Banks to Dump Big Oil," *New York Times*, March 21, 2023, https://www.nytimes.com/2023/03/21/cli mate/climate-change-protests-oil-banks.html.

56. Act.TV, "Justin Pearson at the StopMVP Rally in DC," June 8, 2023, YouTube video, https://youtu.be/6V6PgYrfOYk?si=NH3yJbWYTwLMzKyu.

Epilogue

1. Jonathan Mingle, "Even 'Safe' Places Are Experiencing Climate Chaos in America," *New York Times*, July 13, 2023, https://www.nytimes.com/2023/07/13/opin ion/floods-vermont-new-york-heat-climate-change.html.

2. United Nations, "It's Official: July 2023 Was the Warmest Month Ever Recorded," UN News, August 8, 2023, https://news.un.org/en/story/2023/08/1139527.

3. Robert Barnes and Rachel Weiner, "Supreme Court Clears the Way for Pipeline Construction Favored by Manchin," *Washington Post*, July 27, 2023, https://www.was hingtonpost.com/politics/2023/07/27/supreme-court-mountain-valley-pipeline/.

4. Southern Environmental Law Center, "U.S. Supreme Court Rules Mountain Valley Pipeline Can Proceed through National Forest," news release, July 27, 2023, https://www.southernenvironment.org/news/u-s-supreme-court-rules-mountain-val ley-pipeline-can-proceed-through-national-forest/.

5. Lisa Friedman, "A Republican 2024 Climate Strategy: More Drilling, Less Clean Energy," *New York Times*, August 4, 2023, https://www.nytimes.com/2023/08/04/cli mate/republicans-climate-project2025.html.

6. The section of the Project 2025 blueprint that calls for unraveling the Department of Energy's clean energy programs—and that also calls for major expansions in gas in-frastructure—was written by a conservative lawyer named Bernard McNamee. Before McNamee was appointed by Trump to the Federal Energy Regulatory Commission in 2018, he had worked for nearly a decade as a partner at McGuireWoods, the Richmond law firm that represented Dominion in many legal and political arenas. After his stint at FERC, McNamee returned to the firm's Richmond office, and to his former work of lobbying on behalf of industry clients like Dominion. Prior to his Project 2025 author-ship, McNamee's most famous piece of writing was perhaps an op-ed he wrote in 2018 praising fossil fuels and advocating for more of them to be burned, timed to coincide with Earth Day. Scott Waldman, "Conservatives Have Already Written a Climate

Plan for Trump's Second Term," Politico, July 28, 2023, https://www.politico.com /news/2023/07/28/far-right-climate-plans-00107498.

7. Valerie Volcovici, "White House Launches Methane Emission Task Force to Boost Leak Detection," Reuters, July 26, 2023, https://www.reuters.com/business/envi ronment/white-house-launches-methane-emission-task-force-boost-leak-detection -2023-07-26/.

8. Euan Nisbet, "Rising Methane Could Be a Sign That Earth's Climate Is Part-Way through a 'Termination-Level Transition,'" *Conversation*, August 14, 2023, https:// theconversation.com/rising-methane-could-be-a-sign-that-earths-climate-is-part -way-through-a-termination-level-transition-211211.

9. Ayesha Tandon, "'Exceptional' Surge in Methane Emissions from Wetlands Worries Scientists," Carbon Brief, March 20, 2023, https://www.carbonbrief.org/ex ceptional-surge-in-methane-emissions-from-wetlands-worries-scientists/.

10. Frank Jordans, "UN Chief Says Fossil Fuels 'Incompatible with Human Survival,' Calls for Credible Exit Strategy," Associated Press, June 15, 2023, https:// apnews.com/article/climate-talks-un-uae-guterres-fossil-fuel-9cadf724c9545c7032522 b10eaf33d22.

11. Brad Plumer, "Climate Report Card Says Countries Are Trying, but Urgently Need Improvement," *New York Times*, September 8, 2023, https://www.nytimes.com /2023/09/08/climate/paris-agreement-stocktake.html.

12. David Knowles, "Extreme Rainfall in Hong Kong, Brazil and Greece Leaves Dozens Dead after Flash Flooding," Yahoo News, September 8, 2023, https:// news.yahoo.com/extreme-rainfall-in-hong-kong-brazil-and-greece-leaves-dozens -dead-after-flash-flooding-202946277.html.

13. Carrie Hodousek and Jeff Jenkins, "Winifrede Hollow Residents Say Monday's Flash Flooding Is Worst They've Seen," West Virginia MetroNews, August 28, 2023, https://wvmetronews.com/2023/08/28/winifrede-hollow-residents-tell-stories-of -survival-as-water-rescues-continue-in-eastern-kanawha-county-flood/.

14. Katherine Blunt, "Dominion Sells Natural Gas Utilities to Enbridge for $9.4 Billion," *Wall Street Journal* (Eastern ed.), September 5, 2023, https://www.wsj.com /business/energy-oil/dominion-sells-natural-gas-utilities-to-enbridge-for-9-4-bil lion-bd4533ca.

15. Charlie Paulin, "Dominion Reviving Plans to Build a Natural Gas Peaker Plant in Chesterfield," *Virginia Mercury*, June 14, 2023, https://www.virginiamercury.com/20 23/06/14/dominion-reviving-plans-to-build-a-natural-gas-peaker-plant-in-chester field/.

16. Dominion was far from alone in its enthusiasm for more methane-fueled in-frastructure. A Sierra Club analysis of seventy-seven utilities in 2023 found that, col-lectively, they planned to add 53 new gigawatts of gas-fired capacity through 2030—a huge jump over what they had planned in 2022. See Cara Fogler and Noah Ver Beek, "The Dirty Truth about Utility Climate Pledges," Sierra Club, October 2023, https:// coal.sierraclub.org/sites/nat-coal/files/dirty_truth_report_2023.pdf.

17. Wisteria Johnson, interview, August 3, 2023.

Index

Page numbers in *italics* indicate photographs and figures.

About the Author

Jonathan Mingle is an independent journalist. He has written
about the science and politics of
climate change, energy, technology, public health, resource issues,
and other subjects for the *New
York Review of Books*, the *New
York Times*, *Undark Magazine*,
Yale Environment 360, *Slate*,
the *Boston Globe*, and other outlets. As a 2020 Alicia Patterson
Foundation Fellow, he reported
on the political, legal, and grassroots battles over new natural gas
(a.k.a. methane) infrastructure
and its local impacts and global

climate consequences. A recipient of the Middlebury Fellowship in
Environmental Journalism, he lives with his family in Vermont. His
first book is *Fire and Ice: Soot, Solidarity, and Survival on the Roof of
the World.*